Women in Southeast Asian Nationalist Movements

Women in Southeast Asian Nationalist Movements

A Biographical Approach

Edited by

Susan Blackburn and Helen Ting

NUS PRESS
SINGAPORE

Published with support from the Nicholas Tarling fund

© 2013 Susan Blackburn and Helen Ting

Published by:

NUS Press
National University of Singapore
AS3-01-02, 3 Arts Link
Singapore 117569

Fax: (65) 6774-0652
E-mail: nusbooks@nus.edu.sg
Website: http://www.nus.edu.sg/nuspress

ISBN 978-9971-69-674-0 (Paper)

National Library Board, Singapore Cataloguing-in-Publication Data

Women in Southeast Asian Nationalist Movements: a biographical approach /
  edited by Susan Blackburn and Helen Ting. – Singapore: NUS Press, 2013.
  pages cm
  ISBN: 978-9971-69-674-0 (paperback)

  1. Women—Political activity—Southeast Asia—Biography.
  2. Nationalism—Southeast Asia—History. I. Blackburn, Susan, 1947–,
  editor. II. Ting, Helen, 1964–, editor. III. Title.

HQ1236.5.A785
320.0820959 — 23   OCN843004744

Cover: Albert Leeflang

Printed by: Mainland Press Pte Ltd

Contents

LIST OF MAPS

LIST OF PHOTOGRAPHS

Gendered Nationalist Movements in Southeast Asia

Susan Blackburn

There is quite an extensive literature on gender and nationalism but less on women in nationalist movements, particularly from a biographical perspective, and very little on either of these in relation to Southeast Asia.[1] These are gaps that this book seeks to address.

This introductory chapter opens up discussion of some of the concepts and questions that are central to the chapters that will follow. They relate to gender and nationalist movements, and the special contribution that is offered by the biographical approach. The Introduction reflects on what is specific to Southeast Asia from the point of view of women in nationalist movements. A brief overview of the chapters is also provided.

Gender and Nationalist Movements

"Nation" and "nationalism" are contested terms. Nationalism involves the identification of a people with a place and a community, to which they refer as a nation and to which they feel a sense of belonging and loyalty, and which confers rights and commands obligations. What forms the core of that identification, how it emerges, the discourse of nationalism and how people are mobilised behind it constitute some of the key questions exercising the minds of scholars of nationalism.[2] For most of our Southeast Asian protagonists, living in the first half of the 20th century, fighting to free the land and society in which they lived from foreign colonial powers was something obvious and worthy of their pursuit. For them, nationalism entailed the responsibility to

1

struggle to liberate the nation from foreign domination and establish their own nation-state. Yet this seemingly straightforward agenda concealed a number of tensions and contradictions that could not be ignored as time went on.

Even in the course of the anti-colonial struggle, it was clear that nationalists were divided by class, ethnicity and religion that led them to pursue different visions of the nation. Once the colonial yoke had been thrown off, the nation was openly revealed as lacking solidarity, however hard nationalist leaders worked to conceal it. One of the most intractable problems was the issue of ethnicity and how it was to be negotiated in Southeast Asia's multi-ethnic and multi-religious societies. Some ethnic groups envisaged the nation as the place where they could preserve and sustain their own cultures and religions, which would otherwise be subordinated or even annihilated in a state dominated by other groups. Relatively few in Southeast Asia saw the nation in liberal terms as conferring rights on its citizens, including multicultural rights.

Nationalism posed problems of ethnic and religious identity for a number of the protagonists featured in the chapters that follow. As women they also found that gender was added to the mix, and their lives reveal considerable tension at times between the social construction of gender and the obligations they felt they owed to the nation. The notion of modernity and the need for nationalists to come to terms with it emerged early in the history of Southeast Asian nationalist movements. Ideals associated with both modernity and nationalism, such as equality and personal autonomy, challenged practices of traditional politics as well as well-established gender relations and the vested interests associated with those practices. How compatible with a modern nation, therefore, were customary approaches to gender relations? Did a modern nation confer equal rights on men and women? What role were women to play in nationalist movements? While some women expected that a modern nation would open new doors to them, men — and other women — were not always so ready to welcome social transformation. Should that transformation have been deferred until after national independence was won? Or, alternatively, was it acceptable for women to undertake unconventional roles during the struggle for independence but once that goal was achieved to retreat back to what were considered to be "normal" gender relations in that society? As we shall see, women have had to engage with different answers to these questions in Southeast Asia.

The Significance of Gender in Southeast Asian Nationalist Movements

For Southeast Asians, being seen as a nationalist, at least within the dominant group, has often been a way of acquiring prestige — and it may even be a path to power. In Southeast Asia in the past, nationalist movements have been viewed in a romantic light as struggles against imperialism, and many people associated with such movements have been elevated to the position of national heroes. They are seen as the founders of the nation-states of Southeast Asia today, since all the countries of the region, barring Thailand, were colonised by Western powers (Dutch, English, French, Spanish, Portuguese and American). They won their independence after World War II, during which the whole of the region was occupied by another colonial power, the Japanese. The leaders (usually male) of the winning form of nationalism were seen in the most positive light, and it is interesting to see what share of that hero worship was bestowed upon women and why.

Some decades after independence, however, nationalism has been viewed more ambivalently, for several reasons. First, the much vaunted struggle for independence was followed by far less heroic years in which several Southeast Asian countries, led by famous nationalists such as Sukarno of Indonesia, did not live up to the expectations of those who had sacrificed themselves for the sake of independence. Serious reassessment of the longer-term outcomes of nationalist movements began. Most relevant to this work, questions such as "What has independence done for women?" began to be asked. Minority ethnic groups often also felt that independence had favoured majority groups and neglected their interests. Even at the stage of anti-colonial struggle, and certainly once the goal of nationhood had been achieved, questions arose about the rights of citizens, about the kind of nation that should command loyalty. Looking back to the anti-imperialist nationalist movements themselves, can we find the roots of those problems in the ways those movements treated women (and minority ethnic groups)? In the case of women, did the movements campaign for the recognition of women's rights before independence? If so, to what effect? Our book will pursue such questions.

A second reason for the growing ambivalence about nationalism is that some Southeast Asian governments have used nationalist history for their own purposes, which has served to discredit it, or at least to discredit the official version. Authoritarian regimes in Burma,

Indonesia, Vietnam and elsewhere have instilled a particular interpretation of their nationalist movements in their people, with carefully selected national heroes. Such official versions of history have largely ignored women, or presented only a few sanitised female nationalists for public consumption. This has done a disservice to the pluralism of most nationalist movements and the role of women in them.

Third, nationalist movements did not disappear once the new Southeast Asian countries took form after the Western colonial powers withdrew. The region, one of the most diverse in the world, is well-known for continuing separatist movements driven by ethno-nationalism, as various ethnic groups seek to carve out nation-states for themselves. Burma is the country most affected: groups such as the Shans, Karens and Chins claimed the right to their own states separate from the Burman majority. In Indonesia, East Timorese, Acehnese and Papuan struggles for independence from Jakarta's rule have proved to be "pebbles in the shoe" of government, as an Indonesian foreign minister once put it. In Thailand and the Philippines, Muslim minorities have kept up resistance struggles for independence. Nationalism has thus turned to bite the nationalists, who have in turn been accused of behaving as colonialists. Since many of these separatist movements have involved armed struggle, they pose particular issues in relation to gender: what place do they accord to women, and how have women been involved in practice?

A final reason for the recent growing scepticism about nationalism is that some separatist movements have been associated with Islam and have featured in the international discourse on the "war against terror". The Moro liberation struggle in the southern Philippines is the best-known of these Islamist rebellions, but the Pattani movement in Southern Thailand and Acehnese separatists in Indonesia have been tarred with the same brush. Just as to French colonialists in Vietnam nationalists were terrorists, so now in other parts of Southeast Asia nationalists who might once have been seen as freedom fighters are now regarded much more suspiciously. Since Islamist movements are particularly male-dominated, the role of women within them is especially problematic.

Thus, analysts of Southeast Asian political history are forced to grapple with different views of nationalist movements. In this volume we take an inclusive approach, accepting that nationalist movements are of many kinds and are not limited to the colonial period. In some cases Communist movements can be considered nationalist, if they claim to liberate the nation from colonial/imperialist/neo-colonial domination and if their followers see them in that light. Religion too may be inextricably entwined with nationalist aspirations. Our book features women who have been involved in nationalist movements of different kinds and at different periods, thus allowing us to explore the significance of these variations for our subjects. Obviously an early 20th-century struggle against colonialism occurred in a very different context from a current ethno-nationalist struggle in a world that is wary of the destabilising effect of ethno-nationalism but embraces a belief in human rights. What particularly interests us is how women have perceived nationalism in its various manifestations, and how they have negotiated the mixed agendas that nationalist movements adopt and the mixed reactions they receive internationally. Conversely, how have those movements treated the women in their ranks? Do different kinds of movements take different views of gender relations, and how do they constrain or direct the way women act within them?

The notion of "movement" deserves further clarification, particularly as it affects women. A nationalist movement is a particular form of social movement (that is, it consists of a collectivity of some sort working to promote change) that makes a claim for territorial sovereignty.[3] While social and political movements have a core of leaders and formal organisations, the notion of "movement" implies something wider, encompassing a mass base. The base includes adherents undertaking many roles, including attending rallies, raising funds and providing other material support, and spreading the movement's ideas through the media or in schools, families and community groups. When we consider women's roles, it is especially necessary to take this wider view of nationalist movements. It is usually male leaders and male-dominated nationalist parties that monopolise attention, yet women may play very diverse and essential supportive and even innovative roles.[4]

The Biographical Approach

Taking a biographical approach to women's roles in nationalist movements allows us to see the true diversity and importance of women's contributions, and the impact of those movements on the lives of individuals. Contributors to this volume were asked to write chapters exploring views and roles of the chosen women as actors in the nationalist movement rather than full biographies.

In Southeast Asia there are very few biographies of women nationalists. In some countries, such as Indonesia, selected individuals are designated as official National Heroes, whose lives, in very abbreviated and sanitised form, are celebrated and studied by schoolchildren. A small minority are women. In large part this is due to a restricted identification of nationalist movements with leaders and formal parties, which, as already stated, are almost entirely dominated by men. Until fairly recently, moreover, Southeast Asia lacked a strong biographical tradition, partly because it was unusual to single out individuals for attention as distinct from the collectivity to which they belong — the kinship, religious group or ethnic group. In the past autobiographies were even rarer, for similar reasons.[5] With the expansion of the publishing industry in the region biographies are now quite popular, but they still rarely feature women as nationalists. Our contributors will say more about their countries' historiography in relation to women nationalists.

This book presents a number of examples of women in nationalist movements and asks various questions about them, intended to illuminate their experiences and significance. Why did they identify with a nationalist movement, and what did nationalism mean to them? The intention is to probe the origins of their identification with the nationalist movement, with its gendered dimension. If the nation was an "imagined community", and undoubtedly in many Southeast Asian countries the very notion of nationhood had to be invented from scratch, how did women imagine it? How were they affected by the gendered ideas of their nationalist movement, for instance the notion that women were guardians of tradition? Did they attempt to include the rights of women within the agenda of their nationalist movement — and if so, to what effect? What were the cultural, social and political factors that made them more or less successful? Did women nationalists tend to come disproportionately from particular social classes and ethnic groups? What role did modern education play in their attraction to nationalism, as against, for instance, the influence of friends and family? Our authors address such questions.

A distinct advantage in taking a biographical approach is that it enables us to escape the more common focus on "how nationalist movements envisage gender relations", in which women are treated as objects of nationalist discourse, which in turn is dominated by men.[6] We concentrate on individual women as actors carving out their own niche in nationalist movements. Of course there are restrictions imposed on them by the gendered nationalist discourse, but in surprisingly many cases these women manage to evade or circumvent the restrictive impact of such discourse. How do these women deal with it? If the perceived bias of nationalist discourse on gender is reinforced by dominant religious or ethnic norms, is it insurmountable, or does it unexpectedly offer new opportunities for some women? By examining the agency of these women, we gain a sense of the constraints posed by the wider social and political structures on them, and what it was like to live in their given time and space. The particularity of their experience of struggle in their movement enriches our understanding of the spectrum of possible responses improvised or devised by these women within their respective socio-cultural contexts. Insofar as our knowledge of women's role in some of the nationalist movements remains deficient, the lives of these women offer us illustrative — if not always representative or comprehensive — cases of their gendered experience.

The unifying theme among these women is their participation in the struggle for national autonomy. Yet the nationalist organisations they joined often competed with alternative ones in the same time and place. Through the life histories of the women, we wish to explore the statement made by Ranchod-Nilsson and Tétreault that "there is no single 'woman's view' of the nation" and that "there is no unambiguous 'woman's side' in nationalist conflicts".[7]

Those who recognise that nationalist discourse is gendered in ways that privilege men often resent women's "exploitation" by nationalist movements. They inveigh against the ways in which women are used and then cast aside once independence is achieved.[8] This may or may not correspond with the subjective views of women actors in nationalist movements. Like Marxists criticising conservative workers as having false consciousness, there is among some feminists a view, going back to the famous 1938 pronouncements of Virginia Woolf,[9] that women are deceived by nationalism and should rather be fighting for their own rights, which nationalist leaders have no intention of recognising. On the other hand, Jill Bystydzienski argues that nationalism has "empowered millions of women. It has created pride in indigenous cultures, a demystification of innate superiority of foreign oppressors, and a recognition of community."[10] Moreover, a book edited by Lois West (1997) argues that there can be such a thing as "feminist nationalism", which combines the struggles for women's rights with the right to national self-determination. By taking a biographical approach, we want to understand women's political involvement from their own perspective. Did they feel "used"? Alternatively, did they themselves personally benefit from their involvement in a nationalist movement? How did they understand the meaning of their engagement and experiences? How did they exercise their agency as social actors in their own right? Did they manage to pursue women's rights within the nationalist movement, producing a kind of "feminist nationalism"? If so, were they able to influence the male-dominated mainstream nationalist movement? Each contributor applies her perspective as a scholar to assess these issues in relation to the experience of the woman in question.

In her pioneering work on feminism and nationalism, based on Third World country studies, Kumari Jayawardena has critiqued the limitations of feminist struggles fought in the context of bourgeois-led nationalist movements. She observes that women's struggles were destined to be "subordinate to the political struggle and to the male groupings in political parties".[11] On the other hand, she is more positive towards "revolutionary movements" involving female peasants and workers, which were able not only to transform society but also to improve the position of women.[12] Our studies include women who operated within both "bourgeois-led" and "revolutionary" nationalist movements, so we are in a position to test the validity of Jayawardena's distinction, at least as it relates to some individuals' experiences. Obviously we need to be cautious and discerning in treating their experience as representative of other female colleagues. There is nothing like biography for making one aware of how special every human being is, and our chapters certainly reveal a collection of extraordinary women.

Another attribute of nationalist movements that may well be pertinent for gender relations is the salience of armed struggle. There is certainly a case for arguing that nationalist movements that predominantly pursue violent methods are least likely to give prominence to women and their concerns. Cynthia Enloe has stated that "militarization puts a premium on communal unity in the name of national survival, a priority which can silence women critical of patriarchal practices and attitudes".[13] Yet those who take up arms for the nation are often later treated as heroes, so this may be a route to national recognition for those women who become combatants. Our book contains examples of women who have actively participated in armed struggles, so we are in a position to discover how such nationalist movements have treated them.

This treatment relates also to the way in which history has treated women nationalists more generally. Have their contributions been recognised? If so, how, and if not, why not? As we shall see in the chapters that follow, although women have received little attention, there are some exceptions — and it is instructive to account for them too. They shed light on the continuing nationalist discourse, the shaping of citizens' thinking about gender and nation.

Why Is Southeast Asia of Interest?

Colonialism shaped Southeast Asian nationalist movements. Its imposition of new state borders helped homogenise some ethnic groups into new nation-states (what Anthony Reid has called "imperial alchemy"[14]) and antagonised others, often with lasting effects. The region thus includes many ethnic groups that almost miraculously came to identify with a nation that had never existed previously, and ethnic groups that were excluded or did not wish to be part of the new nation. Our authors provide examples of women who followed both routes.

As already noted, little has been written about women in Southeast Asian nationalist movements, despite the ubiquitous and diverse nature of those movements in the region. This neglect is surprising too in view of the common assumption of historians and anthropologists that women have had a high status in Southeast Asia, especially when compared to other regions of Asia where there have been egregious instances of discrimination against women (such as foot binding in China and widow burning in India). In large part this positive impression is based on economic factors. Visitors to Southeast Asia have long noted the way in which men and women work side by side in the fields and women dominate local markets and petty trade (Reid 1988).[15] The idea that women are the financial managers of the household is widely accepted in the region. Anthropologists[16] also refer to kinship systems as accounting for the greater autonomy of women: the prevalence of bilateral kinship and neolocal or matrilocal marriages strengthens women's position in relation to in-laws and provides support in cases of marital discord or break-up. The high incidence of divorce in Islamic Southeast Asia is sometimes interpreted as evidence of the independence of women.[17]

Yet it is obvious that such evidence of women's relatively high status in Southeast Asia does not translate into political prominence. Women may be very visible publicly in the economic and social spheres, but in politics women have been as under-represented in Southeast Asia as in most parts of the world, despite a few high-profile women leaders such as Corazon Aquino, Megawati Sukarnoputri and Aung San Suu Kyi. As in other regions, politics is seen as a man's domain. Of particular interest, then, is the involvement of women in nationalist movements, an overtly political activity. Taking a bio-graphical approach, as our contributors do, sheds light on the way in which individual women negotiate these tensions. It may also help us to understand why women are frequently overlooked as part of nationalist movements, since their roles are often not interpreted, by themselves or others, as being political. They are presented rather as being involved in women's movements or religious or social movements, which are not seen as connected to the nationalist move-ment. In the following chapters we will see that this is often far from the truth.

Scholars have often grappled with the vexed question of what shapes Southeast Asia as a region. The question is particularly difficult to answer because of the ethnic and religious diversity of Southeast Asia, its fragmented past, and the way in which its nations have been shaped and divided by colonialism. While the "status of women" factor is held up as a regional indicator, this too can be questioned. Our contributors illustrate considerable diversity in relation to women's roles in nationalist movements.

Our Choice of Subjects

The biographical study of Southeast Asian women is in its infancy. In inviting people to contribute to this book we could not call on scholars who had written biographies of women nationalists, for we knew of none. Rather, we were limited to our knowledge of people who had studied both Southeast Asian women and nationalist move-ments. We aimed to include a range of countries, types of nationalist movements, and women who had different roles in those movements. This avoids the "celebratory" style that assumes that anyone who participated in a nationalist movement is to be admired for their lofty goals and self-sacrifice. We are more interested in how (and why) individual women thought and acted. The resulting stories are bound to be as diverse as individuals are. These are people who identify not just with their nation's cause but with other competing identities such as member of a particular ethnic or religious group, mother, wife, daughter, and worker. Over their lifespan they may feel pulled in different directions. One woman's life obviously cannot give rise to new generalisations, but it may challenge some already in vogue.[18] This publication is just the first step towards what we hope to stimulate: a much more substantial exploration of women's roles in nationalist movements in Southeast Asia. Our aim is to gain insights and raise new questions for further research.

The Chapters

Each chapter of the book focuses on one or a maximum of two women active in nationalist movements, covering the whole of the region with the exception of Thailand, Singapore, Cambodia and Brunei. Although nationalism certainly exists in all of the countries we have omitted, we knew of no one able to write a biographical study of a woman in those countries who could be said to have taken a role in a nationalist movement. The omission is again indicative of the early stage such studies are at.

The order of the chapters is roughly chronological, depending on the period in which the woman was active. In total, they illustrate women's activities in nationalist movements ranging from the 1920s to the present day. Although it may well be possible to group our chapters in some other way, such as according to women who resorted to violent methods of pursuing nationalist goals as against those who took more moderate paths, there are advantages in taking a chronological approach. Earlier nationalist movements in Southeast Asia were aimed at ending European colonial rule, which gives the women actors of this period some things in common, such as their responses to modern education, which was new to the region at that time. In recent times nationalist movements have encountered a very different international environment, with greater support for movements such as those in East Timor and Burma, which can make a case for sympathy on human rights grounds. Moreover, the source materials for writing about women in the earlier period are rather different from those of the later chapters. Our authors have not had the chance to interview women subjects who are no longer alive, whereas the last three chapters of the book make ample use of contemporary interviews, especially those conducted by the authors. Indeed, the issue of sources in writing biographies is a controversial one in its own right, and our authors have had to wrestle with the limitations of their sources, as I will comment in my summary of the chapters that follow.

In the first chapter, Chie Ikeya has chosen to write about Daw San, one of Burma's best-known women nationalists, who was active in the anti-colonial movement in that country from the 1920s to the 1950s. Her education, based both in Buddhist Burmese tradition and in British schooling, clearly raised many tensions that she worked through in a strongly nationalist way. Claiming to be committed to both nationalism and feminism, Daw San (1887–1950) was a well-known journalist and editor, and a leader in women's organisations of the time. In her latter role she had links with the nationalist movement in adjacent India, since Burma was treated as part of Britain's South Asian empire: the Indian example provided her with inspiration. The nationalist movement in which she participated was the mainstream movement that gave rise to the first government of the independent nation in 1948. Nevertheless, she has received almost no official recognition for her activities. In this way her treatment has been very similar to that of Suyatin Kartowiyono in the following chapter on Indonesia. As a writer, Daw San has left a good legacy for historians such as Chie Ikeya, and her publications make clear her identification with the Buddhist Burman ethnic majority and her lack of sympathy for the minority ethnic groups that splintered the nationalist movement in Burma. In this way the chapter on Daw San forms a background to the later one on Zipporah Sein, which presents the viewpoint of the Karen nationalists who found they could not live in a Burman-dominated country.

In the following chapter, Micheline Lessard focuses on Nguyen Thi Giang (1906–30), a member of the Vietnamese Nationalist Party in the 1920s. The party modelled itself on the Chinese Nationalist Party (Guomindang) of the time, and was best known for its organisation of the failed Yen Bay Mutiny in 1930. Nguyen Thi Giang played a remarkably prominent role in preparations for that mutiny, after which she committed suicide. She suffered a double eclipse in Vietnamese historiography: not only was she a woman in a country where women's political activities have received little recognition, but she supported a party that represents a historical failure, since the Communist Party subsequently dominated the Vietnamese nationalist movement and has written its history as the winner. For these reasons, and because Nguyen Thi Giang lived under a harsh French colonial regime that made secrecy imperative for nationalists, very little is known about her and Lessard has had to reconstruct a biography largely from French colonial sources, involving much "reading against the grain". As a result there are gaps in our knowledge about Nguyen Thi Giang's social background (we know little more than that she was from the majority Kinh ethnic group and came from the rural north of the country) and about her views on gender relations, and it is difficult to probe her motivation for taking the risks she did in joining a radical nationalist organisation. Nevertheless, there is no doubt about her courage and her passionate opposition to foreign domination. At that time, Vietnamese nationalists had little choice but to take risks.

Suyatin Kartowiyono (1907–83), the subject of my chapter, offers the historian a unique source: she is the only Indonesian woman to have written an autobiography about her political activities. It is an engaging document that reveals her as a strong-minded feminist who nevertheless chose to keep her private life largely out of sight. This and other writings by Suyatin provide good evidence that she saw herself as a nationalist just as much as a leader of the women's movement, which is how she is now remembered, if at all. Being a Muslim Javanese, from the largest ethnic and religious group in Indonesia, Suyatin felt so confident in her ethnicity that she readily criticised what she saw as "feudalist" aspects of Javanese culture and took a sympathetic interest in other religions and cultures. Her tolerance and openness could be seen to result not only from her European-style education but also from a lack of dogmatism in Javanese religious tradition. By implication, she preferred to envisage a nation that would recognise the rights of people of many different backgrounds, and subsequently she was disillusioned with the shape the nation took under autocratic leadership. As a secular nationalist, she strongly supported the anti-colonial movement in Indonesia and helped organise women to provide food to pro-Republican forces and their families during the Revolution of 1945–49. Although the subsequent history of Indonesian nationalism has been dominated by the viewpoint of secular nationalists, it has taken a narrow perspective focusing on male-dominated nationalist parties and has ignored the sacrifice and contribution made by the women's movement and its leaders such as Suyatin. After independence Suyatin played an important role in literacy campaigns in Indonesia and as a leader of women's organisations, but never sought to enter political life.

Rasuna Said (1910–65), the subject of Sally White's chapter, was a contemporary of Suyatin in the Indonesian anti-colonial movement. She was exceptional in becoming a leading figure in a radical male-dominated Islamic nationalist party (Permi) in the 1930s, the first woman to be tried and jailed by the Dutch colonial authorities for her defiantly anti-imperialist speeches. The reasons for her prominence are interesting and include her ethnic background (she was a Minangkabau from the strongly Islamic and yet matrilineal society of West Sumatra). The religious and political ferment in West Sumatra in the early 20th century inspired her, like a number of prominent male leaders, to join the nationalist movement. Having entered the political arena, she went on to become a member of parliament after independence. In Indonesian historiography these events have earned her a place as an officially recognised "National Hero", ignoring some of her less orthodox activities relating to leftist politics and feminism. Rasuna's overtly political career makes her biography different from that of her compatriot, Suyatin. Unfortunately there is no autobiography or good biography of Rasuna Said, but her speeches, newspaper reports and colonial surveillance allow us to see the broad outline of her life, if not her private thoughts.

Daw San, Suyatin and Rasuna all participated in nationalist organisations that gained independence for their countries and formed the new political establishment. The Philippine example brings us back to the realm of parts of a nationalist movement that "failed", plunging their protagonists into obscurity. In this way Salud Algabre (1894–1979), the subject of the chapter by Maria Luisa Camagay, has something in common with Nguyen Thi Giang in Vietnam. She was the only female member of the Sakdal, a peasant movement that challenged the mainstream nationalist movement in the Philippines by launching a peasant revolt in 1935 against US rule and the Philippine landlords who collaborated with the Americans. With the quick suppression of the revolt, Salud and her fellow revolutionaries faded from historical memory, although Salud did not consider their struggle as futile, as revealed in two lively interviews with her later in life. (Unlike Nguyen Thi Giang, she had the advantage of experiencing a much more lenient form of colonialism, and she had a long, if obscure, life after independence.) From central rural Luzon, the main island of the Philippines, she does not appear to have thought about other ethnic groups: she identified herself with the modern secular nationalist movement that began in Luzon in the 19th century and with which her family had been involved. But her family's loss of land influenced her to side with the peasant class, thus alienating her from mainstream nationalist leaders in the Philippines. The scant evidence we have reveals nothing about her views on gender relations, although she herself was obviously very independent-minded and had recognised leadership qualities.

Moving southwest of the Philippines, we have two chapters focusing on women who took part in anti-British nationalist movements in the part of the world we now call Malaysia. There was never a Malaysian nationalist movement, but there were separate nationalist movements in the components that came to make up that federation in 1963. Focusing on British Malaya (now West Malaysia), which in 1957 became the independent Federation of Malaya, Helen Ting compares two Malay women, Shamsiah Fakeh (1924–2008) and Aishah Ghani (1923–2013), who came from similar backgrounds but ended up in different streams of the Malayan nationalist movement. Both their families sent the girls to get a Muslim education in neighbouring Sumatra, where their story overlaps with that of Rasuna Said, since they went to the same school at which she taught and which influenced both of them in their opposition to colonialism. Shamsiah Fakeh started her political career with the left-wing Malay Nationalist Party and then switched to the Malayan Communist Party, joining an all-Malay regiment in the jungle when the party was outlawed by the British. While Aishah Ghani also briefly joined the Malay Nationalist Party, she subsequently shifted to the conservative United Malays National Organisation and became the leader of its women's wing after independence. Clearly they had different conceptions of what an independent Malayan nation should be like, particularly in relation to the place of non-Malays. The chapter uses published memoirs and interviews with both women to unravel why they took divergent paths. Fortunately these sources also enable us to perceive their views about gender relations within the nationalist movement. Given the unsuccessful armed struggle of the Malayan Communist Party, Shamsiah was relegated to the margins of Malaysian history, while Aishah received little more recognition in male-dominated published accounts.

While the political activities of Malay women on the peninsula are better known, Welyne Jeffrey Jehom's chapter sheds light on the struggle of an unusual "Malay" woman who participated in the obscure anti-cession movement in Sarawak in 1946, a movement that resisted the handing over of that territory by its White Rajah into the hands of Britain after World War II. Lily Eberwein (1900–80), the subject of this chapter, was a leader of the women's wing of the Malay party that championed this movement. She was special in being a Western-educated Eurasian who converted to Islam and adopted the Malay cause: her life suddenly changed after the death of her Eurasian father, and she began to identify with her Malay mother's community. As an educated woman who worked in positions not previously taken by Malay women in Sarawak, she knew more about the world than most Malay women and was able to reach out to the Iban community for the cause. A lack of sources, common among supporters of "failed" movements, makes it difficult to uncover Eberwein's motivation and activities. Although we know little of her views, and she saw herself as an educationalist rather than as engaging in politics, she took on unconventional roles for a woman at that time and was perceived by others as a role model.

Moving into the more recent period, Vatthana Pholsena presents two women who were active in the Pathet Lao guerrilla movement in its anti-imperialist struggle in Laos in the late 1950s to early 1970s. Manivanh (mid-1940s–2007) and Khamla (b. middle to late 1950s) belonged to ethnic minority groups but identified with a nationalist and Communist cause dominated by the Lao majority. They make an interesting case of how the mainstream nationalist movement treated ethnic minority women. The nationalist movement reached their remote mountain area because guerrilla leaders needed the cooperation of ethnic minorities: the whole area became a war zone of strategic importance, leaving the minority villagers with few options. It appears that these young women joined the nationalist movement partly in the hope of gaining an education that was not available in their area, yet their years spent in guerrilla struggle equally deprived them of schooling. After the victory of the Pathet Lao, the two women were expected to continue to work to retain the ethnic minority groups' loyalty to the regime. The chapter is based on interviews with the two women, in which they had almost nothing to say about gender relations in the movement, partly because they were not questioned on the subject.

Sara Niner also researched a woman involved in a guerrilla nationalist struggle, this time in East Timor (now officially Timor-Leste). Rosa de Camara (b. 1963), better known as Bisoi, was part of the armed movement from the 1970s to the 1990s. Like the two Laotian women of the previous chapter, she was from a poor, illiterate rural background and was encouraged by her uncle to join the nationalist struggle. Although her cause triumphed in the winning of independence for East Timor, she was bitter at the lack of government recognition of and support for female armed combatants like herself. The chapter is largely based on interviews with Bisoi, who spoke frankly about the difficulties facing women in rural society, in the nationalist movement, and in post-independence Timor-Leste. Those who had been combatants had missed out on the education so important for advancement.

Finally, Ardeth Maung Thawnghmung and Violet Cho present a female leader of an ongoing nationalist struggle in Burma. Zipporah Sein (b. 1955) is the first female general secretary of the Karen National Union, which has long waged an armed campaign for an independent Karen State. She comes from a prominent Karen rebel family, her father being one of the leaders of the armed movement, yet her own expertise has been mainly in education and in organising women. Using extensive interviews with Zipporah, this chapter sheds light on the challenging task of reorientating a movement in view of changing international and national environments. Unlike anti-colonial movements of the early 20th century, the Burmese opposition movement has found some degree of support internationally, due to the widespread condemnation of the oppressive behaviour of the Burmese junta, yet few outsiders are willing to condone armed resistance. The international community offers support for diplomatic negotiation and gender equality, which has favoured Zipporah Sein. The chapter illustrates well the problems faced by a female civilian leader in a movement dominated by soldiers, and investigates the reasons why Zipporah took on this challenge. With this last biographical study we have returned full circle to Burma, a nation riven by competing nationalisms. While the nationalist movement that Daw San joined had no place for female leaders, by the 21st century it was possible for a woman to become a leader of the Karen nationalist organisation that had long conducted an armed struggle for independence from Burma.

Thus, our chapters cover 12 women from 7 different countries and 9 ethnic groups and from different religions (Muslim, Buddhist and Christian). Their ethnicity and religious affiliation in most cases strongly affected their vision of the nation. While most of them were from moderately well-to-do families and received a modern education, the women from Laos and East Timor were exceptions. It is noticeable that those from wealthier and better-educated backgrounds were able to play more prominent roles, while the uneducated were relegated to relatively subservient positions and were more susceptible to being discriminated against. Although they did not all join a nationalist movement from entirely patriotic motives, they soon became committed nationalists and their commitment dominated at least part of their lives. It is not possible to know whether all 12 women addressed gender issues in their nationalist movements: while a few of them (Daw San, Suyatin, Bisoi and Zipporah) openly embraced feminism and contested discrimination against women, others either identified rather less strongly with the cause of women or had a very different understanding about gender relations (Rasuna, Shamsiah and Aishah). In the cases of Nguyen Thi Giang, Salud Algabre, Lily Eberwein, Manivanh and Khamla, there is no evidence that they reflected on what it meant to be a woman in a nationalist organisation. This may, of course, merely reflect the lack of available data. Unless the source materials contained interviews that directly posed questions about gender, it is unlikely that some women would broach the topic.

Six of the women joined armed resistance movements, which placed them at considerable risk: one lost her life in the course of the struggle. The other five suffered from spending years in the jungle: at the very least, their family life and education prospects were affected. Although the nationalist organisations that at least four of them joined cannot be said to have achieved their aims, there is no indication that these women regretted their involvement. Very few of them could be said to have gained personally from their involvement in a nationalist movement, and only one of them (Rasuna Said) has received official recognition for her contribution to a nationalist cause. Yet only Bisoi and Zipporah openly voiced complaints. There may be a psychological dimension to this stoicism: perhaps the kind of woman who took the unusual and adventurous step of participating in a nationalist movement had a positive outlook on life that protected against disappointment.

Because our chapters focus on individual women, it is hard to generalise from them about women's participation in nationalist movements. However, it is worth noting the different capacities in which women participated. As mentioned before, social movements are broad and can accommodate many activities. In this book we find women acting as journalists, members of clandestine armed organisations, leaders of women's organisations, providers of support for armed combatants, and leaders of mainstream nationalist parties. Armed conflict, so often a reason for women taking on unconventional roles, proved very important in the recruitment of more than half of our subjects: Nguyen Thi Giang, Salud Algabre, Shamsiah Fakeh, Khamla, Manivanh, Bisoi and Zipporah. Some of them, such as Rasuna and Zipporah, gained considerable media attention for their nationalist roles; others worked in greater obscurity necessitated by state oppression or by male leaders or through their own choice. While they rarely claimed to be participating in politics, that is precisely what they were doing by joining the nationalist cause. Thus they have contributed their experiences to a neglected field of study in Southeast Asian gender relations. Women may not have been so inactive in politics as is sometimes claimed: observers have just not been looking in the right places.

Conclusion

This introduction serves to raise questions that we have thought worth pursuing about women and nationalist movements. Why have women joined nationalist movements? How have they envisaged the nation? What roles have they played in nationalist movements? How have they negotiated gender relations within those movements? What have they gained or lost by such involvement? Because our contributors have been asked to address such questions from a biographical perspective, by the end of the book we will be in a position to draw together the diverse threads that emerge from an analysis of 12 lives. In the last chapter Helen Ting offers some reflections by way of the Conclusion, drawing out comparisons between the personal experiences of the women into whose lives as nationalists we have gained some valuable insights.

Notes

1. Literature on gender and nationalism includes works such as I. Blom, K. Hagemann and C. Hall (eds.), *Gendered Nations: Nationalisms and Gender Order in the Long Nineteenth Century* (Oxford: Berg, 2000); N.G. Chong, *Women, Ethnicity and Nationalisms in Latin America* (Aldershot: Ashgate, 2007); C. Cockburn, *The Space between Us: Negotiating Gender and National Identities in Conflict* (London: Zed Books, 1998); K. Jayawardena, *Feminism and Nationalism in the Third World* (London and

New Jersey: Zed Books, 1986); T. Mayer (ed.), *Gender Ironies of Nationalism: Sexing the Nation* (London: Routledge, 2000); V.M. Moghadam, *Gender and National Identity: Women and Politics in Muslim Societies* (London: Zed Books, 1994); S. Ranchod-Nilsson and M.A. Tétreault (eds.), *Women, States and Nationalism: At Home in the Nation?* (London and New York: Routledge, 2000); S. Walby, "Woman and Nation", in *Mapping the Nation,* ed. G. Balakrishnan (London and New York: Verso, 1996); L.A. West (ed.), *Feminist Nationalism* (New York: Routledge, 1997); R. Wilford, "Women, Ethnicity and Nationalism: Surveying the Ground", in *Women, Ethnicity and Nationalism: The Politics of Transition,* ed. R. Wilford and R.L. Miller (London: Routledge, 1998); B.F. Williams (ed.), *Women out of Place: The Gender of Agency and the Race of Nationality* (New York: Routledge, 1996); N. Yuval-Davis, *Gender and Nation* (London: Sage, 1993); and N. Yuval-Davis and F. Anthias (eds.), *Woman-Nation-State* (London: Macmillan, 1989). In Asia there is a rich and growing literature on women in the Indian nationalist movement: works include A. Basu, "A Nationalist Feminist: Mridula Sarabhai (1911–1974)", *Indian Journal of Gender Studies* 2 (1995): 1–24; G. Forbes, *Women in Modern India* (Cambridge: Cambridge University Press, 1996); L. Kasturi and V. Mazumdar (eds.), *Women and Indian Nationalism* (New Delhi: Vikas, 1994); V. Menon, *Indian Women and Nationalism: The UP Story* (New Delhi: Shaku Books, 2003); P.N. Premalatha, *Nationalism and the Women's Movement in South India: 1917–1947* (New Delhi: Gyan Publishing House, 2003); and B. Thakur, *Women and Gandhi's Mass Movements* (New Delhi: Deep and Deep, 2006). Honourable exceptions to the neglect of gender in relation to Southeast Asian nationalism include C. Dobbin, "The Search for Women in Indonesian History", in *Kartini Centenary: Indonesian Women Then and Now,* ed. A. Zainu'ddin (Clayton: Monash University, 1980); C. Doran, "Women, Nationalism and the Philippine Revolution", *Nations and Nationalism* 5, 2 (1999): 237–58; A. Khoo, *Life as the River Flows: Women in the Malaysian Anti-colonial Struggle* (Monmouth: Merlin Press, 2007); V. Lanzona, *Amazons of the Huk Rebellion: Gender, Sex, and the Revolution in the Philippines* (Madison: University of Wisconsin Press, 2009); P. Laungaramsri, "Women, Nation, and the Ambivalence of Subversive Identification along the Thai-Burmese Border", *Sojourn: Journal of Social Issues in Southeast Asia* 21, 1 (2006): 68–89; S. Sutjiatiningsih (ed.), *Biografi Tokoh Kongres Perempuan Indonesia Pertama* [*Biographies of Leaders of the First Indonesian Women's Congress*] (Jakarta: Departemen Pendidikan dan Kebudayaan, 1991); S.C. Taylor, *Vietnamese Women at War: Fighting for Ho Chi Minh and the Revolution* (Lawrence: University Press of Kansas, 1999); M.A. Tetreault, "Women and Revolution in Vietnam", in *Vietnam's*

Women in Transition, ed. K. Barry (London: Macmillan, 1996); K.G. Turner, *Even the Women Must Fight: Memories of War from North Vietnam* (New York: Wiley, 1998); and C. Vreede-de Stuers, *The Indonesian Woman: Struggles and Achievements* ('s-Gravenhage: Mouton, 1960).

2. A brief introduction to political debates on nationalism is to be found in David Miller, "Nationalism", in *The Oxford Handbook of Political Theory*, ed. John S. Dryzek, Bonnie Honig and Anne Phillips (Oxford: Oxford University Press, 2006), while discussions of historical interpretations, especially for Southeast Asia, are to be found in A. Reid, *Imperial Alchemy: Nationalism and Political Identity in Southeast Asia* (Cambridge: Cambridge University Press, 2010).

3. I take this definition from Susan Olzak, "Ethnic and Nationalist Social Movements", in *The Blackwell Companion to Social Movements*, ed. D.A. Snow, S.A. Soule and H. Kriesi (Oxford: Blackwell Publishing, 2004).

4. A revealing example of the important contribution of women to a nationalist movement is contained in Susan Geiger's article about women in the Tanganyikan nationalist movement. She stresses the success of women's dance associations in producing nationalism, and argues that women were far more active than men "in organising and mobilising both women and men for the nationalist cause" (S. Geiger, "Tanganyikan Nationalism as 'Women's Work': Life Histories, Collective Biography and Changing Historiography", *Journal of African History* 37 [1996]: 472).

5. For insightful discussions of biography and autobiography in the Indonesian and Philippine contexts, see C.W. Watson, *Of Self and Nation: Autobiography and the Representation of Modern Indonesia* (Honolulu: University of Hawaii Press, 2000); A.W. McCoy, "Introduction: Biography of Lives Obscure, Ordinary, and Heroic", in *Lives at the Margin: Biography of Filipinos Obscure, Ordinary, and Heroic*, ed. A.W. McCoy (Quezon City: Ateneo de Manila University Press, 2000); and D.T. Hill, "In the Shadow of Other Lives: Reflections on Dan Lev and Writing Biography", *Review of Indonesian and Malaysian Affairs* 42, 2 (2008): 147–60. An anthropologist who encountered difficulties trying to collect autobiographies in South Sulawesi recounts her experiences in B. Rottger-Rossler, "Autobiography in Question: On Self-presentation and Life Description in an Indonesian Society", *Anthropos* 88 (1993): 365–73.

6. Examples of such an approach include P. Chatterjee, *The Nation and Its Fragments: Colonial and Postcolonial Histories* (Princeton: Princeton University Press, 1993). In Southeast Asia such analyses are rarer but include C. Brown, "Sukarno on the Role of Women in the Nationalist Movement", *Review of Indonesian and Malaysian Affairs* 15, 1 (1981): 68–82; and D. Marr, "The 1920s Women's Rights Debates in Vietnam", *Journal of Asian Studies* 35, 3 (1976): 371–89.

7.   Ranchod-Nilsson and Tétreault, *Women, States and Nationalism*, p. 7.

8.   See, for example, Ranchod-Nilsson and Tétreault, *Women, States and Nationalism*, p. 3. For a passionate denunciation of the abuse of women due to Japanese nationalism, see C. Ueno, *Nationalism and Gender* (Melbourne: Trans Pacific Press, 2004).

9.   I refer to her statement in *Three Guineas* that since women lack equal rights they have little incentive to fight for their country. Women are outsiders: "… in fact, as a woman, I have no country. As a woman I want no country. As a woman my country is the whole world … [F]rom this indifference certain actions must follow. She will bind herself to take no share in patriotic demonstrations; to assent to no form of national self-praise …." (V. Woolf, *A Room of One's Own and Three Guineas* [Oxford: Oxford University Press, 1992], pp. 313–4).

10. J.M. Bystydzienski, "Conclusion", in *Women Transforming Politics: World-wide Strategies for Empowerment*, ed. J.M. Bystydzienski (Bloomington and Indianapolis: Indiana University Press, 1992), p. 209.

11. Jayawardena, *Feminism and Nationalism*, p. 258. She further concludes that "in the period of nationalist struggles, men were the main movers of history. They organised nationalist movements and political parties, set the parameters for the struggle, even determined the role that women should play. In this sense, with a few exceptions, the women worked within the boundaries laid down by men" (pp. 260–1).

12. Ibid., p. 10.

13. C. Enloe, *Bananas, Beaches and Bases: Making Feminist Sense of International Politics* (London: University of California Press, 1989), p. 56.

14. A. Reid, *Imperial Alchemy*.

15. A. Reid, *Southeast Asia in the Age of Commerce 1450–1680, Vol. 1: The Lands below the Winds* (New Haven: Yale University Press, 1988).

16. For instance, L. Dube, *Women and Kinship: Comparative Perspectives on Gender in South and Southeast Asia* (Tokyo: United Nations University Press, 1997).

17. See G.W. Jones, *Marriage and Divorce in Islamic South-East Asia* (Kuala Lumpur: Oxford University Press, 1994), pp. 230–1.

18. See J. Chapman, "A Khmer Veteran Remembers: Herstory and History", *Indian Journal of Gender Studies* 17, 1 (2010): 1–24 for the use of a short biography to challenge statements about the Khmer Rouge period in Cambodia. Clearly one must take a very cautious approach to such stories, which contradict received history. Apart from the critical analysis to which every first-hand account must be subjected, "one swallow does not a summer make".

CHAPTER 1

The Life and Writings of a Patriotic Feminist: Independent Daw San of Burma

Chie Ikeya

Introduction

Throughout Southeast Asia, the 1920s and 1930s witnessed a marked intensification in reformist, anti-colonial and nationalist activities. In Burmese history this period of late colonialism marks a watershed, when disparate political developments — party politics, university boycotts, labour strikes and nonviolent protests — emerged to signify a new kind of *nain ngan yay* (politics) and the birth of the *wunthanu* (protector of national interests) movement. In 1920, a faction led by young members of the Young Men's Buddhist Association (YMBA), the most famous and influential lay Buddhist organisation in colonial Burma,[1] formed the General Council of Burmese Associations (GCBA), the first organisation with explicitly political goals that focused on securing representative political rights. Within a few years, the GCBA had 12,000 branches throughout Burma.[2] Buddhist monks also involved themselves in political activity and played a key role in the formation of *wunthanu athin* or village-level "patriotic associations" that advocated non-cooperation with the British government in various forms, such as refusal to pay taxes, defiance of orders of the village headmen, boycott of foreign goods, and use of indigenous goods. Despite government attempts to suppress the activities of political monks throughout the 1920s, *wunthanu athin* developed into influential political institutions in the countryside, as demonstrated by

Daw San in the late 1940s. Photo from
Sape Beikman 1967, p. 53

the central role they played in the Saya San Rebellion of 1930–32,
the largest peasant uprising in Burmese history.[3] At the same time,
leftist student activism in the 1930s led to the formation of Dobama
Asiayone (Our Burma/Burmese Association), modelled after the Sinn
Féin Party in Ireland.[4] The Dobama Asiayone was known popularly as
the Thakin Party, and members titled themselves *thakin* (master) as a
symbol of the idea that the Burmese people, not the British, were the
rightful masters of Burma and as an expression of their goal to transform Burma into a classless society of only masters. Dobama Asiayone
served as the umbrella organisation that linked the rapidly expanding
number of nationalist youth groups in urban and rural Burma.

The 1920s and 1930s also saw growing participation of Burmese
women, for the first time, in organised politics, university boycotts,
labour strikes and anti-colonial protests. Yet, the nationalist meta-
narrative in Burma, written by and about leading nationalists (all
men) who became elite political figures in independent Burma, has
either ignored this or relegated the historical past of women to a foot-
note. While some accounts mention the participation of women in
nationalist movements, they merely "insert" women into the national
epic for the purpose of glorifying the anti-colonial struggle led by the
Burma Independence Army, the predecessor of the current military
regime.[5] Such narrow analyses offer little, if any, insight into how
women themselves experienced, perceived and shaped the political
landscape of colonial Burma.

This chapter begins to fill this gap in the historiography of colonial Burma by examining the relationship of one particular woman, Independent Daw San (1887–1950),[6] to the Burmese nationalist movement. The founder and editor of the popular weekly newspaper *Independent Weekly*, published during the 1920s and 1930s, Daw San was a prolific writer known for political and social commentary. She was also a leading member of the Burmese Women's Association, an elite women's organisation established to reinforce the activities of the GCBA as well as to protect and advance the intellectual and spiritual growth and well-being of Burmese women. Through an analysis of her writings and her involvement in the Burmese nationalist and women's movements, I explore how she viewed, experienced and articulated the complex relationship between feminism and nationalism. The mounting nationalist efforts in the 1920s urged the participation of women in the anti-colonial movement, albeit in supporting roles.[7] Women's associations were not autonomous but were subsidiary branches of the main political organisations under male leadership. Yet, the subsidiary position of a women's group in a male-dominated nationalist movement should not lead us to underestimate the feminist content of the women's movement.[8] In her examination of the relationship between nationalism and female subjectivities in early 20th-century China, Joan Judge has shown that the conjoined nature of "the national question" and "the woman question" "enabled women to reposition themselves (or to be repositioned) in pre-existing webs of cultural relations", even as this existing cultural matrix informed national feminine identities that were subsequently fashioned.[9] For Daw San, also, the project of "protecting the interests of the nation" was inextricably intertwined with the "woman question": her emancipation from subordination within the patriarchal structure of family and society. The inseparability of the *wunthanu* and women's movements necessitated and facilitated her role simultaneously as a nationalist and a feminist.

Early Childhood and Education

"Daw San" was the pen name of Ma San Youn,[10] who was born in February 1887 in Mandalay, just two years after the third and final Anglo-Burmese War (1885) ended with the defeat of the last Burmese dynasty (Konbaung dynasty, 1752–1885), the exile of the last Burmese

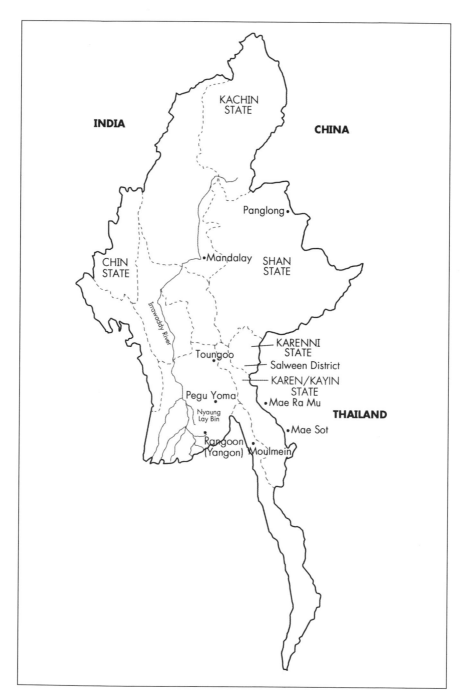

Map 1. Burma/Myanmar

monarch and his immediate family to the western coast of India, the desertion and desecration of the royal palace in Mandalay, and the beginning of British colonial rule over Burma.[11] (See map 1 for places mentioned in this chapter and in chapter 10.) The oldest of five children, Ma San Youn was born into a well-to-do family that specialised in the craft of *shwe chi hto* or gold thread embroidery: tapestry featuring gold, silver and coloured threads; sequins; semi-precious gems; and colourful cut glass. For generations, the family had produced intricate embroidered works including clothing and regalia for members of the royal family, ministers and high-ranking officials. Daw San's mother, Daw Shu, grew up socialising with the children of the chief queen, which contributed significantly to her knowledge and appreciation of Burmese and Buddhist literature. Wanting to raise her children to be similarly learned, Daw Shu instructed them extensively in grammar, traditional Burmese metaphysics, history, poetry and Buddhist scriptures since their early childhood. Daw Shu probably saw this Burmese Buddhist education as a necessary supplement and corrective to the formal education her children were receiving under the British.

Over the course of the 19th century, Buddhist monastic schools gradually lost their prerogative as the chief providers of education; privately and governmentally supported lay and mission schools that offered a vernacular, Anglo-vernacular and English co-educational system of public instruction increased in number.[12] With the support of grants-in-aid administered by the colonial administration, Christian missionaries made headway especially in the area of female education, which Buddhist monastic schools in Burma did not provide.[13] As a result, an unprecedented number of women gained access to education, leading to a rise in female employment. Women employed in the professions of public administration, law, medicine, education and journalism increased by 33 per cent (from 17,760 to 23,588) during the 1920s, with a notable 96 per cent increase (from 3,332 to 6,540) in the field of medicine and 64 per cent increase (from 2,955 to 4,857) in the field of education.[14]

Ma San Youn belonged to this rapidly expanding generation of educated women. She was enrolled in a vernacular school; and in 1900, the year her father — U Pein — passed away from illness, she completed the seventh grade with honours. She was 15 years of age when she received a state scholar prize to attend the Morlan Lane Normal School in Moulmein and began her training to be a teacher at the Christian school. Upon passing the teachers' exam, she was assigned to a normal (teachers' training) school in Toungoo to be a teacher of Burmese *bādā* (language and literature), a subject in which she excelled.

Becoming "Daw San"

Ma San Youn's life in Toungoo had a promising start. Though she received a meagre salary, teaching was clearly her passion and a source of joy. When she was approximately 20 years old, and after teaching at the primary level for three years, she was promoted to teach in the secondary grades. Ma San Youn met and married U Kywet, a fellow secondary grade teacher. By all accounts, the marriage was a happy one and the couple had one daughter and three sons. But the marriage was tragically cut short. After the last child was born, U Kywet was transferred to administer a school in Singu. Not long after his move, he contracted malaria and passed away at the young age of 26. Ma San Youn's grief over the loss of her husband was soon compounded by the death of her two younger sons barely a year after she was widowed. While mourning the death of her loved ones, Ma San Youn sought solace in writing, which led to her first major publication, *Khin Aye Kyi*.

The story, which was published in 1918 in *Thuriya Magazine* as the winner of the monthly's short fiction competition, is titled after its Buddhist heroine. In this semi-autobiographical story, Khin Aye Kyi is born to a wealthy Buddhist couple in Moulmein. When Khin Aye Kyi comes of age, the couple reluctantly enrol her in an American Baptist mission school, fearful on the one hand that their daughter will be converted to Christianity, but anxious on the other that she obtain an education. Fortunately, due to her Buddhist upbringing by her devout parents, the girl is not swayed by the proselytising efforts of her missionary teachers. As in the case of Ma San Youn, Khin Aye Kyi completes the seventh grade shortly after her father, U Ee, passes away and goes on to attend a teachers' training school where she specialises in Burmese *bādā*. She grows into a beautiful woman and a learned teacher single-mindedly committed to the teaching of *bādā*, the propagation of *sāsana* (teachings of the Buddha), and the education of women. She remains utterly uninterested in love and marriage, until one day she narrowly escapes abduction by a lecherous man named Maung Pe Nyun thanks to her friend Maung Thein Pe, who

Burmese Nationalist Movement, 1917–49

1917	Young Men's Buddhist Association (YMBA) passes political and anti-colonial resolutions
1919	Formation of Burmese Women's Association (BWA), Young Women's Buddhist Association (YWBA) and Wunthanu Konmaryi Athin (Patriotic Women's Association)
1920	Establishment of General Council of Burmese Associations (GCBA); first university boycott
1920s	Proliferation of *wunthanu athin* (village-level patriotic associations)
1930	Formation of Dobama Asiayone; first anti-Indian riots
1930–32	Saya San Rebellion
1936	Second university boycott
1937	Separation of Burma from India
1938	1300 Revolution; second anti-Indian riots
1939	Establishment of Communist Party of Burma (CPB)
1942–45	Japanese occupation
1945	Formation of Anti-Fascist People's Freedom League (AFPFL); British reoccupation of Burma
1946	CPB is expelled from AFPFL
1947	Panglong Agreement; assassination of Aung San; formation of the Karen National Union (KNU)
1948	Burma gains independence from Britain; armed insurgency by CPB; mutinies in the army
1949	Armed campaign for an independent state by KNU

has been courting Khin Aye Kyi unsuccessfully. The story concludes with Khin Aye Kyi's happy marriage to Maung Thein Pe, her saviour, with the blessings of her mother, Daw Kyi.[15]

This story, published under the pseudonym Buddha bādā myanmar ma (a Buddhist Burmese woman), encapsulates what turned out to be an important and lifelong cause for Ma San Youn: feminist nationalism. The story is about a "protectress of national interests" who believes that *all* Burmese people should respect and honour their *bādā* and *sāsana* as she does. It is no coincidence that at about this time, organised politics in Burma and the *wunthanu* movement were beginning to take shape, as in colonial Lanka, in the form of Buddhist revivalist movements and the related campaign for Buddhist education.[16] Just one year before the publication of *Khin Aye Kyi*, the YMBA passed resolutions of a political and anti-colonial nature that included, most famously, a strong protest against Europeans' wearing shoes in pagoda precincts, contrary to Burmese custom.[17] And only a few years thereafter, the GCBA and its affiliated women's organisations urged women in Burma to defend the *sāsana* by abstaining from marrying non-Buddhist men. The *wunthanu* movement in Burma was formulated from the beginning for the protection and revival of Buddhism.

Bādā also served as a rallying point for the "national education movement" — an outcome of the 1920 student strike at Rangoon University — to establish "national schools" as alternative and independent educational institutions where "love of country and love of nation are no less assiduously cultivated and nurtured" through "the invaluable services of Burmese literature and Burmese history".[18] As the motto of the Dobama Asiayone shows, *bādā* continued to be a pillar of the *wunthanu* movement in the 1930s:

> Burma Is Our Country
> Burmese Is Our Literature
> Burmese Is Our Language
> Love Our Country
> Cherish Our Literature
> Uphold Our Language[19]

Khin Aye Kyi was an early — perhaps the earliest — feminine model of *wunthanu* and *dobama*. It was not until the 1930s that the *thakin* articulated a coherent notion of the *dobama*; nor did discussions of the *myo chit may* (female patriot) become popular in the Burmese media until the late 1920s. Long before such feminine representations of patriotism emerged, Ma San Youn fashioned a "Buddhist Burmese woman" who cherished and loved the language, literature and religion of the Burmese people.

It is worth stressing that in *Khin Aye Kyi*, Ma San Youn goes to great lengths to emphasise the necessary relationship between "the national" and "the woman's" question. Accordingly, Khin Aye Kyi proposes: "if women could contribute alongside men, but in their own and separate way, ideas, suggestions, and plans on how to make the *a myo* (nation),[20] *bādā* and *sāsana* prosper, then I don't think Burmese men would be oppressed and subjugated by the British." The importance of female education to the nationalist struggle of colonial Burma was repeated again through Khin Aye Kyi's father, U Ee, during a conversation with his wife about whether or not to enrol Khin Aye Kyi in the American Baptist mission school: "It's because young women have little education that we Burmese people find ourselves under colonial rule. Future generations of Burmese will be able to better govern society and the country if young girls like Khin Aye Kyi are given an education. You know very well why women are so important right now." Ma San Youn offered the colonial experience of humiliation and subjugation as a painful but edifying lesson in the indispensability of female education, framing the issue of female education in nationalist discourse. In this instance, the experience of colonisation was perceived to "enable women to doubt the hegemonic patriarchal discourse of their own society" and "lead to a desire to develop new possibilities".[21]

To the extent that the "conditions of women" had become the scale for measuring the readiness of a country for national self-determination, the gender disparity in literacy and education represented a national problem. Yet, to argue in 1918 that women needed to not only get educated but also educate others for the sake of the *a myo* was to take a radical stance. Here, the descriptive "a Buddhist Burmese woman" that Ma San Youn used to publish *Khin Aye Kyi* is instructive. Was the self-identification as "a Buddhist Burmese woman" a strategy to deflect criticism of the story — specifically, its determined promotion of the intellectual and vocational aspirations of young Burmese women — as the work of a Westernised woman who had been indoctrinated by a Christian and colonial modern education? Ma San Youn must have anticipated that her support for female education might be construed as support for the Christian missionary and/or the colonial project. In all likelihood, she positioned herself as Buddhist and Burmese to contend with the question of whether she would be rendered a collaborator with the colonial project. The consequence of this strategy, however, was the conjuring up of a limited community of "Buddhist Burmese" compatriots, which rendered the identification by minority groups, both Buddhist and non-Buddhist, problematic.

Khin Aye Kyi was nothing short of groundbreaking. The acclaimed "patriot-writer" Saya Lun (1876–1964), for instance, wrote a *lay gyo* (four-stanza poem) praising Ma San Youn as a rare literary genius who surpassed some of the most celebrated women court poets from the Toungoo and Konbaung periods. Such recognition by a man described as "the single most revered literary figure in modern Burma"[22] no doubt boosted Ma San Youn's reputation as a woman of letters. Ma San Youn soon found herself writing short stories and essays regularly for *Thuriya Magazine* under the name "Daw San".[23]

From Daw San to Independent Daw San

Daw San's entry into Burmese literary circles resulted in her second marriage — to somebody who had also lost a spouse, U Ba Than, then an editor for *Thuriya Magazine*. In 1922, Daw San resigned from her teaching position in Toungoo and joined U Ba Than in Rangoon (Yangon). Her decision to resign, remarry and relocate may have been facilitated by the fact that at around this time, the British administration issued a decree that all schoolteachers must apply for permission from the commissioner of education to write in newspapers and magazines. She chose to resign and to start a new life in Rangoon.

Her second marriage lasted only a few years, due apparently to U Ba Than's alcohol addiction, and Daw San made yet another attempt at a fresh start. In 1925 she divorced U Ba Than, moved with her children to a new home, and set up her own paper, tellingly named *Independent Weekly*. Daw San explains that the name of the paper, which was inspired by the Irish nationalist paper the *Irish Independent*, signified her desire for Burma's freedom but also her "determination to never return to the shackled life of a salaried worker or a married woman".[24] This rejection of colonisation, wage labour and matrimony as analogous forms of subjugation and exploitation presented a radical critique of marriage — which functioned in this context as a metaphor for gender norms and relations — at a time when the family and the home were still very much defined and naturalised as the primary responsibilities of a woman. *Independent Weekly* symbolised Daw San's conjoined nationalist and feminist aspirations. Mirroring her endeavour to be independent, Daw San single-handedly ran the paper, not only authoring the editorials, headline news and all of its various columns, such as "Kwa Si e mhattan" (Mr Kwa Si's Journal), "Ma Shwe e diary" (Miss Parrot's Diary) and the ladies' column "Yuwadi kye hmoun" (Young Ladies' Mirror), but also managing the day-to-day operations of the press.

At about this time, Daw San also emerged as a leader of the first women's organisation in Burma, the Burmese Women's Association (BWA), established in 1919.[25] The BWA played a supporting role to the anti-colonial struggle of the GCBA. Critical of the British government's economic policy for undermining local industries and impoverishing the Burmese common folk, the GCBA advocated the use of local goods, the boycott of imported products, and the picketing of stores that sold imported items. Accordingly, the BWA condemned the use of imported goods and promoted wearing blouses made of *pinni* (light brown, homespun cotton) and longyi with local *yaw* designs originating in the western hill tracts of Burma.

In addition to discouraging Burmese women from marrying men of religious faiths other than Buddhism in the name of *sāsana*, the group campaigned assiduously for legislative reforms to ensure that a Burmese woman who married a non-Buddhist did not lose her Buddhist spousal rights. Though the Special Marriage Act of 1872 provided the forms and procedures for Buddhists and non-Buddhists to contract valid marriages, women in such marriages were not protected under Burmese Buddhist law.[26] As a result of the persistent lobbying by the BWA, the colonial government drafted the Buddhist Marriage and Divorce Bill in 1927; and the BWA continued to push for the bill until it finally went into effect in 1939. The BWA was thus a protector not only of Buddhism but also of Burmese tradition. To signify their role as bearers and wearers of tradition, members of the BWA, including Daw San, wore scarves woven with a design of a peacock, the symbol of the last Burmese dynasty, on top of *pinni* and *yaw* longyi.

The association was also an advocate of female education, believing that "women's rights" had less to do with suffrage and more to do with education.[27] In support of its educational mission the BWA opened a library — one of the few in the country — for its members immediately upon its inception.[28] Aware of the reluctance of Burmese parents to send their adolescent daughters to school unaccompanied, the association advocated successfully for women-only sections in city trams for the transportation of female students to school. Daw San and other members of the BWA chaperoned young women to and from school in their endeavour to reassure wary parents and encourage them to allow their daughters to pursue higher education.[29]

That the feminist struggle was no less pressing than the *wunthanu* movement for Daw San is also clear from a 1927 demonstration in support of women's rights to vote and to stand for parliamentary elections that she led with Daw Mya Sein (1904–88), another prominent member of the BWA.[30] On the morning of 3 February 1927, Daw San and Daw Mya Sein led a group of more than 100 women on the premises of the Rangoon Municipal Hall and the legislative council to show support for a proposal — scheduled to be debated in the council the same morning — to abolish "the sex-disqualification clause" that prohibited women from running for parliamentary posts. The demonstrators shouted out the following chant:

> Burmese women, don't be afraid
> Wait and see what will become of the act
> Banning us women from ministerial positions
> Burmese women, be watchful and active
> In Britain, women have attained seats in the parliament.[31]

This endeavour to engender legislative reforms might be attributed to similar initiatives of Burmese male politicians to establish a firm footing in electoral politics and to obtain greater Burmese representation in the legislative council. According to Daw Mya Sein, the women demonstrators were well aware that any attempt by Burmese women to be elected to the council would be construed as nationalist, but she stressed that the demonstrators objected to the sex-disqualification clause primarily as feminists.[32] As the protesters' chant suggests, what prompted the demonstration were the concurrent struggles in England and India by women to remove sex disqualification on voting and to attain posts in supreme legislative bodies. The demonstrators strove in unison with international feminist associations such as the International Alliance of Women for Suffrage and Equal Citizenship and the British Commonwealth League, which urged the British government "on behalf of the women of the Empire" to grant Burmese women the right to run in elections for the legislative council.[33]

   The connection between these early women's movements in Burma and similarly urban, elite and middle-class international feminist movements is not surprising given that the 1920s and 1930s represented "the high tide of internationalism" for the women's movement.[34] In fact, the 1927 demonstration was featured in *Stri Dharma* (Woman's Duty), a well-known women-run journal in India that had emerged in the 1920s and 1930s as "an international feminist news medium targeted at Anglo-Indian, Indian, and British women readers".[35] And, according to Daw Mya Sein, the 1927 demonstration had been sponsored by the National Council of Women in Burma (NCWB),[36] which had a mixed membership of British, Indian, Anglo-Indian, Anglo-Burmese and Burmese women, of which Daw San was also a member. Established in 1926 and led by mostly British women, the NCWB was an affiliate of the National Council of Women in India and a local branch of the International Council of Women, which claimed to represent 36 million women by 1925.[37] What little documentation exists on the NCWB indicates that it was concerned with improving the lives of women and child labourers in Burma in 1929, well before *thakin* and other politicians turned their attention to the plight of the working class.[38]

Subsequently, in 1931, Daw San along with other Burmese members of the NCWB formed the Myanmar Amyothami National Council (Burmese Women's National Council), described by some scholars as a splinter organisation established by those who had "come to feel that the NCWB was too international in outlook, and did not adequately address the nationalist aspirations of its Burmese members".[39] Again, little is known about the goals and activities of the Myanmar Amyothami National Council apart from the fact that it contested writings on Burmese women in foreign newspapers that the council deemed harmful to Burmese women.[40] According to Ba Khaing, the author of one of the earliest Burmese-language books to chronicle the history of nationalist movements in Burma, the members of the group were "wives of government officers or wealthy men", "out of touch with the ordinary women", who refrained from political activities because they "could not afford to oppose the government".[41]

Many aspects of Daw San's involvement in local and translocal women's movements would suggest that she was a conservative and elitist feminist. As the examples discussed above illustrate, Daw San's role and authority as a pioneering leader of women's movements seems to have rested on the suffering and then salvation of exploited and "helpless" women, not unlike British imperialist-feminists and Indian nationalist-feminists who endeavoured to rescue their powerless — and mostly non-Western — sisters who suffered from various forms of "enslavement" such as lack of education, employment in prostitution, polygamy, and child marriage.[42] Yet her writings in *Independently Weekly*, which she continued to use throughout the 1930s as a platform for participating in and supporting anti-colonial and nationalist movements, demonstrate that she was a vociferous critic of both the "pro-government" and anti-government political elites in Burma.

The editorial in the 29 June 1935 issue, for instance, discusses the well-known political feud among three prominent members of the legislative council[43] and chastises council members for allowing political infighting to hinder them from fulfilling their duty to safeguard the welfare of their country and to assist the poor and the needy.[44] The column "Mr Kwa Si's Journal" in the same issue of *Independent Weekly* similarly reinforced Daw San's critique of the political elites, rebuking Burmese ministerial officials for "not giving a damn about their poverty-stricken country men and women and their hardships. Instead, they are demanding a raise." Mr Kwa Si compares the Burmese ministers to Mahatma Gandhi, describing the latter as "a true national leader" who does not spend more than 10 pya[45] a day on himself and dedicates himself to the affairs of his country, and concludes: "When people who emulate the likes of Gandhi appear in Burma, only then will our ministers feel ashamed of their own behaviour."[46]

In the editorial of 26 March 1938, devoted to a discussion of the Burma oilfield strike, Daw San again lambasted the ministers for their hypocrisy and lack of patriotism. The oilfield workers' strike was the pivotal event in the "1300 Revolution", the final act in the political upheavals in pre-war Burma.[47] It began in January 1938 with a strike by workers from the Burmah Oil Company in Chauk who were protesting low wages and other oppressive measures taken by the oil companies. It culminated in a countrywide general strike by the entire workforce in Burma, with 34 concurrent strikes involving an estimated 17,645 workers in foundries; dockyards; public transportation; civil service; and the oil, rice, cotton, match, rope and rubber industries.[48] The editorial sharply criticises the political leadership: "The ministers claim to sympathize with the plight of the oil field workers as they [ministers] take their 15 kyat daily stipend, sit in cool meeting rooms under fans, and accuse the supporters of the strike for embezzling money that they collected on behalf of the poor strikers."[49]

The articles express Daw San's frustration with the political elites, a feeling shared by many members of the Burmese public. As Robert Taylor points out, the majority of Burmese peasantry and youth became increasingly disillusioned with and suspicious of the political elites and "did not look to the elected legislators as their leaders, spokesmen or protectors".[50] The articles also show that far from being absorbed in elite and legislative politics that had little connection with — or significance for — popular nationalist and labour movements, Daw San sought to make the government and the political elites accountable to the masses.

More Trials and Tribulations

Daw San worked hard to keep *Independent Weekly* running. Initially, she insisted on managing the paper on her own. Her children recalled that they were basically raised by their maternal aunts while Daw San devoted herself to her paper and political activism.[51] That *Independent Weekly* lasted for over a decade — a remarkable feat considering the speed and frequency with which papers came and went at the time — attests to Daw San's abilities both as an editor and a writer. Ill fortune struck, however, and her printing press was destroyed in the three-month-long anti-Indian riots of 1938.[52] *Independent Weekly* never recovered.

It was not until after World War II that Daw San resumed writing. *Yuwadi Journal* (Young Women's Journal), a journal written, edited and managed entirely by women, was founded in 1946 by Dagon Khin Khin Lay (1904–81), a literary prodigy. Daw San was a founding member of the editorial board of *Yuwadi Journal*. She revived the "Kwa Si" column for the journal, except she wrote as Daw Kwa Si or "Auntie Kwa Si" whereas she had previously written as Mr Kwa Si. Her continued dedication to the promotion of female education, authorship and readership is evinced not only by her contributions to *Yuwadi Journal*, but also by her role as the vice-president of the Burmese Women Writers Association, another brainchild of Dagon Khin Khin Lay, established in 1947.[53]

Her writings in *Yuwadi Journal* show that Daw San remained deeply concerned about the fate of her country in the post-war years. She frequently urged the people of Burma to rally behind the cause of nation building and to *ā masho*, or "don't let up", so that "it shan't be long before Burma gains independence".[54]

Another recurrent theme in the "Auntie Kwa Si" column was that of national unity, the subject of the column published in the 18 May 1947 issue. Daw San begins by referring to the looming partition of India. She explains that Mohammad Ali Jinnah and the Muslim League are talking of creating a Muslim nation called Pakistan because they cannot agree with the visions and policies of the Indian National Congress, led by Jawaharlal Nehru, adding that "princes and rajas have joined the bandwagon and are asking for their own independent nation called Rajasthan". Daw San notes that such talks of partition are not taking place in India alone:

> In Kwa Si's Burma as well, the Rakhines are saying that they don't want to live alongside Burmans and are demanding an Arakanistan. Chins, Kachins, and Shans are already asking for the right to one day secede from an independent Burma and form their own states. And don't even talk about the Karens. The Karens have already gone to Britain to ask for their own sovereign nation, Karennistan. The *kabya* (mixed population) too. They cooperated with Burmans for independence, but on the eve of independence, they say they can't mingle with Burmans, that they will live separately. They have apparently already mapped out their own sovereign territory.[55]

Ironically, the Panglong Agreement of 1947, which secured, in principle, the allegiance of the leaders of the "hill tribes" and the Shan states to the Union of Burma and the Rangoon-based government led by the predominantly Burman Anti-Fascist People's Freedom League (AFPFL) under the leadership of Aung San, had been reached only a few months prior — in February. Nonetheless, and for reasons discussed in the chapter on the Karen nationalist Zipporah Sein in this volume (chapter 10), there was, on the one hand, enduring mistrust of minority ethnic groups as untrustworthy British collaborators and, on the other, a growing perception that the AFPFL had neither the willingness nor the capability to address the concerns of the ethnic minorities, particularly the Karen Christian community. Concurrently, the rivalry between the Communist and non-Communist leaders of the AFPFL only intensified on the eve of independence. Not surprisingly, Daw San warned that Burma was on the brink of disintegration: "If people here secede and people there secede, leaving Burma a tiny entity, and if that tiny Burma splinters into many separate associations and societies that follow disparate goals and ideologies, then how can Burma have any strength left?" According to her, the solution to political discord was not separation but cooperation; she was evidently reluctant or unable to envision a Burmese nation without the Shans, Karens and other indigenous ethnic groups.[56] She reminisced about times past when people in Burma "worked together in unison" to empower the nationalist movement. Having reminded her readers of the political efficacy of unity and cooperation, she suggested that people in Burma would be better off "splitting the gold instead of the land".[57] As it turned out, these were prescient warnings. Barely half a year after independence, the Burmese government was facing armed insurrections by the Communist Party of Burma and Karen separatist groups. (For a more extended discussion of the armed ethnic struggle in Burma, see chapter 10 by Ardeth Maung Thawnghmung and Violet Cho in this volume.) By 1949, more than half of the army had mutinied.

Through the column "Auntie Kwa Si", Daw San sought to impress upon her readers the exigency of nation-building efforts and to edify the public on how to serve their country and fulfil their patriotic duties. She likewise utilised her weekly talks on Burma Broadcasting Services — which she started in the late 1940s — to expound on urgent political and social issues raised by Burma's independence. No doubt she would have carried on her lifelong endeavour to advance and "protect the interests of the nation" and her countrymen and women, had she not discovered that she had cancer. She was only 62 years of age when she succumbed to the illness.

Reflections on the Life of a Forgotten Heroine

The prominent writer Daw Khin Myo Chit has argued that it was due to the growth of nationalist movements "that women were encouraged to come out from the narrow precincts of their homes and contribute towards the national cause".[58] Nationalists in colonial Burma certainly encouraged Burmese women to contribute actively to public life, and many Burmese women did in fact do so, particularly through their participation in organised politics. Yet the growing visibility of politicised and organised women in colonial Burma must be understood as having been shaped by both *wunthanu* and feminist efforts to mobilise women. There is widespread belief even today that Burma has simply never needed feminism and that "no legislation in modern times has been considered necessary, as customary laws ensure for women a position suitable to present-day concepts of equality".[59] As this brief biographical account of Daw San has shown, contrary to such views, some people in Burma perceived the need to mobilise against gender discrimination and took organised action to intervene in the sufferings of Burmese women.

Moreover, there is little evidence to suggest that the *wunthanu* movement itself sought to alter the position of women. Scholarship on Third World feminism has suggested that nationalism thwarted the feminist aspirations of women's movements in the Third World and that although women's movements in many Asian countries achieved official political and legal equality, they were unable to alter women's subordination within the patriarchal structure of family and society.[60] The case of Burma reinforces this argument. Nevertheless, the task of spreading a feminist nationalist programme was paramount to many patriotic women such as Daw San. Members of the early women's associations promoted liberal reforms such as female education and suffrage alongside political tactics that relegated women's activism to morally bound and symbolic critiques of colonialism. Under the nationalist banner, they pursued agendas that benefited Burmese women — especially their less privileged Burmese sisters — and confirmed their feminist identity. Daw San was a patriot and a feminist, jointly and simultaneously, and articulated her critiques of political, social and economic inequities and oppressions from the location of a feminist nationalist.

Despite her stature as one of the pioneering and leading women nationalists and rare women editors, and the staunch political and nationalist stance of her paper, barely a few references are made to Daw San in nationalist histories of Burma; and only a fraction of her voluminous writings has been preserved for posterity. The obvious explanation for this historical amnesia is what Barbara Andaya has described as the "hegemony of the national epic in Southeast Asian historiography", a phenomenon that has privileged the writing of metanarratives that are centred around the lives of male individuals "to whom evolution or liberation from foreign control is attributed".[61] Historians of Burma have accorded little importance to accounts by or about women, or to women's and gender issues. I also suspect, however, that the reason behind the forgetting of Daw San concerns the fact that she was an unconventional woman who challenged existing gender norms and expectations and flouted in many ways normative notions of femininity. She aspired to be an independent and autonomous woman, to such a degree that she renounced marriage. A single widow and divorcee without a college degree, and yet she dared to publicly criticise the exclusively male political elite.

I have elsewhere critiqued the notion of the "traditional" high status of women in Southeast Asia and the prevalent representations of Burmese women as historically independent and equal to men.[62] What claims about the freedom and independence of Burmese women disregard is that the active role of women as economic agents — the very attribute that gave women their autonomy and power — had paradoxically subordinated them to men socially, spiritually and politically. As in other Buddhist societies in the region, literati and experts on medicine, arithmetic and astrology were traditionally monks or former monks.[63] Administrators and communal authorities were principally men.[64] Female authority and leadership in the sphere of administration and governance were virtually unknown until the late colonial period.

The posthumous treatment of Daw San belies the frequent evocations of the image of the unfettered and independent Burmese woman. It points to the uneasy relationship that women in Burma have had — and continue to have — with authority and autonomy in the religious, political and cultural spheres. In life and afterlife, the patriotic and feminist Daw San sheds light on the difficulties that women have faced in struggling to become producers, arbiters and transmitters of knowledge, and to increase their presence and influence in the political arena.

Notes

1. The YMBA was originally a non-political group established by middle-class, educated Burmese elites to organise conferences on social and religious issues and serve as the nodal point connecting disparate lay organisations in Burma.

2. R.H. Taylor, *The State in Myanmar* (London: Hurst, 2008), p. 183.

3. J.C. Scott, *The Moral Economy of the Peasant: Rebellion and Subsistence in Southeast Asia* (New Haven: Yale University Press, 1976); P.M. Herbert, *The Hsaya San Rebellion (1930–1932) Reappraised* (London: Department of Oriental Manuscripts and Printed Books, British Library, 1982); M. Aung-Thwin, "Genealogy of a Rebellion Narrative: Law, Ethnology and Culture in Colonial Burma", *Journal of Southeast Asian Studies* 34, 3 (2003): 393–419.

4. Dobama Asiayone has also been translated as "We Burman Association". *Do* means either "our" or "we", and *bama* can be used as a designation for the Burman ethnic majority. *Bama* also refers, however, to all the people in Burma, irrespective of their ethnicity.

5. Thakin Thein Pe Myint, *Ko twe mhattan* [*Memoirs*] (Yangon: Taing Chit, 1950); U Nu, *Burma under the Japanese: Pictures and Portraits* (New York: St. Martin's Press, 1954); Hla Pe, *U Hla Pe's Narrative of the Japanese Occupation of Burma* (Recorded by U Khin, Vol. 14. Ithaca:

Southeast Asia Program, Cornell University, 1961); Htin Aung, *The Stricken Peacock: Anglo-Burmese Relations, 1752–1948* (The Hague: Martinus Nijhoff, 1965); Ba Maw, *Breakthrough in Burma: Memoirs of a Revolution, 1939–1946* (New Haven: Yale University Press, 1968); Burma Socialist Programme Party, *Myanmar nainngan amyothami mya e nainnganay hlouk sha mhu* [*The Political Movements of Women in Myanmar*] (Yangon: Sape Beikman, 1975).

6. The prefixing of the title of newspapers and periodicals to the names of editors and columnists is a practice that remains common to this day. The practice appears to have sprung from the absence of surnames in Burma. In order to distinguish famous or public figures, who often possess matching names, an identifier of some sort is prefixed to their names.

7. C. Ikeya, *Refiguring Women, Colonialism, and Modernity in Burma* (Honolulu: University of Hawaii Press, 2011).

8. Not all women and men involved in women's movements can be considered feminists. In this paper, I use the term "feminist" to refer to Daw San because her political activism was oriented not only towards addressing "the conditions of women" and mobilising "women" as a constituency, but also towards challenging certain systemic gender inequalities in Burma. For a useful discussion of the distinctions between women's and feminist movements, see P. Dufour, D. Masson and D. Caouette, "Introduction", in *Solidarities beyond Borders: Transnationalizing Women's Movements*, ed. P. Dufour, D. Masson and D. Caouette (Vancouver and Toronto: University of British Columbia Press, 2010), pp. 13–5.

9. J. Judge, "Talent, Virtue, and the Nation: Chinese Nationalisms and Female Subjectivities in the Early Twentieth Century", *American Historical Review* 106, 3 (June 2001): 768.

10. There are no surnames in Burma, and therefore Burmese names appear in their full form at every occurrence in the chapter. Where appropriate, honorifics such as Daw and Ma — rough equivalents of "Ms" and honorifics for older and younger women respectively — have been added to names, but these prefixes do not appear in the bibliography.

11. Biographical information on Daw San has been taken largely from Yin Yin Htun, *Independent Daw San* (Yangon: Pinnya than saung poun hneik taik, 2009); Saw Moun Nyin, *Bamar amyothami* [*Burmese Women*] (Yangon: Thiha poun hneik htaik, 1976); Kyan, "Amyothami mya ne sanezin lawka" [Women and the World of Journalism], in *Sanezin htamain sa tan mya* [*Essays on the History of Journalism*] (Yangon: Sape Beikman, 1978), pp. 279–312; and correspondence between her relatives and the author.

12. Each type of education was distinguished by the language of instruction and examination.

13. For a detailed discussion of educational reforms in colonial Burma, see Kaung, "A Survey of the History of Education in Burma before the British Conquest and After", *Journal of Burma Research Society* 46, 2 (Dec. 1963): 1–129; K. Dhammasami, "Between Idealism and Pragmatism: A Study of Monastic Education in Burma and Thailand from the Seventeenth Century to the Present", PhD diss., Oxford University, 2004; Ikeya, *Refiguring Women.*

14. Government of India, *Census of India, 1921, Vol. 10: Burma* (Rangoon: Office of the Superintendent, Government Printing and Stationery, 1923), and *Census of India, 1931: Part One, Report, Vol. 11: Burma* (Rangoon: Office of the Superintendent, Government Printing and Stationery, 1933).

15. Daw San [Buddha bādā myanmar ma, pseud.], "Khin Aye Kyi", *Thuriya Magazine* (Aug. 1918).

16. See E.C. Braun, "Ledi Sayadaw, Abhidhamma, and the Development of the Modern Insight Meditation Movement in Burma", PhD diss., Harvard University, 2008.

17. E.M. Mendelson, *Sangha and State in Burma: A Study of Monastic Sectarianism and Leadership* (Ithaca: Cornell University Press, 1975), pp. 196–235; Maung Maung, *From Sangha to Laity: Nationalist Movements of Burma, 1920–1940* (New Delhi: Manohar, 1980), p. 13.

18. Aye Kyaw, *The Voice of Young Burma* (Ithaca: Southeast Asia Program, Cornell University, 1993), p. 36. What distinguished the "national schools" from the public schools was not so much the curricula or even the language of instruction (since vernacular schools all taught in Burmese) but the rules regulating student conduct. National school students were allowed to read any newspapers, for example, whereas public school students were not permitted to read any, and they were not required to wear European-type shoes. Instead of observing British Empire Day, the King's Birthday, and Saturday and Sunday as holidays, national schools designated as holidays the Buddhist pre-Sabbath and Sabbath days and the anniversary of the student boycott day (Aye Kyaw, *The Voice of Young Burma*, pp. 36–7).

19. Khin Yi, *The Dobama Movement in Burma, 1930–1938* (Ithaca: Southeast Asia Program, Cornell University, 1988), p. 5.

20. The term *a myo* actually refers variously to race, kin, breed, lineage, family, rank, caste, kind, sort and species. In colonial Burma, however, *a myo* took on the meaning of "a nation or ethnic group".

21. I. Kwon, "'The New Women's Movement' in 1920s Korea: Rethinking the Relationship between Imperialism and Women", *Gender and History* 10, 3 (1998): 399.

22. A. Allott, "Thakin Ko-daw Hmaing", in *Far Eastern Literatures in the 20th Century: A Guide*, ed. Leonard S. Klein (New York: Ungar Publishing Company, 1986), p. 6.

23. She is known to have also written for the political column "Matali and Wee Takyoun Talk Politics" in *Pinnya alin* (*Knowledge Magazine*). According to Daw Kyan, Daw San voiced her criticism of the British colonial administration through this political column, for which she drew frequent warnings against sedition from the British administration (Kyan, "Amyothami mya ne sanezin lawka", pp. 282–93). Unfortunately, I have not come across this column in my examination of *Pinnya alin* and have been unable to locate any copies of Daw San's writings for the column.

24. Quoted in Yin Yin Htun, *Independent Daw San*, p. 25.

25. When the BWA was formed in 1919, it was an elite women's organisation with approximately 300 members, mostly educated women, wives of officials, and prosperous women entrepreneurs. Also in 1919, the Young Women's Buddhist Association (YWBA) and Wunthanu Konmaryi Athin (Patriotic Women's Association) were formed as subsidiary branches of the YMBA and *wunthanu athin*.

26. The benefits of the status of a married woman under Burmese Buddhist law included, but were not limited to, an equal share in the property acquired by the couple during the marriage, and joint custody of all the children, whom the husband had to support through their years as minors in the event of divorce (Maung Maung, *From Sangha to Laity*, pp. 61–72).

27. L. Edwards and M. Roces (eds.), *Women's Suffrage in Asia: Gender, Nationalism and Democracy* (London and New York: RoutledgeCurzon, 2004), p. 10.

28. Burma Socialist Programme Party, *Myanmar nainngan amyothami mya e nainnganyay hlouk sha mhu*, p. 30.

29. Ibid., p. 41.

30. The superintendent of a national girls' high school at the time of the conference, Daw Mya Sein was the daughter of U May Oung, a well-known barrister and Indian Civil Service officer who served as home member on the legislative council, one of the highest government positions open to Burmese people in colonial Burma, from 1924 until his death in 1926. Daw Mya Sein had graduated from secondary school as well as university with distinction, earned a master's degree from St. Hugh's College, Oxford University, in 1927 and a diploma in education in 1928, and continued to have a successful career in education.

31. Burma Socialist Programme Party, *Myanmar nainngan amyothami mya e nainnganyay hlouk sha mhu*, p. 71.

32. Mya Sein, "The Women of Burma: A Tradition of Hard Work and Independence", *Atlantic Monthly* (Feb. 1958): 123; Mya Sein, "Myanmar amyothami" [Burmese Women], in *Myanmar amyothami kye moun* [*A Looking Glass of Burmese Women*] (Yangon: Myanmar nainggan sape hnik sanezin ahpwe, 1998, originally published in 1958), p. 190.

33. International Alliance of Women for Suffrage and Equal Citizenship, "Letter to the Under-secretary of State, India Office, 1927", in file "Status of Women under New Constitution", L/P&J(B) 512, India Office Records.
34. L. Rupp, *Worlds of Women: The Making of an International Women's Movement* (Princeton: Princeton University Press, 1997), p. 43.
35. M.A.E. Tusan, "Writing *Stri Dharma*: International Feminism, Nationalist Politics, and Women's Press Advocacy in Late Colonial India", *Women's History Review* 12, 4 (2003): 623.
36. I have yet to come across another source that confirms this attribution (Mya Sein, "Towards Independence in Burma: The Role of Women", *Asian Affairs* 59, 3 [Oct. 1972]: 296).
37. National Council of Women in Burma, 1927; Rupp, *Worlds of Women*, p. 15.
38. The NCWB investigated the labour conditions of women and children in Rangoon and its vicinity in 1929 and submitted a report to the Royal Commission on Labour in India (National Council of Women in Burma, 1929). This is the only such documentation that I have come across. While the government made an inquiry into the standard of living of the working class in Rangoon at around the same time, the brief paragraph on "employment of women and children" states merely: "there are not many women and children employed in factories in Rangoon" (Government of Burma, *Report of an Enquiry into the Standard and Cost of Living of the Working Classes in Rangoon* [Rangoon: Labour Statistics Bureau, 1928], p. 89).
39. R.J. Carlson, "Women, Gender, and Politics in Burma's Nationalist Movement, 1900–1931", MA thesis, Cornell University, 1991, p. 107.
40. Sape Beikman, "Myanmar konmaryi athin mya" [Burmese Women's Associations], in *Myanma swe soun kyan* [*Myanmar Encyclopaedia*] 10: 57–9 (Yangon: Sape Beikman, 1966), p. 59.
41. H-B. Zöellner (ed.), "Material on Ba Khaing, *Political History of Myanma*", Working paper no. 10:5, Southeast Asian Studies, Universität Passau, 2006, pp. 3, 52.
42. A. Burton, *Burdens of History: British Feminists, Indian Women, and Imperial Culture, 1865–1915* (Chapel Hill and London: University of North Carolina Press, 1994), pp. 169, 175.
43. On the political feuding among U Ba Pe, Dr Ba Maw and U Chit Hlaing, then minister of forestry, minister of education and president of the council respectively, see J.F. Cady, *A History of Modern Burma* (Ithaca: Cornell University Press, 1969), pp. 360–86; Taylor, *State in Myanmar*, pp. 168–73.
44. Daw San, "The Coming Council Session", *Independent Weekly* (29 June 1935), p. 1.
45. There are 100 pyas to 1 kyat.

46. Daw San [Kwa Si, pseud.], "Mr. Kwa Si's journal", *Independent Weekly* (29 June 1935), p. 2.

47. The event is named after the Burmese calendar year, which is lunisolar. There have been a number of eras in Burmese chronology, the current era having commenced in 639 CE.

48. Khin Yi, *Dobama Movement in Burma*; Maung Maung, *From Sangha to Laity*, p. 177; Taylor, *State in Myanmar*, pp. 214–5. Women members of the Dobama Asiayone, known as *thakinma*, also joined in the strike, leading the effort to collect donations for striking Burmah Oil Company workers, about 100 to 150 of whom were women. Also among the workers who joined the 1300 Revolution were 200 women from Yaykyaw Ma Sein Nyunt's cheroot factory and approximately 1,000 more from rope and match factories in Rangoon. For details of the strike, see Burma Socialist Programme Party, *Myanmar nainngan amyothami mya e nainnganyay hlouk sha mhu*, pp. 101–23; Maung Maung, *From Sangha to Laity*, pp. 171–94.

49. Daw San, "Burma Oil Fields' Affairs", *Independent Weekly* (26 Mar. 1938), p. 1.

50. Taylor, *State in Myanmar*, p. 187.

51. Daw San later recruited her two sisters to write for the paper.

52. The riots were occasioned by a mass meeting of Burmese Buddhist monks and laymen at the Shwedagon Pagoda on 26 July 1938. The meeting had been organised to protest an anti-Buddhist book first published seven years earlier and republished a few months prior to the riots. Those gathered for the meeting marched to the Soortee Bara Bazaar and, upon arrival there, began throwing stones and attacking Indians. Looting and damaging of Indian mosques, shops and homes spread throughout Burma immediately following the unrest at the bazaar, extending into September 1938 (Riot Inquiry Committee, *Interim Report of the Riot Inquiry Committee* [Rangoon: Office of the Superintendent, Government Printing and Stationery, 1939]).

53. I have not been able to find any information on Daw San's role in the association.

54. Daw San [Kwa Si, pseud.], "Daw Kwa Si", *Yuwadi Gyanay* 1, 24 (16 Mar. 1947): 24.

55. Daw San [Kwa Si, pseud.] "Daw Kwa Si", *Yuwadi Gyanay* 1, 33 (18 May 1947): 23.

56. It is unclear, however, to what extent she objected to or, conversely, sympathised with the nationalist and separatist claims of the minority ethnic groups. Likewise, I am unable to determine, from the writings of Daw San that I have come across or discussion with her family and relatives, how precisely she envisioned the position of ethnic minorities in an independent Burma.

57. Daw San [Kwa Si, pseud.], "Daw Kwa Si", *Yuwadi Gyanay* 1, 33 (18 May 1947): 23.

58. Khin Myo Chit, *Colorful Burma: Her Infinite Variety; A Collection of Stories and Essays* (Rangoon: KMCT Sazin, 1976), p. 193.

59. Mi Mi Khaing, *The World of Burmese Women* (London: Zed Books, 1984), p. 26.

60. K. Jayawardena, *Feminism and Nationalism in the Third World* (London and Totowa: Zed Books, 1986); B. Ray, "The Freedom Movement and Feminist Consciousness in Bengal, 1905–1929", in *From the Seams of History: Essays on Indian Women*, ed. Bharati Ray (Delhi: Oxford University Press, 1995).

61. B.W. Andaya, *The Flaming Womb: Repositioning Women in Early Modern Southeast Asia* (Honolulu: University of Hawaii Press, 2006), p. 3.

62. Ikeya, *Refiguring Women*; C. Ikeya, "The "Traditional" High Status of Women in Burma: A Historical Reconsideration", *Journal of Burma Studies* 10 (2005/2006).

63. Mendelson, *Sangha and State in Burma*.

64. Though village headmanships as well as chieftainships in the Shan hill states have been known to descend in the female line, hereditary lineages of female headmanship were rare. Richard James Carlson, who has examined in some detail the evidence for female hereditary lineage in his dissertation on women, gender and nationalist politics in Burma, concludes that by the 18th century at least "such lines were, with one recorded exception, non-existent above the village level and outside of the Pagan area" (Carlson, "Women, Gender, and Politics", p. 15).

CHAPTER 2

"I Die Because of My Circumstances": Nguyen Thi Giang and the Viet Nam Quôc Dan Dang

Micheline Lessard

On 17 June 1930, at dawn, a young woman by the name of Nguyen Thi Giang, disguised as a peasant woman, stood on the edge of a field near the town of Yen Bay, northwest of Hanoi. (See map 2 for places mentioned in this chapter.) Standing quietly beside a number of onlookers, she watched as a man by the name of Nguyen Thai Hoc, along with 12 of his fellow "co-conspirators", was marched into a nearby field in order to be executed by French colonial authorities. Hoc and the others had been arrested and convicted of organising the Yen Bay Mutiny, one of a number of unsuccessful uprisings planned by the Viet Nam Quôc Dan Dang (VNQDD), the Vietnamese Nation-alist Party.[1] According to some newspaper accounts, French colonial authorities had kept the exact date of the executions secret. In order not to attract too much attention, the 13 condemned to death had been transported by special train only the night before from Hanoi.[2] Hoang Van Dao, author of a history of the VNQDD, claims that Nguyen Thi Giang learned from a fellow revolutionary that Nguyen Thai Hoc and the 12 others had been taken to Yen Bay. Wishing to make her way there without detection, she boarded a train apparently "helped by comrades who ... disguised themselves as coal burners and mechanics".[3] It is not clear what Nguyen Thi Giang may have been thinking as she watched the first 12 releases of the guillotine blade and as she waited for the final execution, that of Nguyen Thai Hoc. As she stood quietly watching the grisly spectacle of her lover's execution

Map 2. Vietnam during the French colonial period

by guillotine,[4] no one, not even French colonial authorities present, suspected that the young woman in peasant clothing was Nguyen Thi Giang, herself wanted in conjunction with the organisation of the Yen Bay Mutiny and for her numerous revolutionary activities as a member of the VNQDD. Noting that Nguyen Thai Hoc had been "calm" at the moment of his execution, the chef des services de police et de sûreté au Tonkin (the French police chief and head of the Surete, the secret police, in Tonkin) simply noted that the execution had been witnessed by approximately 60 people, "mostly women and young people".[5] Nguyen Thi Giang had managed, as she had countless times before, to elude French police officers who had been looking for her for quite some time.[6]

Following her fiancé's decapitation on the orders of the French colonial administration and at the hands of a Vietnamese executioner,[7] Thi Giang left quietly, undetected by authorities. Two days later, in Dong Khe (also sometimes written as Dong Ve),[8] Nguyen Thai Hoc's native village, a peasant discovered the body of a young woman in a nearby rice field. The woman, dressed in mourning clothes, had apparently died of a self-inflicted gunshot wound to the head.[9] Two letters found in the young woman's pocket allowed officials to identify her as Nguyen Thi Giang. One of Thi Giang's sisters, Nguyen Thi Tinh, was also called upon to identify the body. In one of her letters, Thi Giang explained her suicide, stating that she could not bear to live following the execution of her husband, and that she wished to "follow him into heaven".[10] In order to reach her beloved once again, Thi Giang had used the revolver Hoc himself had given her. Nguyen Thi Giang had allegedly asked Nguyen Thai Hoc to allow her to carry the pistol "so that if he should meet a fatal end, she would use it to kill herself".[11]

The tragic deaths of these two Vietnamese patriots, often re-counted in highly romanticised terms, point to a number of serious problems in the writing of Vietnamese women's history. First, with respect to Nguyen Thi Giang, historians — Vietnamese and non-Vietnamese alike — have focused mainly on her suicide and on her admission that life without Hoc would be intolerable. As such, she has become one more in a pantheon of Vietnamese woman patriots to choose suicide.[12] According to Vietnamese historians, in the first century of the Common Era the Trung sisters chose suicide over capitulation before Chinese forces. Two centuries later, another woman willing to take up arms for the national cause, Ba Trieu, also chose suicide over surrender. She too had led an armed insurrection against

Chinese troops. The Trung sisters and Ba Trieu may not have opted for suicide because they could not conceive of life without their loved ones, but their decisions to take up arms were nonetheless considered to be motivated by a desire to avenge the deaths of their husbands and their fathers at the hands of Chinese invaders. In each of these cases, these women are depicted as devoted daughters or wives. Devotion to nation and devotion to the men in their lives are depicted as synonymous, as equally heroic, the family but a microcosm of the nation. And in spite of their outstanding achievements as patriots, their filial piety is what has made their forays outside the "inner quarters" acceptable and even respectable. For historians, such an interpretation not only shifts the focus away from that of the women's accomplishments, but it is also anachronistic. The historiography of the Trung sisters and Ba Trieu attributes to them Confucian ideals and qualities that had yet to reach Vietnam at that point.

The Trung sisters and Ba Trieu are an essential element of Vietnamese historiography and Vietnamese national identity. The willingness of Vietnamese women to take up arms when the nation was in danger highlights Vietnam's numerous independence struggles against enemies who were often much more militarily powerful, struggles that therefore required the use of all available resources, including women.[13] Within the specific context of the period of French colonial rule in Vietnam (1858–1954), the focus of historians studying Vietnamese women has been on the development of a women's movement, and almost exclusively on those women who participated in anticolonial resistance within the confines of the Indochinese Communist Party (ICP). One striking example of this historiographical phenomenon is the first serious study on Vietnamese women, Mai Thi Thu and Le Thi Nham Tuyet's *Women of Vietnam*.[14] In their study the authors depict the heroic acts of Vietnamese women in the 19th century and then skip to the creation of the ICP in 1930, thereby ignoring the hundreds of women who participated in anti-colonial movements and activities between 1900 and 1930. Furthermore, the story also links the development of women's emancipation movements with that of the creation of the ICP even though the VNQDD itself had called for the emancipation of women and had created a women's section as well as women's groups and cells.

Nguyen Thi Giang's place in Vietnamese history has therefore been dictated largely by the overwhelming emphasis placed on the ICP. Nguyen Thi Giang, as a member of the VNQDD, engaged in revolutionary activities similar to those of her counterparts in the ICP, and yet she has mostly been ignored (as has the VNQDD). While revolutionary women who belonged to the ICP, such as Nguyen Thi Minh Khai and Nguyen Thi Dinh, have been the subject of numerous memoirs, biographies and scholarly studies, Nguyen Thi Giang's attempts to free Vietnam of French rule have hardly been examined. Since victors often command historical analysis, those movements or parties, such as the VNQDD, not present at the moment of success tend to be relegated to the background, present but very much out of focus. Women like Nguyen Thi Giang, whose political activities preceded the founding of the ICP, are absent from the historical narrative. It seems that "within this framework, Vietnamese women's political consciousness appears virtually non-existent before the formation of the Indochinese Communist Party in 1930".[15] In addition, much of what is written about her follows a Marxist line and yet focuses primarily on a "love story" rather than on her participation in anti-colonial activities. Ironically, the Marxist interpretation and focus depicts Nguyen Thi Giang as an idealised Confucian widow rather than the fierce nationalist she happened to be.

What has been lost in this approach to the study of Nguyen Thi Giang specifically is the fact that her actions were not merely those of a lovelorn woman. She was, by all accounts, an important and influential member of the VNQDD. Memoirs and historical accounts have grossly ignored her contributions to this nationalist movement in two significant ways. First, Nguyen Thi Giang's adherence to the VNQDD is attributed to the fact that she was the fiancée of one of its founders, Nguyen Thai Hoc. Second, the actual work she did for the VNQDD is either excluded from historical analyses or is barely mentioned, while her suicide is exalted. What follows on these pages, then, is an attempt to elucidate the life of Nguyen Thi Giang the patriot, her work as one of the most important members of the VNQDD. An analysis of the sources reveals that Nguyen Thi Giang's contribution to the VNQDD included her work as a propagandist, a liaison officer, a recruiter, an organiser and an intelligence officer. Before delving into her life, however, it is necessary to comment on the sources used in this study.

First, secondary sources pertaining specifically to Nguyen Thi Giang are scarce. There are no monographs devoted entirely to her life, her political ideas, or her specific role and activities within the VNQDD. So far, the only major study of the VNQDD is Hoang

Van Dao's *Viet Nam Quoc Dan Dang: A Contemporary History of a National Struggle, 1927–1954*.[16] While Hoang Van Dao does acknowledge Nguyen Thi Giang's prominence within the VNQDD, and while his monograph does offer glimpses into her life as a party member, the focus is clearly not on her. Still, Nguyen Thi Giang occupies more space in Hoang Van Dao's study than she does in other publications. She does figure in a chapter titled "Nguyen Thi Giang" in a larger study of anti-colonialism in Vietnam: Lang Nhan's *Nhung tran danh Phap: Tu Ham Nghi den Nguyen Thai Hoc, 1885–1931*.[17] Here Nguyen Thi Giang's work is recognised briefly, in general terms. The events surrounding Hoc's execution are mentioned as well, but most of the rest of the chapter focuses on Thi Giang's suicide and on her parting letters.[18]

As for archival documents, taken individually, the sources available (French colonial administration memos and correspondence, interrogations, Vietnamese revolutionary memoirs) are problematic. French colonial sources carry their own biases. While French Sûreté officers' information pertaining to Vietnamese patriots' activities tended to be fairly accurate, the officers nonetheless often made much of Vietnamese women's relationships with male revolutionaries, assuming that these women joined the resistance based only on a submissive sense of filial piety. A clear example of this can be found in a 1929 police report written up following an assassination that had been committed by members of the VNQDD, it was suspected, at the Hanoi Botanical Gardens. While enumerating a list of possible VNQDD suspects, including some women, the authors of the police report simply described the women in reference to their respective male companions: "Nguyen Thai Hoc's mistress is Nguyen Thi Gian (*sic*); Pho Duc Chinh has Nguyen Thi Tham for a mistress."[19] As this author has stated elsewhere, "it seldom occurred to these authorities that it was possible to be both filial and politically conscious".[20] As such, the portrait they paint of Nguyen Thi Giang is strictly that of a young revolutionary woman whose fiancé was a founder of the VNQDD. The crucial role played by Nguyen Thi Giang within the VNQDD sometimes emerges indirectly when we examine the interrogations carried out by the Sûreté of arrested VNQDD members. It is imperative, however, that the motives of the "confessions" elicited by these interrogations be taken into account. It is quite possible that those interrogated and who provided information about Nguyen Thi Giang's activities may have implicated her and others in order to save them-selves. It is also worth keeping in mind that the "confessions" of these VNQDD members may have been obtained through coercive or violent means. It is necessary, therefore, that the information gleaned from these interrogations or confessions be corroborated by other sources.

As for memos and correspondence written by French colonial administrators, they tend to draw, with broad strokes, what they con-sidered to be threats to the French presence in Vietnam. These threats included any overt demonstrations of nationalist sentiment or any expression in favour of Vietnamese independence. The so-called enemies of the French presence in Vietnam covered a wide political spectrum, from collaborating Vietnamese who sought to improve the economic and educational conditions of their countrymen through constitutional means, to groups, such as the VNQDD, who called for armed rebellion against French colonial rule and who also advocated social and political revolution such as the elimination of the Viet-namese monarchy and the establishment of a Vietnamese republic. In most instances, French colonial officials were quick to dismiss these Vietnamese nationalists as failures, as intellectually and morally deficient.

Vietnamese revolutionary memoirs of course tend to glorify the actions of revolutionaries. For the most part, revolutionary memoirs (*hoi ky cach manh*) published by the Democratic Republic of Vietnam after 1945, and by the Socialist Republic of Vietnam after 1975, have focused almost exclusively on those revolutionaries who were mem-bers of the ICP. There are but a few that offer a glimpse into the lives and actions of VNQDD members. In these memoirs, the role of Nguyen Thi Giang is depicted in glowing terms, but she is still por-trayed mostly as the fiancée of Nguyen Thai Hoc. There is also in these memoirs a tendency to focus on the star-crossed lovers' fate rather than on Nguyen Thi Giang's own revolutionary fervour and political ideology. Most of these memoirs highlight only the events surrounding the patriots' lives or those that reflect what may be con-sidered a "revolutionary" outlook or past. As such, much information is excluded from the narratives, and the portraits that emerge are rather unidimensional. While these memoirs do provide interesting details surrounding events, they are nonetheless often mere chrono-logical accounts of events with little analysis. Equally problematic is the paucity of citations and notes in these biographical accounts or memoirs. In addition, they often provide contradictory versions of events or different details.[21]

Newspaper accounts are easier to analyse since there was then no attempt to provide an unbiased view of the news. The images of revolutionaries such as Nguyen Thai Hoc and Nguyen Thi Giang that emerge from newspapers depend on the political slant of the papers themselves. While French colonial newspapers such as *L'avenir du Tonkin* referred to the likes of Thi Giang and Hoc as terrorists, newspapers such as *l'Humanité*, published in France, depicted them as martyrs. There is, of course, a broad spectrum between those two polar views. While on their own these sources can be problematic, taken together they allow us to better understand the role played by Nguyen Thi Giang within the VNQDD. While the purpose of this essay is to focus on the importance of Nguyen Thi Giang's role within the VNQDD, it is necessary to first provide a measure of historical context concerning that political movement. Therefore, we will briefly examine the role of Nguyen Thai Hoc in the formation of the VNQDD as well as the political aims and the organisation of the party itself. This will allow for a better understanding of Nguyen Thi Giang as a member of the VNQDD.

Historical Background

The establishment of French colonial rule in Vietnam began with a Franco-Spanish attack on the port of Da Nang in 1858. The premise for this attack was the protection of Catholic missionaries who had been subjected to the severe repression and persecutions called for in a number of Nguyen imperial edicts in the 1820s. By 1862 the ruling Nguyen dynasty, recognising its military inferiority, signed a treaty (the Treaty of Saigon) that ceded to France Saigon and three provinces of southern Vietnam. The Nguyen subsequently signed other treaties that ceded further provinces to France, and by 1884 French military troops had made their way to northern Vietnam. That year, a treaty was signed that essentially placed all of Vietnam under French control. French administrators in Vietnam then divided the country into three separate administrative regions: Tonkin in the north, Annam in the centre, and Cochinchina in the south. While Cochinchina was transformed into a colony under direct French administration, Tonkin and Annam were administered as protectorates. In Annam and Tonkin the Vietnamese monarchy and the bureaucracy were

Vietnamese Nationalist Movement

1885   Can Vuong Movement (Loyalty to the Emperor Movement) started by scholars in support of Prince Ham Nghi against French takeover

1905   Phan Boi Chau starts the Dong Du Movement (To the East Movement)

1907   Phan Chu Trinh opens the Dong Kinh Nghia Thuc (Tonkin Free School) in Hanoi, promoting *quoc ngu*, the Vietnamese Romanised script, and developing a Western, modern curriculum

1917   Creation of the Constitutionalist Party by a group of educated Vietnamese based in Saigon. It called for reforms in education and in economic policies

1925   Founding of Thanh Nien (Revolutionary Youth League) by Ho Chi Minh, a party inspired by Marxist-Leninist principles

1927   Founding of the Viet Nam Quôc Dan Dang (Vietnamese Nationalist Party) by Nguyen Thai Hoc and others

1930   Yen Bay Mutiny, organised by VNQDD

1931   Founding of the Indochinese Communist Party by Ho Chi Minh

1941   Creation by Ho Chi Minh of the Viet Minh, an alliance of Vietnamese nationalist groups, for the purpose of overthrowing French rule in Vietnam

1945   The August Revolution leads to the Viet Minh seizure of power following the Japanese surrender. Declaration of independence of Vietnam

maintained, but they answered to the French colonial administration established in Hanoi.

Vietnamese resistance to French rule and domination was immediate. The Treaty of Saigon marked the beginning of what came to be known as the Scholars' Resistance Movement. Some scholars who had been appointed to various levels of the imperial bureaucracy chose to resist colonial rule by refusing to continue to serve the Nguyen court and by rejecting any collaboration with France. A number of these scholars retreated to their native villages, where they often worked as schoolteachers. Others, such as Phan Dinh Phung, chose the path of armed resistance, mounting attacks against French troops and against Catholic villages.

In 1905, inspired by the Japanese victory over Russia, a Vietnamese patriot by the name of Phan Boi Chau spearheaded the Dong Du (To the East) Movement. Chau's nationalism found expression in what he believed to be Vietnam's three affinities with Japan: race, language and culture. Like Phan Dinh Phung, Chau favoured armed resistance. His principal goal was to send young Vietnamese men to Japanese military schools. Another Vietnamese nationalist and a contemporary of Phan Boi Chau's was Phan Chu Trinh, who believed that Vietnam's autonomy would be possible only after educational, political and social reforms. In 1907 Trinh opened, along with cofounders such as Luong Van Can, the Dong Kinh Nghia Thuc (Tonkin Free School), providing a Western-style modern education to both Vietnamese boys and girls. While colonial authorities shut down the school in 1908 because of its alleged "nationalist" curriculum and activities, a new generation of Vietnamese nationalists emerged, the products of the French colonial education system.

The emergence of these new nationalist currents coincided with the development of the mass press in Vietnam in the 1920s. Through various newspapers, young Western-educated Vietnamese expressed their political views.[22] Their political leanings covered a broad spectrum of the political scale. Some advocated economic nationalism based on the development of Vietnamese commerce, industry and handicrafts.[23] Such demands had also been made by more moderate nationalists such as Bui Quang Chieu after the creation of the Constitutionalist Party in 1917 in Cochinchina, the southernmost administrative region of French-controlled Vietnam.[24]

While some advocated Vietnamese autonomy through constitutional means and through collaboration with France, others, influenced by revolutions in China and in the Soviet Union, were more radical in nature, calling not only for Vietnam's independence but also for political and social revolution. Such was the case of Thanh Nien, the Revolutionary Youth League, a political movement founded by Ho Chi Minh while in exile in Canton. Thanh Nien was inspired by the Marxist-Leninist approach adopted by Ho Chi Minh while he was a student in Moscow in the early 1920s. Thanh Nien would later become the Indochinese Communist Party. The Viet Nam Quôc Dan Dang, founded in Vietnam in 1927, was more vague about its ideological leanings. Its members nonetheless viewed themselves as revolutionaries.

The Viet Nam Quôc Dan Dang

The VNQDD was founded by a group of Western-educated Vietnamese including Nguyen Thai Hoc, who was born in 1903 and trained as a schoolteacher. Unable to persuade the French colonial authorities of the need for reforms, including freedom of the press, he decided to organise a political movement. The VNQDD was modelled on the Chinese Nationalist Party (Guomindang). It originated in 1925 with the establishment of a bookshop in Hanoi (Nam Dong Thu Xa), intended to provide a "center for study and propaganda".[25] According to French colonial authorities, the bookshop, which was housed in the home of a schoolteacher named Pham Tuan Tai, was intended also to engage in publication.[26] Those affiliated with the study centre, including Nguyen Thai Hoc, had been greatly influenced by Sun Yat Sen and the 1911 Revolution in China. The group focused primarily on nationalism and carried out propaganda and recruitment campaigns — mostly in student circles in the urban areas but also, to some extent, among factory workers and rural peasants.[27] From the study centre emerged the VNQDD in 1927. By then the Guomindang "was sweeping to political power in China".[28] According to the historian Alexander B. Woodside, young Vietnamese nationalists such as Nguyen Thai Hoc "fervently hoped" the Guomindang would "support a Pan-Asian movement of confrontation with Western colonialism".[29] When such a movement failed to materialise, Nguyen Thai Hoc created a Vietnamese version of the Guomindang. French colonial officials, while seriously concerned about the creation of yet another anticolonial organisation, nonetheless derisively referred to the VNQDD as but a "servile" copy of the Chinese model.[30]

Most VNQDD members were young, French-educated Vietnamese: students, teachers and journalists.[31] However, the party was also able to recruit members from among Vietnamese soldiers and traders. Colonial administrators attempted to explain the growth of the VNQDD by suggesting that it had been the outgrowth of political ferment in 1926 in Vietnamese schools. For a period of one year, Vietnamese students had engaged in school strikes, mostly to protest the fact that they could not openly mourn the death of the patriot Phan Chu Trinh.[32]

While the party's ideological orientation was neither sophisticated nor complex, its one driving force was the call for Vietnamese independence through armed struggle if necessary. The party also called for the establishment of a Vietnamese republic. The VNQDD was not a Communist movement per se, but its structure was nonetheless similar to that of Communist organisations. Such had also been the case with its Chinese counterpart, the Guomindang, which in Canton benefited from the advice afforded by the presence of political advisers from the Soviet Union.[33] In spite of such influences, however, the VNQDD, according to Vu Van Thai, was characterised by "vagueness in its social programs" and by the fact that it was "without a solid doctrinal basis".[34] The VNQDD was organised into local branches of approximately 19 members. Beneath the local branches were small cells of three members.[35] The branches also had subcommittees: propaganda, organisation, finance, intelligence.[36] Part of the party's agenda was the emancipation of women. There were women's branches in addition to the general branches. The purpose of these was to group women in order to educate them about issues such as equality and emancipation. Though it is impossible to quantify the level of women's participation in the VNQDD, it is clear from archival documents that not only were women present in the women's branches but also, as was the case with Nguyen Thi Giang and Nguyen Thi Bac, some women served the party beyond the women's branches and held positions of leadership within the party.

All members were asked to take an oath of loyalty and willingness to sacrifice "life and property for the party".[37] Betrayal of the party or of its members could result in severe retribution, including death. Between 1928 and 1929 the party expanded rapidly. Hoc and his fellow revolutionaries had been successful in recruiting students, small business owners and civil servants.[38] By 1929 the party boasted 1,500 members and at least 120 cells.[39] By 1930 the party, it is estimated, counted 70,000 members, attesting to the talent and to the success of its recruiters and propagandists.[40]

The VNQDD planned for its revolution to take place in four phases. The first phase was organisational in nature. This included recruitment and the establishment of branches and cells. It was during this first phase that members were to be educated in revolutionary theories and practices. The second phase was to consist of various types of covert activities, such as bombings and targeted assassinations, which would eventually lead to a major insurrection. These violent actions were to serve two purposes. In the first place, the targets were those structures, institutions and people considered to be symbolic of French colonial rule in Vietnam. It was also hoped that such attacks would destabilise French colonial rule. The third phase was that of the major insurrection.[41] The hope was that the agitation fomented in the second phase would mobilise large masses of Vietnamese into a major armed offensive. The fourth and final phase would be that of "reconstruction", when the VNQDD would seize power and establish an independent Vietnamese state.[42]

However, informants had made their way into some branches of the VNQDD. In fact, official colonial administration documents reveal that there had been informants within the party since its creation in 1927. Because of this, the French Sûreté was aware of nearly all party meetings, of who attended the meetings, and of the decisions taken at these meetings. This explains why, shortly after the party was founded, Nguyen Thai Hoc was already being followed closely by the French Sûreté in Vietnam.[43] The VNQDD came under even greater scrutiny after February 1929, when René Bazin, a French recruiter (for work on plantations), was assassinated. Believing that the VNQDD was responsible for Bazin's death, French colonial authorities quickly rounded up and arrested VNQDD members.[44] A professed admirer of Sun Yat Sen, Hoc drew a parallel between this situation and that of the Guomindang in 1911, in particular the "heroic deaths of the 72 Youth Heroes in an abortive revolt in Canton on the eve of the 1911 Chinese revolution".[45] Hoc decided that the time was ripe to prepare for the general insurrection. Aware of the presence of infiltrators and to ensure its survival, the party therefore organised, in 1929, the assassination of members it deemed to have betrayed the party cause.[46] In spite of such measures, the safety of the party was further undermined by "a series of accidents involving explosions in homes of VNQDD members manufacturing explosives".[47] These incidents, of course, further alerted the French Sûreté in Vietnam, and Nguyen Thai Hoc believed that if the party was to survive the revolution had to begin as soon as possible. Such was the context within which a number of successive attacks, including one in Yen Bay, were planned.

The Yen Bay Mutiny, also referred to as the Yen Bay Uprising, took place in February 1930. After months of planning, on 10 February 1930 armed VNQDD rebels attacked the French military garrison at Yen Bay. Despite the ultimate failure of the uprising, what proved to be most disturbing to French colonial authorities was the fact that the VNQDD had been successful in recruiting Vietnamese soldiers and that the attack on Yen Bay was to be followed by a series of other attacks on French garrisons. Similar attacks were carried out five days later in Phu Duc, Vinh Bao and a number of other towns, with the participation of Vietnamese soldiers. During the attacks, a number of French officers were killed and the rebels were able to confiscate weapons. A Vietnamese district administrator, Hoang Gia Mo, was reported to have been "captured, tried and sentenced by the people and beaten to death".[48] The attacks were followed by demonstrations, protests and general unrest.

All of the attacks carried out by the VNQDD were quickly repulsed by local militia led by French officers. Repression against the VNQDD was swift and efficient. French colonial authorities also used bombing strikes in the surrounding countryside to further halt the rebellion. Eleven days after the uprising, one newspaper reported that there had been more than 300 arrests.[49] By 20 February Nguyen Thai Hoc was already captured in Hai Duong province, east of Hanoi, after a 40-day manhunt.[50] One month later, the sentence of execution came down for Hoc and 12 of his comrades.

Nguyen Thi Giang

Nguyen Thi Giang was born in 1906[51] in the village of Bac Giang, near Phu Lang Thuong in northern Vietnam. Thi Giang was one of three sisters, and all of them eventually engaged in nationalist movements. Very little is known about the socio-economic circumstances of the family. Given that both Thi Giang and her older sister Thi Bac were literate, it is safe to assume that they had spent time in the Franco-Vietnamese educational system and that their family could afford to send them to school. Thi Giang first met Nguyen Thai Hoc in 1929, shortly before the VNQDD became widely known to French colonial authorities and before many of its members were arrested or driven underground.[52] She was only 22 years old when Hoc convinced her and Thi Bac to join the VNQDD.[53] The sisters' initial functions within the party involved "relations and propaganda".[54] As Nguyen Thi Giang was soon able to demonstrate her commitment and her abilities to the party, her responsibilities within it became more significant. It became clear that Nguyen Thai Hoc trusted her implicitly with sensitive information.[55]

If historiography has ignored the work of Nguyen Thi Giang as a member of the VNQDD, French colonial authorities were very much aware of the depth of her involvement and her influence within that movement. In his report on anti-colonial movements, Sûreté chief

Louis Marty stated that the VNQDD had a women's section and that the women involved in it played a "not-negligible" role.[56] With respect to Nguyen Thi Giang specifically, Marty described her as one whose "revolutionary activity surpassed that of Nguyen Thai Hoc".[57] One of Thi Giang's key roles was that of a propagandist. The VNQDD's propaganda service was multifaceted. One of its aims was the writing, publication and dissemination of books, periodicals and pamphlets explaining the party's aims and principles. In addition, a "military" section of the propaganda service was created in order to recruit into the VNQDD Vietnamese soldiers in the colonial army.[58]

As a propagandist, Nguyen Thi Giang travelled extensively throughout northern Vietnam in order to inform Vietnamese of the VNQDD's mission and activities. Thi Giang would explain the VNQDD's political agenda and strategies either to individuals sympathetic to the cause of Vietnamese independence, or to groups, even entire villages. The propagation of the party's ideas also entailed the clandestine publication of numerous political tracts and pamphlets, many of which had been written by Nguyen Thi Giang herself. The role of propagandist carried with it significant dangers, for in colonial Vietnam there was neither freedom of expression nor freedom of assembly. Any small group of Vietnamese gathered to engage in political discussion was in danger of arrest and imprisonment. Speakers at such gatherings were considered to be leaders of an anti-French movement and faced serious penalties, such as lengthy prison terms and hard labour. If they were convicted of having incited any form of violent political action, they could be executed. The travels of Nguyen Thi Giang were made all the more difficult by the fact that French colonial authorities had begun the practice of requiring the acquisition of identification papers for Vietnamese travelling throughout French Indochina. Nguyen Thi Giang, once she became known as a member of the VNQDD, would have to resort to the use of disguises as well as counterfeit identity papers. She was indeed engaging in risky business. Between 1929 and 1930, French colonial authorities, largely through the use of informants, were aware of Nguyen Thi Giang's travels and of her work as a propagator of the VNQDD's political ideas. After having found some explosives in the village of Noi Vien (in Bac Ninh province), Sûreté officials reported to the résident supérieur du Tonkin that Nguyen Thi Giang was a frequent visitor to the village, where she participated in "revolutionary conferences".[59] In the course of these propaganda campaigns, Thi Giang was often accompanied by her sister

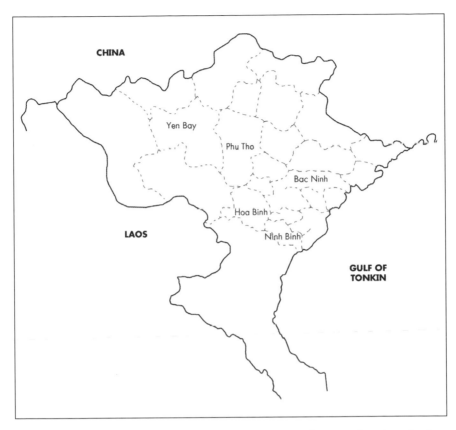

CHINA

Yen Bay

Phu Tho

Bac Ninh

Hoa Binh

LAOS

Ninh Binh

GULF OF
TONKIN

Map 3. Provinces of northern Vietnam (Tonkin) under French colonial rule

Nguyen Thi Bac. As indicated in one of its reports, The French Sûreté acknowledged the VNQDD's success when it came to propaganda:

> The propaganda was well received by young civil servants, particularly teachers and students. It also found great favour in military circles. Many indigenous sub-officers in the artillery, infantry, financial administration and aviation had joined the party.[60]

As the scholar Oscar Chapuis has noted, "a significant number of those Indochinese guards had rallied VNQDD thanks to the propaganda network led by two women, Cô Giang (Nguyen Thi Giang), and Cô Bac (Nguyen Thi Bac)".[61]

While travelling throughout Tonkin, Nguyen Thi Giang was also able to exercise other functions. As one of the party's liaison officers, she ensured effective communication between cells, branches and other VNQDD members. Thi Giang's liaison work allowed the VNQDD to inform its spread-out members about upcoming actions, about potential dangers (such as the presence of informants within cells or branches), and about the arrests and imprisonment of some of their fellow members. In addition, rather than using the postal system (where mail could easily be confiscated by colonial authorities), liaison officers carried with them written instructions and correspondence between members of the VNQDD. In and of themselves, each of these documents was highly incriminating. According to Hoang Van Dao's history of the VNQDD, Nguyen Thi Giang was also able to successfully conduct "any work the party gave her", thus enhancing her standing within its ranks: "When Nguyen Thai Hoc disguised himself and lay low in the provinces of Hoa Binh, Ninh Binh, and Phu Tho [see map 3], where the mountains provided extra difficulties and dangers, she always brought him news and information and conveyed his instructions to the party local chapters."[62] Nguyen Thi Giang's work as a liaison officer therefore allowed the VNQDD to continue to plan and to carry out its objectives even though many of its members, especially its leadership, were forced underground because they were already in the French Sûreté's cross hairs. Without capable liaison officers, the VNQDD could not have carried out a significant number of its planned activities. Such was the assessment of Sûreté officials who stated in a 1934 report that Nguyen Thi Giang had served as a liaison officer between her lover, the imprisoned Nguyen Thai Hoc, and the new leaders of the party.[63] Following the arrest of Nguyen Thai Hoc in February 1930, Le Huu Canh had taken over the leadership of the VNQDD. Thanks to Nguyen Thi Giang, Canh was able to effectively communicate with Hoc while the latter was held in Hoa Lo Prison in Hanoi.[64] By this time, Thi Giang had become the VNQDD's principal adviser.[65] French Sûreté chief Louis Marty stated in one of his reports that Nguyen Thi Giang had been an "indefatigable" liaison officer.[66]

The significance of Nguyen Thi Giang's efforts to continue the VNQDD's activities and to establish communications between Le Huu Canh and Nguyen Thai Hoc needs to be highlighted here, for the efforts reveal much about Thi Giang's devotion to the cause of Vietnamese national independence. Prior to the Yen Bay Uprising, in late 1929, a measure of dissension had developed within VNQDD ranks. Some members had objected to Nguyen Thai Hoc's position that immediate armed insurrection should take place. The dissidents believed that the time was not ripe for such actions, that they could be dangerous to the party and to the cause. This small faction was led by Le Huu Canh. One of Canh's followers, Nguyen Doan Lam, had even broken his oath to the VNQDD by refusing, on a number of occasions, to execute orders given to him by Nguyen Thai Hoc. Hoc was so angry with Canh that he called him a traitor and ordered his assassination. The assassination attempt failed, but the incident nonetheless created a rift within the party between those who supported Nguyen Thai Hoc and those who agreed with Canh.[67] Once Hoc was arrested following the Yen Bay Uprising and Le Huu Canh had taken over the leadership of the VNQDD, Nguyen Thi Giang opted to work with Hoc's rival in order to ensure the survival of the VNQDD. By becoming the liaison between Hoc and Canh, Nguyen Thi Giang was able to keep intact her loyalty to both Hoc and the VNQDD. She was also able not only to inform Hoc about the VNQDD's actions, but also to keep him fully involved as a party leader and member, his position therein having been inevitably compromised by his imprisonment. Furthermore, she contributed greatly to the party's ability to continue its activities while under the threat of severe repression from French colonial authorities. By ensuring that communications took place between Hoc and Canh, Thi Giang also contributed to mending the rift between the party's factions. These actions demonstrate that Nguyen Thi Giang was not merely a "follower" of Nguyen Thai Hoc, but also a highly capable strategist.

Liaison work also allowed the VNQDD to plan concerted actions against specific targets. Since Nguyen Thi Giang was a liaison officer, her safety hinged upon her ability to elude informants, Sûreté officers and the police. According to an unsigned short biography of Nguyen Thi Giang, the work of liaison officer was an "exhausting assignment" for her.[68] Like many liaison officers of illegal political parties or movements, Nguyen Thi Giang conducted much of her work in disguise. Up until her death in June 1930, she had been able to escape security agents. At one point, while she was meeting with another VNQDD leader, Doan Tran Nghiep, the police broke into the house and Nghiep was immediately arrested. Nguyen Thi Giang somehow managed to escape amid the confusion.[69] This was no small feat given that her work within the VNQDD was well-known to the Sûreté and given that "her description was known to all the colonialist agents".[70] Thi Giang was easily identifiable since she had a specific physical characteristic: she was severely cross-eyed. Thi Giang's ability to outwit and to elude the Sûreté proved crucial to the VNQDD as she often aided other VNQDD members in their attempts to hide from French colonial authorities. During the manhunt that followed the Yen Bay Uprising, for example, Nguyen Thi Giang helped VNQDD member Nguyen Van Hien by finding and taking him to the home of a fellow VNQDD member, Thi Truyen, where he was to remain in hiding until it was safe for him to travel. Thi Giang later accompanied Hien when she took him to an isolated home in Haiphong from which he was able to escape from Vietnam to China.[71] Such aid, provided to wanted members, proved crucial to the survival of the VNQDD because after the severe repression that had followed the Yen Bay Uprising and after the execution of Nguyen Thai Hoc and the suicide of Nguyen Thi Giang, the VNQDD was able to regroup by moving its operational bases to southern China.

Nguyen Thi Giang's work within the VNQDD also included the planning and organisation of covert actions and plots against both French political figures and institutions, and against Vietnamese considered to be traitors to the VNQDD. In December of 1929, for example, the Sûreté found, in a ditch in the village of Noi Vien in Bac Ninh province, at least 150 explosive devices hidden in large urns. The Sûreté arrested six men suspected of having fabricated the explosive devices. One of the accused, a man by the name of Dang Xuan Lien, claimed that the bombs had been crafted at the home of a schoolteacher named Thang under the instructions and the orders of Nguyen Thi Giang.[72]

During the Yen Bay Uprising itself, Nguyen Thi Giang had been more than a mere bystander or companion to her fiancé. Nguyen Thai Hoc had called upon her and her sister Nguyen Thi Bac, and a third woman by the name of Do Thi Tam, to form the Yen Bay troop unit.[73] Present throughout the planning stages, it was Nguyen Thi Giang who had informed Nguyen Thai Hoc that the ICP, not wanting to be upstaged by the VNQDD, was also planning political and military actions in the area.[74] The ICP had also distributed a number of flyers announcing the VNQDD's imminent attack upon the Yen Bay garrison.[75] On the day of the uprising, while Nguyen Thai Bac and others, disguised as Vietnamese peasant women selling produce, transported caches of weapons by train from Phu To to Yen Bay, Nguyen Thi Giang was already in Yen Bay, steering troop units to safety in the nearby Rung Son mountains.[76] From there she was in constant, direct communication with the commanders of the troop units.[77] In spite of its ultimate failure, the Yen Bay Mutiny had been able to get off the ground because of the efforts of Nguyen Thi Giang.

Following the Yen Bay Uprising in 1930, it became clear that members of the VNQDD were in grave danger. French colonial authorities immediately cracked down on the movement, searching out and arresting suspected members of the party. Not only were Nguyen Thai Hoc and other leaders arrested, but so too was Nguyen Thi Bac, Thi Giang's sister. Thi Bac was taken to Hoa Lo Prison in Hanoi prior to the trial in which she was convicted of having endangered the security of French Indochina. Thi Bac was sentenced to 20 years in prison.[78] She was then deported to Con Dao Prison (Poulo Condore), where she remained until 1936, when the metropolitan French Popular Front government freed a number of colonial political prisoners.[79] Upon her release, Thi Bac would continue to work for Vietnamese independence as she reportedly allowed Vietnamese revolutionaries to gather at her home in Bac Ninh (just north of Hanoi).[80]

Immediately after the Yen Bay Uprising, the colonial administration asked the French Sûreté in Vietnam to conduct an inquiry into the causes and sequence of the events. The minutes of the inquiry's sessions reveal that Nguyen Thi Giang was a key player in the Yen Bay Uprising. The interrogation of a suspected VNQDD member, Le Van Canh, centred around a plot to assassinate Governor General of Indochina Pierre Pasquier. Canh testified that he had written a document, dictated by Nguyen Thi Giang, in which the assassinations of Pasquier as well as numerous others (high-level French administrators, Vietnamese mandarins, and Vietnamese traitors to the VNQDD) were mandated. The document had been written in invisible ink on the orders of Nguyen Thi Giang and stated that it was time to remove the capitalist yoke that was oppressing Vietnam and that the assassination of Pierre Pasquier would serve as a lesson.[81] Le Van Canh explained further that Nguyen Thi Giang's instructions included comments about positive and negative policies. The positive policies called for the recruitment of as many party members as possible, while negative policies called for the assassination of as many enemies of the party as possible.[82]

Pasquier's "death sentence", as dictated by Thi Giang, echoes the party's ideology and purpose: "The country lost, the family dispersed, the race decimated for almost one century, our Annamite[83] people are ruthlessly under the boot of the French imperialists and the capitalists, and are painfully reduced to the condition of beasts of burden."[84]

The words Thi Giang used to justify Pasquier's execution were very similar to those she wrote in one of her suicide letters. In the letter, addressed to Nguyen Thai Hoc's parents, Nguyen Thi Giang alluded to the pain of the loss of national sovereignty:

> Dear Father and Mother, I die because of my circumstances. I cannot convey the harm done to my family and I cannot avenge the insult to my country. I offered my chaste heart in Hung Vung temple. Now, I return to our father's native land[85] and use this pistol to end my life. Please be generous and accept your ungrateful daughter-in-law's respectful prostration. Respectfully yours, Nguyen Thi Giang.[86]

In her letter Nguyen Thi Giang also expressed her regret at not being able to die under the tricolour flag of her country, and at leaving "in danger" her fellow revolutionaries.[87]

It is also likely that in addition to high-level French colonial administrators, Nguyen Thi Giang was responsible for the assassination of VNQDD members suspected of having betrayed the party. According to French colonial intelligence reports, Thi Giang in all likelihood ordered the assassination of Nguyen Van Ngoc, a suspected Sûreté informant.[88] Ngoc, who had been arrested with other VNQDD members, was found strangled in prison in 1930. A few days later, according to Sûreté officials, Thi Giang ordered the assassination of another VNQDD "traitor": Pham Thanh Duong. Duong had apparently provided information to the Sûreté to lead them to the party's bomb reserves.[89] According to the Sûreté, Nguyen Thi Giang was also directly involved in the assassination of a man by the name of Nguyen Binh. On 30 May 1930, two VNQDD members attacked and killed Binh, an administrator responsible for "payments" who was carrying 10,000 piastres. Binh was killed in broad daylight on a Hanoi street.[90] On the night of Binh's assassination, a meeting took place in which Nguyen Xuan Huan, one of the co-conspirators in the assassination plot, identified a woman named Thi Lê as also being present at the meeting. When arrested, Huan was shown a police photograph of Nguyen Thi Giang, whom he identified as Thi Lê.[91] The police then became aware that Thi Lê was one of Nguyen Thi Giang's numerous aliases. The purpose of the meeting had been to determine what to do with the funds stolen from Nguyen Binh.[92] According to the Sûreté, 5,000 piastres had been sent to the Yunnan section of the VNQDD and the rest of the money had been sent to businesses in Hanoi and

Haiphong whose purposes and profits were intended to finance the VNQDD's activities.[93]

After the mutiny and after the arrests of Nguyen Thai Hoc and other VNQDD members, Nguyen Thi Giang, who had escaped but who was being sought by the Sûreté, had proposed a plan to attack Hoa Lo Prison in Hanoi in order to free Hoc and the others. Unable to accomplish this by the time of Hoc's execution, Nguyen Thi Giang made her way to the execution grounds in Yen Bay — but not merely to be a silent witness to her fiancé's execution. She had developed a plan to bomb the execution grounds and to free Hoc and his comrades. Fearing the possibility of such actions, French colonial authorities had brought in an additional 400 soldiers to provide security and to monitor the area. Thi Giang was therefore unable to follow through with her plans.

Conclusion

The aim of this chapter was to demonstrate that Nguyen Thi Giang's participation and work in the VNQDD was considerable. Thi Giang's work as a propagandist, a liaison officer and an organiser allowed the VNQDD to develop a political programme, to recruit significant numbers of members and to mount several "military" actions against colonial rule. The point here is not to glorify the violent actions of Nguyen Thi Giang and the VNQDD or to ponder upon the necessity of an anti-colonial armed insurrection. As noted above, French colonial officials recognised Nguyen Thi Giang's prominent role within the VNQDD, even stating that she may have been more revolutionary or more politically active than Nguyen Thai Hoc. Ironically, in spite of such recognition, Sûreté reports focus almost exclusively on Nguyen Thai Hoc and his male compatriots within the VNQDD, making clear a gender bias. Given her prominence and her level of activity within the VNQDD, Nguyen Thi Giang should be given, at the very least, equal consideration to that of Nguyen Thai Hoc. Nguyen Thi Giang's contributions to the Vietnamese nationalist cause deserve to be part of the historical landscape. While sources are scarce and varied, they nonetheless clearly point out that she was a patriot and that she had chosen the VNQDD as a means towards national independence. The evidence also demonstrates that she was an important and influential member of the party.

While she was engaged (perhaps even married) to Nguyen Thai Hoc, much of her work was accomplished on her own, since the couple's revolutionary activities seldom allowed them to spend time together. She was not a mere follower of Nguyen Thai Hoc but rather a genuine companion in arms. While her suicide was indeed a spectacular gesture, and while one of her final letters was a testament to her love for Nguyen Thai Hoc as well as an expression of regret that she could not avenge the harm that Hoc's execution had wreaked upon their family, what is most often ignored is the patriotic tone of those letters as well as her commitment to the VNQDD's aims: "I have not restored to my country its glory, I have not avenged my family. Although I am still young, I have already sacrificed myself for the cause of the people. But the road to progress is long."[94]

To focus simply on her devotion to Nguyen Thai Hoc is reductive at best. It is clear that Nguyen Thi Giang was equally devoted to the cause of Vietnamese independence and was a nationalist in her own right.

Notes

1. The Yen Bay Mutiny, also referred to as the Yen Bay Uprising, took place in February 1930 when members of the Viet Nam Quôc Dan Dang attacked the French military garrison at Yen Bay. See Nicola Cooper, *France in Indochina: Colonial Encounters* (Oxford: Berg Publishers, 2001), pp. 93–4.

2. "Les treize exécutions de Yen-Bay", *Le petit parisien* (18 June 1930), p. 1. This was also reported in a Vietnamese newspaper: "Nguyen Thai Hoc va Pho Duc Chinh", *Phu Nu Tan Van* (26 June 1930).

3. Hoang Van Dao, *Viet Nam Quoc Dan Dang: A Contemporary History of a National Struggle, 1927–1954*, transl. Huynh Khue (Pittsburgh: Rose Dog Books, 2009), p. 491.

4. There is no evidence that Nguyen Thi Giang and Nguyen Thai Hoc were married, although Thi Giang did mention a ceremony of sorts in her suicide note. Historians have referred to Thi Giang as Thai Hoc's fiancée, while other sources, such as official colonial sources, have referred to her as his mistress.

5. Archives nationales d'outre mer (hereafter ANOM), Fonds ministériels (hereafter FM), Nouveaux Fonds (hereafter NF), Dossier 2626, Police de l'Indochine, Service de la Sûreté du Tonkin, *Note confidentielle 7880*.

6. "Nguyen Thai Hoc va Pho Duc Chinh da bi hanh hinh hom 17 Juin. Co Giang la vo Nguyen Thai Hoc da tu van theo chong va theo dang" [Nguyen Thai Hoc and Pho Duch Chinh Executed June 17. Co Giang, Wife of Nguyen Thai Hoc, Commits Suicide to Follow Her Husband and the Party], *Phu Nu Tan van* [*Women's News*], 26 June 1930.

7. "Nguyen Thai Hoc va Pho Duc Chinh da bi hanh hinh hom 17 Juin". In one of her letters Thi Giang alluded to a ceremony and vows, which meant that she may have married Hoc. In any case this would have been a second marriage for Hoc since he was already married to another woman when he met Nguyen Thi Giang.

8. An unnamed source cites Tho Tang as Hoc's native village: *Co Giang: Follow Him to Heaven*, Virtual Vietnam Archive, Douglas Pike Collection: Unit 08 Biography, Item #48929. On the other hand, the sociologist Trinh Van Thao claims Hoc was born in the village of Vinh Tuong: Trinh Van Thao, *Vietnam: Du Confucianisme au Communisme* [*Vietnam: From Confucianism to Communism*] (Paris: L'Harmattan, 1990), p. 43. Yet another source explains that Tho Tang is a village adjacent to Dong Khe (or Dong Ve): Lang Nhan, *Nhung tran danh Phap: Tu Ham Nghi den Nguyen Thai Hoc, 1885-1931* [*Fighters against France: From Ham Nghi to Nguyen Thai Hoc, 1885-1931*] (Houston: Zieleks, 1987), p. 208.

9. One source claims that Thi Giang shot herself in the heart: *Co Giang: Follow Him to Heaven*. However, photos found in the colonial archives, and taken upon the discovery of her body, reveal instead a wound to the head.

10. *Co Giang: Follow Him to Heaven*.

11. Hoang Van Dao, *Viet Nam Quoc Dan Dang*, p. 490.

12. For an analysis of the rise in women's suicide rates in the 1920s, see Linh Vu, "Drowned in Romances, Tears, and Rivers: Young Women's Suicide in Early Twentieth Century Vietnam", *Explorations* 9 (2009): 35–46.

13. This notion is examined closely in Kathleen Gottschang Turner and Phan Thanh Hao, *Even the Women Must Fight* (New York: John Wiley and Sons, 1998).

14. Mai Thi Thu and Le Thi Nham Tuyet, W*omen of Vietnam* (Hanoi: Foreign Languages Publishing House, 1978).

15. Micheline Lessard, "More than Half the Sky: Vietnamese Women and Anti-French Political Activism, 1858–1945", in *Vietnam and the West: New Approaches*, ed. Wynn Wilcox (Ithaca: Southeast Asia Program, Cornell University, 2010), p. 92.

16. Hoang Van Dao, *Viet Nam Quoc Dan Dang*.

17. Lang Nhan, *Nhung tran danh Phap*.

18. It should also be noted that this particular study suffers from a lack of citations.

19. ANOM, Gouvernement général de l'Indochine (hereafter GGI), Dossier 65537, *Note de l'inspecteur René Veyrenc sur le meurtre commis dans la nuit du 5 au 6 octobre au jardin botanique de Hanoi sur la personne de l'émissaire de la commission criminelle nommé Nguyen Van Kinh*.

20. Lessard, "More than Half the Sky", p. 92.

21. Most discrepancies concern specific dates. In some cases the sources differ when it comes to birth dates or the ages of the protagonists. In other instances precise dates are not available.

22. For a more thorough analysis of the role of the Vietnamese press in creating a public sphere for political debate, see Shawn Frederick McHale, *Print and Power: Confucianism, Communism, and Buddhism in the Making of Modern Vietnam* (Honolulu: University of Hawaii Press, 2004).

23. ANOM, GGI, Dossier 65517, *Rapport du président de la commission criminelle, Viet Nam Quoc Dan Dang et Viet Nam Thanh Nien Cach Menh Dong Tri Hoi*, p. 12.

24. Ibid.

25. Study by the Senior Liaison Office, U.S. Embassy, Vietnam, "Nationalist Politics in Vietnam", Douglas Pike Collection, Unit 06 Democratic Republic of Vietnam, Item #2321601006.

26. ANOM, GGI, Dossier 65517, *Rapport du président de la commission criminelle*, p. 12.

27. Ibid.

28. Alexander B. Woodside, *Community and Revolution in Modern Vietnam* (Boston: Houghton Mifflin, 1976), p. 59.

29. Ibid.

30. Louis Marty, *Contribution à l'histoire des mouvements politiques de l'Indochine franÁaise* [*Contribution to the History of French Indochinese Political Movements*] (Hanoi: Imprimerie d'Extrĺme Orient, 1933), p. 8.

31. A study conducted by Gail Kelly in 1971 demonstrated that members of the VNQDD tended to be "more literate and better educated than the communists" and "by far better educated than the population as a whole". Gail P. Kelly, "Education and Participation in Nationalist Groups: An Exploratory Study of the Indochinese Communist Party and the VNQDD, 1929–1931", *Comparative Education Review* 15, 2 (June 1971): 232.

32. For a more detailed analysis of these school strikes, see Micheline Lessard, "We Know the Duties We Must Fulfill: Modern 'Mothers and Fathers' of the Vietnamese Nation", *French Colonial History* 3 (2003): 119–41; and Micheline Lessard, "The Colony Writ Small: Vietnamese Women and Political Activism in Colonial Schools during the 1920s", *Journal of the Canadian Historical Association* 18, 2 (2007): 3–23.

33. Senior Liaison Office, U.S. Embassy, Vietnam, "Nationalist Politics in Vietnam".

34. Vu Van Thai, "Vietnam: Nationalism under Challenge", *Vietnam Perspectives* 2, 2 (Nov. 1966): 5.

35. Ibid.

36. Ibid.

37. Ibid.

38. Senior Liaison Office, U.S. Embassy, Vietnam, "Nationalist Politics in Vietnam".

39. Scott McConnell, *Leftward Journey: The Education of Vietnamese Students in France, 1919-1939* (New Brunswick: Transaction Books, 1989).
40. Senior Liaison Office, U.S. Embassy, Vietnam, "Nationalist Politics in Vietnam".
41. Ibid.
42. Marty, *Contribution à l'histoire*, p. 14.
43. *Nguyen Thai Hoc. The Schoolteacher Patriot* (Virtual Vietnam Archive, Texas Tech University, Douglas Pike Collection, Unit 08: Biography, Item #2361209096), p. 30.
44. Ibid.
45. Senior Liaison Office, U.S. Embassy, Vietnam, "Nationalist Politics in Vietnam".
46. Ibid.
47. Ibid.
48. Ibid.
49. "Les événements du Tonkin," *La tribune indochinoise* (21 Feb. 1930), p. 1.
50. Ibid.
51. Phuong Bui Tranh, "Femmes vietnamiennes pendant et après la colonisation française et la guerre américaine: réflexions sur les orientations bibliographiques" [Vietnamese Women during and after French Colonisation and the American War: Reflections on the Bibliographical Orientations], in *Histoire des femmes en situation coloniale* [*History of Women under Colonialism*], ed. Anne Hugon (Paris: Karthala, 2004), p. 78.
52. Lang Nhan, *Nhung tran danh Phap*, p. 205.
53. *Co Giang: Follow Him to Heaven*, p. 33.
54. Phut Tan Nguyen, *A Modern History of Vietnam, 1802-1954* (Hanoi: Nha San Khai Tri, 1964), p. 380.
55. Lang Nhan, *Nhung tran danh Phap*, p. 205.
56. Marty, *Contribution à l'histoire*.
57. Ibid.
58. ANOM, GGI, Dossier 65517, *Rapport du president de la commission criminelle*, p. 32.
59. ANOM, *Service de liaison avec les originaires des territoires français d'outre-mer* (hereafter SLOTFOM), Série 3, Carton 131.
60. Marty, *Contribution à l'histoire*, p. 24.
61. Oscar Chapuis, *The Last Emperors of Vietnam: From Tu Duc to Bao Dai* (Westport: Greenwood Press, 2000).
62. Hoang Van Dao, *Viet Nam Quoc Dan Dang*, p. 488.
63. Marty, *Contribution à l'histoire*, p. 20.
64. Ibid.
65. Hoang Van Dao, *Viet Nam Quoc Dan Dang*, p. 127.
66. Marty, *Contribution à l'histoire*.
67. Ibid., p. 20.

68. *Co Giang: Follow Him to Heaven*, p. 34.
69. Ibid.
70. Ibid.
71. ANOM, GGI, Dossier 65444, *Déclarations de Nguyen Van Hien, dit Nguye Huy Hien, dit Thien Nhien, dit Vuong Tien Vinh, dit Hong The Huong, Octobre 1937.*
72. ANOM, SLOTFOM, Série 3, Carton 131.
73. ANOM, SLOTFOM, Série 3, Carton 131, p. 73.
74. Ibid., p. 90.
75. Ibid.
76. Ibid., p. 91.
77. Ibid.
78. Thu Ha (ed.), *Danh Nu Trong Truyen Thuyet va Lich Su Viet Nam* [*Women in Legend and History of Vietnam*] (Hanoi: Nha Xuat Ban Lao Dong, 2009), p. 112. Some sources claim that Nguyen Thi Bac had been sentenced to death. This discrepancy may likely reflect the fact that the sentence was reduced to 20 years in prison at Con Dao after an appeal. French colonial archival documents are replete with the commutation of convicts' sentences after appeal.
79. ANOM, Résidence Supérieure du Tonkin (hereafter RST), Dossier 2244.
80. Ibid.
81. ANOM, Police de Sûreté, Commissaire Spécial, Procès verbal, RST, 1930.
82. Ibid.
83. The French referred to the Vietnamese as Annamites, from the name "Annam", used by the Chinese in past occupations and signifying the Pacified South. In spite of the pejorative and negative connotations of this term (pacification serving as a euphemism for colonialism), it was used not only by the French but by Vietnamese as well.
84. ANOM, *Déclaration du VNQDD sur la sentence de mort d'un serviteur de capitalistes impérialistes franÁais à Gouverneur général de l'Indochine Pasquier.*
85. The term "native land" here refers to the native village.
86. Hoang Van Dao, *Viet Nam Quoc Dan Dang*, p. 490.
87. ANOM, GGI, Dossier 65536, Police de l'Indochine, Service de la Sûreté du Tonkin, *Suicide de Nguyen Thi Giang.*
88. Marty, *Contribution à l'histoire*, p. 20.
89. Hoang Van Dao, *Viet Nam Quoc Dan Dang*, p. 79.
90. Marty, *Contribution à l'histoire*, p. 21.
91. ANOM, RST, *Commissariat special de la Sûreté, 21 Août 1930.*
92. Ibid.
93. Marty, *Contribution à l'histoire*, p. 21.
94. ANOM, GGI, Dossier 65536, Police de l'Indochine, Service de la Sûreté du Tonkin, *Suicide de Nguyen Thi Giang.*

CHAPTER 3

Suyatin Kartowiyono: A Nationalist Leader of the Indonesian Women's Movement

Susan Blackburn

In Indonesian history Suyatin Kartowiyono (1907–83) is remembered, if at all, as a leader of the women's movement from the late 1920s to the 1950s. Starting in 1928 as an organiser of the first Indonesian women's congress, she went on to be active in the women's federations established in the 1930s, 1940s and 1950s and was a founder of the secular women's organisation Perwari (Persatuan Wanita Republik Indonesia, Union of Women of the Indonesian Republic). She is not remembered as part of the nationalist movement. The purpose of this chapter is to show that during the struggle against Dutch colonialism, she identified herself — and indeed the women's movement generally — as nationalist. The questions addressed in this chapter are: Why did she become a nationalist, and what did that concept mean to her? Why did she become a leader of the women's movement rather than of the mainstream nationalist movement? What was her contribution to the nationalist movement? How did her identification with that movement influence her life? And why has Indonesian nationalist historiography omitted all reference to her?

Unlike most Indonesian women leaders, Suyatin Kartowiyono left behind some written reflections on the Indonesian women's movement and an autobiography, *Mencari Makna Hidupku* [*Searching for the Meaning of My Life*], published in 1983. Because by the time the autobiography was written she was quite ill (she died at the end of 1983), it was produced with the help of Hanna Rambe, a well-established journalist and author who volunteered her services because she had known and admired Suyatin from childhood.[1] Comparing the autobiography with earlier writings by Suyatin,[2] it seems clear that the work was very substantially in her own words. Probably Hanna Rambe recorded conversations with her and helped to structure the book with the aid of Suyatin's notes and diaries.[3]

It is doubtful whether, left to her own devices, Suyatin would ever have written her autobiography. Indonesians of that era, especially women, wrote little about themselves. Hers is the only such work by a female leader from the colonial period. The Indonesian publishing industry and the reading market were in their infancy, limiting the scope for publication, and traditions of modesty may have inhibited some Indonesian leaders from appearing to blow their own trumpet.[4] Apart from her own writings, moreover, very little has been published about Suyatin Kartowiyono, although her activities in the women's movement are quite well recorded. For insight into her own motivation, this chapter depends heavily on her own accounts.[5] In them, Suyatin often refers to her own emotions and opinions, although she reveals very little about her private life, reflecting her views about what was appropriate for publication. Defying the well-known Javanese traditional preference for harmony and avoidance of confrontation, and perhaps reflecting Western literature — of which she was an avid reader — Suyatin does not shy away from recounting some of the conflicts in which she was involved and defends her own position strongly. Focused on her public role, her autobiography clearly exemplifies what Watson refers to as "the sense of contributing to the definition of a nation", which he regards as the "distinctively Indonesian consciousness" informing the 20th-century autobiographies he has examined.[6]

Becoming a Nationalist

At no point in her autobiographical writings does Suyatin Kartowiyono pinpoint a moment when she became an Indonesian nationalist or why. Born in the Dutch colony of the Netherlands Indies, she grew up with the nationalist movement, moving in the 1920s, along with thousands of other educated young Indonesians, from an ethnic-based organisation to an identification with Indonesia as a nation. It was as if she absorbed the ethos of the time, what has been called "The age of movement", the age of the *pergerakan*.[7] In this her father, Mahmud

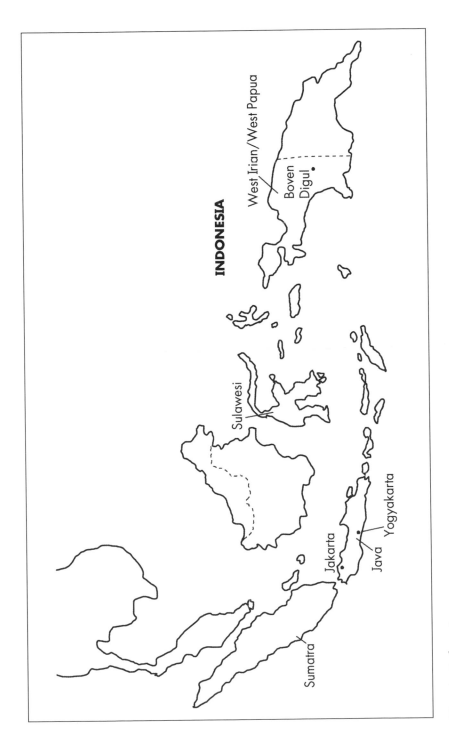

Map 4. Indonesia

Joyodirono, was clearly very influential — not in the sense of instilling nationalist ideas, but rather in his intense involvement in organisations, in the new kind of groupings that came with modern life, and in his attitudes. As Suyatin put it, her father "formed my personality as someone who couldn't stand to see injustice or oppression. I was always moved to defend people who were deprived of their rights."[8] By contrast, her mother, R.A. Kiswari, appears to have had less influence in shaping her character.

Suyatin Kartowiyono, a Javanese by ethnicity, was born in a village in central Java, the dominant island in the Indonesian archipelago. (See map 4 for places mentioned in this chapter.) Her father, a railway official, was a well-read man and provided a modern education for his four daughters and his only son, who was born after Suyatin. This was most unusual for the times: only a small proportion of Indonesians went to school, and girls received even less education than boys. At an early age Suyatin became an avid reader, and as she advanced into her teenage years she followed her father into organisational activities. Her father had founded a branch of Budi Utomo, a Javanese organisation started in 1908, which came to be identified as a forerunner of the nationalist parties although it was not overtly political.[9] It was inspired, as Suyatin and her father clearly were, by the aim of improving life for Javanese.

When Suyatin Kartowiyono entered a Dutch secondary school in 1922 at the age of 15 she became active in the women's wing of Jong Java (Young Java), an organisation for educated young Javanese who felt a sense of duty towards their motherland.[10] She took on the editorship of the organisation's journal. By this time, she notes quite casually in her autobiography, "I had long known that the colonial system was evil", although she admired a number of good Dutch people.[11] In 1926, when Suyatin was 19, together with other young teachers she established and became president of Puteri Indonesia (Indonesian Girls), the women's wing of a new overtly nationalist organisation for young educated people, Pemuda Indonesia (Indonesian Youth).[12] She had begun to attend nationalist meetings, especially those addressed by the up-and-coming secular nationalist leader Sukarno, the founder of the PNI, the Nationalist Party of Indonesia. "I was attracted," she noted in her autobiography, "to the idea of unifying the whole of Indonesia. Really that was the only way to fight the Dutch."[13] In 1928 Pemuda Indonesia held its second congress and launched what is regarded as a landmark in the Indonesian nationalist movement, the Youth Oath, whereby young Indonesians pledged

Indonesian Nationalist Movement, 1908–49

1908	Establishment of first modern proto-nationalist organisation, Budi Utomo (Noble Endeavour)
1912	Founding of first nationalist organisation, Sarekat Islam (Islamic Union), and first women's organisation, Puteri Merdeka (Free Women)
1920	Founding of Indonesian Communist Party, Partai Komunis Indonesia (PKI)
1927	Founding of secular nationalist organisation Partai Nasional Indonesia (PNI), led by Sukarno
1926–27	Unsuccessful anti-colonial revolts by PKI
1928	Youth Oath congress of Pemuda Indonesia (Indonesian Youth)
1928	First Indonesian women's congress
1930	Founding of radical Islamic nationalist organisation Persatuan Muslimin Indonesia (Permi)
1931	Arrest and exile of Sukarno and other nationalist leaders
1939	Creation of GAPI, a nationalist coalition for democracy
1942–45	Japanese occupation
1945	Declaration of independence and founding of Indonesian republic
1945–49	Indonesian Revolution (struggle against reimposition of Dutch rule)
1949	Transfer of sovereignty from Dutch to Indonesian republic

loyalty to their nation, Indonesia, and stated that its language was Bahasa Indonesia, which was based not on Javanese but on Malay.[14]

It is hard to appreciate now how revolutionary those ideas were. The nation of Indonesia had no precedents. The very name was new, invented by a 19th-century anthropologist. The only thing that held together this archipelago of hundreds of islands and ethnic groups was that they had been conquered, bit by bit over several centuries, by the Dutch and brought together into what was then known as the Netherlands Indies or Dutch East Indies. At that time the colony had no common language except Dutch, which Suyatin — like her educated friends in Pemuda Indonesia — spoke fluently. By the late 1920s, becoming a nationalist meant taking on a new identity, identifying with a huge archipelago rather than just one's own ethnic group, and learning what was for most people an entirely new language. None of these ideas came directly from the schooling they had received at the hands of the Dutch, who had no interest at all in promoting a concept of nationhood in their colony, although of course Western education familiarised its recipients with the history of nationalist struggles. Writing about it much later, when the independent Republic of Indonesia was well established, Suyatin Kartowiyono seemed to have forgotten the novelty of the nationalist movement in the 1920s. Her progress from Jong Java to Pemuda Indonesia is presented as something obvious, as indeed it may have been to many educated young Indonesians who absorbed ideas of nationalism through their reading and from hearing these ideas propagated by the privileged few — nationalist leaders such as Mohammad Hatta, who had gone to the Netherlands for higher studies, or Sukarno, who had been nurtured in home-grown political organisations such as Sarekat Islam.

Nevertheless, Suyatin Kartowiyono was aware that she had been swept up in a time of change that entailed standing out against narrow ethnic-based traditions and Dutch colonial rule. She writes of having to take Malay lessons in order to be able to follow the nationalist speeches of people like Sukarno, to read the nationalist press for herself to be part of that movement, to make her own public speeches, and to write for the nationalist media.[15] Although a Javanese, she easily rose above her ethnicity; and although a Muslim, she identified most strongly with the secular stream in the nationalist movement. In both respects Suyatin had much in common with other Western-educated Javanese who operated with ease among people of different ethnic and religious backgrounds.

Relations with the Mainstream Nationalist Movement

Yet Suyatin did not become active in mainstream nationalist organisations led by men such as Sukarno, much as she admired him at the time. Again, this is something she does not explain in her writings: why in the late 1920s she took the decision to devote herself to the burgeoning women's movement rather than to the organisations with which she had identified up to that time. Inspired by the nationalist fervour of the Youth Oath of October 1928, in December of the same year, at the age of 21, she was one of the three organisers of the first Indonesian women's congress, which is regarded as the starting point of the national women's movement. It involved inviting women's organisations from around the archipelago to attend a conference with the aim of promoting unity and national identity among them. Not surprisingly, the conference organisers all lived in Yogyakarta, which has long nurtured tolerant cooperation among people of different faiths. Catholic, secular and Islamic organisations were represented, and it was Suyatin's first experience of negotiating the open tensions between them on the question of marriage law, and steering them towards an agreement to work together.[16]

In taking up this leadership position, apparently Suyatin Kartowiyono did not consider herself to be making a choice between two different movements. To her, the women's movement went hand in hand with the nationalist movement, and her commitment was not so much to a particular women's organisation as to something more novel, to forging an Indonesian national women's movement. As she put it later, "The feminist struggle was especially stimulated by the spirit of nationalism and the sense of justice."[17] The first women's congress succeeded, as Suyatin hoped it would, in raising women's awareness of belonging to the Indonesian nation, and resulted in them forming an umbrella organisation of Indonesian women's groups.[18]

The reasons why she committed herself to both the nationalist and the women's movements derive from her passionate opposition to discrimination. In her autobiography she credits her parents with a strong sense of egalitarianism, of raising their children to feel comfortable mixing freely with people of different classes, races and creeds.[19] For her, nationalism did not come with blinkers. At school she learned the meaning of justice, "a word that was very sweet to me: it has ever since been very important."[20] From an early age, according to her own account, she hated invidious distinctions to be made between people, herself included. Although her parents were obviously very liberal in their views, they still expected boys and girls to behave differently; and when this involved what Suyatin Kartowiyono regarded as discrimination, she objected strongly. For instance, why should she have to help her mother in the kitchen when this was not expected of her brother?[21] She was particularly wounded to learn from her sisters that her father, to whom she felt very close, had been disappointed at her birth because he wanted a boy.[22] Regardless of the fact that he soon was proud of her, more so than of her brother born a few years later, the very idea that parents would prefer boys to girls was objectionable to Suyatin.

Often in later life Suyatin Kartowiyono acknowledged the profound influence on her of the published letters of Radeng Ajeng

Kartini, regarded as the first modern feminist in Indonesia.[23] Kartini's letters to Dutch friends, published in 1911 after her death, are full of resentment against the restrictions placed on upper-class Javanese girls like herself: restrictions such as lack of access to post-primary education, early arranged marriages, forced deference to men and to those older than themselves, and the polygamous practices of aristocratic men. Although not subjected to such restrictions, Suyatin Kartowiyono was well aware of the plight of girls in the Javanese aristocracy, since her mother was related to the court of Yogyakarta. She became very critical of aristocratic life, and her autobiography relates a number of instances where she came into conflict with members of that class. For instance, in her teens she refused to bow down to the sultan of Yogyakarta, or to address high-ranking Javanese people in Javanese: she preferred to use the very egalitarian Malay language rather than the status-inflected Javanese.[24] This "anti-feudal" behaviour caused a sensation at the time.[25] What Suyatin also learned from Kartini's fate (she was married off to a polygamous man and died early in childbirth) was that it was imperative for women to be able to support themselves.[26] She made sure that she worked throughout her life to earn an income.

Her identification with Kartini from her early teenage years showed that Suyatin Kartowiyono took to feminist ideas with great ease. In her autobiography she wrote: "My years in MULO [secondary school] determined my career for life. My struggle from that time onwards, until 1960, was devoted to improving the rights and destiny of Indonesian women."[27] She adopted the same causes as Kartini, advocating education for girls, the abolition of early arranged marriages, and opposition to polygamy (or, more correctly, polygyny). This last cause became critical for Suyatin several times during her life. Her first encounter with polygamy is implicit, and not directly faced, in her autobiography. In her writings Suyatin Kartowiyono rarely addressed very personal matters that, one senses, may have been painful not only to her but to other members of her family. The fact was that she herself was the daughter of a polygamous father, yet she never in writing criticised her father for behaviour to which she objected in principle. She was obviously too close to him, far closer than to her mother, who, being unable to read or write, did not share many of her interests.[28] Later encounters with polygamy were not so intimate but certainly influenced Suyatin Kartowiyono's life. While she was in her early twenties, her public criticism of the practice of Javanese royalty in taking multiple wives (*selir*) earned her a caution from the Dutch, who protected the privileges of the court: she was threatened with being banned from the principalities if she persisted in such subversive behaviour.[29] Later in life she learned to negotiate diplomatically the minefield that polygamy constituted in the Indonesian women's movement: it caused great tension between Islamic women's organisations and more secular ones. A testing choice was made by her in 1937 on this issue, as described below. And finally, in the 1950s as leader of the women's federation she came into direct conflict with the powerful President Sukarno when he took a second wife.

For all these reasons, then, Suyatin threw herself into the women's movement in the late 1920s and remained a leader in it until age and ill health, and perhaps the tenor of the times, rendered her inactive by the 1960s. In all this there is an implicit question: Could Suyatin Kartowiyono have pursued her causes within the embrace of the mainstream nationalist movement? There are a number of issues here, including leadership and gender differences. It was very hard for a woman to be a leader in male-dominated nationalist parties such as Sukarno's Indonesian Nationalist Party, founded in 1927. The fact that the public meetings organised by these parties were often held at night deterred many women. Suyatin recalled that although she often attended nationalist meetings, at night she sat with Sukarno's wife of the time, Inggit Garnasih, because few women came.[30] Women did make occasional public speeches to such audiences, but it was rare. One of the very few women nationalist leaders of the colonial period was Rasuna Said, who is the subject of the next chapter in this book. She became the leader of a radical Islamic party, Permi (Persatuan Moeslimin Indonesia, Union of Indonesian Muslims), and was imprisoned by the Dutch in the 1930s for her outspoken attacks on colonialism. It was dangerous to be a nationalist leader in the late 1920s and the 1930s: such leaders ran the risk of being arrested and exiled, although Indonesian nationalists did not experience the level of repression that the Vietnamese did, at the hands of the French, as illustrated in the case of Nguyen Thi Giang (chapter 2). Nevertheless, the dangers probably deterred many women, or at least their protective families. Suyatin Kartowiyono herself appears to have been remarkably fearless and independent-minded, despite police surveillance at times.

Suyatin had a very egalitarian relationship with her husband, emphasising in her autobiography that she chose him over other young men because he was truly supportive of her chosen work, which she described as "national independence and improvement in the status of women".[31] They were married in 1932, when she was 25 and already working as a teacher, as she continued to do after marriage. Having a young family in the 1930s must, however, have somewhat restricted what she could do in public life. In her autobiography she is rather defensive about the arrangements she made to combine work, activism and family duties, and it is unclear precisely what supportive roles were played by her husband and unnamed kin or domestic workers.

There is no evidence that Suyatin found it difficult to work with men. Her autobiography shows she admired and was close to a number of male nationalist leaders, including Ki Hajar Dewantara and Haji Agus Salim.[32] They seem to have treated her as a protégé rather than as an equal, which is not surprising considering the age difference between them. Suyatin's relations with her male peers could be ambivalent, and she was firm about the need to be autonomous. Thus she emphasised many times that women should always have their own income, as she had done, and on some occasions she stood up to male leaders, especially to Sukarno in the 1950s when he took a second wife. Attending a women's congress in India in 1953, she reacted against the advice of Vijaya Lakshmi Pandit that "We should always be nice to men so that we can achieve our goals quicker". "In my heart I grumbled, 'But women can't be nice to them all the time. We demand justice!'"[33]

However, in her own life Suyatin Kartowiyono made some concessions to differentiated gender roles. For instance, she claimed that she always put her family first, as a mother should.[34] Moreover, although she felt she found equality in her marriage, she fell into line with Indonesian tradition so far as to insist that her husband was the head of the household. Even in this admission, however, she was unconventional: whereas the New Order regime, during which she wrote her autobiography, preached that men and women were equal because women took leadership in the home while men were leaders in public life, Suyatin reversed the order, saying, "In the office and in organisational life I became a leader. At home, my husband was the head of the household." For her this reflected their "meeting of minds".[35] Neither of these concessions seems to have cramped her style, however: she was an independent and outspoken woman.

This raises another serious point. From colonial times to the present, it seems that while the nationalist movement was regarded as political, the women's movement was always labelled "social". The Dutch were inclined to regard the women's movement quite indulgently for this very reason. Only a few individuals in it, such as Rasuna Said, were seen as too close to radical nationalists and therefore political; but women who concerned themselves with education and marriage reform were considered harmless to the regime.[36] Yet such clear distinctions could not be drawn, as Suyatin Kartowiyono was well aware. Congresses of the women's movement began with the singing of the nationalist anthem that had been adopted by the Youth Congress of 1928, and at the second women's congress in 1929, held in Jakarta in the hall used by the nationalist movement, Suyatin noted that people kept calling out "*Merdeka!*" (Freedom), which made the police threaten to close the meeting.[37] In 1941 the women's federation joined the nationalist umbrella organisation Gabungan Politik Indonesia (Indonesian Political Federation), which was attempting to wrest democratic reforms from the colonial government.[38] Immediately after the declaration of independence in 1945 a new women's federation was set up. Suyatin was the leader of the conference that established it, and she emphasised that it was "integrated with the struggle for freedom" since its first task was to support the new republic.[39]

The causes Suyatin championed within the women's movement were clearly political in that they involved radical changes in society and in public policy. Some of them were too subversive for much of the male-dominated nationalist movement. Leaders such as Sukarno frequently warned the women's movement that "women's issues" should be put on hold until the country had gained independence, and indeed the conception of national interest expounded by the male leaders should always be given priority. There was an implicit acknowledgement that many "women's issues", such as marriage reform, were too divisive to contemplate and that they threatened male prerogatives.

At one point in her life Suyatin Kartowiyono was forced to make the choice that Sukarno urged upon the women's movement. In 1937 the Dutch colonial government held out the prospect of a law that allowed Indonesians to choose a civil marriage that enforced monogamy. This was a radical departure from the religion-based marriage laws of the day, whereby one married according to the law of the religion or customary group to which one belonged. Thus the vast majority of the Indonesian population, being Muslims, were subject to Islamic family law, which permitted polygyny. The reform proposed by the Dutch was intended in part to meet the demands of many women's organisations for a fairer alternative for women, especially a law that would allow Muslim women to escape the threat of polygyny.[40] But when the government sought the support of the women's movement, Suyatin Kartowiyono and most other women leaders rejected the offer. Like male nationalist leaders, Suyatin claimed the proposal was a stratagem to divide the nationalist movement, and indeed it threatened to split the Islamists from the rest. She concurred with Sukarno that marriage law reform would have to wait until the country was independent: "I was certain that it was better for Indonesia to first achieve national independence as the absolute condition for improving the lives of women."[41] Thus she proved her nationalist credentials. Unfortunately she was to find that after the transfer of sovereignty in 1949, the governments of independent Indonesia shied away from the divisive issue of marriage reform and it was not until 1974 that a government was strong enough to defy Islamic opposition and force through a uniform marriage code.[42]

Benedict Anderson has referred to nations as "imagined communities",[43] an idea that raises the question of how nationalists opposing foreign rule imagined their independent nation would form a community. Although Suyatin never spelled out her vision of the "imagined community" of Indonesia, it is possible to deduce it from her writings and activities. It was clearly based on the notions of justice and equality, and her view of Indonesia was open and inclusive. She never labelled groups as "other", seeking to exclude them from the nation; rather, she recognised the diversity of Indonesia and revelled in it, as shown by her interest in other religions and ethnic groups. In this way her nationalism was more clearly aligned with the secular nationalists than with most Islamic nationalists. She appears to have been more inclusive than many secular nationalists in that she did not treat Chinese Indonesians as aliens, as frequently happened in Indonesia.

Her Role in the Nationalist Movement

As stated, Suyatin Kartowiyono saw the women's movement as working hand in hand with the male-dominated nationalist movement to prepare the country for independence. It mobilised women, raising their awareness of the nation and of the need to create a modern state in which men and women were truly equal. The scene had been set in 1928 at the Youth Oath ceremony, where both men and women took the nationalist oath, and it culminated in the constitution of the

Republic of Indonesia in 1945, which declared that men and women were equal. As Suyatin put it in her autobiography:

> As early as 1926 women's organisations began to be political in the sense that what they were demanding was no longer just improvement in women's situation and equality of rights in marriage and citizenship, but they began to oppose colonialism and oppression of one nation by another. By the time of the arrival of the Japanese, both the women's movement and the nationalist movement were struggling for the independence of the nation. Then the feeling of unity among women's organisations, and the feeling of nationalism among men and women, rose markedly between 1942 and 1949.[44]

Compared with some other nationalist movements, in Indonesia few efforts were made to mobilise the masses of men and women against colonialism. Unlike in India, for example, men and women were not recruited to support huge demonstrations of opposition to colonial rule. In part this was a result of careful Dutch policies to restrain Indonesian nationalists: when the movement showed signs of becoming too radical its leaders were arrested and exiled. However, few Indonesian organisations showed any real interest in recruiting mass support, and most women's organisations were similarly reluctant — with the exception of Islamic organisations, which recruited on the basis of religion rather than nationalism. During the colonial period Suyatin, like most other women leaders, appeared satisfied with building small organisations of largely urban, educated women. At one point in her career, in 1931, she had the opportunity to make contact with poor working women, yet she was satisfied with drawing the attention of existing women's organisations to the plight of these women rather than seeking to involve such women themselves in organisations.[45] Although, given the constraints of the time, it would indeed have been difficult for her to do so, even after independence she never seems to have contemplated such a move or regretted not being able to do so. Thus, her notions of a nationalist movement and of a women's movement, which she saw as intertwined, were limited, as were those of most other leaders during the colonial period.

Even if one followed the prevailing trend to regard the women's movement as social, not political, and therefore not really nationalist, there is a strong case to be made for Suyatin Kartowiyono's direct contribution to the nationalist cause during the Indonesian Revolution of 1945–49, the period of heroic struggle by Indonesians to prevent the Dutch from re-establishing colonial rule after the Japanese occupation. Vastly inferior to the Dutch in military terms, the Indonesian resistance movement — consisting largely of revolutionary youth and guerrilla soldiers, and employees of the new Republican government — depended on the voluntary support of the people. The nationalist movement and the women's movement, working together, operated on a mass scale during the Revolution.

A basic requirement was to feed members of the resistance movement and their families at a time when food production and transportation were disrupted by the end of the Japanese occupation and the efforts of the Dutch to reassert control, opposed at every step by Indonesian Republican supporters. Women immediately took on the task of feeding the Republicans through the organisation known as WANI (Wanita Negara Indonesia, Women of the Indonesian State). WANI appointed Suyatin to supervise the transportation of food in Java, and she travelled widely around the island as part of this mission, reporting to the Republican government in Yogyakarta. Her autobiography dwells eloquently on the trials of this period.[46] For instance, she describes how, even when heavily pregnant, she squeezed into and out of overcrowded trains and secreted on her person incriminating papers and objects when Dutch soldiers came on board to check people's identities and arrest revolutionaries.

As her autobiography sums up:

> For independence I did my utmost, even while pregnant. I rode trains at night, perched on the coupling between carriages, with the soot from the engine flying over my head; I rode bicycles with flat tyres while heavily pregnant; I walked far into the night when called to meetings in Yogyakarta and elsewhere; and I did all this wholeheartedly.[47]

There was no doubt in her own mind that she was a very active participant in the nationalist movement.

How Being in the Nationalist Movement Influenced Her Life

As a result of her nationalist convictions, before the Japanese occupation Suyatin Kartowiyono suffered some harassment and police surveillance at the hands of the Dutch colonial government, which was implacably opposed to the notion of independence.[48] During the colonial period, Suyatin's being a nationalist meant that both she and her husband refused to be employed by the colonial government. Trained as a teacher, she taught in private schools even though the pay was far less than she would have received in the state system.[49] Interestingly, she had no objection to working for the Japanese during the occupation even though she recognised they were far more brutal than the Dutch.[50] Presumably, like Sukarno, she anticipated that Indonesia would win its independence under the Japanese.

After independence Suyatin Kartowiyono was in a good position to benefit from her nationalist credentials and get a well-paid position in the new government bureaucracy. For several years she was able to pursue one of her life goals through a government position promoting literacy. She was delighted to be able to travel around much of the vast archipelago in this capacity, visiting places she had barely heard of before. In the process she was also able to help build the network of her organisation, Perwari, a secular women's organisation spread throughout Indonesia — as its president from 1953 to 1960, Suyatin helped it establish schools and literacy courses, mother-and-child health clinics and a women's legal centre — as well as to participate in campaigns for women's causes.[51] In 1957 she finally resigned her high-ranking government job in protest against governments that refused to oppose polygamy and against President Sukarno when he embarked upon a polygamous marriage.[52]

From her autobiography and other writings, one gains the impression that Suyatin Kartowiyono devoted her life to the nationalist movement and the women's movement, conceiving of them as inextricably intertwined insofar as their common goals were to seek an independent nation with an egalitarian society. Her husband and six children, although obviously vital to her private life and the source of great satisfaction, did not impinge on the public persona and received very little attention in her autobiography.[53] Another short account of her life pays tribute to her humanity, her generosity in sharing her knowledge and helping women, and her courage, honesty and sincerity in thought and action.[54]

Did Suyatin Kartowiyono benefit from her involvement in the nationalist movement? Her autobiography leads one to believe that it enriched her life immeasurably. She was grateful for the opportunity to serve her country and in the process get to know it better. From time to time the autobiography waxes rhapsodical as she admires the Indonesian regions she visited and the remarkable people she met, mostly ordinary people who overcame great odds. The opportunity to benefit materially or personally is not mentioned; Suyatin appears to have lived frugally without feeling deprived, and she sought no honours although she did pick up three national awards along the way for her social work and service to the women's movement.[55]

Any regrets Suyatin mentions concern not herself personally but the causes she espoused. President Sukarno disappointed her: from having admired him when young, she turned against him in the 1950s when he embarked on his first polygamous marriage. The battle for marriage law reform was dispiritingly long, but she was grateful when a law was finally passed in 1974, although she felt it still had weaknesses.[56] There are indications that she was disturbed during her final years by trends in the women's movement under the New Order. The emergence of "wives' organizations" (i.e., organisations comprising wives of state employees) weakened her organisation, Perwari, and led to a lack of leadership in the women's federation, Kongres Wanita Indonesia (Indonesian Women's Congress).[57] However, she chose to dwell on the progress she had perceived through her lifetime:

> The position of our women, with such good opportunities to gain an education since independence, is far different from what it was during Kartini's life. Our struggle to gain a national marriage law has been achieved, twenty years after Indonesia's independence.

What remained, she thought, was to ensure that single women were treated as equals, allowed to live their own lives.[58]

How History Has Treated Her

Suyatin Kartowiyono has been sadly neglected in the writing of Indonesian history. Long dominated by the state's version of nationalism, Indonesian historiography presents a story of triumphant struggle for independence, but only a limited number of individuals are given recognition as having played important roles.[59] The country has a National Heroes Board, which oversees the selection and promotion of an official list of National Heroes, carefully developed over the years to ensure each region has its own names and to reflect the ideology of the regime in power. The list consists mainly of selected individuals who resisted the imposition of colonial rule before there was any conception of an Indonesian nation, of leaders of nationalist parties, and of military leaders, especially from the period of the Revolution. Very few women are mentioned, and the few that are are an incongruous bunch.[60] Kartini features prominently, although she did not oppose Dutch rule or identify as an Indonesian. Founders of early modern schools for girls are mentioned: Dewi Sartika in West Java, Walanda Maramis in Sulawesi, and Rahmah El Yunusiah in Sumatra. None of these women were part of the male-dominated nationalist movement more narrowly conceived: their contributions were seen as social rather than political. Leaders of the women's movement, including Suyatin Kartowiyono, do not feature in the pantheon of National Heroes. The only woman who is occasionally mentioned as belonging to the "political" nationalist movement is Rasuna Said, because she was a leader of a male-dominated party in the 1930s[61] (see the next chapter in this book).

Literature about the nationalist movement, at home and abroad, mentions almost no women outside the official pantheon. A.K. Pringgodigdo, whose early approach to chronicling the history of what he called the "Indonesian people's movement" was unusually pluralistic, distinguished different strands within the nationalist movement, including religious, youth and women's streams; but in writing about the women's stream he mentions almost no individuals except his wife of the time, Suwarni Pringgodigdo.[62] Other historians have an even narrower view.

Those who have documented the history of the Indonesian women's movement have been kinder to Suyatin Kartowiyono. Although there is no full biography of her (and indeed few have been published of any of her female contemporaries),[63] there are tributes to her in a number of records of the growth of the women's movement and its consolidation after the Japanese occupation.[64] But this merely confirms the line drawn between the nationalist and women's movements: they are seen to be quite separate — at best parallel but not overlapping.

Just as there were advantages to women in joining the women's movement rather than the male-dominated nationalist movement, one can argue that the memory of a woman like Suyatin Kartowiyono perhaps benefits from being ignored by official nationalist propaganda. As a number of critics have shown, the "approved" versions of the lives of National Heroes reduced them to "cardboard cutouts"[65] and contributed to the decline of interest in history in Indonesia under the New Order. With the revival of more independent historical and biographical writing in the post-Suharto era, it is to be hoped that

Indonesians will recognise that their nationalist movement was pluralistic and that different streams within it, such as the women's movement under the leadership of nationalists like Suyatin Kartowiyono,
projected inspiring alternative visions for Indonesia.[66]

Notes

1. Sujatin Kartowijono, *Mencari Makna Hidupku* [*Searching for the Meaning
    of My Life*] (Jakarta: Penerbit Sinar Harapan, 1983), pp. 7–11.
2. I shall often refer to Suyatin Kartowiyono by her first name, which is
    common practice in Indonesia, where many people (such as Sukarno)
    have only one name and family names are often not used. In any case,
    Kartowiyono was Suyatin's husband's family name, and before they were
    married she was usually known just as Suyatin.
3. The autobiography contains, for example, an extensive account of
    Suyatin's overseas trips in the 1950s, which was probably based on her
    own records and photos of the time.
4. See, for instance, Anderson's discussion of the memoirs of Sutomo, who
    wrote more about those who had influenced him than about himself
    (Benedict Anderson, "A Time of Darkness and a Time of Light: Trans-
    position in Early Indonesian Thought", in *Perceptions of the Past in
    Southeast Asia*, ed. Anthony Reid [Singapore: Heinemann, 1979]). How-
    ever, Sutomo wrote in the 1930s; by the 1980s, when Suyatin's auto-
    biography was published, leaders were becoming more accustomed
    to writing about themselves. A few male nationalists published their
    memoirs — for instance, Sukarno (Soekarno, *Sukarno, an Autobiography
    as Told to Cindy Adams* [Indianapolis: Bobbs-Merrill, 1965]); Hanifah
    (Abu Hanifah, *Tales of a Revolution* [Sydney: Allen & Unwin, 1972]);
    Subardjo (Ahmad Djojoadisuryo Subardjo, *Kesadaran Nasional: Oto-
    biografi* [*National Consciousness: An Autobiography*] [Jakarta: Gunung
    Agung, 1978]); Sastroamijoyo (Ali Sastroamijoyo, *Milestones on My
    Journey: The Memoirs of Ali Sastroamijoyo, Indonesian Patriot and
    Political Leader* [St. Lucia: University of Queensland Press, 1979]) — but
    Suyatin was unique among female leaders in doing so.
5. Most of Suyatin's writings were published before the spelling of Indo-
    nesian had been standardised. In this chapter I have modernised the
    spellings of names. Under the old system, based on Dutch pronunciation,
    her name was Sujatin Kartowijono. Apart from her autobiography, her
    main writings concerning her life are "The Awakening of the Women's
    Movement of Indonesia", in *Indonesian Women: Some Past and Current
    Perspectives*, ed. B.B. Hering (Bruxelles: Centre d'étude du Sud-Est
    asiatique et de l'Extreme Orient, 1976); *Perkembangan Pergerakan Wanita*

Indonesia [*The Growth of the Indonesian Women's Movement*] (Jakarta: Yayasan Idayu, 1977); "Ny. Sujatin Kartowijono: Tokoh Pergerakan Wanita Indonesia" [Ny Sujatin Kartowijono: A Leader of the Indonesian Women's Movement], in *Sumbangsihku Bagi Pertiwi: Kumpulan Pengalaman dan Pemikiran* [*My Contribution on Behalf of Women: A Collection of Experiences and Reflections*], ed. Lasmidjah Hardi (Jakarta: Yayasan Wanita Pejoang, 1981); and "Pengalaman Seorang Pemimpin Organisasi" [Experience of an Organisation's Leader], in *Perjuangan Wanita Indonesia 10 Windu Setelah Kartini 1904–1984* [*The Indonesian Women's Struggle 80 Years after Kartini 1904–1984*] (Jakarta: Departemen Penerangan RI, 1984).

6.   C.W. Watson, *Of Self and Nation: Autobiography and the Representation of Modern Indonesia* (Honolulu: University of Hawaii Press, 2000), p. 15.

7.   The idea of *pergerakan* is developed by T. Shiraishi (*An Age in Motion: Popular Radicalism in Java, 1912–1960* [Ithaca: Cornell University Press, 1990]), who makes no acknowledgment of women's participation.

8.   Kartowijono, *Mencari Makna Hidupku*, p. 13.

9.   Ibid., p. 26.

10.   Ibid.

11.   Ibid., p. 31.

12.   Ibid., p. 40.

13.   Ibid., pp. 36–7.

14.   Although the Javanese comprise the largest ethnic group, there is no majority ethnic group in Indonesia. Malay was chosen as the basis for the national language partly because it had been the lingua franca of traders in the archipelago, partly because newspapers had developed it for modern usage, and partly because, unlike the very hierarchical Javanese language (which has different levels according to the person addressed), it was egalitarian in nature and therefore considered more suitable for a modern nation.

15.   Kartowijono, *Mencari Makna Hidupku*, pp. 37, 68.

16.   See Susan Blackburn, *The First Indonesian Women's Congress of 1928* (Clayton: Monash University Press, 2008).

17.   Kartowijono, "Awakening of the Women's Movement", p. 3.

18.   Kartowijono, *Mencari Makna Hidupku*, p. 41.

19.   See, for example, Ibid., p. 30. In her autobiography, Suyatin makes a point of recounting the family friendships with Eurasians and Chinese and notes her early interest in other religions besides her own Islam: she sought out information about Buddhism, Christianity and theosophy, in all of which she clearly found something sympathetic.

20.   Ibid., p. 31.

21.   Ibid., p. 19.

22.   Ibid., p. 25.

23.   Ibid., pp. 25–6.
24.   Ibid., p. 28.
25.   Ibid., p. 37.
26.   Suyatin stressed this point several times in her autobiography. In parti-
       cular she recorded a conversation with others in the women's movement
       when, discussing polygamy, she pointed out that it was essential for
       wives to earn their own living so that they were not dependent on hus-
       bands who might decide to take another wife (Ibid., pp. 218–9).
27.   Ibid., p. 29.
28.   Ibid., p. 22. Suyatin's ambivalent attitude towards her father is explored
       by Soe Tjen Marching, *The Discrepancy between the Public and Private
       Selves of Indonesian Women* (Lewiston: Edwin Mellon Press, 2007), pp.
       211–8.
29.   Kartowijono, *Mencari Makna Hidupku*, p. 44.
30.   Ibid., p. 37.
31.   Ibid., p. 43.
32.   Ibid., pp. 144–5.
33.   Ibid., p. 94.
34.   Ibid., pp. 49–50.
35.   Ibid., p. 234.
36.   This attitude of the Dutch is clear from their official reporting on Indo-
       nesian activities in intelligence documents such as the survey of the
       "native" press (*Overzicht van den Inlandsche en Maleisch-Chineesche Pers*
       [*Survey of the Native and Chinese Malay Press*] [Batavia: Landsdrukkerij]);
       confidential official reports as found in R.C. Kwantes, *De Ontwikkeling
       van de Nationalistische Beweging in Nederlandsch-Indie: Bronnenpublikatie:
       Derde stuk 1928–1933* [*The Development of the Nationalist Movement
       in the Netherlands Indies: Sourcebook, Vol. 3: 1928–1033*] [Groningen:
       Wolters-Noordhoff, 1981]); and their report on the women's movement
       published in the 1930s (*De Inheemsche Vrouwenbeweging in Nederlandsch-
       Indie en het aandeel daarin van het Inheemsche Meisje* [*The Native
       Women's Movement in the Netherlands Indies and the Role in It of the
       Native Girl*] [Batavia: Landsdrukkerij, 1932]).
37.   Kartowijono, *Mencari Makna Hidupku*, p. 41.
38.   Kartowijono, "Awakening of the Women's Movement", p. 5.
39.   Ibid., p. 7.
40.   See Susan Blackburn, *Women and the State in Modern Indonesia* (Cam-
       bridge: Cambridge University Press, 2004), pp. 125–7.
41.   Kartowijono, *Mencari Makna Hidupku*, p. 221.
42.   See Blackburn, *Women and the State*, chapter 5.
43.   Benedict Anderson, *Imagined Communities: Reflections on the Origin and
       Spread of Nationalism*, 2nd ed. (London: Verso, 1991).
44.   Kartowijono, *Mencari Makna Hidupku*, p. 68.

45. I refer here to Suyatin's participation in 1931 in an investigation into the situation of exploited women batik workers in Lasem, central Java. She discusses this issue briefly in her autobiography (*Mencari Makna Hidupku*, pp. 43–4), and I deal in more detail with the relationship between the Indonesian women's movement and poor working women in *Women and the State in Modern Indonesia*, chapter 7.

46. Kartowijono, *Mencari Makna Hidupku*, pp. 55–6.

47. Ibid., p. 221.

48. Ibid., pp. 43–4.

49. Ibid., p. 46.

50. Ibid., p. 50.

51. Sri Sutjiatiningsih (ed.), *Biografi Tokoh Kongres Perempuan Indonesia Pertama* (Jakarta: Departemen Pendidikan dan Kebudayaan, Direktorat Sejarah dan Nilai Tradisional, Proyek Inventarisasi dan Dokumentasi Sejarah Nasional, 1991), p. 69.

52. Kartowijono, *Mencari Makna Hidupku*, p. 228.

53. It is striking that in her autobiography — written during the New Order, when women were supposed to be predominantly mothers — Suyatin makes almost no mention of her children: not only does she never give their names, but she even refrains from saying how many children she had.

54. Sutjianingsih, *Biografi Tokoh Kongres Perempuan Indonesia Pertama*, p. 72.

55. In 1961 Suyatin received the Satya Lencana Kebaktian Sosial from the Ministry for Education and Culture for her social work, and in 1968 the Ministry for Social Affairs awarded her the Satya Lencana Pembangunan for her 40 years of devotion to the women's movement. In 1978 President Suharto awarded her the gold medal for Perintis Pendidikan Wanita (pioneer of women's education) (Kartowijono, *Mencari Makna Hidupku*, pp. 231–2).

56. Ibid., p. 233.

57. Kartowijono, "Awakening of the Women's Movement", pp. 16–8. It is notable that an obituary to Suyatin was headed "Leaving with a Feeling of Anxiety about the Quality of the Leadership of the Women's Movement" (*Kompas*, 4 Dec. 1983).

58. Kartowijono, *Mencari Makna Hidupku*, pp. 234–5.

59. See Timothy P. Barnard, "Local Heroes and National Consciousness: The Politics of Historiography in Riau", *Bijdragen tot de Taal-, Land- en Volkenkunde* 153, 4 (1997): 509–26; and Rommel A. Curaming, "The State and the Historians in the Construction of Nationalist Historical Discourses in Indonesia and the Philippines: A Preliminary Consideration", in *Asian Futures, Asian Traditions*, ed. Edwina Palmer (Folkestone: Global Oriental, 2005).

60.   In her 1976 work (p. 3), Suyatin lists the official National Heroines as Martha Christina Tijahahu, Tjut Nyak Dien, Tjut Nyak Meutia, Nyi Ageng Serang (all involved in anti-colonial resistance before the rise of Indonesian nationalism), Maria Walanda Maramis, Kartini, Dewi Sartika, Nyi A. Dahlan and Rasuna Said. She goes on to note that there were many more women activists.

61.   For a discussion of the process of selection of National Heroes since the New Order, see Charnvit Kasetsiri, "The Construction of National Heroes and/or Heroines", in *Southeast Asia over Three Generations*, ed. James T. Siegel, Audrey Kahin and Benedict Anderson (Ithaca: Cornell University Press, 2003).

62.   A.K. Pringgodigdo, *Sedjarah Pergerakan Rakjat Indonesia* [*A History of the Indonesian People's Movement*], 3rd ed. (Djakarta: Pustaka Rakjat, 1950).

63.   The only book-length biographies relating to the organised women's movement in Indonesia concern Maria Ullfah Santoso/Subadio (Gadis Rasid, *Maria Ullfah Subadio: Pembela Kaumnya* [*Maria Ullfah Subadio: The Defender of Her Race*] [Jakarta: Bulan Bintang, 1982]) and S.K. Trimurti (Soebagio, *S.K. Trimurti: Wanita Pengabdi Bangsa* [*S.K. Trimurti: A Woman Devoted to Her Nation*] [Jakarta: Gunung Agung, 1982], and Agus Salim, *S.K. Trimurti* [Bandung: Jembar, 2007]). It may be significant that both these women were the first female ministers in Republican cabinets, which probably indicates that becoming part of the male-dominated political system has been the only way to make women's political contribution visible in Indonesia.

64.   See, for example, Panitia Peringatan 30 Tahun Kesatuan Pergerakan Wanita Indonesia, *Buku Peringatan 30 Tahun Kesatuan Pergerakan Wanita Indonesia, 32 Des. 1928–22 Des. 1958* [*Commemorative Book for the 30th Anniversary of the Indonesian Women's Movement Association, 22 Dec. 1928–22 Dec. 1958*] (Djakarta: Pertjetakan Negara, 1958); Cora Vreede-de Stuers, *The Indonesian Woman: Struggles and Achievements* ('s-Gravenhage: Mouton, 1960); Kongres Wanita Indonesia, *Sejarah Setengah Abad Pergerakan Wanita Indonesia* [*History of Half a Century of the Indonesian Women's Movement*] (Jakarta: Balai Pustaka, 1978); and Sutjiatiningsih, *Biografi Tokoh Kongres Perempuan Indonesia Pertama*.

65.   Gerry van Klinken, "The Battle for History after Suharto: Beyond Sacred Dates, Great Men, and Legal Milestones", *Critical Asian Studies* 33, 3 (2001): 323–50.

66.   It is heartening to see that school textbooks are now beginning to recognise the Indonesian women's movement as part of the nationalist movement. The secondary school history textbook by Nana Nurliana Soeyono and Sudarini Suhartono *Sejarah untuk SMP dan MTS* [*History for Secondary Schools*] (Jakarta: Grasindo, 2006) has a section on the women's

movement as part of the chapter on the nationalist movement. Suyatin Kartowiyono receives a mention on p. 85. On the other hand, the historian Siti Fatimah wrote in 2008 that of the more than 1,700 books on Indonesian history published in the previous decade, only 2 per cent discussed women ("Perspektif Jender Dalam Historiografi Indonesia" [Gender Perspective in Indonesian Historiography], in *Titik Balik: Historiografi di Indonesia* [*Turning Point: Historiography in Indonesia*], ed. Doko Marihandono [Jakarta: Wedatama Widya Sastra, 2008], p. 387).

CHAPTER 4

Rasuna Said: Lioness of the Indonesian Independence Movement

Sally White

Rasuna Said is one of the few Indonesian women accorded the status of National Hero. Born in Maninjau, West Sumatra, in 1910, Rasuna is honoured for her contribution to the nationalist movement in the years leading up to Indonesia's independence and for the official roles she undertook once independence had been achieved. Often referred to as Singa Betina (lioness) or Srikandi (warrior princess), an epitaph reportedly given to her by Indonesia's first president, Sukarno, Rasuna is regarded as the embodiment of a female fighting spirit.[1] She is identified strongly with the Minangkabau ethnic group, from which she and many other nationalist leaders came, a people known for their combative nature and deep sense of Islamic piety.

Rasuna came to national prominence in November 1932 when she became the first woman in the Netherlands Indies to be arrested and charged by the Dutch colonial government for "sowing hatred" against the Dutch. In the offending speech, she expounded on the platform of the Islamic political party to which she belonged, Permi, arguing that Islam taught that imperialism was wrong and that independence would surely come one day, forcing the Dutch from Indonesian lands. Rasuna's political career began when she was in her late teens. She took leadership positions in a number of organisations in the colonial period, culminating in her becoming a parliamentarian in independent Indonesia. She was also an educator, devoting several decades to teaching girls and women in her native Minangkabau and then North Sumatra. Outspoken, personally devout, and strong enough to take on the challenges of participating in a nationalist movement and revolutionary war, Rasuna Said is a fascinating figure worthy of greater scholarly attention.

Unfortunately, Rasuna Said has left no autobiographical writings. This chapter is thus based largely on Indonesian-language biographies, on Rasuna's journalistic writings, and on newspaper and Dutch reports produced while she was still alive.[2] In this chapter, I consider what we learn from Rasuna's biography, writings and speeches regarding her understanding of nationalism and why she became involved, at great personal cost to herself and her family life. A passionate advocate for education for girls and women and for women's political involvement, how did she reconcile her gender activism with her equally strong Islamic faith?

Historical Background

The first half of the 20th century, into which Rasuna was born, was a volatile and exciting period when anti-colonialism was growing in Indonesia. Contestations and exchange among proponents of ideas rooted in Communist ideology, in secularism, and in Islamic tradition or reform added great complexity to the nascent nationalist movement. From the early decades of the century, religious conflicts arose between the reformists known as the *kaum muda* (young group) and the *kaum tua* (old group), and the customary leaders aligned with the colonial authorities. The *kaum muda* were returning students, particularly from Cairo, with new ideas on how to revitalise and modernise Islamic practice and enable Muslim nations to throw off (Christian) colonial rule, while the *kaum tua* rejected the need for substantial reform of Islamic practice.

In Java, the nationalist movement was led largely by a small elite who had received a Western education either in the Indies or in the Netherlands. They formed political parties that differed in ideologies, tactics and strategies. Two of the best known were the Partai National Indonesia (Indonesian Nationalist Party), led by the future Indonesian president Sukarno, which espoused a populist ideology rooted in a blend of Marxist, nationalist and Islamic ideas; and the Partai Sarekat Islam Indonesia (Indonesian Islamic Union Party, PSII) which was the only Islamic-based party in Java. Mass-based Islamic organisations such as Muhammadiyah, which was dedicated to religious and social reform and did not engage directly in politics, nevertheless strongly influenced the growth of a sense of one national community rooted in the majority faith of its populace, Islam. (Key dates for the Indonesian nationalist movement are found in the text box in the previous chapter. For place names mentioned in this chapter, see maps 4 and 5.)

In West Sumatra, the home of the Minangkabau ethnic group, the nationalist movement developed somewhat differently. Long a centre for Islamic reform, West Sumatra was the site of the Paderi Wars (1820–37), a conflict that broke out between the purveyors of new Islamic ideas brought back by a number of religious leaders who studied abroad, and the traditional elite. The latter defended the blend of local custom and Islamic belief that had developed over centuries in the region, including its matrilineal inheritance system, against a stricter interpretation of what was Islamic.[3] The conflict between the *kaum muda* and *kaum tua* in the early years of the 20th century was in some ways a continuation of this older contestation. But what began as a religious reform movement in West Sumatra became increasingly nationalist in ideology and outlook; for the younger generation of Minangkabau leaders, there was no contradiction between these two currents of thought.

Schools were at the centre of the reformist project in West Sumatra. The first school to break away from a traditional model of education to introduce secular subjects was the Diniyah School, founded in Padang Panjang in 1915 by the prominent Islamic reformist Zainuddin Labai El Yunus. More important, Zainuddin's sister, Rahmah El Yunusiah, established a version of the Diniyah School for girls in 1923 and thus became a central figure in the development of modern Islamic education in Indonesia, particularly for girls. The fame of her school spread, attracting pupils from as far away as Malaysia and Singapore, as noted in chapter 6 by Helen Ting in this volume. By 1926 it had become a boarding school for girls that taught a mixture of religious subjects and domestic science.

Rahmah's motto for her school was that girls must be educated to become educators in the home, in the school and in society.[4] Despite the matrilineal inheritance system, which gave Minangkabau women some economic independence, a woman's primary function was considered to be her role as wife and mother, as it was elsewhere in the Indies at this time. A basic education was thought adequate for girls

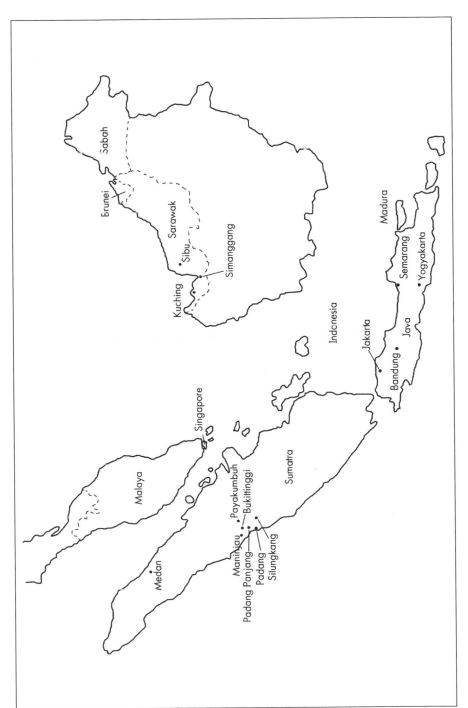

Map 5. Malaysia and western Indonesia

who married young. Some religious knowledge was considered necessary, but even girls from pious families generally received only a rudimentary religious education. The Islamic reformist movement changed this attitude. The *kaum muda* established religious organisations and schools specifically for girls, arguing that women had the same rights to religious education as men because, just like men, they were accountable before God for their deeds on Earth. Further, women had the responsibility to spread Islam to other women through involvement in organisations such as Aisyiyah, the women's wing of Muhammadiyah, to further the interests of Islam in Indonesia. Thus women required education related not just to their roles in the family, but also to their religious roles.[5] Rahmah's school was the embodiment of such an attitude, and Rahmah herself was a strong, independent woman who impressed people with her single-mindedness and the firmness of her convictions.

Another figure pivotal to the Minangkabau reformist movement, Haji Abdul Kasim Abdullah, known as Haji Rasul, founded a second important school network in 1918 with the establishment of the first Thawalib school, also in Padang Panjang. Inspired by the Diniyah School, Haji Rasul's school introduced graded classes, textbooks, and more modern methods of teaching and curriculum. The Thawalib schools specialised in teaching theoretical and philosophical aspects of Islam. The goal was to produce graduates who could think for themselves and act as teachers and religious reformers in the community.[6] This emphasis on students reflecting on their social and political circumstances and those of Muslims in the Indies led many students into political involvement. The original school in Padang Panjang became heavily influenced by Communist ideology, causing Haji Rasul, a fervent anti-Communist, to resign — but the network continued to grow, producing many of the region's younger leaders. Among such leaders, Communist ideology often blended with Islamic ideas about social justice and anti-imperialism to produce interesting alliances between Communists, traders and some of the *kaum muda* in the major cities of the region.[7]

By 1930, there were various strands of the *kaum muda* movement. Muhammadiyah, the Islamic organisation founded in Java in 1912, was introduced into West Sumatra by Haji Rasul in 1925 and began to experience strong growth.[8] The PSII was also gaining in popularity. Both Muhammadiyah and the PSII were more radical in West Sumatra than in Java. Then in November 1928, the Sumatra

Thawalib Union, an organisation for Thawalib students, was established. It was set up with the goal of unifying the various Thawalib schools and modernising the curriculum, but its sphere of interest soon grew to include issues of social and political transformation.[9] As some of the more radical Minangkabau leaders tried to take Muhammadiyah in a more political direction, the central leadership in Java came under increasing pressure from the Dutch authorities to weed out such elements and purge the West Sumatran branches of "extremists".[10] Matters came to a head in 1930, resulting in the founding by the leaders of the Sumatra Thawalib Union of a new organisation, Persatuan Moeslimin Indonesia (Permi, Union of Indonesian Muslims).[11] It attracted the more political elements of the West Sumatran *kaum muda*, including those dissatisfied with the apolitical direction of Muhammadiyah.

Permi combined Islam and nationalism as its two pillars, differentiating itself from the secular-oriented parties led by Dutch-speaking intellectuals such as the future president, Sukarno, but also from most other Islamic organisations not involved in politics, such as Muhammadiyah. Its motto was "Islam to achieve the nobility of Islam, nationalism to achieve an independent Indonesia".[12] The widespread appeal of Permi and its leaders immediately attracted the attention of Dutch authorities concerned about the combination of political radicalism and Islam.[13] At its third congress in Padang in December 1932, Permi officially became a political party with 160 branches throughout West Sumatra, its primary base of support, and in most regions of Sumatra.[14] Of the 10,000 or so Permi members in 1933, several thousand were women.[15]

Rasuna: The Early Years

Born during a period of turbulence, Rasuna Said came from a family known for their religiosity and well regarded in the village in which they lived, near the marketplace of the bustling town of Maninjau. Rasuna grew up in the home of her uncle because her father, a successful trader, was often away for long periods. She was reportedly the only one of her siblings to receive a religious education rather than a secular education in a Dutch school after she left primary school.[16] After graduating from primary school, she studied at an Islamic school near her home before moving to Padang Panjang to attend the Diniyah School.[17]

While studying at the Diniyah School, Rasuna began to teach younger students — a practice common among gifted students. She also came into contact with the founder's sister, Rahmah El Yunusiah, who was six years older than Rasuna. They reportedly took lessons together with some leading *kaum muda* scholars, most notably Haji Rasul. Although he is known for a number of his less enlightened views on women,[18] Haji Rasul nevertheless believed in the importance of religious education for girls. When Diniyah Girls School was established in 1923, Rasuna became an assistant teacher there while continuing her studies. She also attended a school in Padang Panjang that taught girls household skills.

In 1926 Rasuna returned to Maninjau for a couple of years following a major earthquake in Padang Panjang that destroyed the newly constructed Diniyah Girls School.[19] While there, she continued her religious education, studying primarily at the Thawalib school under the directorship of Haji Udin Rachmany, a reformist Muslim involved in both the political and religious movements, from whom she also took private lessons. Rasuna excelled, completing the four-year course in just two years.[20] She was also involved in establishing a school to combat illiteracy, the first of its kind in the town. During this time, Rasuna acquired many of the skills that were to mark her participation in the nationalist movement. After sunset prayers each evening, Haji Rachmany reportedly talked to his students about the nationalist movement and the need to achieve Indonesian independence. He also gave his students weekly lessons in public speaking and debating, and Rasuna sometimes made speeches that lasted an entire afternoon.[21]

A Political Career

Haji Rachmany was the person who introduced Rasuna into the world of political organisations. Like many of the Minangkabau *kaum muda*, he had been attracted to the anti-colonial and anti-imperialist stance of the Communist Party and become a member, but he was expelled when he questioned the party's position on religion in 1925.[22] However, he continued his association with the Sarikat Rakyat (People's Union), a Communist-affiliated organisation popular in West Sumatra, and it was no doubt Rachmany who convinced his young student Rasuna to join that organisation in 1926, becoming either branch secretary or propagandist.[23] While she was a member of Sarikat Rakyat, the Communist Party staged a disastrous abortive revolt in West Sumatra — in the town of Silungkang — in 1927.[24] Both Rachmany and Rasuna were reportedly involved in preparations for the revolt in Maninjau, and following its suppression, Sarikat Rakyat was disbanded.[25] This ended Rasuna's formal involvement with left-wing politics, but some of its ideologies continued to inspire her.

In 1928 Rasuna joined a branch of Partai Sarikat Islam (later renamed PSII), again with Rachmany, who became its leader in the West Sumatran region in 1929. Rasuna held a position in the central leadership of the Maninjau branch. Sometime in 1928–29 Rasuna returned to Padang Panjang, to her position of assistant teacher at the Diniyah Girls School under Rahmah El Yunusiah, and once again she immersed herself in the social and political ferment of the town.[26] In 1929, at the age of 19, she married Duski Samad, a politically active teacher at the Sumatra Thawalib School in Padang Panjang. This she did against the wishes of her family, choosing a partner who shared her political aspirations.[27] Rasuna's actions here demonstrate not only her strength of character and independent mind, but the extent to which she was moving away from tradition, presumably under the influence of the Islamic reform movement. After her marriage, Rasuna continued to teach at the Diniyah Girls School while becoming increasingly political through her membership of Permi.

It is notable that from the beginning women were integral to Permi's central leadership, something that had never happened in an Islamic organisation in Java. Although Permi did form a women's wing, in which Rasuna Said was also involved, women in Permi were not simply relegated to a separate section of the main party, subordinate to it structurally, as was the usual case in Indonesia. Rasuna Said was one of three female leaders of Permi and the only one appointed to the central board in 1931, as a "propagandist". The other two women, Rasimah Ismail and Ratna Sari, were added to the party's leadership the following year, along with a number of other women.

What makes Rasuna's involvement in the Permi leadership and her role as propagandist so interesting is that her appointment to this role happened a year after Haji Rasul took on the Muhammadiyah leadership from Java over the issue of a woman addressing a mixed gathering, an act he considered *haram* (prohibited) and against custom, although it was common practice in Java.[28] As this incident indicates, there were differences in attitude towards women's participation in the public sphere both within and between Muslim groups. Alfian has argued that reformist Islam as it developed in Minangkabau was more puritanical than in Java; it was more concerned with a faithful following of the central tenets of Islam than with the modernising aspect of the reformist project, and this led to different attitudes on women's roles and a greater polarisation in West Sumatra on the issue than in Java.[29] Abdullah also recounts a 1927 visit by Haji Fachruddin, a leading Muhammadiyah figure from Yogyakarta, to West Sumatra, where he told his audience that Islam was now more progressive in Java than in Sumatra.[30] Like other Islamic reformist movements going back to the Paderi War, Muhammadiyah was also critical of the matrilineal inheritance system in Minangkabau, which was seen as backward.[31] Nevertheless, in Minangkabau women participated in Muslim organisations, including Muhammadiyah, in large numbers. Rasuna apparently threw herself into her new job as propagandist for Permi, travelling around the region to address public meetings and attempting to persuade other women to join the movement in fighting for Indonesian independence. Her husband did the same, and it is said that the marriage suffered: the two often did not see each other for weeks at a time and divorced in the early 1930s, with Rasuna retaining custody of their young daughter.[32] But the two remained friends for the rest of Rasuna's life, and they continued to work together in the party leadership.

In 1930 the relationship between Rasuna and Rahmah El Yunusiah, who continued to be her employer at the school in Padang Panjang, fell apart over the issue of the teaching of politics. In a legendary episode, Rasuna is said to have begun to teach her young students, both in class and outside, about the importance of political action in order to achieve an independent Indonesia.[33] Because of the situation in their homeland, they, as the future leaders of Minangkabau, needed to be involved in the political movement. Rasuna's request to have politics taught as a separate subject was rejected by Rahmah, on the grounds that faith must form the bedrock of all education: without it, all political action was meaningless and possibly dangerous because it would be open to exploitation. The teaching of politics would also endanger the school, bringing it to the attention of the Dutch authorities and causing disputes among teachers, pupils and parents. If pupils wanted to engage in politics, they could do so after graduation, and their religious education would give them a firm foundation on which to base their actions.[34]

Nevertheless, Rasuna continued to engage her students in political discussions and, given her prominence in the Permi movement, was a figure of great charisma, revered by many of the girls, who became so absorbed in the political maelstrom around them that they began to neglect the regulations of the boarding school, including communal prayers.[35] When it became clear that no agreement could be reached between these two strong-willed women, Rahmah took the matter to the School Council, which agreed that politics should not be taught in the school. Consequently, in 1931 Rasuna left Diniyah Girls School and moved to Padang.

The move was fortuitous for Rasuna, given that the central board of Permi had moved to Padang, which became the centre of the Islamic nationalist movement.[36] In Padang Rasuna was shocked by what she saw as the backward state of women, and she launched an attack on the local traditions and customs that denied girls education and political participation.[37] She formed a Permi group specifically for women and girls, founded a primary school in Padang, and taught at the Thawalib Putri School. Under Permi's direction, literacy schools were set up all over West Sumatra that also served to provide political education and draw people into the movement, and Rasuna taught in these too. She then left her primary school in Padang and went to teach at a teacher training school in Bukittinggi, after the school director, the charismatic Permi leader Muchtar Loethfi, requested the Permi leadership board that she take up this position because he was so impressed by her.[38] She still held this position in December 1932, when her life took a dramatic turn.

Rasuna's Arrest and Trial

Dutch authorities had become increasingly concerned about the nationalist sentiments being expressed by the more radical Indonesian organisations. The role of women in stirring up nationalist sentiments in West Sumatra was commented on by one Dutch official in 1933. "More than elsewhere," he stated, "women on the West coast tend to be interested in the political movement, and to drive this movement, whereby they sometimes deliberately put the men to shame." Women such as Rasuna Said and Rasimah Ismail, he continued, were no exceptions; and in many meetings, women were in the majority and often expressed themselves "more sharply and passionately than the other sex".[39] Rasuna Said had thus begun to acquire a reputation for fearlessly expressing radical political ideas.

Rasuna gave a speech at a public meeting of the women's wing of Permi in Padang Panjang on 23 October 1932 titled "Steps to the

Independence of the People in a Greater Indonesia".[40] After giving a history of the nationalist movement in Indonesia, she argued that Dutch rule had destroyed people's livelihoods, which in turn had destroyed the character and values of the Indonesian people. The Quran, she continued, taught that imperialism ruined their lives and those of their grandchildren. According to the report of the meeting, Rasuna quoted "a wise person": "Man is born free, it is only society that makes him into a slave, sinning against religion and nation." It went on: "The speaker raised the spirits of the gathering with these words: 'It is better that we ask Allah for death than that we are not of service to the nation'." In these short excerpts we see some of the reasons for Dutch concern. The critique of imperialism is typical of sentiments expressed by the confluence of radical and Islamic ideas in West Sumatra. And it comes close to a call to arms, linking nationalist ideas with those of serving God.

Less than a month later, after another speech in Payakumbuh, Rasuna Said was arrested and charged with contravening articles 153 and 154 of the Criminal Code, the "hate sowing" articles designed to be used against those who intentionally disturbed public order or expressed feelings of hatred or contempt for the Dutch government in the Indies. Rasuna gave the speech at a public session of the women's section of Permi on the principles and goals of Permi. She began by explaining Permi's policy of treating imperialism as the enemy, and of not joining any of the councils established by the Dutch to allow limited political participation by Indonesians. Permi, she said, was working towards an independent Indonesia, and the councils were there only to improve the Netherlands Indies, not Indonesia. At this stage of the speech, an official intervened and warned Rasuna to watch her words. She continued with the theme of Islam as the enemy of imperialism on the basis of the Quran. She then moved on to defend Permi against accusations that it was not aligned with the national movement but rather based on Islam, which was international, and stated that Permi would treat all Indonesians who were not Muslims justly in accord with what was written in the Quran. Finally she called on the daughters of Payakumbuh to "move" and not to be feeble as they had been so far: "We must achieve Indonesian independence, independence must come." The speech, according to the newspaper report, was well received by the public, who numbered about 1,000.[41]

Rasuna Said was held in custody until her trial on 28 December 1932. Although she was the first woman to be charged with what was known as a *spreekdelict* (speaking offence), she was soon joined by her fellow Permi member Rasimah Ismail, who was arrested after a speech at a Permi meeting on 23 November. The arrest of the two women caused a stir locally, but after Rasuna's trial, where she received a sentence of 15 months' imprisonment, her case became a national cause célèbre. The response was in part because of the novelty factor: she was the first woman to be imprisoned for speaking out against Dutch rule. But more important, it was because of her demeanour and the sentiments she expressed at her trial. Rasuna was unrepentant. In a letter she sent to the Permi board while awaiting trial, she stated: "We struggle with conviction! If we win in our struggle, we will get two benefits. First, Indonesia will be free; second, paradise as promised by God. And if we fail — but we are not allowed to — then indeed a free Indonesia will not be achieved, but paradise still awaits. This is our conviction!"[42]

People flocked from all over West Sumatra to attend Rasuna's trial before the local court in Payakumbuh. Up to 1,500 people, some from the towns but others from Islamic boarding schools in the villages, waited outside the courtroom. The charges were read out: that she, in a public meeting of around 1,000 people, had planted feelings of hostility, at the very least sowing hatred towards the Dutch government. The offending words singled out by the authorities were: "The people demand Indonesian independence. Until they are independent, the people of Indonesia will be considered lowly and abject by the world. Permi bases its politics on non-cooperation, it does not participate in Councils created by the Dutch government."[43] Rasuna was then cross-examined on what she meant by various sentiments expressed in the speech. She answered every question without hesitation and gave unadorned answers, often causing a stir among the audience. For example, when she was asked what she meant by her opening words in the meeting — "Happy greetings to the sons and daughters who are not yet free, but will become free, and the Dutch government will disappear" — Rasuna explained that the people of Indonesia were not yet free but "sooner or later will achieve independence. I know, and the whole world knows, that every people has the right to independence. It is also clear that when the time comes when Indonesia is independent, then the Dutch government that is in power now will disappear, itself fall." When asked why she made the statement, she said it was in order "to hold out the promise of the times to come. Also to raise the spirits of my people."

Under questioning, Rasuna explained that the struggle against oppression was a natural law, that the Indonesians were enslaved by Dutch regulations and norms, and that they were victims of imperialism. Her goal was to increase the spirit of the people to struggle to achieve independence. When the judge asked the meaning of her statement "If my brothers feel afraid to join the struggle, won't they feel embarrassed if Indonesian independence is achieved by women?" she replied (confirming Dutch views about the way women were egging men on to join the movement) that she said this to "increase the fuel" of the movement among men. The audience, she said elsewhere, consisted of women and some men, some of whom were educated, but all of whom understood the meaning of her speech. When asked how she knew this, she replied, "They had tears in their eyes while I spoke."

News of Rasuna's sentence and trial spread across the archipelago. The way in which she conducted herself and used the court as a forum to disseminate Permi's political views and agitate for Indonesian independence met with widespread approval. Permi received letters and telegrams of admiration and support from a number of political parties and individuals. Dr Sutomo, a well-known Javanese nationalist leader, called Rasuna a "model for Indonesian leaders and heroes".[44] Locally, Rasuna Said was compared to the nationalist leader Sukarno, who had given a famous speech at his trial in Bandung in August 1930. While awaiting her transfer to the women's prison in Semarang, Java, where she would serve out her sentence, Rasuna was inundated by gifts of food from the local women of Payakumbuh, and it was also reported that at least five women had named their daughters Rasuna, with one woman stating, "May my child be like Rasuna."[45] When the ship arrived in the harbour near Padang to take Rasuna and Rasimah Ismail, who had been sentenced to nine months by the local court in Bukittinggi, to Tanjung Priok in Java, over 1,000 people flocked to bid them farewell.

Rasuna Said's trial represents the peak of her involvement in the political stream of the nationalist movement. The public recognition and support she received made her for a short time the most prominent woman in that movement. However, her involvement came at great personal cost to this young woman, who was accompanied to the women's prison in Semarang by her baby daughter. The same opinion writer who compared her so favourably to Sukarno in a later piece also pointed out the differences between the two. Sukarno, he wrote, was an engineer, a graduate of higher education, with a high level of knowledge and experience in the world of politics. Rasuna, on the other hand, was a primary school graduate who could not speak Dutch and had very little experience of politics, especially outside her region. For the defence teams at his trial Sukarno had top men from across Java; Rasuna had only one defence advocate, from the neighbouring province.

Rasuna Said was the first of the Permi leaders tried and imprisoned by the Dutch. Dutch authorities instituted a range of repressive measures against the remaining leaders, including restrictions on movement, a prohibition on teaching, and a ban on holding public meetings. The three main leaders were arrested in August and September 1933 and exiled to Boven Digul in Papua, as were other leading figures including Rasuna's former husband, Duski Samad. Others left the region because they feared government reprisals. In the end, there was almost no one left to run the main office in Padang. Ratna Sari, another prominent Minangkabau woman, became Permi's first female president, also taking on the role of secretary, and the first female to head any political party in Indonesia. Unfortunately, she did not remain president for long: her family placed pressure on her to return home, which she then did. Permi limped on for some years, before finally disbanding in October 1937.

Post-Imprisonment

When Rasuna was released from prison in 1934, she returned to a very different world. Dutch repressive activity had succeeded in taking the steam out of the nationalist movement, especially in West Sumatra. In Java, a celebration had been planned for her and Rasimah's release, but it could not be held due to a ban on public meetings.[46] Rasuna returned to Padang and studied for four years at the Islamic College, a teacher training institute established by Permi in 1931.[47] She began her journalistic career, writing for the college journal *Raya*, as well as teaching at a girls' school she had founded.[48] According to J. Jahroni, Rasuna wrote several harsh critiques of the Dutch for causing misery to Indonesia, with *Raya* becoming a rallying point for the movement in West Sumatra. However, she became disillusioned with the demise of Permi and the cowardly attitude of some Permi leaders.[49] The Dutch continued to exercise strict control over the nationalist movement in Padang, and as a result of all these factors Rasuna eventually moved to Medan in North Sumatra, probably around 1938. There she established a girls' school and edited the journal *Menara Putri*, a weekly magazine focusing on issues to do with women and Islam.[50] Politics was taught at the school, with girls told that they had an important role to play in the nationalist movement and that they had the right and responsibility to contribute to the social, economic and political fields rather than simply running the household, although this was also important.[51]

Rasuna's only appearance in the public spotlight during these years came with the release of a Draft Marriage Ordinance by the Dutch authorities in June 1937. The ordinance allowed Muslim couples to voluntarily register a marriage contract that prohibited polygamy and permitted divorce only before a judge in a civil court.[52] It caused such an outcry among Islamic groups that it was withdrawn from discussion before it was formally introduced. Although the ordinance was meant to apply only to Java and Madura, ad hoc committees to fight it were set up in numerous cities outside of Java, including Medan. Rasuna Said gave the keynote address at a meeting of the Medan committee in August 1937, before 500 women.[53] In her speech Rasuna defended Islamic marriage law, including polygamy and provisions for divorce, while acknowledging there were problems with its implementation in Indonesia. Her argument was that although there was a "flood" of divorces, leaving many women and children destitute, and men took a second wife without thinking deeply about their actions, these shortcomings had to do with the state of society, not with the marriage law itself. Islam, she argued, regulated marriage perfectly. Polygamy was necessary in some cases because it was preferable to men taking mistresses and having children out of wedlock, leaving women and their families in a precarious legal situation without the rights accorded to them as legitimate family members. Divorce was an escape clause from an unhappy marriage. Forcing men, and especially women, to appear before a court of law to provide evidence of the need for a divorce would be deeply shaming and would deter divorce applications, so that women would be unable to remarry and would be forced to live in poverty.

The contents of Rasuna's speech reflected the general attitude of Islamic groups to the draft ordinance. She acknowledged there were problems but disagreed with the remedy proposed, instead seeing the solution in better education for Islamic marriage officials responsible

for implementing Islamic marriage law, and in giving greater autonomy to Muslims to marry, reconcile and divorce according to the
teachings of Islam. In her speech, Rasuna identified herself clearly
within an Indonesian Islamic women's movement and differentiated
herself from the nationalist movement. As Muslim women, she argued,
members of her movement had an insight into the state of marriage
that had as much validity as that of either the men and women of
the nationalist movement, or the government. While secular women's
groups were fighting for stronger protection for women in marriage,
although they mostly rejected the draft ordinance — as chapter 3 on
Suyatin Kartowiyono points out — Muslim women's groups defended
marriage law based on orthodox interpretations of the Quran and
regulated by Muslims themselves. Marriage law was a major stumbling
block to the unification of the women's movement in Indonesia in
the pre-independence period, especially given the numerical strength
of the Muslim women's organisations, and continued to be a sticking
point in the newly formed republic until at least the 1970s.

Interestingly, Rasuna's tone was altogether different from that
of her earlier speeches. She began by praising the Dutch authorities
for their good intentions in wanting to improve the ailing state of
marriage in Indonesia, while politely disagreeing with their proposals
for reform. She presented her arguments with conviction, but in a
respectful and reasoned way, and ended by calling on the Dutch
government to withdraw the draft ordinance in a manner well removed from the fiery speeches she had made before her arrest.
From her time in Medan, Rasuna allegedly became associated more
with left-oriented political movements, although the primary evidence
for such accusations seems to be her second marriage to Bariun
AS, a known leftist.[54] Yet there is no sign here of her earlier anti-
imperialism, or of leftist sentiments. Perhaps this is tactical; she had
clearly learnt from her earlier experience of incarceration. But the
views she expressed concerning Islam and the importance of Islamic
practices and institutions in daily life are consistent with her strong
Islamic identity. Her biographers noted that throughout her life
Rasuna dressed in what was regarded as an Islamic way: a long batik
skirt, flowing tunic, and headdress pinned neatly under the chin. She
also strictly observed Islamic dietary requirements and was respected
for her piety and religious knowledge. Rasuna was both a strong
advocate for the rights of women and a committed Muslim who

believed her reformist beliefs provided women with a platform from which to reform society and press for those rights.

The Later Years

Rasuna returned to West Sumatra in 1942 following the Japanese occupation of Sumatra during World War II. On her return she joined the short-lived Pemuda Nippon Raya, an organisation founded by Chatib Sulaiman to bring all the youth organisations in the region under one umbrella and, under the guise of supporting the Japanese, to work towards Indonesian independence. When the Japanese disbanded the movement, suspicious of its goals, they arrested the leaders, Rasuna included, but soon released them to avoid causing popular unrest.[55] In October 1943, prompted by the Japanese for strategic reasons to aid their own defence, Chatib Sulaiman established a volunteer military force known as Giyu Gun. From the beginning, Giyu Gun had strong nationalist aims. It became a vehicle to prepare for Indonesian self-government, by establishing networks of communication and self-help across the region as well as developing military skills and arming those trained.[56]

Sulaiman enlisted young leaders from across West Sumatra to recruit and support the forces, including Rasuna, Rahmah El Yunusiah and Ratna Sari. They founded a woman's section of the Giyu Gun called Hahanokai, which acted as a support organisation, helping with the logistics of feeding and clothing the fledgling force and providing them with moral support. The women were also active as propagandists, drumming up community support for the troops and inspiring potential recruits to join the organisation. Rasuna travelled widely and worked tirelessly for Hahanokai. According to one story, Rasuna's friends visited her at home and were surprised to meet Bariun AS, her second husband, there — Rasuna having largely kept her marriage a secret. Bariun is reported to have told the women, "Yes, Kak Una [Sister Una] is my wife, but actually she is married to the struggle." And Rasuna herself is said to have concurred: "No matter how much I need Bung Bariun [Brother Bariun], the struggle is more important."[57]

After the declaration of Indonesian independence on 17 August 1945, Rasuna continued to be involved in politics at the regional level but also increasingly at the national level. Unfortunately, it is difficult to find detailed reports of her activities from the period 1945 till her death in 1965, but she seems to have played an important and perhaps idiosyncratic — or at least individual — role in national life. At the regional level, when independence was declared, Rasuna worked together with a number of leading figures to form organisations supporting the new republic. When Vice-President Mohammad Hatta, himself a West Sumatran, visited Bukittinggi on 29–30 July 1947 and established an organisation called Fron Pertahanan Nasional (National Defence Front), Rasuna became part of the central leadership of the organisation and headed the women's section. The organisation brought together the various elements of Minangkabau society, including religious and customary leaders and mass organisations, political parties, and women's and youth groups, in an attempt to avoid the types of social and political divisions that were causing major problems elsewhere in Indonesia and becoming apparent in West Sumatra.[58] The fact that Rasuna was chosen to play a prominent role in this and other organisations shows the prestige she enjoyed in the region.

One organisation to which Rasuna belonged that is not mentioned in any of the biographies is the Volksfront, an organisation established by Chatib Sulaiman and Barius AS in mid-March 1946 as a local chapter of the Persatuan Perjuangan (Struggle Union), founded by the Communist leader Tan Malaka.[59] At a conference in Java, Tan Malaka had presented a seven-point programme that he wanted the government to adopt. The Republican government considered three of these points unacceptable: 100 per cent independence (this was a time when the republic was involved in negotiations with the Dutch to form part of a federation), the seizure and control of plantations belonging to the enemy, and the seizure and control of industries belonging to the enemy.[60] In West Sumatra the Volksfront began to assume many of the functions of the regional government, and relations between the two bodies became increasingly tense. When the Volksfront introduced measures that would make the 100 rupiah note invalid, its leaders were arrested and detained.[61] Rasuna Said was among those arrested, but she was given house arrest. All the leaders were released after a week, on the proviso they did not attempt to seize economic control again.[62]

Rasuna soon became more involved at the level of national politics. In January 1947, she was one of 14 members chosen by the West Sumatran chapter of the Indonesian National Committee to represent the region in the Central Indonesian National Committee, a quasi parliament established to assist the president. According to her bio-graphies, she became a member of the Working Party of the Central Indonesian National Committee, a legislative body established to increase the power of the Committee vis-à-vis the president.[63] Rasuna supported the ratification of the Linggajati Agreement, which had been drawn up in November 1946, recognising Indonesian sovereignty over Java and Sumatra within a Dutch Federal Republic. Her support for the Linggajati Agreement is interesting, given her involvement in the Persatuan Perjuangan, which had demanded "100% indepen-dence", and the continued opposition to the agreement of some left-wing groups, headed by Tan Malaka, and the reformist Islamic party Masyumi.[64] This is evidence of Rasuna's support for President Sukarno, with whom she is said to have had a close relationship.

After the transfer of power from the Dutch to the republic in 1950, Rasuna was appointed to the transitional parliament intended to advise the president until elections could be held. Her appointment was as a representative of women's groups, and she was part of the Finance Committee of the parliament. She was also a member of the steering committee of a body set up by the parliament to coordinate efforts to bring West Irian (now West Papua) under Indonesian control. When Sukarno formed the National Council, an advisory body to the cabinet meant to represent functional groups in society, Rasuna was appointed a member in July 1957. And when that body was transformed into the Supreme Advisory Council, as part of the move towards authoritarian rule in Indonesia, she retained her membership.[65] She stayed in parliament until her death from breast cancer in November 1965, a time when the country was in turmoil as the transition began between the old order under Sukarno, and the New Order under Suharto. Before her death, she is said to have de-voted more and more time to trading activities, having acquired capi-tal through her political connections and become a wealthy woman.

Although details are hard to come by, there are a number of interesting facets of Rasuna's later career and life. First, Rasuna refused to join the Muslim political party Masyumi, unlike many of her former colleagues from Permi, and despite being urged to do so. Second, she became directly involved in the nationalist women's movement, joining Perwari, a secular women's organisation established in late 1945 to fight for social justice for women and for all society, and to assist in the struggle for Indonesian independence (see chapter 3 on Suyatin Kartowiyono).[66] Perwari was particularly associated with the struggle during the 1950s for a marriage law, a struggle in which there was much tension between Muslim women's organisations and other women's organisations. It is unclear how long Rasuna was a member and in what capacity, but she was associated with the organisation until at least 1954, when she was said to have been its vice-president.[67] Third, Rasuna became involved in the peace movement in the 1950s, attending peace congresses in Copenhagen, Budapest and Beijing as well as organising a peace conference in Jakarta. According to a Dutch report in 1954, she was a "well-known figure" in "the Communist women's and world peace movement".[68] Finally, Rasuna strongly rejected the Revolutionary Government Republic of Indonesia rebellion in West Sumatra, which involved many of her old colleagues, including Rahmah El Yunusiah. The rebellion (1958–61) arose through widespread disillusionment with the radical direction the Sukarno government was taking and received support from many *kaum muda* Muslims, including several in the Masyumi party.[69] Rasuna denounced the actions of a number of her former friends, speaking with Sukarno at a public rally in Bandung, calling on the rebels to return to the nationalist fold, and stating that the rebellion made her feel ashamed to be a daughter of Minangkabau.[70]

Perhaps Rasuna's path in later life was informed by a more left-wing world view, developing out of the earlier period when she was influenced by ideas combining Islamic anti-imperialism with leftist thought, while not necessarily adopting other Marxist ideas, especially regarding the role of religion in daily life. Perhaps with the establishment of the republic she became more secular in her outlook, in the sense that — like many other committed Indonesian Muslims, including her fellow Minangkabau Hatta — she came to believe that religion should not form the basis of the state. If so, it is a clear rejection of some of the ideas she expressed in her days of involvement in Permi, where Islam and nationalism were the twin pillars. Nevertheless, Islam remained central to her own life and to her legacy as a strong Muslim woman fighting for what she believed in: the nation, and the rights of women to education and full participation in social and political life.

A National Hero

Rasuna was awarded the title National Hero on 13 December 1974. This made her only the ninth woman to achieve such recognition in Indonesia and the first to be honoured for her contribution to the nationalist struggle. Previously women were recognised either for their participation in regional struggles against Dutch rule, which took place before the national movement originated, or for their general contribution to the women's movement, fighting for education and the rights of women.[71]

Rasuna Said lived during tumultuous times. Like many of her generation she was born into a colonial state, lived through a period of Japanese occupation, participated in a revolutionary war, and became part of the first democratic period of rule in Indonesia. Through all of these changes, she demonstrated a deep commitment to the nationalist cause, to Islam and to the interests of women. The locus of her activities changed from regional to national, but even in her time as a propagandist for Permi, it was clear that her loyalties lay with an entity far larger than just West Sumatra. Her faith informed her anti-imperialism; how she understood the role of the non-Muslim minority within an independent state is unclear. Her faith also taught her that women needed to be educated and were religious subjects whose rights and duties were the same as men's, even if their social roles differed. The twin pillars enshrined as Permi's ideological basis of Islam and nationalism made Rasuna a passionate advocate for the need for women to become educated and involved in politics, an attitude that made her different from the mainstream of Islamic reformists and Muslim women's organisations who believed that women should be active in the Islamic reform movement but not nationalist politics.

There is, however, much about Rasuna's motivations and ideological commitment that remains elusive. The speeches we have from the height of her political engagement in the nationalist movement do not specifically mention issues of women's rights, beyond the need for women to participate in the nationalist cause. At times she identified strongly with the reformist Islamic movement, for example on the issue of marriage reform; at other times her nationalism appeared to be the strongest motivating force. In the later decades of colonial rule, Sukarno claimed to be "a convinced nationalist, a convinced Muslim, a convinced Marxist".[72] Rasuna's life story shows a similar commitment to nationalism and Islam. While Sukarno may have added Marxism, Rasuna, less overtly leftist in her ideology, added a commitment to the rights of women.

Notes

1. On Srikandi and other strong images of women in Javanese mythology, see P. Carey and V. Houben, "Spirited Srikhandhis and Sly Sumbadras: The Social, Political and Economic Role of Women at the Central Javanese Courts in the 18th and Early 19th Centuries", in *Indonesian Women in Focus: Past and Present Notions*, ed. E. Locher-Scholten and A. Niehof (Dordrecht: Foris Publications, 1987).

2. The "official" biography (Team Fact Finding Badan Pembina Pahlawan Pusat, *Haji Rangkayo Rasuna Said: Kesimpulan Team Fact Finding, Badan Pembina Pahlawan Pusat* [*Haji Rangkayo Rasuna Said: Conclusions of the Fact Finding Team, Working Group for Selection of National* Heroes] [Jakarta: No publisher, 1974]) was written to justify her candidature for National Hero. The problem with this and other biographies used here is that there are few references, so it is difficult to check the veracity of events, especially where contradictory accounts are given.

3. T. Abdullah, *Schools and Politics: The Kaum Muda Movement in West Sumatra (1927–1933)* (Ithaca: Cornell Modern Indonesia Project, Cornell University, 1971), pp. 5–7.

4. A. Rasyad, "Perguruan Diniyyah Puteri Padangpanjang: 1923–1978. Suatu Studi Mengenai Perkembangan Sistem Pendidikan Islam" [Diniyyah Puteri Padangpanjang Teachers' Training: 1923–1978. A Study of the Development of the Islamic Education System], PhD diss., Institut Agama Islam Negeri, Syarif Hidayatullah, Jakarta, 1982, p. 2.

5. S. White, "Reformist Islam, Gender and Marriage in Late Colonial Dutch East Indies, 1900–1942", PhD diss., Australian National University, 2004.

6. Abdullah, *Schools and Politics*, pp. 34–6, 56–62.

7. A. Kahin, *Rebellion to Integration: West Sumatra and the Indonesian Polity, 1926–1998* (Amsterdam: Amsterdam University Press, 1999).

8. Alfian, *Muhammadiyah: The Political Behaviour of a Muslim Modernist Organization under Dutch Colonialism* (Yogyakarta: Gadjah Mada University, 1989), p. 252.

9. Abdullah, *Schools and Politics*, pp. 125–8.

10. Muhammadiyah had been able to grow so strongly in West Sumatra in part because it capitalised on opposition to reports that the Dutch planned to introduce restrictions on religious teaching in the region (the so-called Guru Ordinance). Many Muhammadiyah members sought to maintain this confluence of Islam and politics, and wanted a discussion with the central leadership in Java over the organisation's acceptance of government subsidies for its schools (Ibid., pp. 93–4).

11. Initially the organisation was referred to by the initials PMI, and only after 1932 was it called Permi. However, I will refer to it as Permi to avoid confusion.

12. T. Djaja, "Rasuna Said (1910–1965): Srikandi Indonesia yang pertama masuk penjara karena politik" [Rasuna Said (1910–1965): The First Indonesian Heroine to Be Jailed for Political Reasons], *Nasehat Perkawinan* [*Marriage Advice*] 75 (1978): 29; and Abdullah, *Schools and Politics*, p. 131.

13. Kahin, *Rebellion to Integration*, p. 65.

14. Ibid., p. 55.

15. H. Poeze, "Inleiding" [Introduction], in *Politiek-politioneele overzichten van Nederlandsch-Indië: bronnenpublikatie* [*Political Police Reports on the Netherlands Indies: A Sourcebook*], ed. H. Poeze and Koninklijk instituut voor taal-, land- en volkenkunde (Pays-Bas) (Dordrecht and Providence: Foris publications, 1988), p. xlii.

16. According to Jahroni, this was according to her own wish (J. Jahroni, "Haji Rangkayo Rasuna Said: Pejuang Politik dan Penulis Pergerakan" [Haji Rangkayo Rasuna Said: Political Fighter and Movement Writer], in *Ulama Perempuan Indonesia* [*Indonesian Women Islamic Scholars*], ed. J. Burhanuddin [Jakarta: Penerbit PT Gramedia Pustaka Utama bekerja sama dengan PPIM IAIN Jakarta, 2002], p. 70).

   According to Tamar Djaja, it was because her father hoped that she would continue her education in Egypt (Djaja, "Rasuna Said", p. 27).

17. There are discrepancies in the accounts regarding Rasuna's schooling. I have largely followed the account given in the "official" biography, with additional information taken from Jahroni ("Haji Rangkayo Rasuna Said") and Djaja ("Rasuna Said").

18. J. Hadler, *Muslims and Matriarchs: Cultural Resilience in Indonesia through Jihad and Colonialism* (Ithaca: Cornell University Press, 2008), pp. 165–8.

19. It was quickly rebuilt, at great personal expense to Rahmah, and continued to grow in strength and influence.

20. Team Fact Finding, *Haji Rangkayo Rasuna Said*, p. 6.

21. Jahroni, "Haji Rangkayo Rasuna Said", p. 76.

22. Abdullah, *Schools and Politics*, p. 68.

23. According to most accounts, she was appointed secretary. The *Ensiklopedia Minangkabau* (Padang: Pusat Pengkajian Islam, 2005), however, writes that she became a propagandist. While there is no evidence either way, the fact that Rasuna was only 16 at the time makes a position of propagandist more likely.

24. Kahin, *Rebellion to Integration*, pp. 46–9.

25. Team Fact Finding, *Haji Rangkayo Rasuna Said*, p. 8.

26. Djaja, "Rasuna Said", p. 28. Djaja also comments that Rasuna was "very attractive in appearance".

27. Jahroni, "Haji Rangkayo Rasuna Said", p. 87.

28. Hadler, *Muslims and Matriarchs*, pp. 164–5; White, "Reformist Islam, Gender and Marriage", pp. 106–8.
29. Alfian, *Muhammadiyah*, pp. 259–62.
30. Abdullah, *Schools and Politics*, p. 78.
31. Hadler, *Muslims and Matriarchs*, pp. 21–5.
32. Her first child, a boy, is said to have died shortly after birth.
33. The story is recounted with slight variations in all the biographies of Rasuna. The original version is contained in *Boekoe Peringatan 15 Tahoen "Dinijjah School Poeteri" Padang Pandjang* [*Commemorative Book for the 15th Anniversary of "Dinijjah Girls' School" Padang Pandjang*], 2nd ed. (Padang Pandjang: Dinijjah School Poeteri, 1936). My account is based on this original version, plus the versions in D. Noer, *The Modernist Muslim Movement in Indonesia, 1900–1942* (Kuala Lumpur: Oxford University Press, 1973); Rasyad, "Perguruan Diniyyah Puteri Padangpanjang"; and Jahroni, "Haji Rangkayo Rasuna Said".
34. Noer, *Modernist Muslim Movement*, pp. 54–5.
35. Rasyad, "Perguruan Diniyyah Puteri Padangpanjang", pp. 170–1.
36. Kahin, *Rebellion to Integration*, p. 54.
37. *Pewarta*, 21 Aug. 1933.
38. Ibid.
39. R.C. Kwantes (ed.), *De Ontwikkeling Van De Nationalistische Beweging in Nederlandsch-Indië: Bronnenpublikatie, Vol. 3* (1928–Aug. 1933) (Groningen: H.D. Tjeenk Willink, 1975), p. 843.
40. *Tjaja Sumatra*, 27 Oct. 1932.
41. She also gave a second speech at the public meeting on Islamic opposition to imperialism, but it was the first speech that got her into trouble.
42. M. Pandoe, "Dua Singa Betina Dibuang" [Two Female Lions Jailed], in *Jernih Melihat Cermat Mencatat: Antologi Karya Jurnalistik Wartawan Senior Kompas* [*Watching Clearly and Noting Carefully: An Anthology of Senior* Kompas *Journalists' Writings*], ed. Julius Pour (Jakarta: Penerbit Buku Kompas, 2010), p. 68.
43. This account is based on an article that includes a transcript said to be from the trial (Ibid.).
44. *Tjaja Sumatra*, 24 Jan. 1933.
45. Ibid., 18 Jan. 1933.
46. Djaja, "Rasuna Said", p. 30.
47. Kahin, *Rebellion to Integration*, p. 82.
48. Djaja, "Rasuna Said", p. 28; and Team Fact Finding, *Haji Rangkayo Rasuna Said*, p. 7.
49. Jahroni, "Haji Rangkayo Rasuna Said", pp. 80–1.
50. Djaja, "Rasuna Said", p. 31.
51. Jahroni, "Haji Rangkayo Rasuna Said", p. 81.

52. For a detailed description of the ordinance and Muslim reactions to it, see White, "Reformist Islam, Gender and Marriage", pp. 294–320.

53. "Poeteri Medan menentang Ordonansi Kawin. Pidato Rgkj. Rasoena Said. Doea kali dapat ketokan dari polisi", *Adil* 64 and 65 (1937): 12 and 3–4.

54. Jahroni, "Haji Rangkayo Rasuna Said", pp. 93–4.

55. G. Saydam, "Rasuna Said: Tokoh Politik, Singa Betina yang Orator Ulung" [Rasuna Said: Political Leader, a Lioness Who Was an Excellent Orator], in *55 tokoh Indonesia asal Minangkabau di pentas nasional* [*Fifty-five Indonesian Leaders from Minangkabau in the National Arena*] (Cet. 1.) (Bandung: Alfabeta, 2009), p. 213.

56. Kahin, *Rebellion to Integration*, pp. 99–103.

57. Jahroni, "Haji Rangkayo Rasuna Said", p. 84.

58. Badan Pemurnian Sejarah Indonesia Minangkabau (BPSIM), *Sejarah Perjuangan Kemerdekaan Republik Indonesia Di Minangkabau, 1945–1950* [*A History of the Independence Struggle for the Indonesian Republic in Minangkabau, 1945–1950*], Vol. 1 (Jakarta: Badan Pemurnian Sejarah Indonesia — Minangkabau, 1978), p. 321.

59. Tan Malaka was born in Payakumbuh, in West Sumatra, where he had always been popular and rose to national prominence after the declaration of independence. On Tan Malaka and Persatuan Perjuangan, see A. Reid, *The Indonesian National Revolution, 1945–1950* (Hawthorn: Longman, 1974), pp. 88–90.

60. BPSIM, *Sejarah Perjuangan Kemerdekaan Republik Indonesia Di Minangkabau*, p. 318.

61. Kahin, *Rebellion to Integration*, p. 117.

62. BPSIM, *Sejarah Perjuangan Kemerdekaan Republik Indonesia Di Minangkabau*, p. 321.

63. M. Ricklefs, *A History of Modern Indonesia since c.1300*, 2nd ed. (Basingstoke: Macmillan, 1994), p. 218.

64. Reid, *Indonesian National Revolution*, pp. 96–8.

65. According to her official biography, she was appointed to the National Council to represent women's groups. According to Kahin (*Rebellion to Integration*, p. 196) and Saydam ("Rasuna Said", p. 214), it was as a representative for West Sumatra. Both Saydam and Kahin mention a story about Ratna Sari, Rasuna's old comrade, criticising her appointment because she "had lived too long in Jakarta and no longer understood the feelings of the people of her home region".

66. S. Kartowijono, "The Awakening of the Women's Movement in Indonesia", in *Indonesian Women: Some Past and Current Perspectives*, ed. B.B. Hering (Bruxelles: Centre d'étude du Sud-Est asiatique et de l'Extreme Orient, 1976), p. 7.

67. Secret document in the Dutch Cabinet archives, dated 16 November 1954 and labelled Minvor kab GS 16002 geheim, www.historici.nl/

Onderzoek/Projecten/Nederlands-IndonesischeBetrekkingen1950–1963/ Document/19065. According to her official biography, Rasuna was on the central board of Perwari from 1948 to 1953 (Team Fact Finding, *Haji Rangkayo Rasuna Said*, Appendix, p. 2).

68. Ibid. It must be remembered, however, that this was a time when the spectre of Communism was present everywhere and many anti-imperialist organisations were labelled "Communist".

69. Ricklefs, *History of Modern Indonesia*, pp. 262–5.

70. R. Said, "Pidato Rasuna Said" [Rasuna Said's Speeches], in *Tidak ada kontra revolusi bisa bertahan: Amanat Presiden Soekarno dan Pidato Rasuna Said pada Rapat Pantja Sila di Bandung tanggal 16 Maret 1958* [*Counter-revolution Cannot Last: The Address of President Soekarno and the Speech of Rasuna Said to the Pantja Sila Meeting in Bandung on 16 March 1958*] (Djakarta: Penerbitan Chusus, Kementrian Penerangan RI, 1958).

71. The first group consisted of Cut Nyak Dhien and Cut Nyak Meutia, both from Aceh; Marta Christina Tijahahu from Maluku; and Nyi Ageng Serang from Central Java. The second group consisted of Dewi Sartika, Kartini, Maria Walanda Maramis and Nyai Ahmad Dahlan. The female most recently (2006) awarded the honour of National Hero, Opo Daeng Risadju from South Sulawesi, is the only other woman who participated in the nationalist movement and war of independence.

72. Reid, *History of Modern Indonesia*, p. 7.

CHAPTER 5

Salud Algabre: A Forgotten Member of the Philippine Sakdal

Ma. Luisa T. Camagay

Born in 1894, Salud Algabre was a member of the Sakdal, a Philippine peasant organisation founded in 1930 by Benigno Ramos. The organisation protested against the mainstream nationalist movement led by Manuel Quezon, because the Sakdalistas considered that it was not seeking genuine independence from the American colonialists and that it was dominated by landlord interests. Salud figured prominently in an uprising on 2 May 1935 in the town of Cabuyao, Laguna, when she led a group of Sakdalistas who blocked the railroad, cut telegraph lines and patrolled the national highway.

For this act, Salud was arrested by the authorities and stood trial on the charge of being a member of an illegal association. The case lasted for four years. The court found her guilty, and she was fined and sentenced to imprisonment for six to ten years — the only woman Sakdalista to be so punished. However, she served less than two years of her sentence as she was pardoned by Quezon, president of the Commonwealth of the Philippines. After World War II Salud continued her fight against big landholders until she died at the age of 85 in 1979.

In books containing short biographies of Filipinos in history, there are few women, and Salud does not figure in the list. There is more documentation of Filipino women who struggled to be given the right to vote.[1] The fact that this was a cause spearheaded by educated and professional women who were able to document their struggle made them by default visible in the historical narrative. Absent or rare,

Philippine Nationalist Movement

1896   Outbreak of the Philippine Revolution against Spanish rule

1898   Declaration of independence of the Philippines, followed shortly afterwards by the takeover of the country by the United States

1930   Benigno Ramos establishes the Sakdal movement, whose objective is to accuse and expose government officials whose acts are detrimental to the country

1934   US Congress passes the Tydings-McDuffie Act, which provides that independence will be granted to the Philippines in ten years

1935   A constitutional convention in the Philippines approves the constitution on 8 February 1935, and the US president does the same on 23 March 1935

The Sakdal Uprising takes place on 2–3 May 1935 to register rejection of the Tydings-McDuffie Law and to demand independence by 31 December 1935

The Commonwealth Government provided for in the 1935 Constitution is inaugurated on 15 November 1935

1942   Japanese forces land in the Philippines

1943   A Japanese-sponsored republic is proclaimed on 14 October 1943

1945   General Douglas MacArthur proclaims the liberation of the Philippines from the Japanese

1946   The United States grants the Philippines independence on 4 July

however, is the documentation of women who were active in the nationalist movement but came from the lower class. Legitimate though the causes of both these types of women, struggles by peasant women remain absent or marginalised in the pages of the nation's history.

It is also notable that those few women who are generally recognised as having participated in the nationalist movement in the 20th century identified with the mainstream and were part of the elite that led it. The Sakdal movement has been relegated to the sidelines, even though it was part of a long history of peasant movements that combined nationalism with a struggle for land in the Philippines. Except for the discussion of Sakdalism in David Sturtevant's book

Salud Algabre in 1977. Courtesy of
Nestor Castro

(1976), the history of the movement has not been extensively documented, so the role of Salud Algabre in the Philippines nationalist
movement has received very little attention. In effect, not until very
recently have women in such peasant movements been the subjects of
historical study.[2]

This chapter relies on a few lesser-known interviews of our
protagonist. Salud was interviewed in 1935 by the *Sunday Tribune
Magazine* and in 1966 by the historian David Sturtevant.[3] These tran-
scribed interviews provide invaluable insights into her personality
and her convictions. Eleven years later, Salud was interviewed by the
Filipino historian Isagani Medina. Salud was by then 83 years old. The
result of this interview was an article written in 1996 by Thelma B.
Kintanar and Carina C. David.[4] So far, these three interviews remain
the major sources of information about Salud.

As a female member of a section of the Philippine nationalist
movement that combined the demands for independence and rights
for peasants, Salud Algabre has been lost from view in the history of
Philippine nationalism. This chapter will attempt to return her to the
ranks of notable nationalists.

Filipino Women in the Nationalist Movement

The Philippines is home to the first nationalist movement in Southeast Asia to have declared independence from Spanish colonial rule and established a modern nation-state. In the 19th century modern-style nationalist organisations were formed, and in 1896 the Philippine Revolution led to the end of Spanish colonial rule and the declaration of a short-lived independent Philippine Republic in 1898. US colonialism almost immediately displaced the Spanish. Admittedly, it was of a much more benign type than the Spanish colonialism, and the Americans claimed to be preparing the Philippines for independence, but the actual transfer of sovereignty did not occur until after World War II, in 1946.

In the 20th century the mainstream Philippine nationalist movement, which had resorted to armed rebellion against the Spanish, was led by a landed elite who cooperated with the Americans, taking positions in the Philippine Commonwealth structures created by the colonial power in preparation for eventual independence. The Jones Law of 1916 was the first articulation by the United States of its decision to grant the Philippines independence on the condition that a stable government was established. It also created an all-Filipino legislature composed of a House of Representatives headed by Sergio Osmena and a Senate headed by Manuel Quezon. Members of both chambers came from the landowning class. This elite used their political clout to protect their economic interests. Members of the Philippine missions sent to the United States to work for independence laws also originated from the landed class. There was no room in this mainstream nationalist movement for peasants, who constituted the majority of the population and included many tenants of the large landlords. Nor was there much room for women, even of the elite class.

The Philippine nationalist movement contained a few notable women, but colonialism had made it difficult for many women to become involved in such public political activities. Efforts were made by the Spanish colonial power, and particularly the Catholic Church, to reduce Filipino women to a position of subordination in relation to men. This kind of socialisation, impressed through education and the publication of moral codes about how women should behave, may have had an impact on the elite but affected ordinary Filipino women far less. After all, the creation story of the Filipinos, wherein man and woman emerged from a single node of a bamboo, underscored the

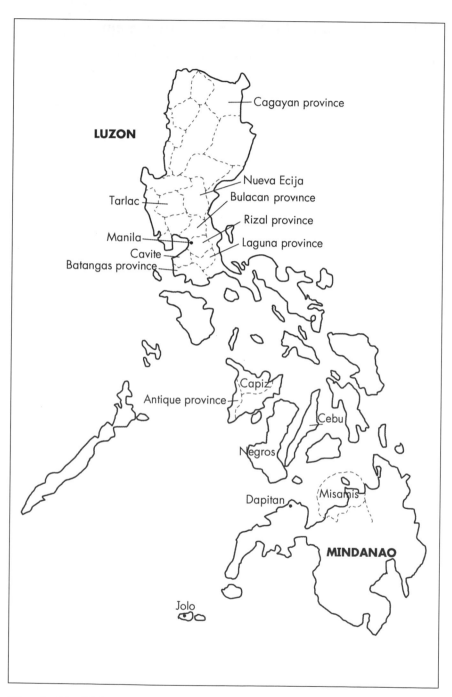

Map 6. The Philippines

egalitarian status of man and woman in rural society. Women's political activity began in the 19th century. Filipino women established a Masonic Lodge dedicated to women and formed a women's chapter in the Katipunan, a secret organisation that aimed to overthrow Spanish rule in the Philippines.[5]

In the early 20th century, under US rule, some Filipino women entered male-dominated professions (such as medicine and law) and demanded the right to vote in the electoral assemblies established by the Americans. They finally acquired the right to vote through a provision in the 1935 Constitution.[6]

In this context Filipino women were emboldened to get involved in the affairs of the nation. The women included Salud Algabre, who took up the fight to improve the situation of peasants, for which she saw the independence of the country as indispensable.

The Sakdal Movement

The Philippines has a long history of agrarian unrest, caused by land tenure problems. By the 19th century, land became an important economic asset not only for food production but also for commercial crops. Early in that century, the Spanish finally opened up the Philippines to world trade, which created a demand for certain crops such as sugar, tobacco, abaca hemp and rice. At that time, landowners were of two types: religious corporations and private individuals. The former owned vast tracts of lands devoted to cash crops. The majority of Filipino landowners, who owned two to three hectares of land, were compelled to borrow capital for the cultivation of cash crops. Loans were extended by rich landowners who imposed usurious rates and readily acquired the land once the farmer defaulted in paying his debt. With an economy based on agriculture and the landholding class confined to a few, tenancy became the norm rather than the exception.

Protests against vast estates owned by Catholic orders such as the Dominicans contributed to the Philippine Revolution. These estates were found in most provinces of southern Luzon, the main island of the Philippines. (For places mentioned in this chapter, see maps 6 and 7.) One of the revered leaders of the 19th-century nationalist movement, Jose Rizal, came from the province of Laguna, which was practically a Dominican estate, where tenants were ruthlessly exploited. Laguna was also the native province of Salud Algabre. Land tenure problems persisted there, even though land was purchased by private owners under US colonialism.

The pattern of farmers losing their land to big landowners, as described above, persisted during the US period. It did not help that many Filipinos did not have legal title to their land since the process of getting a title required money, education and time, all of which the ordinary Filipino farmer lacked. Hence Filipino society during the early decades of the 20th century continued to be dominated by large landowners.

The Depression of the 1930s worsened the lot of farmers in the Philippines, which fuelled peasant uprisings, including the Sakdal movement. Unlike the more common spontaneous peasant Millenarian uprisings, however, Sakdal was also a nationalist organisation.

Ramos, the founder of the Sakdal movement, was an employee of the Philippine Senate who fell out with the nationalist leader, Manuel Quezon, who was the Senate president and had been responsible for getting Ramos his job. Ramos vowed henceforth to be a critic of Quezon as well as the government. In 1930 he founded an organisation and a newspaper, both bearing the name "Sakdal", a Tagalog word meaning "to accuse" or "to strike". The objective of the organisation was "to accuse governmental officials before the public of acts which Ramos declared detrimental to the country and especially to the common people".[7] Ramos urged his followers not to participate in government, not to vote, and not to pay the *cedula* or poll tax. The field notes gathered by Sturtevant, a historian of this period of Philippine history, yielded testimonies of arrested Sakdal members who refused to pay their poll tax. Salud Algabre's husband was one of them.[8]

One issue of the newspaper *Sakdal*, dated 16 August 1930, set out the nationalist ideas of the organisation. It argued that independence was not something to be granted by the United States; it was a right declared by the Filipinos. It was wrong, therefore, for leaders such as Quezon to send missions to Washington to seek independence: the nationalist movement should seize independence.

In 1933, the Sakdal movement became a political party. A convention was held on 29 October, and Sakdal produced a constitution and by-laws.

The Tydings-McDuffie Law, which provided for a transition government to last for ten years, was approved by the Philippine Legislature on 1 May 1934. Ramos explained Sakdal's rejection of the Tydings-McDuffie Law in this manner:

We do not believe the Tydings-McDuffie Act ... Since 1898, the United States has again and again repeated the statement: We will recognize the independence of the Philippines and has designed legislation to permit independence. But they never carried it out. By saying that they will recognize independence in ten years, the Americans are doing nothing more than suppressing independence agitation for ten years. The Americans, who have over and over promised to recognize our independence and have always broken their promise, have now enunciated a new promise called Tydings-McDuffie Act. So why should they be believed this time? We have affirmed that at whatever cost we must secure independence by our own strength.[9]

In July of 1934, a constitutional convention took place to draft a constitution that was to be ratified through a plebiscite on 14 May 1935. On 2–3 May the Sakdal Uprising took place, registering the Sakdal's rejection of the constitution. By this time the movement had adherents in the provinces of Laguna, Rizal, Nueva Ecija, Bulacan, Tarlac, Batangas, Tayabas, Cavite, Capiz, Cebu, Negros, Cagayan, Antique and Misamis. These provinces had large estates and landless tenants. At the time of the uprising, the Sakdal movement advocated land reform, the dismantling of large estates or haciendas, and immediate, complete and absolute independence from the United States.

Clearly, the agrarian discontent in the Philippines attracted peasants to the movement. This was the situation of the Sakdal movement when Salud Algabre became a member.

Personal Antecedents of Salud

Salud Algabre was born two years before the beginning of the Philippine Revolution of 1896. She was the daughter of Maximo Algabre, a landowner from Cabuyao, and Justina Tirones, a seamstress. She had nine siblings, but only six survived.

The Algabre family had a history of resistance against colonisers starting from the Spanish period. According to Salud, her grandfather and father fought the Spaniards during the Philippine Revolution. Her grandfather, who was a gobernardorcillo (head of a town), slashed his own throat as a protest against the threat of the Spanish civil authorities to banish him to a far-off place for refusing to kiss the hand of a priest. An uncle was a member of the Katipunan, the secret organisation that spearheaded the Philippine Revolution. Some relatives were exiled to Dapitan and Jolo in Mindanao for their revolutionary activities.[10] Salud mentioned that during the war against Spain her grandfather and father were soldiers who faced the Spaniards in Calamba and Santa Cruz, two towns in Laguna. Both fought under General Juan Cailles, who would later become governor of Laguna during the US period.

In her interview in 1966,[11] Salud recalled that her paternal grandfather had extensive landholdings and five granaries. The fact that he owned land qualified him to get elected as gobernadorcillo during the Spanish period. She did not mention how her grandfather lost his lands. It is likely that he became indebted in some way and due to his inability to pay back the loan his land was acquired by the lender.

Both Salud's parents had formal schooling, having spent about six years in Manila. When it was Salud's turn to study, she too was sent to Manila during the years 1903–9. Living with an uncle in Tondo, she was able to finish grade four. Her mother, however, made her stop schooling out of fear that her American music teacher, Mrs Brown, would take her to the United States. Salud had fond memories of this teacher and also remembered her English teacher, Mrs Domondon, and her sewing teacher, Mrs Emilia Flores. With her schooling halted, Salud was entrusted by her mother to a private tutor until the first year of high school.[12]

According to Salud, her patriotism was sparked by her appreciation for a subject in elementary school that must have been civics, a subject introduced by the Americans to the curriculum and focused on training for citizenship. Salud recalled that it was through this subject that she internalised her identity as a Filipino and her love for her country. In her later interview with Isagani Medina, Salud sang from memory the patriotic song *Philippines, My Philippines* composed by Francisco Santiago.[13] When she was 19 years old Salud featured as one of the town belles of Cabuyao, in Laguna, in the annual parade on 30 December 1913 to commemorate the death anniversary of the national hero Jose Rizal.[14]

In her 1966 interview, Salud admitted to having several suitors but said it was Severo Generalla who won her heart. She mentions that by this time both her parents were gone and that the match was initiated by the father of Severo, who was the master baker in a bakery in Pandacan, a suburb of Manila. Salud mentions that Severo studied nine years in Manila and attended night school at the Liceo de Manila, where he obtained an Associate in Arts degree. Salud was

21 years old and was working as a seamstress when she married Severo in 1915.[15]

Severo left his job as a baker and became a cigar maker at Tabacalera, a private tobacco factory, where he became president in Pandacan of the Union Obreros de Tabaco de Filipinas (Tobacco Workers Union of the Philippines). Salud described her husband as a "strong union man" and mentioned that Severo's affiliation to the union "would lead to some trouble" (using her own words) that necessitated their leaving Manila and returning to the province of Laguna. Severo owned a stall in the Calamba public market and also went into farming.[16]

Although Salud and Severo may have started life as members of the Filipino educated elite, they experienced growing impoverishment. The loss of their lands in the provinces may have resulted in their relocation to Manila in search of job opportunities in the city. Severo's involvement in the labour movement in Manila then forced him and Salud to return to their place of origin, now as landless peasants. This marked a turning point in Salud's life. It was back in Laguna that Salud would become a member of the Sakdal movement.

Salud as a Member of the Sakdal Movement

A reversal of the family's fortunes, added to the fact that she had some education, made Salud Algabre analyse the situation not only of herself but of the peasant class to which she now belonged. Salud eloquently articulated the plight of the dispossessed, which is evident in an interview given in 1935 after she was arrested.[17]

For Salud, no number of petitions sent to the US government or consultations with Filipino leaders — who in her mind had become stooges of the Americans — would ameliorate the condition of the peasants. In her 1966 interview she expressed the injustice that had befallen tenant farmers in these words:

> When we worked the land, we were cheated. The terms on the estate were 50-50. If the tenants harvested 1,000 tons, 500 were to go to the *proprietario* [landowner] and 500 to the farmers. But we never got the agreed 50 per cent. We would get a mere 25 per cent, sometimes even less.[18]

Salud was convinced that there was no one to turn to but her fellow peasants, who had to organise themselves. This realisation moved her to join the Sakdal movement.

Salud became a member of Sakdal in 1930, when she was 36 years old. Her interest in the movement was awakened when her grandfather Lino handed her a copy of the newspaper *Sakdal*. For Salud, the contents of the newspaper expressed succinctly the plight of peasants like her who were attracted to the objectives of the Sakdal movement, which worked for the distribution of land and the independence of the Philippines from the United States.[19]

In her 1966 interview, Salud stated that independence was indispensable and was an important precondition for improving the plight of peasants:

> Nothing could solve our problem except independence, as the United States had promised. Freedom was the solution ... With independence, the leaders would cease to be powerful. Instead, it would be the people who were powerful. The people would have their freedom. We would have our own lands; they would no longer be the monopoly of the *proprietarios* and of government officials. As it was, we had nothing.[20]

Salud's words, recorded in an interview after she was captured in 1935, describe vividly the plight of peasants during the 1930s:

> We cannot send the children to school without money. Times are bad. What mother wouldn't send her children to school if she could. Two years ago we made a sugar crop for Julia Lumpaco in Calamba. We were to take what they gave us after the sugar was sold. We harvested 122 tons of cane. We have received no pay as yet. We owe Julia P137.00 The account is mixed up. Some times [*sic*] when we got a peso she would put down P1.15 or P1.20. When we got P5.00 she would put down P5.75. We were dissatisfied. Couldn't stand the charges so we left. She said for every ton we harvested she would collect fifty centavos on the land. We were supposed to get a fourth of the harvest. They wouldn't let us raise chickens. We needed chickens to get spending money for the children; where we are now we are getting P1.20 a week for the chickens, have fruit trees and get odd jobs cutting cane. We had two carabaos [buffaloes], but both have been sold. We borrowed P400.00 on a mortgage when my child got sick. A surveyor agreed to survey our solar [farm] and get title for P50.00. He did it in our absence and made mistakes in the boundary. Then he sued us for P130.00. We spent the P50.00 we had to pay for the title in the lawsuit. We haven't been able to pay the land tax for four or five

years. My husband was put in jail because he had no cedula. We
are against the Constitution. We are against the leaders because
they promise us independence and never get it. We think there is
no hope for us in our hardships without independence.[21]

When they met Benigno Ramos, the founder of the Sakdal movement,
in 1930, Salud and her husband agreed to help organise the movement
in the town of Cabuyao. In her 1966 interview Salud described Ramos
as "a good man" and said that she and her husband agreed completely
with his purpose. Organising the movement in Cabuyao meant distri-
buting free copies of the newspaper *Sakdal* and explaining its contents
to other peasants.[22]

Eventually Salud's home became a regular meeting place every
Sunday. Salud recalled later that Mass was celebrated in the morning,
officiated by the head of the newly established Iglesia Filipina Inde-
pendiente (Philippine Independent Church), Gregorio Aglipay.[23]

This church played an important part in the Philippine nationalist movement. In 1898, during the Philippine Revolution, Aglipay,
a Filipino secular priest, was appointed by Emilio Aguinaldo as the
chief chaplain of the Filipino armed forces. He was summoned by
the Manila Ecclesiastical Tribunal, a church body controlled by the
Spaniards, for having accepted such an appointment and for other
breaches to the canonical discipline. Aglipay never appeared before
the tribunal and as a result was excommunicated. In 1902, the Philippine Independence Church was formally established with Father Aglipay
as its first bishop, independent of the Pope in Rome. It drew many
adherents among the Filipinos because its liturgy was similar to the
Catholic faith. The only difference was that it had severed its ties with
Rome. This was why the Philippine Revolution considered it to be a
national church; its clergy was entirely Filipino, and it was headed
by a Filipino.

Sakdal delegations from nearby provinces such as Tayabas,
Batangas, Cavite, Rizal and Bulacan congregated in Salud's house. At
one point there were about 500 Sakdalistas present. Salud commented
in the 1966 interview: "It was exciting. Religion in the morning and
politics all day." These meetings assumed a festive air, with everyone
bringing their own food and Ramos and Aglipay in regular attendance:
"Cooking fires burned all day and well into the night."[24] Starting in
late 1931, meetings were held regularly until the Sakdal Uprising on
2–3 May 1935.

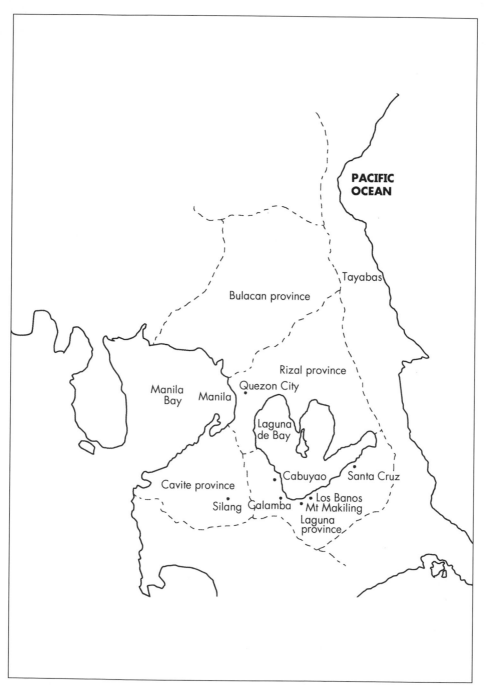

Map 7. Provinces of southern Luzon, Philippines

The town authorities were suspicious. The police would barge in and inquire why people were gathering. They would disperse the group and deny them freedom of assembly and freedom of speech. Arrests of Sakdal members took place as well.[25]

The non-payment of *cedula* became a convenient excuse for arresting Sakdalistas. Salud's husband was one of those jailed for not paying *cedula* and was made to wear a uniform with stripes like those of the tiger. In her 1966 interview Salud recounted:

> I took a picture of Severo in that tiger shirt and mailed it to the United States. I wanted the Americans to know what their compatriots here in the Philippines were doing to the people. What kind of government did we have if men who refused to pay the *cedula* were forced to wear tiger suits. Nothing happened. I don't know whether they received it or whether it was intercepted.[26]

In a meeting of local leaders held in Salud's house on 7 April 1935, it was agreed that an uprising would be held on 2 May 1935. Salud's role was to inform the Sakdal leaders in the nearby towns of Cabuyao such as San Pedro, Calamba, Los Banos and Caluan of the impending uprising. She instructed them that the uprising would consist of their occupying the municipal hall of the town, raising the Sakdal flag and proclaiming independence.[27]

The Sakdal Uprising in Cabuyao

In her 1966 interview, Salud Algabre gave an extensive account of her part in the Sakdal revolt of 1935. On 30 April 1935 she went to San Pedro, Calamba, Los Banos and Caluan to inform Sakdal leaders of the forthcoming uprising. She was back in Cabuyao the following day, 1 May. According to her, the Sakdalistas were armed with *bolos* (knives), clubs, sickles, some shotguns and revolvers.[28]

On the afternoon of the appointed day, 2 May, Salud led a group of Sakdalistas assembled near the railroad station and blocked the railroad and cut the telegraph lines. Salud was garbed in a white long-sleeved shirt, a red skirt with a blue tapis (a piece of cloth wrapped around the skirt) and a white headband.[29] The colours red, white and blue echoed the colours of the Philippine flag.

Other Sakdalistas converged in the municipal hall of Cabuyao. At that time, the municipal mayor tried to dissuade them from occupying the town hall. Seeing that he had failed to stop them, the mayor admonished them not to touch anything found inside the building. Even the guns in the armoury of the municipal hall were not touched by Sakdalistas. They raised the red Sakdal flag and sang the Sakdal hymn.[30]

Salud and her group proceeded to the highway and felled trees to block the road. Traffic was stopped at the highway at six in the evening. At seven o'clock, Salud and her group stopped a car carrying Marines from Los Banos. A sergeant asked Salud why they were being stopped. Salud introduced herself and her companions as Sakdalistas and said that they were demanding "immediate, complete and absolute independence". She asked for the Marines' firearms and the key of their vehicle, and issued a receipt for the confiscated items. Salud gave food to the Marines and stayed with them until the morning. Because the Marines seemed frightened by the Sakdalistas with their *bolos*, Salud then released them.[31]

Following is an account recorded in 1935 by one of those stopped by Salud:

> Salud Algabre, the *generala* was a thin, slight woman and she must have been around forty. But her frailty ended then and there. In her attire, her brisk manner and her speed, she affected a martial disposition. She had on a white long sleeved *camiseta* [a shirt], a red skirt and a white piece of cloth for a *tapiz*. These together with a white headband made her a perfect picture of a war general. We noticed too that she was restlessly walking hither and yon, inspecting detained cars, issuing receipts for confiscated revolvers. Later on, she made it emphatic that only those revolvers belonging to Filipinos would be returned to their owners. Americans, Chinese and other foreigners would have to give up their weapons for lost.[32]

The confiscation of weapons belong to Americans, Chinese and other foreigners by Salud, with the parting shot that they should be considered as lost, implies that these people were considered as oppressors of Filipino peasants and therefore deemed as enemies. The same account mentioned that in issuing receipts for confiscated items, Salud borrowed a fountain pen from the author of the account. She cut off a piece of her skirt and said: "Now take this piece of cloth as a receipt of your fountain pen and as soon as the war is over, just show me this receipt and you can have your pen back." We do not know whether the promise was fulfilled, but what was significant was the expression of Salud's word of honour.

Salud's married name, Generalla, was easily transformed into *Generala*, which was the Spanish term for "woman general". In fact, despite being expected to assume the surname of her husband, Salud retained her maiden name, Algabre. In a sign of her independence, she explained, "It's my custom not to use my husband's name. I don't want my maiden name to die."[33]

Around eight in the morning, Salud returned to her house to get some rice. It was at this time that the governor of the province, Juan Cailles, and his soldiers stormed the Cabuyao municipal hall. When news reached Salud that the constables were after her, she went to the house of a friend to check on her children and hid in an irrigation canal. At the time of the uprising, the eldest of Salud's five children was 16 years old and the youngest 14 months. She remained there until 1.30 in the afternoon. Salud recounted:

> Hardly had I reached home when I was informed that a number of Constabulary soldiers led by Governor Cailles were on the way to arrest me. Leaving my children crying, I went to the river about five meters from the house, and submerged myself in the water. I kept my head under the water as long as I could stand it without breathing, then I would rise for a breath of fresh air.
>
> I heard Governor Cailles giving orders to shoot me down on sight. I was fearful the soldiers, angered at not finding me, might shoot my children. I expected to hear their shots anytime. Governor Cailles and his men waited at the house for almost an hour. I thought I would go crazy if they did not go away soon. At last they left, and I sneaked into the house and told my children to be good for I was going away. Then I went to *Pulong Kahoy* in Cavite where I hid until the Constabulary came last Sunday.[34]

In her escape towards Silang, Cavite, Salud later recalled meeting a soldier along a dike. He ordered her to come close to him. She said:

> I drew myself straight and tall and walked up to him. He had on a Constabulary hat, but was wearing only an undershirt and trousers. He had also a rifle with a fixed bayonet in his hands. We just stared at each other over the bayonet. After a long time, he lowered the rifle, turned and left. I continued on across the paddies.
>
> I believe he knew who I was. Perhaps he had heard that I had a powerful *anting-anting* [amulet]. People said I did. But my only *anting-anting* was help from God.[35]

Salud continued to elude the soldiers as she crossed rivers and hiked through rice paddies. She even mentioned that there was an airplane searching for her. After she reached Silang, she was walking along the bank of the river when she encountered a huge pile of rocks. As she turned back, Salud would have fallen into the river had not her tresses got entangled in the branch of a tree. She recounted how scared she was at nightfall, imagining supernatural beings lurking around but at the same time mesmerised by the myriad of fireflies that lighted the place where she was hiding. She recalled having staved off hunger by eating raw eggs from a hen's nest that she chanced upon.[36]

One of her uncles, Miguel de la Cueva, a fellow Sakdalista who was also searching for her, discovered Salud hiding in a grove of bamboo. He convinced her to give herself up. She was presented to the authorities of Silang and then brought back to Cabuyao and then to Santa Cruz, the capital of Laguna province. She was incarcerated from 5 May 1935 to 1 October 1935, when she was set free upon payment of bail amounting to 2,000 pesos.[37]

While in jail, Salud was visited and interviewed by some American authorities. One of them asked her why she and the Sakdalistas had staged an uprising. Salud replied that the Sakdalistas were after "immediate, complete and absolute independence". Participating in the plebiscite scheduled to accept or reject the Tydings-McDuffie Law providing for a ten-year transition before the granting of independence by the United States was unacceptable to the Sakdalistas. Salud thought that the Americans appreciated her reply.[38]

It must have helped Salud that her husband shared her aspirations since he too was a member of the Sakdal movement. Severo was a delegate to a Sakdal Convention, representing Laguna province. According to Salud in her 1966 interview, after the uprising Severo escaped to Mount Makiling, where he hid for seven months. He secretly went back to Manila but was later captured and imprisoned. He was released before World War II.[39] Sturtevant mentioned that Severo, being a labour leader and aware of the fate of popular movements, counselled moderation, which Salud rejected.[40]

While Salud was incarcerated her children were left in the care of an aunt, which she confessed made her feel guilty. One of Salud's sons recounted that one time they left behind their youngest sibling with a dog that had recently given birth. They heard the child crying, apparently out of hunger. When the siblings got to her, they saw her suckling from the dog.[41]

The trial of Salud and the Sakdalistas took four years. It was held in Intramuros, Manila. According to Salud, her children followed her during these hearings as this was the only opportunity for her to see them. A court decision was handed down on 3 January 1939. It read:

> Wherefore, it having been proved beyond reasonable doubt that the Lapiang Sakdalista (Sakdalista Party) is an association which has for its objective the overthrow of the Government through forcible means, an act punished by the Penal Code, and that the defendants are members of the said party, some of them being also officers and organizers, the Court finds the said defendants (with the exception of Benigno Ramos who has not yet been tried) guilty of the crime of illegal association and hereby sentences them.[42]

Salud was the only woman Sakdal member who was imprisoned for being one of the leaders of the Cabuyao Uprising.

According to Salud,[43] she was sentenced to a term of six to ten years of imprisonment and fined 5,000 pesos but she did not serve the full term. After being imprisoned for one year, seven months and three days, she was pardoned by Manuel Quezon, president of the Commonwealth government, the very person whom the Sakdalistas detested. The Sakdalistas viewed Quezon as being in cahoots with the Americans in withholding independence from the Filipinos. They perceived him as misleading the people by saying that the Commonwealth government was transitional when in reality he wanted US interests to continue in the Philippines. According to the Sakdalistas, Quezon was from the privileged class and the government that he headed catered to the interests of the elite and not to the lower class. Moreover, the Sakdalistas referred to Quezon as *dugong Kastila* (Spanish blood), which reminded the ordinary folk of the cruel and oppressive Spanish colonialists.

Struggle after the Uprising

After accusing Quezon of collaborating with the Americans, during the liberation of the Philippines from the Japanese Salud herself was accused of being a Japanese collaborator and imprisoned. She was arrested by the 48th Infantry Regiment of the United States Armed Forces of the Far East guerrillas on 4 February 1945 and was arraigned in court on 17 October 1945.[44]

In her testimony, Salud stated that Benigno Ramos, founder of the Sakdal movement, had invited her to be a member of the Makabayan Katipunan ng mga Pilipino (MAKAPILI, Association of Patriotic Filipinos). This organisation was described in the court "as an organization of military character for the purpose of giving material support and physical as well as moral assistance and aid to the Empire of Japan and the Japanese Imperial Forces in the Philippines".[45] It is pertinent to point out that Ramos had sought asylum in Japan in December 1934 and directed the activities of the Sakdal movement from that country. Ramos was welcomed by radical Japanese Pan Asianists who claimed Japan should take a leading role in liberating Asia from Western imperialism. Ramos convinced the Japanese to support popular anti-colonial movements such as the Sakdal. During the Japanese occupation of the Philippines, Ramos returned to his homeland and worked with the Japanese.

Salud testified in court that Ramos' invitation came a month before she was arrested. She said that she was told to oversee a MAKAPILI plantation in Barrio San Jose and was given five Filipino guards by the Japanese to protect the plantation. According to Salud, the Japanese provided rice for the 60 Filipinos working on the plantation. She added that she was given a .38 calibre pistol by the Japanese and mentioned that four Japanese officers frequented her home.

On 16 December 1946, the People's Court (a court established to try cases of collaboration in the Philippines) ordered the provisional dismissal of the case against Salud "on the ground that witnesses which the prosecution intended to present in this case are not available".[46]

Salud denied that the Sakdalistas were in league with the Japanese.[47] It is possible to conjecture that Salud, like other Sakdal members, saw the Japanese as liberators of the Filipinos from the American colonialists. Japan's Greater East Asia Co-Prosperity Sphere espoused Asia for Asians but with Japan as the leader. Many of the mainstream nationalist Filipino elite also worked with the Japanese during the war, for similar reasons or out of self-interest, making the issue of collaboration a very murky one.

After the war, Salud continued to oppose the rich who held on to big landholdings. In one of her battles she took on the Tuason family over the Tatalon Estate in Quezon City. Salud said: "The reason why I neglected my children is because I helped fight the avidity of the Tuasons in Tatalon."[48] Thus she continued to cast her lot with the dispossessed, although it is notable that she did not join the Hukbalahap movement, which began during World War II and claimed to fight for both independence and peasants' rights to land. Perhaps the Communist ideology of the Hukbalahap did not appeal to Salud.

Salud's Legacy

When interviewed at the age of 72 by Sturtevant and asked whether there was bitterness in her heart after the failed Sakdal Uprising, Salud replied: "I was not bitter. I did what I thought was right. We lost and I was punished. The principles we fought for, and my faith in God, strengthened me."[49]

Looking back to that fateful day of 2 May 1935, when the uprising was quelled by government forces, Salud felt that it was not a failure. Her words were: "no uprising fails. Each step is a step in the right direction."[50] These words echoed Salud's thinking that change, whether economic or political or both, constituted a process, be it evolutionary or radical. One piece of evidence for this optimism was that as an aftermath of the Sakdal Uprising, the Commonwealth government adopted measures to improve the conditions of peasants through Manuel Quezon's Social Justice Program.

Salud considered the Sakdal Uprising a shining moment in the history of the Philippines. It probably represented a high point in her life too. She explained that despite being advanced in age, talking about the Sakdal movement rejuvenated her:

> We have talked a long time, but I am not tired. Whenever there is talk about the Sakdalistas, I become younger and stronger. I feel like it is 1935 again. *That was the moment.* [My emphasis.] Everything led up to the uprising. That was the high point of all our lives. Afterwards things were never the same. Later people and principles became confused. Few people think well of Sakdalism these days. They should remember what happened in May 1935. They should also remember why.[51]

Asked if she had any words to impart to the youth of the Philippines, Salud answered: "I no longer have anything to say. It's really up to them. They should love their country. They're Filipinos. They should help their fellow Filipinos rise."[52]

By some strange coincidence, Salud passed away on 2 May 1979, on the 44th anniversary of the Sakdal Uprising in which she had played a key role. She was 85 years old. Her fellow Sakdalistas acted as pallbearers when she was interred at the North Cemetery in Manila. Jeremias Addia, a fellow Sakdalista, recited the following verse before her coffin was lowered:

> Ang gawaing maglingkod sa lahi at bayan,
> Kakambal ng dusa at kamatayan,
> At ang maaring ngayo'y kasalanan
> Bukas makalawa ay kabayanihan.
> (To serve one's race and country,
> Is intertwined with suffering and death,
> And what today may be considered a crime
> May tomorrow be a heroic act.)[53]

Addia's prophecy was not fulfilled in the case of the Sakdal in general and Salud Algabre in particular, reflective perhaps of the continued marginality of the appreciation of the peasants' struggle in the national history of the Philippines. The political struggle and fragments of the life story of Salud were fortunately documented in the interviews used in this chapter. They serve as an argument for the use of oral history as a method in the documentation of women in nationalist movements, especially women from the peasant class. It is the only way their story can be heard and preserved for posterity.

Notes

1.   See Tarrosa Subido, *The Feminist Movement in the Philippines 1905–1955* (Philippines: National Federation of Women's Clubs in the Philippines, 1989); and Mina Roces, "Is the Suffragist an American Colonial Construct? Defining 'the Filipino Woman' in Colonial Philippines", in *Women's Suffrage in Asia: Gender, Nationalism and Democracy*, ed. Louise Edwards and Mina Roces (London and New York: RoutledgeCurzon, 2004).

2.   Vina Lanzona, *Amazons of the Huk Rebellion: Gender, Sex and Revolution in the Philippines* (Madison: University of Wisconsin Press, 2009).

3.   Pablo Anido, "Face to Face with the Generala", *Sunday Tribune Magazine*, 12 May 1935, p. 3; David Sturtevant, *Popular Uprisings in the Philippines (1840–1940)* (Ithaca and London: Cornell University Press, 1976), pp. 279–80, 288–99.

4.   Thelma B. Kintanar and Carina C. David, "Salud Algabre, Revolutionary", *Review of Women's Studies* 6, 1 (1966): 75–84.

5.   Teodoro Agoncillo, *History of the Filipino People* (Quezon City: Garotech Publishing, 1990), pp. 146, 163.

6. See Subido, *Feminist Movement in the Philippines*; and Roces, "Is the Suffragist an American Colonial Construct?"
7. Joseph Ralston Hayden, *The Philippines: A Study in National Development* (New York: Arno Press, 1972), p. 383.
8. Sturtevant, *Popular Uprisings in the Philippines*.
9. Cited in Grant Goodman, "An Interview with Benigno Ramos", *Philippine Studies* 37 (1989): 218.
10. Kintanar and David, "Salud Algabre, Revolutionary", p. 76.
11. Sturtevant, *Popular Uprisings in the Philippines*, p. 288.
12. Ibid., p. 289.
13. Kintanar and David, "Salud Algabre, Revolutionary", p. 76.
14. Sturtevant, *Popular Uprisings in the Philippines*, p. 289.
15. Ibid., pp. 289–90.
16. Ibid., p. 290.
17. Ibid., pp. 279–80.
18. Ibid., p. 290.
19. Kintanar and David, "Salud Algabre, Revolutionary", p. 77.
20. Sturtevant, *Popular Uprisings in the Philippines*, pp. 290–1.
21. Ibid., pp. 279–80.
22. Ibid., p. 292.
23. Ibid.
24. Ibid.
25. Ibid., p. 293.
26. Ibid.
27. Ibid., pp. 293–4.
28. Ibid., pp. 293–8.
29. Anido, "Face to Face with the Generala", p. 3.
30. Sturtevant, *Popular Uprisings in the Philippines*, p. 294.
31. Ibid., pp. 294–5.
32. Anido, "Face to Face with the Generala".
33. Kintanar and David, "Salud Algabre, Revolutionary", p. 77.
34. Anido, "Face to Face with the Generala".
35. Sturtevant, *Popular Uprisings in the Philippines*, p. 296.
36. Kintanar and David, "Salud Algabre, Revolutionary", p. 80.
37. Sturtevant, *Popular Uprisings in the Philippines*, pp. 296–7.
38. Ibid., p. 297.
39. Ibid., p. 298.
40. Ibid., pp. 286–7.
41. Kintanar and David, "Salud Algabre, Revolutionary", p. 81.
42. Cited in Carmen Tiongco-Enriquez, "Revolt within the Grassroots", in *Filipino Heritage*, ed. Alfredo Roces (Metro Manila: Lahing Pilipino Publishing, 1978), p. 2519.
43. Sturtevant, *Popular Uprisings in the Philippines*, p. 298.

44. People's Court Files. Box #133, Folder #1, Case #4573. Case of Salud Algabre, 1946 (University of the Philippines Main Library).

45. Ibid.

46. People's Court Files. Box #133, Folder #1, Case #4573 (University of the Philippines Main Library).

47. Sturtevant, *Popular Uprisings in the Philippines*, p. 298.

48. Kintanar and David, "Salud Algabre, Revolutionary", p. 81.

49. Sturtevant, *Popular Uprisings in the Philippines*, p. 298.

50. Ibid., p. 296.

51. Ibid., p. 299.

52. Kintanar and David, "Salud Algabre, Revolutionary", p. 82.

53. Herky del Mundo, "Salud Algabre-Sakdalista", *WHO Magazine* 2 (1979): 40–2.

CHAPTER 6

Shamsiah Fakeh and Aishah Ghani in Malaya: Nationalists in Their Own Right, Feminists Ahead of Their Time

Helen Ting

This chapter compares the political involvement of two contemporaries, Shamsiah Fakeh (1924–2008) and Aishah Ghani (1923–2013), who grew up in British Malaya. Aishah and Shamsiah shared many similarities in terms of their ethnic origins and childhood education, but their fate and life journeys differed radically as adults. Born into the matrilineal Minangkabau culture, both went through Malay primary schooling and even continued their education in the same well-known Arabic-medium Islamic school in Padang Panjang, West Sumatra, which is discussed in greater detail in chapter 4 of this book (Sally White). Both of them were initiated in their political involvement within the left-wing Malay Nationalist Party (MNP), the first Malay political party formed after World War II.[1] Both of them also became famous as the head of AWAS (Angkatan Wanita Sedar), the women's wing of the MNP. Aishah left the MNP after ten months and Shamsiah came in to replace her, staying on with the MNP until it was outlawed.

Subsequently, Aishah joined the United Malays National Organisation (UMNO) and became its women's wing leader after independence. Entering the government, she was appointed as the general welfare minister in 1974 — a position she held until 1984, when she retired from politics. Aishah is well known for having promoted

Thirteen-year-old
Shamsiah Fakeh with
her mother and brother
before both siblings
left for Sumatra in
1938 to study. Photo
from *Memoir Shamsiah
Fakeh*, courtesy of
Strategic Information
and Research
Development Centre,
Petaling Jaya

Shamsiah Fakeh, 1960. Photo
from *Memoir Shamsiah Fakeh*,
courtesy of Strategic Information
and Research Development
Centre, Petaling Jaya

Aishah Ghani (standing, middle) with friends at Diniyah Putri School in Padang Panjang, 1937; seated is Ibu Rahmah El Yunusiah, the principal of the school. Courtesy of Arkib Negara, Malaysia

Aishah Ghani at Hyde Park, London, 1956. Courtesy of Arkib Negara, Malaysia

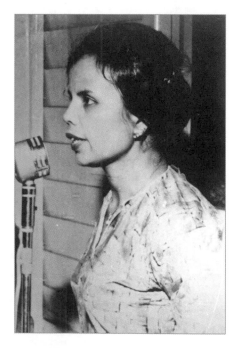

Aishah Ghani speaking at the general election campaign in Kampung Datuk Keramat, Kuala Lumpur, 1964. Courtesy of Arkib Negara, Malaysia

Syariah legal reform by overseeing a high-level committee that negotiated, deliberated and put together a comprehensive set of family laws
based on an enlightened interpretation of the Islamic laws.[2] Unfortunately, this set of laws was subverted by conservative religious scholars
and officials in various states who were unhappy that she had made
polygamy almost impossible for Muslim men.[3]

Shamsiah ended up joining the anti-British armed insurrection
led by the Malayan Communist Party (MCP). When a state of
Emergency was declared in June 1948, she was confronted with the
dilemma faced by many other left-wing leaders: either retreat into the
jungle or, like thousands of others, be detained without trial at the
pleasure of the colonial power. She became part of the all-Malay 10th
Regiment of the Malayan National Liberation Army formed by the
MCP in the jungle. In 1957 she was sent by the MCP to further
her studies in China, and she worked in the Malay section of Beijing
Radio as a broadcaster for more than three years. In 1965 the party
sent Shamsiah to Indonesia to do international representation work,
but she was detained there for two years by the Indonesian military.
In December 1967, she and her husband together with two other
comrades were released and allowed to return to Beijing. Influenced
by the Cultural Revolution in China, the MCP leaders there became
involved in factional conflicts. As a consequence, Shamsiah and her
husband were suspended from party membership in 1968 and kept
under house arrest for two years. Shamsiah and her family were subsequently allowed by the Chinese government to live as ordinary
foreign sojourners rather than be placed under the MCP.[4] After waiting
for ten years, their application to return to Malaysia was finally approved in 1994.

Some Methodological Considerations

In this comparative analysis, the most important sources of information are the autobiographies of Shamsiah[5] and Aishah. In 1991 a
Malay magazine, *Dewan Masyarakat*, published a seven-part series of
articles on Shamsiah.[6] At that time Shamsiah was in exile in China,
waiting for the Malaysian government to allow her to return. The feature was written by Fatini Yaacob, a journalist for *Dewan Masyarakat*,
based on her extensive research and interviews with people who were
related to or had worked with Shamsiah at various times. The contents

of the articles, while colourful and informative, should be taken with a pinch of salt. For instance, the background of Shamsiah's father as depicted by Fatini differs from that described by Shamsiah in her memoirs. Nonetheless, these articles give a feel for the popular image of Shamsiah in the Malay community. As for Aishah, there are a couple of academic works about the women's wing of UMNO[7] that provide third-person accounts of her life.

In their memoirs, the articulation of the self-identity of Aishah and Shamsiah is undoubtedly intertwined with their lifelong political commitment. Writing about memoirs and autobiography, Mark Freeman has noted that they may be understood as the "re-writing of self" as the autobiographer looks back at the life path travelled from the vantage point of the historical position and perspective he or she has arrived at.[8] While such dynamics of re-interpretation imply that the perspective articulated may not always reflect the original point of view in real time, it is nonetheless a perspective the person has evolved by virtue of successive political decisions, lifelong actions and practices. In this sense, the writing of memoirs can be understood as an attempt at making sense of the self and evaluating the meaning of one's past deeds as inscribed in the larger sociopolitical context. To a lesser or greater extent, their narratives inevitably reflect or challenge the dominant narrative of Malaysian national history, depending on which side of the political divide their struggle was situated.

From another point of view, we may also understand the lives and self-identities of Aishah and Shamsiah as having been forged progressively by virtue of their continued actions and practices that committed them further to the political struggle they were engaged in.[9] The everyday choices they made and the actions they took not only resulted in their being assigned to different historical positions in the grand narratives of Malaysian national history, but also led them to subscribe to the general political understanding of their immediate community of struggle. By comparing the interpretations of two persons on opposite sides of the struggle, we can gain some insights into the perspectives of actors on both sides of the divide, however partial they may be. In the meantime, for the analysis to do them justice, we need to be attentive to possible variations in terms of their embrace of the general sociopolitical — be they ideological, gender, class and/or ethnic — positions of the respective nationalist move- ments they participated in.

Historical Context

British Malaya consisted of three different colonial political systems of direct and indirect rule over the Malay states. The states of Selangor and Negri Sembilan, in which Aishah Ghani and Shamsiah Fakeh were born respectively, were part of the Federated Malay States under the indirect rule of the British. The British practised a racial policy of divide and rule, building their political legitimacy as protectors of the Malay people against the Chinese and Indian population who migrated to carry out various new economic functions such as tin-mining and rubber plantation activities. During the first half of the 20th century, the predominantly depressed socio-economic conditions of the Malay population led to a sense of alarm and urgency among the Malay intelligentsia to uplift the community in the face of the more urbanised non-Malay population.

The hardship suffered under Japanese occupation between 1941 and 1945 stirred political awareness among the Malayan population. The predominantly Chinese Malayan People's Anti-Japanese Army (MPAJA), which was formed by the MCP, saw more Malays who were tired of the tyrannical Japanese rule joining their ranks towards the mid-1940s. Fatefully, the brief period of political vacuum after the Japanese surrender and before the return of the British, termed the interregnum period, saw violent Sino-Malay clashes occurring in isolated locations in Malaya due to some overzealous, reckless Chinese leaders of the MPAJA punishing Malays who collaborated with the Japanese. In retaliation, some local Malay leaders such as Kiai Salleh organised paramilitary groups that went about killing Chinese indiscriminately, regardless of whether or not they were MPAJA members. These violent ethnic clashes formed the historical context in which a popular Malay movement emerged against the Malayan Union Plan, the civilian political system proposed by the British to replace the British Military Administration. Inaugurated on 1 April 1946, the short-lived Malayan Union was replaced by the Federation of Malaya on 1 February 1948.

By then, there were three main pan-Malayan political movements in post-war Malaya: the left-leaning MNP, which was formed in 1945; the MCP, which had existed since the 1930s; and UMNO, which was formed at the first Anti-Malayan Union Congress attended by state-level Malay associations throughout the peninsula in March 1946. The MNP was invited to join the Anti-Malayan Union Congress but

Malayan Nationalist Movements

1874	Direct British intervention begins in sultanates on Malayan Peninsula
1895	Britain establishes Federated Malay States
1928	Formation of Nanyang Communist Party, renamed Malayan Communist Party (MCP) in 1930
1945	Formation of Malayan Nationalist Party (MNP)
Mar. 1946	Formation of United Malays National Organisation (UMNO)
Apr. 1946	Malayan Union formed
July 1946	Tripartite (sultans, UMNO representatives and British officials) secret negotiation begins on alternative to Malayan Union
Dec. 1946	Pan-Malayan Council of Joint Action (PMCJA) formed
Jan. 1947	MNP resigns from PMCJA and forms PUTERA, before rejoining PMCJA to form AMCJA-PUTERA
May 1947	Publication of draft Anglo-Malay Federation Agreement
July/Aug. 1947	AMCJA-PUTERA finalises the People's Constitutional Proposals for Malaya
Oct. 1947	All-Malaya strike against the Federation of Malaya Agreement
Feb. 1948	Federation of Malaya formed
June 1948	Declaration of state of Emergency throughout Malaya
1955	Federal Legislative Councillors elected
1957	Independence of Federation of Malaya
1963	Formation of Federation of Malaysia
1989	Peace treaty signed between Malaysian government and MCP

withdrew from it after three months. Even though the Malayan Union was put in place as planned, the British authority gave in to Malay pressure and negotiated a replacement with the Malay sultans and UMNO representatives in the form of an Anglo-Malay agreement. This gave rise to the Federation of Malaya, which imposed far more stringent conditions in granting political status to the non-Malay population. In response, non-Malays and leftist groups (including the MNP) came together to form a multi-ethnic platform called PUTERA-AMCJA[10] to propose an alternative political system to the Federation of Malaya.

Even before the declaration of the state of Emergency in June 1948, British colonial power had tightened its control over union activities and cracked down massively on leftist sympathisers. MCP leaders and members as well as some of those from the MNP retreated into the jungle to escape arrest and regrouped to take up guerrilla warfare. Malaya was effectively plunged into a civil war.

Incremental political autonomy was granted by the British, in part as a strategy to thwart the anti-colonial political edge of the MCP armed insurrection. In an attempt to cater to a multi-ethnic mix of voters in municipal elections, a temporary collaboration between UMNO and the Malayan Chinese Association (MCA) gave rise to the emergence of the Alliance, a coalition of UMNO, the Malayan Chinese Association and the Malayan Indian Congress. This required the national leaders of UMNO to switch radically from the organisation's founding rhetoric of exclusionary Malay nationalism to a more accommodating Malayan nationalism in partnership with the Malayan Chinese Association and the Malayan Indian Congress. The management of internal contradiction arising from this tension among different factions within UMNO presented a constant and ongoing challenge to its national leaders.[11] It was to the Alliance leaders that the British subsequently handed over the political control of British Malaya minus Singapore.

As the Federation of Malaya achieved political independence in 1957, the pro-British and staunchly anti-Communist political elites of the Alliance were not interested in negotiating a peace settlement with the MCP. Even though the security forces managed to drive MCP guerrilla forces farther north to the Thai border, they were not able to eradicate the latter completely. A peace accord was signed between the Malaysian government and the MCP leadership only in December 1989 — in Hatyai, Thailand, witnessed by Thai government officials.

Childhood Memories of Aishah

Aishah Ghani was born in 1923 in Kampung Sungai Serai, Hulu Langat, in the state of Selangor. (For place names in this chapter, see maps

Map 8. Malaya

5 and 8.) As the youngest among five children, she was the apple of her parents' eye. Aishah excelled in studies and received an offer to continue her education in an English convent school in Kajang, a town near her village. Her father strongly opposed this, as he believed studying in an English Christian school would bring about "many sins" (*bersekolah Inggeris akan membawa banyak dosa*).[12] Aishah later recounted that she was extremely sad but had to obey her father's wish. After having completed five years of primary education in a Malay-language school, she was offered a place at the age of 11 to be a trainee teacher — but her parents rejected that option as well because they did not want her to stay away from home.

Aishah then had to confront her worst fear: her parents wanted to marry her off, as was the fate of most young Malay girls of her age and time. Her mother asked her to prepare embroidered bed linen, an essential item in a Malay bride's dowry. She protested with all her might, screaming, crying and throwing away materials her mother handed her for the embroidery work. She began a few days of hunger strike, threatening that "something bad" would happen if her plea to continue her studies did not materialise.[13] Subsequently, her Indonesian brother-in-law Abdul Halim, who was a religious teacher, managed to persuade Aishah's parents to send her to a religious boarding school for girls in West Sumatra. In fact, it was also thanks to Abdul Halim, who believed in the importance of educating girls, that Aishah had gone to primary school, unlike her two illiterate elder sisters.

Aishah also recounted an unforgettable experience that influenced her greatly when she was in grade four in the Malay school: the visit of Miss Kontik Kamariah binti Ahmad. Aishah was impressed by the fact that Kontik, who was in her early twenties, arrived at the school driving a red sports car. Even more impressive, she saw her school principal nodding constantly to whatever Miss Kontik had to say throughout her stay at the school. Aishah mentioned that this experience had given her the belief that in order to advance, besides being educated a woman should be brave in overcoming any resistance. She said that she was "spellbound" (*terpesona*) and "dazed" (*terpegun*) by the thought that a young lady like Kontik could drive her own car and give instructions to a male school principal.[14] Kontik was the first school inspector of the Malay schools in the state of Selangor. She was also the first Malay woman to pass the Senior Cambridge examinations.

Aishah successfully completed grade seven at the Arabic-medium primary Diniyah Girls School in Padang Panjang, West Sumatra, within four years (1936–39), despite her very elementary linguistic competence in the Arabic language at enrolment. In 1940 she continued her studies in Kolej Islam, an Islamic teachers' training college in Padang, but her education was interrupted by the Japanese occupation. She managed to return home and worked briefly as a teacher.

Shamsiah's Childhood

Shamsiah Fakeh was born in 1924, a year after Aishah, in Kampung Gemuruh, Kuala Pilah, in the state of Negeri Sembilan. She was the second among eight brothers and sisters. Unlike Aishah, Shamsiah grew up in poverty. Her father, of Sumatran origin, was a peddler selling vegetables, fish and home-made medicine. Shamsiah recalled that her father was often chased away by the police because he did not have a legal trading licence, and he was once detained in the police station for a few days. In order to supplement the household income, her mother also went from house to house selling cloth to villagers.

In 1938, after her Malay-medium primary education, Shamsiah's father sent her to an Islamic school in Padang Panjang, accompanied by her younger brother. In her memoirs, Shamsiah mentioned that the school inculcated a nationalist spirit among its young Indonesian students.

Due to the unstable international political situation, her father brought her back to Malaya in 1940 to continue her studies in a recently founded local Islamic school, the Islamic High School in Pelangai — but that did not last long. Within a year the founder of the school, Tuan Guru Lebai Maadah, arranged with the respective parents for Shamsiah to be married to a rich farmer's son, her classmate. She stopped schooling after her marriage. According to Shamsiah, Lebai Maadah arranged the marriage to get monetary contributions from the parents involved so as to expand his school.[15] Thus, unlike Aishah, Shamsiah was not able to escape the common fate of early marriage. As a rich farmer's son, Shamsiah's husband, Yasin Kina, did not work and relied on his parents for financial support. His parents also gave the couple some farmland and built a small house for them. Shamsiah recalled that she had to help with farming activities, which she was not used to. In June 1944, eight months' pregnant and after being married for three years, she was divorced without any valid reason by

Yasin. Both the children she bore with Yasin died in infancy due to malnutrition.

While Shamsiah felt bitter about Yasin's inconsiderate treatment, her even shorter marriage with her second husband, J.M. Rusdi, was no better. Rusdi was a womaniser and a spy for the Japanese. He divorced Shamsiah after five months of marriage, again without any valid reason. As a consequence of these two marriages, Shamsiah developed strong feelings about male oppression of women. In addition, she felt sorry that her education had been interrupted by marriage and the poverty of her family.

Common Political Roots Going Separate Ways

Aishah Ghani and Shamsiah Fakeh shared a common starting point in their experience of political initiation in a turbulent post-war era, when anti-colonialism was on the rise but Sino-Malay conflicts prevented a united anti-colonial nationalist movement.

Shortly after the end of World War II, Aishah was employed as a lead writer by the MNP for its party organ, *Pelita Malaya*. She was initially highly enthusiastic about MNP's anti-colonial cause. Besides holding publishing responsibilities, she was also asked to head the women's wing, AWAS. As the head of AWAS, she followed party leaders — in particular Ahmad Boestamam, who headed the male youth wing, API (Angkatan Pemuda Insaf) — to various corners of British Malaya to mobilise popular support for MNP and recruit women villagers into AWAS. When Aishah left MNP after ten months, Shamsiah came in to replace her.

Shamsiah explained later that she encountered and became attracted to the anti-colonial discourse of the MNP during her Islamic studies in Bagan Serai, in the state of Perak, after the war. In her memoirs, she said, "It was from here that I began to be attracted to the nationalist struggle or the struggle to demand independence."[16] With the blessings of her father, she was able to follow closely seminars and public forums organised by both the MNP and UMNO. She got to know some of the MNP leaders, and once she even stood up and gave a spontaneous speech at a public meeting organised by the MNP.

When she became the women's wing leader, Shamsiah also followed other party leaders to various places around the country to rally people to the cause of anti-colonialism, to expand party membership and to form local branches. Shamsiah was highly spirited and a gifted, fiery speaker. She was able to utilise her religious knowledge in her speeches, quoting verses from the Quran and the Prophet's Hadith. She became a well-known anti-colonial Malay woman leader. She was also a member of the MNP Central Committee from December 1946 until the party was banned in 1948.

Why did Shamsiah stay on in the MNP and then continue her anti-colonial struggle in the MCP, while Aishah left the MNP within less than a year? How did they explain their successive course of nationalist commitment?

A closer look at the underlying logic of how Aishah and Shamsiah explained their nationalist commitment reveals that they reflect fairly standard themes discussed by those on both sides of the political divide. The disagreement with armed struggle as a means to achieve national autonomy and the rejection of Communist ideology are the two main lines of argument used by Aishah to explain why she left the MNP and, correspondingly, to portray UMNO in a positive light.

In her autobiography, Aishah mentioned that from time to time she was sent by the MNP to attend training courses or meetings together with other party leaders in secluded places. After attending them, her doubt regarding the political orientation of the MNP grew. She talked about a meeting in which there were joint discussions with "a lot of" Chinese on how to get support from the Malay population. She asked the MNP leadership why Chinese were present at an MNP meeting, but she did not get a clear answer. In one course the speaker talked about the Bolshevik Revolution in Russia, the success of the Communists in spreading their influence, and their future plans for Southeast Asia. She mentioned that only God knew how she felt at that time, and that she "surrendered" to Him to spare her from going astray.[17] She did not explain why she was so anxious but seemed equally uncomfortable with the fact that the course was held in a desolate slum area inhabited by Chinese farmers and pig-rearers as by the fact that the speaker was advocating the Communist takeover of Southeast Asia through armed revolt.

In early July 1946, after ten months in the party, Aishah decided to quit the MNP when it wanted to send her to Ipoh, in the state of Perak, to take charge of the northern region. She rejected the offer and informed the party that she wished to stop her work at the MNP and withdraw her party membership. She then joined Radio British

Military Administration as a Malay-language broadcaster. The official reason Aishah gave to the MNP party leadership for leaving was that she was getting married to Abdul Aziz bin Abu Hassan. Aishah also gave a second reason in her autobiography. She said that she had lost faith in the MNP's struggle. She felt that party leaders were too ambitious (*cita-citanya ingin menjangkau awan*) and hence did not exercise discretion over whom to befriend or build political alliances with. She noted that the MNP leaders did not believe that British colonialism could end by mere persuasion and hence believed that armed struggle was inevitable and were prepared for it.[18] After the above-mentioned course on the Russian Revolution, she recounted that she argued with a party leader on the wisdom of armed insurrection. Her position was that the Malays in Malaya did not need to start a revolt to secure independence, especially since revolt would entail the loss of lives.[19] She was also critical of MNP leaders' "fantasy" of setting up a *Melayu Raya* empire (which would encompass both Indonesia and Malaysia) in the form of a republic.[20]

Shamsiah, on the other hand, emphasised in her memoirs the anti-colonial credentials of the MNP and MCP, and contrasted them with the complicity of UMNO with the colonial power and the latter's initial reluctance to use the slogan of "*merdeka*" (meaning independence). In defence of the armed struggle of the MCP, she also quoted Samad Idris, a journalist-turned-UMNO politician who in his memoir described his involvement in Barisan 33. Barisan 33 was a relatively unknown paramilitary cell annexed to UMNO youth, with plans to secure firearms and attack police stations, that was secretly organised in the 1950s. Even though the plans were not realised, Shamsiah asked why this plan by UMNO youth for an armed uprising against the British was acceptable to UMNO while Malays involved in armed struggle under the leadership of the MCP in the jungle were branded as "Communist terrorists".[21]

In one of the feature articles about Shamsiah in *Dewan Masyarakat*, the central concern of its author, Fatini, was how such a great, dedicated female anti-colonial nationalist steeped in Islamic knowledge could embrace Communism. Fatini seemed to equate Communism simplistically with atheism, or the rejection of Islamic belief. She suggested that Shamsiah "imbibed Communist ideology" even as her nationalist spirit remained strong.[22] A surrendered MCP member interviewed by Fatini claimed that Shamsiah admitted to being a

"Communist representative", who according to him had to fulfil three conditions: be an atheist, be loyal to MCP, and have strong discipline and understand Communist philosophy and struggle.[23]

Referring to the *Dewan Masyarakat* articles, Shamsiah wrote in her memoirs: "In actual fact, I am not a female leader of the Communist Party of Malaya or a famous female public figure. I am just a woman fighter (*pejuang wanita*) who struggled against the British for the independence of my homeland and for the emancipation of women."[24] She claimed that she was seen as a Malay woman leader who headed the first progressive women's body in Malaya (AWAS) that was not afraid to fight the colonial power.[25] She was proud of what she had done and urged the readers of her memoirs to differentiate between the colonial era under the British and the era after independence.[26]

Aishah did not join UMNO immediately after she left MNP in 1946. She explained in her autobiography that she concentrated on her work as a radio broadcaster and the new family she was building. She joined UMNO only in 1950, when she began to work part-time in order to be able to take care of her two young children. Upon joining UMNO, she was immediately assigned as the secretary of the women's wing of the local branch. From the following year until she went to London for further studies in 1955, Aishah was a regular member of the women's wing delegation to the UMNO general assembly.

How do we make sense of Aishah Ghani's commitment to the cause of Malaya's political independence when, after five years of active political involvement in UMNO, she left the country for further studies just as the country was about to deliberate on its first majority-elected federal legislative council? And how should we understand her perspective in terms of political commitment when she rejected the UMNO president's request to return from London to lead the women's wing of UMNO in 1956?

Aishah mentioned in her autobiography that in 1956, after she completed her English language courses and just as she was about to start her journalism course, the UMNO leader Tunku Abdul Rahman met her in London. He told her that Khadijah Sidek, the leader of the women's wing, had been expelled from the party, and he asked Aishah whether she was willing to return to Malaya to replace Khadijah. She refused straight away, explaining to him that she needed to remain in London to complete her journalism course. She commented that the Tunku's query strengthened her resolve to equip herself with as much knowledge as possible so that she could become an effective leader of consequence rather than feeling handicapped in the face of bigger challenges.[27]

These actions make one wonder whether Aishah perceived the role of the UMNO women's wing as subsidiary and secondary in achieving independence: she did not think it worthwhile to heed the Tunku's request and abandon her journalism training. Indirectly, Aishah explained her stance by proposing a different role for herself. She quoted the Tunku as telling Malayan students in London that although the initial objective of struggle to achieve independence might not take too much time, translating this independence into meaningful reality (*mengisi kemerdekaan*) would then become a heavy responsibility and would take a long time.[28] Aishah seemed to understand this goal as raising the status of the Malay people to the same level as non-Malay Malayans.[29] When she landed at the airport in Kuala Lumpur upon her return from London in December 1958, she mentioned that she praised God for the fact that her homeland had achieved independence, and that she as the daughter of this homeland had returned from her sojourn overseas to contribute to the struggle to *mengisi kemerdekaan*.[30]

It is reasonable to deduce from the above that Aishah was a very rational, determined, even politically ambitious person. From her youth, she seemed to know exactly what she wanted and worked hard to ensure that she could achieve it. While the great majority of UMNO grass-roots members communicated mainly in Malay, it was the English-educated male elites who dominated the national leadership of the party. Aishah seemed to aspire to become part of the English-educated political elites at the top; she was not content with being just a mediocre politician due to her lack of knowledge and exposure. The Tunku emphasised English proficiency as one of the conditions for an UMNO leader to be chosen as an electoral candidate. It was not difficult for Aishah to figure out that should she master English and acquire a professional qualification, she would be well placed — even ahead of some of her Malay-educated male colleagues — to rise up the ranks to the national level.[31]

The Ethnic Dimension

With regard to UMNO's political orientation, Aishah found the "method of struggle to demand independence pursued by the Malay leaders in UMNO more convincing".[32] She believed that the Malay people were still in a position of weakness and that if they demanded something with force, they would face negative consequences. While she acknowledged both UMNO and MNP as Malay nationalist parties aiming to liberate the country, she found the struggle of UMNO "more honest and pure".[33] It is notable that she described UMNO's struggle as fighting for the future of the Malay people[34] rather than for all Malayan people.[35]

In her memoirs Aishah sounded as though she was addressing only Malay readers, despite having been a cabinet minister for a decade. Malaya for her was confined mainly to the Malay community. Her struggle focused on the emancipation of the Malay people rather than decolonisation of the people of all ethnicities in Malaya at that time. In her memoirs, she expressed her unease when mingling with non-Malays in the meetings or training courses conducted by the MNP. It may even be argued that she looked upon non-Malays with a certain degree of mistrust and hostility. Instead of acknowledging the negotiation of independence from the British as the joint efforts of a multi-ethnic united front, she contended that "it was the Malay people who had fought for independence".[36]

In her autobiography, Aishah expressed her admiration for and agreement with the controversial book written by Dr Mahathir Mohamad in the aftermath of the racial riots of 13 May 1969, *The Malay Dilemma*.[37] She referred to non-Malays freely and indiscriminately as "immigrants" (*pendatang*) and wrote approvingly of Mahathir's reference to Malays as the "definitive people" of Malaya. According to her, "immigrants" needed to respect the policy of the land and not go overboard in demanding their rights.[38]

Perhaps, like many among the Malay population, Aishah had a perspective on the Chinese population in Malaya that was skewed by the sporadic Sino-Malay violence that broke out during the interregnum period. She talked about some ruthless and arbitrary atrocities committed by "a group of Chinese" belonging to the MPAJA. Noting that many Malays fell victim to Chinese, she related how she and her relatives had heard her neighbour screaming for help one night in August 1945 and the following morning the neighbour and his son were found to have been killed. Even though she acknowledged that some villagers said it was not the MPAJA that had killed them but the rubber tappers who previously worked under the neighbour, she apparently did not think so.[39]

It is revealing to read her commentaries on the Anti-Malayan Union Movement. She mentioned that Malay papers reminded Malays that if they did not bravely do something to oppose the Malayan Union Plan, they would be faced with consequences worse than the Japanese oppression.[40] She noted that with the implementation of the Malayan Union Plan, "all the people will be given the same rights regardless of their descent, and all will be called 'Malayan'".[41] This argument that all Malayan people being given the same rights would result in "consequences worse than the Japanese oppression" makes sense only if Sino-Malay distrust and hostility are presumed. Notably, among all other leaders who spoke at the Anti-Malayan Union Movement Congress, she quoted Kiai Salleh, the leader of a Malay paramilitary group that indiscriminately killed members of the Chinese population, including defenceless women and children.[42]

Aishah's narrow Malay nationalistic political perspective on Malayan nationhood coincided with the generation of UMNO politicians who rose from the time of Premier Abdul Razak after the racial riots in 1969. Aishah rose to become the women's wing national leader with the changing of the guard from Tunku Abdul Rahman to Abdul Razak. On the other hand, if this was her perspective of nationalism, it is understandable that she felt uneasy in the MNP and with the ambiguous association with the Chinese-dominated Malayan Communist Party and preferred instead UMNO as the vehicle of her political activism.

Shamsiah, on the other hand, appears to have been far more ethnically inclusive in her perspective. From her childhood world of Malay culture and Islamic studies, her political involvement seemed to have widened her horizon and contacts with people of other ethnic communities. In her memoirs, she did not seem to judge or react to people based on their ethnic origins. She never commented in any negative sense on the Chinese community or her Chinese comrades, or on the predominantly "Chinese nature" of the MCP. She did not use the pejorative term *pendatang* (immigrant) to refer to non-Malays as did Aishah (and probably many other Malays of her time).

It was Fatini's articles that referred to Shamsiah's initial public contact with "the Chinese" (synonym for the author with "Communist") in a negative sense. Apparently Aishah Ghani, as one of Fatini's informants, suggested that Shamsiah might have been exposed to Communist ideas in the context of the PUTERA-AMCJA campaign, when she appeared frequently in public with a couple of Chinese women leaders of mass organisations that were seen as fronts for the MCP.[43] PUTERA-AMCJA was formed to campaign against the Federation of Malaya Agreement (proposal of a political structure to replace the Malayan Union), forged between the British colonial power and UMNO and Malay rulers in 1947.

Shamsiah, on the other hand, described the PUTERA-AMCJA collaboration as playing an important and positive role in the history of the struggle against colonialism. She referred to the coalition as the first to provide a platform for cooperation and unity of all ethnic communities in Malaya, preceding the multi-ethnic Alliance coalition.[44] She stressed that AWAS, representing progressive and politically conscious Malay women, was proud to be part of the historic PUTERA-AMCJA cooperation.

There is also the question of how the predominantly Chinese MCP regarded Shamsiah. Fatini was told by her informants, former comrades of Shamsiah who surrendered, that Shamsiah was greatly respected by Chinese MCP members and leaders even though she apparently did not occupy any important official position. In his interview with Fatini, Ahmad Salleh[45] argued that Shamsiah must have abandoned her Islamic faith or else she could not have become someone trusted by the MCP Central Committee.[46] He insinuated that she might have been used by the MCP as a public front to demonstrate the goodwill of the MCP towards the Malay people.

Apparently in response to this report, Shamsiah explained in her memoirs that as a branch level committee member, she was not entitled to carry a pistol and a hand grenade. However, Musa Ahmad, the chairman of the MCP at the time, told the 10th Regiment that she was given the honour of being able to do so as a sign of respect for the leader of AWAS, that is, she stressed, in her capacity as *a Malay woman*. According to her, Musa said that the MCP was worried that its good name might be tainted if she got killed and the enemy found that she did not have a firearm.[47] In fact, the political importance of the all-Malay 10th Regiment cannot be underestimated. The regiment refuted the allegation that the MCP was a "Chinese party" and the shaping of Malay public opinion by British propaganda that caricatured its struggle as a Chinese insurrection. Yet it appears that it was not only the ethnic dimension that mattered in the case of Shamsiah but the fact that she was a woman as well, as she herself stressed.

The Gender Dimension

Both Shamsiah and Aishah faced issues concerning the quality and availability of women leaders in their respective organisations. Aishah spoke about the challenge to find suitable members for local women's wing committees, let alone for heads of those committees. She acknowledged the lack of political ambition among the Malay women who joined UMNO in the name of strengthening Malay unity and helping the party to win as many electoral seats as they could. More detrimentally, some of those in rural areas also frowned on other women who indicated their readiness to play a more active role in the party. Most early local women's wing leaders were older housewives whose husbands were men of wealth or status, such as village head, school principal or district officer.[48] Aishah described their political knowledge and understanding as "very moderate" and pragmatic.[49]

This was clearly not her idea and ideal of a woman political leader. Aishah's reference point might well have been the young, modern and English-speaking Miss Kontik, whom she encountered as a primary school pupil. This might explain the reason for which she decided to leave everything behind to further her studies and master English so as to become a different type of female political leader.

Elsewhere, Aishah mentioned that she was elected consecutively 12 times (1960–72) to the Supreme Council of UMNO without having to campaign much for herself, which was indeed a feat as a female UMNO leader. Interestingly, she mentioned that based on her experience, a woman who wished to become a division chief needed to have strong male supporters.[50] She also said that besides having loyal and skillful supporters, such a candidate needed to fully understand politics as a "game" and be confident that she had mastered well the art of this "game", and yet be wise enough to know the pitfalls to avoid.[51]

Shamsiah, on the other hand, approached the issue of women's participation in politics from a different angle. Given her very down-to-earth and humble perspective of herself and her service to the cause of decolonisation, she empathised with and instilled a sense of mission among her followers. According to her, her message to them was very simple. She would explain that under the yoke of colonisation, the (Malay) people remained poor and low in knowledge. Only when they had a free and independent country would it be possible to build the nation and bring prosperity to society.[52] Using stories about the Prophet Muhammad's wives who sought knowledge and actively conducted various activities outside the home, she encouraged village women to develop their potential and leadership qualities and to go beyond shouldering household responsibilities. She also reminded them to pursue independence hand in hand with men, likening men and women to the two wings of a bird: the lack of one would cripple movement.[53]

Her former comrade in AWAS, Aishah Hussein, recalled that they used to walk three or four kilometres in the rural area of Sungai Long, near Kajang, to recruit women villagers as members. Shamsiah also organised programmes for these women with the aim to conscientise them, such as literacy, cooking and sewing classes, so that they would be confident and know how to conduct themselves in public functions. In order to broaden their world view, those women who knew how to read were asked to buy and read newspapers. These women members also participated in fundraising efforts to support the political activities of AWAS in particular and MNP in general.[54]

Shamsiah explained that her nationalist struggle for independence had made her aware of the oppression of women. She believed that the struggle for men's liberty depended on the same for women. In effect, she noted that while women suffered from all kinds of oppression due to the feudalist, capitalist and imperialist systems, they were also oppressed by men because of traditional customs and religious rules. As an example, she gave her experience of being divorced by her first husband without a valid reason when she was eight months' pregnant.[55] Shamsiah described the responsibility of raising the living standard of women, achieving equal rights for men and women, and liberating women from the chain of oppression as a big and heavy responsibility to be accomplished over the long term. Achieving the independence of her homeland, for her, was the first step towards the liberation of women.[56]

Despite her belief in women's liberation, Shamsiah took a controversial step in her third marriage. She married Ahmad Boestamam, the head of API, as his second wife in December 1946, six months after she started working at the MNP.

Fatini described Shamsiah's third marriage thus: "This was the most sensational marriage in the history of the Malay nationalist struggle. Boestamam and Shamsiah — the API chief and AWAS head — they were a great match!" Nonetheless, her subsequent comments were damaging: "But just as her previous marriages, this marriage also ended in failure. What was wrong with Shamsiah?"[57] When asked, Ishak Hj. Muhammad, a one-time president of MNP, criticised Shamsiah, saying that she "likes to get married" and was "mad about men" and even wanted to elope with Ahmad Boestamam.[58] Nonetheless, her other former comrades defended her. Wahi Anuwar, her fourth husband, said Ahmad was "a bit egoistic and got carried away by his ego".[59] Another unnamed informant referred to Ahmad as follows: "Boestamam's ego is too high. He does not like to be challenged and does not obey any leaders."[60] It appears that Ahmad might have been interested in Shamsiah from the beginning. He may have felt "challenged" when Shamsiah teased him about the shortcomings of API's contribution to the party, and decided to "tackle" her by making her his wife.[61]

In her autobiography, Shamsiah defended her decision to marry Ahmad Boestamam as a way to learn from him:

> At that time I was aware that even though I had high morale for the struggle my ideological and political maturity was still low. I was still green and lacking experience in struggle. This is not something strange. While I needed to learn by doing, I also needed help from people who were experienced. I thought I would get a lot of help from Ahmad if I married him.[62]

She also defended her position as the second wife by saying that from a religious point of view Islam allowed polygyny, and that she maintained a good relationship with Ahmad's first wife, Rabitah. Shamsiah blamed her subsequent divorce with Ahmad on his mother and elder sister, who did not approve of her.[63] Fatini's sources mentioned that Shamsiah was unhappy that Ahmad Boestamam, when convicted of sedition for his writings, sought donations to pay his fine in order to avoid going to jail. She felt that it would have been better for him to suffer in prison rather than beg for people's sympathy to bail himself out.[64]

Another more serious accusation against Shamsiah was made by Musa Ahmad, the former MCP chairman who surrendered to the Malaysian government in 1981. He claimed that Shamsiah threw into the river the child she bore in the jungle with her fourth husband, Wahi Anuwar. Shamsiah denied this in her memoirs. She described the difficult situation she was in after giving birth and struggling to keep her infant son with her. Her hiding place was attacked several times by the British Army.[65] Lacking rest and proper nutrition, she had no milk to feed her baby. So in the end she allowed her comrades who saved her to take him away to be adopted by a family in the nearby village. However, she found out after three years that her baby had been killed by them.[66] When the MCP leaders found out about it, they punished those who were involved after consulting with her.[67] This episode illustrates the dilemma of a woman freedom fighter, who despite doing all she could to save her baby still ended up losing him while she soldiered on with her political struggle. The fact that Aishah took leave from political involvement for a few years after her marriage is perhaps, in a mild sense, the reverse of Shamsiah's bitter experience of the "domestic tension" often faced by women involved in political activities.

Conclusion

The lives of Aishah and Shamsiah are embedded in the larger historical and ideological struggle for independence in British Malaya, and are marked by social conflicts that remained unresolved for decades even after independence. Their private lives and political involvement were also profoundly marked by the cultural norms and religious practices of their ethnic community as Malay and Muslim women. In their own ways, they sought what they understood as the acceptable way to self-emancipation and struggled to enlarge that space.

While knowledge of the wider historical context is indispensable for us to understand more fully the story of their struggle, and how their political involvement gave meaning to their identity, their life experiences also enable us to gain insights into how — as social agents of change on two different sides of the political divide — they participated in and contributed to the ongoing struggle through their respective localised, situated practices. As noted by Roxana Waterson, analysing personal narratives at the intersection with history helps us to understand what it was like to live through "interesting times" and gain insights into wider social and political processes.[68] It is this diversity and distinctiveness of individual experiences, offering particular points of view while reflecting the workings of the larger structural forces, that could be the unique contribution of biographical studies to enriching historical understanding.

Notes

1. In Malay the party is called Parti Kebangsaan Melayu Malaya.
2. Aishah Ghani, *Memoir Seorang Pejuang* [*Memoirs of a Fighter*] (Kuala Lumpur: Dewan Bahasa dan Pustaka and Malaysian Education Ministry, 1992), pp. 198–201. The legislation was described by the renowned Malaysian Islamic feminist Zainah Anwar as one of the most "enlightened" in the Muslim world in the early 1980s. See Zainah Anwar, "What Islam, Whose Islam? Sisters in Islam and the Struggle for Women's Rights", in *The Politics of Multiculturalism*, ed. Robert W. Hefner (Honolulu: University of Hawaii Press, 2001), p. 233.
3. According to Zainah, soon after the adoption of this version of the Muslim family law act in 1984 in the Federal Territories, a Syariah judge allegedly asked a woman who objected to her husband taking a second wife as to whether she wanted to obey the laws of Aishah Ghani or the laws of God (Zainah, "What Islam, Whose Islam?" p. 245). Given that Islam comes under the purview of the state, each state's Islamic authority subsequently resisted amending its Muslim family law act accordingly, or enacted a watered down version of the template legislative proposal. For a brief discussion on this, refer to Helen Ting, "Gender Discourse in Malay Politics: Old Wine in New Bottle?" in *Politics in Malaysia: The Malay Dimension*, ed. Edmund Terence Gomez (London and New York: Routledge, 2007), pp. 75–106.
4. According to an informant, the MCP subsequently reinstated their party membership and apologised to them.
5. Shamsiah Fakeh, *Memoir Shamsiah Fakeh: Dari AWAS ke Rejimen Ke-10* [*Memoirs of Shamsiah Fakeh: From AWAS to the 10th Regiment*] (Bangi: Penerbit UKM, 2004).
6. These feature articles in *Dewan Masyarakat* are all by Fatini Yaacob: "Siapa Sebenarnya Shamsiah Fakih?" (Feb. 1991), pp. 15–20; "Pendidikan, Perkahwinan Dan Perceraian Shamsiah" (Mar. 1991), pp. 21–7; "Shamsiah Fakih Ke Bagan Serai" (Apr. 1991), pp. 20–8; "AWAS Pimpinan Shamsiah mengatur Strategi Menentang Penjajah" (May 1991), pp. 20–6; "Punca Penceraian Shamsiah: Boestamam" (June 1991), pp. 22–30; "Shamsiah Dipengaruhi Komunis?" (July 1991), pp. 24–8; "Benarkah Shamsiah 'Wakil' Komunis?" (Aug. 1991), pp. 24–30. In a separate article some years later, Fatini mentioned that she even managed to fly to Changsha, China, to interview Shamsiah herself, but the results of the interview were not permitted to be published (Fatini Yaacob, "Shamsiah Fakeh", *MASSA* [1998]: 36). Though she did not mention why, it is almost certain she was under pressure from the Special Branch.
7. Virginia Helen Dancz, *Women and Party Politics in Peninsular Malaysia* (Oxford: Oxford University Press, 1987); Lenore Manderson, *Women,*

Politics, and Change: The Kaum Ibu UMNO, Malaysia, 1945–1972 (Kuala
Lumpur: Oxford University Press, 1980); PERTIWI, "Aishah Ghani,
Tan Sri Datin Paduka Seri (Dr)", in *Biografi Tokoh Wanita Malaysia*
[*Biographies of Female Personalities in Malaysia*] (Petaling Jaya: Pelanduk
Publication, 2004), pp. 6–8; Sulasiah Munajir, "Aishah Ghani, Tan Sri:
Menjaga Kebajikan Masyarakat" [Aishah Ghani, Tan Sri: Taking Care
of Social Welfare], in *20 Tokoh Wanita* [*Twenty Female Personalities*]
(Bangi: Medium Publication, 2009), pp. 1–8.

8.   Mark Freeman, *Rewriting the Self: History, Memory, Narrative* (London
and New York: Routledge, 1993), pp. 1–24.

9.   See Dorothy Holland and Jean Lave, "History in Person: An Introduc-
tion", in *History in Person: Enduring Struggles, Contentious Practice, Inti-
mate Identities*, ed. Dorothy Holland and Jean Lave (Santa Fe: School of
American Research Press; Oxford: James Currey, 2001), pp. 3–33; Craig
Calhoun, "The Problem of Identity in Collective Action", in *Macro-Micro
Linkages in Sociology*, ed. Joan Huber (Newbury Park, London and New
Delhi: Sage Publications, 1991), pp. 51–75. This issue will be further
discussed in the concluding chapter.

10.   PUTERA stood for Pusat Tenaga Rakyat, which was a coalition of
several Malay grass-roots organisations as well as the MNP; AMCJA
stood for All Malaya Council for Joint Action and was a coalition of an
assortment of Chinese and Indian grass-roots organisations as well as
chambers of commerce, etc.

11.   Helen Ting, "The Politics of National Identity in West Malaysia: Continued Mutation or Critical Transition?" *Southeast Asian Studies* (Kyoto
University) 47, 1 (June 2009): 29–49.

12.   Aishah, *Memoir Seorang Pejuang*, p. 5.
13.   Ibid.
14.   Ibid., p. 4.
15.   Shamsiah Fakeh, *Memoir Shamsiah*, p. 19.
16.   Ibid., p. 29.
17.   Aishah, *Memoir Seorang Pejuang*, p. 23.
18.   Ibid., p. 31.
19.   Ibid., p. 23.
20.   Ibid., p. 35.
21.   Shamsiah, *Memoir Shamsiah*, pp. 84–8.
22.   Fatini, *Dewan Masyarakat* (Aug. 1991), p. 24.
23.   Ibid., pp. 28–30.
24.   Shamsiah, *Memoir Shamsiah*, p. 12.
25.   Ibid., p. 37.
26.   Ibid., p. 13.
27.   Aishah, *Memoir Seorang Pejuang*, pp. 46–7.
28.   Ibid., p. 46.

29. Ibid., p. 47.
30. Ibid., p. 53.
31. Personally, she regarded mastery of English as the key to a much wider horizon and limitless knowledge. She wrote that previously she felt extremely unhappy with her inability to handle conversations in English, especially when she was confronted by situations that required such a skill. When she worked as a radio broadcaster, she constantly needed to translate the news from English into Malay before reading it, which was a very frustrating experience for her. This resulted in an inferiority complex and lack of self-confidence. Ibid., p. 53.
32. Ibid., p. 30.
33. Ibid., p. 31.
34. Ibid., p. 39.
35. She argued that since UMNO was formed through the sacrifice of numerous Malay associations, it was only proper that UMNO give priority to the Malay population, which was far more backward than other ethnic groups. Ibid., p. 101.
36. Ibid., p. 220.
37. Ibid., pp. 219–22.
38. Ibid., p. 221.
39. Ibid., pp. 21–2.
40. Ibid., p. 24.
41. Ibid.
42. Cheah Boon Kheng, "Sino-Malay Conflicts in Malaya, 1945–1946: Communist Vendetta and Islamic Resistance", *Journal of Southeast Asian Studies* 2, 1 (Mar. 1981): 109.
43. Fatini, "Shamsiah Dipengaruhi Komunis?" p. 24.
44. Shamsiah, *Memoir Shamsiah*, p. 19.
45. Ahmad Salleh was suspected of being a spy in the guerrilla forces. He admitted that he came out of the jungle with a telegram from the Tunku assuring him that he would not be prosecuted.
46. Fatini, "Benarkah Shamsiah 'Wakil' Komunis?" p. 29.
47. Shamsiah, *Memoir Shamsiah*, p. 132.
48. Wazir Jahan Karim, "Malay Women's Movements: Leadership and Processes of Change", *International Social Science Journal* 35, 98 (1983): 719–31.
49. Aishah, *Memoir Seorang Pejuang*, pp. 38–40, 110.
50. Ibid., p. 111.
51. Ibid., p. 112.
52. Shamsiah, *Memoir Shamsiah*, p. 37.
53. Fatini "AWAS Pimpinan Shamsiah mengatur Strategi Menentang Penjajah", p. 21.
54. Fatini, "Shamsiah Fakih Ke Bagan Serai", p. 27.

55. Shamsiah, *Memoir Shamsiah*, p. 44.
56. Ibid., pp. 44–5.
57. Fatini, "Punca Penceraian Shamsiah: Boestamam", p. 22.
58. Ibid., pp. 23, 25.
59. Ibid., p. 25.
60. Ibid., p. 23.
61. Ibid.
62. Shamsiah, *Memoir Shamsiah*, p. 40.
63. Ibid., pp. 43–4.
64. Fatini, "Punca Penceraian Shamsiah: Boestamam", p. 23.
65. Wahi helped her to deliver the baby but parted with her after being attacked by the army. Based on the rumours spread by British intelligence, the MCP was misled to believe that Wahi Anuwar surrendered himself. Shamsiah was upset that Wahi betrayed the cause and became a renegade. That ended Shamsiah's fourth marriage.
66. Her testimony was confirmed by an informant of Fatini, Abdul Rahman Abdullah, who was then tasked to assist her but lost her when attacked by British troops (Fatini, "Benarkah Shamsiah 'Wakil' Komunis?", p. 27).
67. Shamsiah, *Memoir Shamsiah*, pp. 67–72.
68. Roxana Waterson, "Introduction: Analysing Personal Narratives", in *Southeast Asian Lives: Personal Narratives and Historical Experience*, ed. Roxana Waterson (Singapore: NUS Press, 2007), pp. 1–2.

CHAPTER 7

Lily Eberwein: Her Life and Involvement in the Anti-cession Movement in Sarawak

Welyne J. Jehom

This chapter examines the political involvement of Lily Eberwein (1900–80) in what is referred to as the anti-cession movement in Sarawak, now a part of Malaysia. This little-known nationalist movement in the 1940s attempted to retain the "independence" of Sarawak against takeover by Britain. Although it failed to achieve its objective, it did serve to politicise many local people, including women.

Despite being Eurasian by birth, Lily Eberwein identified with the Malay community in the multi-ethnic society of Sarawak and was active as an educationalist and a political leader. She was a pioneer in a number of ways, being the first "Malay" woman offered a job as a telephone operator at the government department in 1927, and then the first "Malay" woman principal of Permaisuri Girls School, the first Malay girls' school in Sarawak, founded in 1930. During the Japanese occupation in Sarawak, the Japanese appointed Eberwein as the leader of the Malay section of the Kaum Ibu, a multi-ethnic women's association.[1] In March 1947 she was elected as the chairperson of the women's wing of the Malay National Union of Sarawak, a leading group in the anti-cession movement.[2] Eberwein resigned from her post as the principal of Permaisuri Girls School in 1947 as a gesture of protest against the cession, but she continued her role as an educationalist by establishing new schools.

From a theoretical point of view, the anti-cession movement is a strange nationalist phenomenon because it supported the continuation

Kaum Ibu MNU, Sarawak, 1946. Courtesy of Datuk Sri Hajjah Hafsah Harun

Lily Eberwein Abdullah,
1980. Courtesy of Datuk Sri
Hajjah Hafsah Harun

of the rule of the "White Rajahs" of Sarawak. Sarawak was traditionally under the suzerainty of the Brunei sultan, who ruled through Malay chiefs. In 1841 the British Brooke family took over, and three generations of Brookes managed to maintain their control over this remote and neglected part of Borneo and generate goodwill and support among the local population. As in other parts of Southeast Asia, however, the Japanese occupation during World War II swept away the old regime; and after the war Britain negotiated with the reigning Brooke Rajah to "cede" Sarawak to the British empire, adding it to their other colonies in the region. Politicised by their experience of Japanese rule, local leaders opposed the cession, wishing to keep Sarawak independent of the British empire. Although it may seem odd to label as nationalist a movement that supported one form of British rule, that of the Brookes, against another, the British empire, it is understandable from the point of view of local Malay elites who identified the Brookes with their long-standing political domination in Sarawak, and from the point of view of the anti-cession movement's vision of a new future for their independent nation.

Focusing on Lily Eberwein helps to draw attention to the involvement of women in the anti-cession movement, a matter that has largely been neglected in historical works — although women's participation has been mentioned by Sabihah Osman,[3] Hasbie Sulaiman,[4] Sanib Said[5] and Robert Reece.[6] Nordi Archie, who wrote about the participation and the role of women in Sarawak politics between 1946 and 1996, briefly discussed their early political engagement in the anti-cession movement in 1946.[7] This chapter is based on very limited archival sources and an interview with Eberwein's daughter who was a former minister of culture, youth and sport in Sarawak, Datuk Sri Hajjah Hafsah Harun.[8]

Historical Background

Sarawak is located on the island of Borneo, separated from West Malaysia (Peninsular Malaysia) by the South China Sea. (For place names in this chapter, see map 5.) It is one of the two states that have made up East Malaysia since the formation of the Federation of Malaysia in 1963. Among the more than 40 ethnic groups in Sarawak, the major ones are the Iban, Chinese and Malay, followed by Bidayuh, Melanau, Orang Ulu and other indigenous groups. Terminology is loose: Ibans and Bidayuh have often been referred to as Dayaks.

Table 1 gives the statistics for the ethnic groups in 1947. The category "Other indigenous" includes groups such as Kayan, Kenyah, Penan, Kelabit, Bisaya, Kajang and Sembop, while the category "Others" includes Indians.

Table 1   Sarawak population by ethnic group, 1947[9]

Malay	97,469
Sea Dayak [Iban]	190,326
Land Dayak [Bidayuh]	42,195
Melanau	35,560
Other indigenous	29,867
Chinese	145,158
Others	5,719
European	691
Total	546,385

Malays in Sarawak were divided into the aristocratic elite (*perabangan*) and commoners — the latter were mainly fishermen, petty traders involved in riverine trade with indigenous people of the interior, and farmers growing rice, coconut and rubber.[10] The indigenous groups practised shifting cultivation, planted sago, or lived by fishing.[11] Chinese cultivation concentrated on smallholdings of cash crops such as rubber and pepper.[12]

Although Malays were a non-indigenous minority, they dominated the area politically. Sarawak was ruled by the Malay Brunei sultanate until the arrival and involvement of James Brooke in the "Sarawak affair" in 1839, when Sarawak was in rebellion against the central power. Brooke assisted the sultan's representative and brought peace to the area, for which he was rewarded in 1841 with the title of Rajah of Sarawak. According to Sanib, "James Brooke and the 'dynasty' which he founded in Sarawak, seen in a larger context of the Malay world, was just another of those Malay kingdoms that mark the history of the archipelago."[13] However, Reece has argued that the Brooke Raj should also be seen as part of the development of European imperialism in insular Southeast Asia, rendering ambiguous later objections to the takeover of Sarawak by the British colonial office. Nevertheless, the Brooke Raj depended on the Malay aristocratic elite to rule Sarawak. In a country where immigrant Malays had been accustomed to rule, apparently there was little objection to having another

The Anti-cession Movement in Sarawak

1839	Arrival and involvement of James Brooke in "Sarawak affair"
1841	Sultan of Brunei rewards James Brooke with title of Rajah of Sarawak
1917	Last White Rajah of Sarawak, Charles Vyner Brooke, takes up his post
1941–45	Japanese occupation of Sarawak
Feb. 1946	Britain announces that Rajah Vyner Brooke has decided to cede his country to the British Crown
July 1946	Sarawak becomes a Crown Colony
1946	Beginning of anti-cession movement
1963	Formation of the Federation of Malaysia, including Malayan Peninsula, Sarawak and Sabah

kind of foreigner as rajah. Under the Brookes, members of the traditional Malay elite were recruited to hold highly respected posts in the civil service, where they gained administrative experience, subordinate only to the Brookes and their European officers.[14]

The last White Rajah of Sarawak, Charles Vyner Brooke, took up his post in 1917 and was forced out of power by the Japanese during World War II. After the war he decided that the best future for Sarawak was to become a British Crown Colony, and so, on 6 February 1946, the colonial secretary announced in the British Parliament that Rajah Vyner Brooke had decided to cede his country to the British Crown. The decision to cede[15] Sarawak to the British Crown was made without consulting the Rajah Muda (Prince) Anthony Brooke,[16] who expected to become the White Rajah after his uncle, Vyner Brooke. According to Reece, "It may have been that his nephew's (Anthony) inflexibility in negotiations with the Colonial Office finally persuaded the Rajah that he should not succeed him and that Sarawak should instead become the colony of the Crown."[17]

During the 1930s, officials of the Colonial Office had toyed with the idea of taking over the Sarawak government from the Brooke regime and considered potential economic opportunities opened up by such a move. At the end of World War II, access to rubber and oil in Sarawak acquired a greater priority in view of the impending independence to be granted to India and Burma.[18] The British arranged with Rajah Brooke for Sarawak to become a Crown Colony on 1 July 1946.[19] Sarawak was to remain under British administration until it joined the Malayan Peninsula with Sabah to form the Federation of Malaysia in 1963. The loss of Sarawak's independence in 1946 was resisted by elements within it, in what was called the "anti-cession movement". This movement indicated the politicisation of important sections of the population in the previous decade.

The Anti-cession Movement

Until the late 1930s, state politics in Sarawak was confined to the Brooke family and the 70 to 80 Europeans in the Sarawak Service.[20] Traditional Malay and a handful of Chinese elites monopolised the representation of native and Chinese interests. Then Malays and Chinese began forming communal organisations that threatened to bypass the traditional leadership. The Ibans also began to assert themselves by establishing a communally based cooperative aimed at competing with Chinese traders.

The catalyst for this social change was education. Christian churches had established mission schools, and the Chinese had also set up schools privately. Elite Malays had the opportunity to be prepared for clerical government posts in the National College, which was founded by the government in 1919.[21] Government provision for Iban education was negligible. However, in the early 1930s there was a considerable increase in educational opportunities in the Sarawak capital, Kuching.[22]

While schooling was spreading among all communities, particularly in the larger towns, employment opportunities were not. The Native Officer Service remained the monopoly of the *perabangan* in spite of the growing number of educated Malays and Ibans who were much better qualified. It was not until 1941 that the government appointed the first Malay native officer who was not an aristocrat. By 1941, there were a substantial number of young educated people of all races whose expectations could not be satisfied by either the Brooke government or the traditional Malay and Chinese leadership.[23]

Fajar Sarawak,[24] founded in 1930 by a small group of educated Malays of non-aristocratic origin, was the first Malay-language newspaper in Sarawak. It showed the first stirrings of Malay political awareness: it was very critical of the *perabangan*, describing them as being more concerned with their wealth than with helping poor Malays, and also hinted that the *perabangan* were doing very little to justify the position of prestige and authority that they had traditionally enjoyed. However, the paper disappeared after a few months, due to lack of support and to active opposition by the *perabangan*.[25]

Haji Abdul Rahman pursued the idea of a pan-Malay organisation, which had been suggested by one of the founders of *Fajar Sarawak*, Rakawi Yusoff. Thus, 1939 saw the formation of Persatuan Melayu Sarawak (Sarawak Malay Union), which was renamed Persatuan Melayu Kebangsaan Sarawak (Malay National Union, MNU) after World War II.[26] Among its many objectives were: to unite Malays and work together for their advancement; to promote business, education, culture and the Malay language; and to protect the Islamic faith.[27] However, the most significant objective that showed dissatisfaction with the traditional form of representation through the *perabangan* was that the MNU aimed to liaise between Malays and the government.[28] Through the MNU, younger Malays sensed that to improve in their social and economic condition, they would have to bypass the *perabangan*.

Before the Japanese invasion, then, there were already manifestations of discontent among the newly educated generation vis-à-vis the traditional leadership. The Japanese regime broke the myth of European political and cultural supremacy. At that time, Ibans were for the first time given the opportunity to participate in government administration by the Japanese. While the Japanese occupation did not provide opportunities for political activity, it did inspire people in Sarawak with the self-confidence to adopt a political stance and to organise what amounted to political parties. By the end of the war, therefore, all the main ethnic groups in Sarawak had become politicised.[29] Subsequently, the MNU, the China Distress Relief Fund committees, and the Dayaks Cooperative Society became the precursors of post-war political parties, two of them in response to the cession controversy in early 1946.

During World War II the Malay National Union (MNU) and educated Malays were not favoured by the Japanese, who followed the Brooke style of governing the masses through the traditional elite.[30] Nevertheless, networks among MNU members were maintained and their branches were revived after World War II, serving the cause of anti-cessionists in mobilising mass support within the Malay community.[31]

Following the announcement on 6 February 1946 by the rajah that the British Crown had consented to taking over Sarawak, the MNU and Sarawak Dayak Association (SDA) emerged as Sarawak's first political parties. For many months, SDA leaders could not come to a clear stand on cession. Both organisations were apprehensive of Chinese domination. There were obstacles before the MNU and SDA could cooperate, due to suspicion that the former were simply using the latter to meet their own ends: this suspicion was fuelled by the patronising attitude to indigenous Sarawakians among MNU conservatives. However, agreement on cooperation was finally achieved as the Ibans were convinced by the close personal friendship between Robert Jitam and Mohd. Nor, and by Suhaily bin Matlayeir, who knew most of the Ibans in Kuching and spoke their language.[32] However, from July until October 1946, the MNU faced internal conflict between the conservatives and younger activists. The latter were mostly English-educated Malays of non-aristocratic origin who found they had more in common politically with Robert Jitam of SDA. MNU members wished to see a reinstatement of the rajah, but not necessarily for the same reasons. For the traditional elite, reinstatement of the Brookes meant a return to the status quo in which they had occupied positions of power and prestige.[33] The motivation of younger Malays in the MNU was more complex because while some just wanted the restoration of Brooke rule, others wanted self-government as promised in the 1941 constitution, which the Rajah had introduced just before the Japanese occupation.[34]

After the war, the rajah made plans to return to Sarawak in March 1946 to revive the 1941 constitution. In order to show that he was ceding the territory to Britain in a proper constitutional manner, the rajah called a meeting of the Council Negri (Council of State), which was held from 15 to 17 May 1946, solely for the purpose of passing the cession bill. Although 10 of the 16 Malay members voted against the bill, most European members (seven out of ten) voted in favour, and the cession bill was passed by 18 votes to 16 on a show of hands.[35] In a cable sent to British Prime Minister Clement Attlee, the Malay leaders Datu Patinggi and Abang Haji Zaini stated that cession did not have the lawful assent of the representatives of the indigenous people and that five of the native members who had voted for cession were "under monetary influence".[36]

The anti-cession campaign took the form of expressions of loyalty to Bertram and Anthony Brooke, Rajah Vyner Brooke's brother and nephew respectively.[37] Datu Patinggi invited Bertram and his son Anthony, who was regarded as the rajah's successor, to return to Sarawak to initiate fresh discussions on the question of cession. In his letter opposing cession Datu Patinggi included a memorandum from MNU leaders and village heads, dated 12 March, pleading that if the rajah felt unable to continue taking charge of the government he should hand over to Anthony Brooke.[38] The anti-cession movement, spearheaded by the MNU, was under way.

After the announcement of cession, there were mixed feelings among the Chinese in Sarawak. Some Chinese assumed that Sarawak would form part of the Malayan Union and that the Sarawak Chinese would enjoy the rights of Malayan Union citizenship. Others mentioned that "all we want is to have our status raised so that we can enjoy equal rights with the natives", while some, although concerned that cession might bring an increase in taxation, looked forward to the development that they anticipated colonial status would bring about. Mission-educated Chinese who had a stake in economic development and modernisation but appreciated many of the features of personal rule were uncertain whether the new government would be able to exercise the same control over some of the Ibans of the interior, whose recent headhunting exploits were well known. Among the Ibans, only those who were mission-educated were aware of the cession. The other Ibans and most of the upriver people continued to think for some time that the rajah was still in authority.[39]

The differing perceptions and reactions of the many ethnic groups in Sarawak determined the amount of support and participation in the anti-cession movement. However, published accounts of the movement give scant attention to women's role in it. The remainder of this chapter focuses on the life of Lily Eberwein. The other important issue that is of interest here is whether those women thought of their action as political and of themselves as nationalists.

Locating Malay Women in the Anti-cession Movement

Among the Malays educated before World War II were women who had access to the first Malay girls' school, Sekolah Permaisuri, which did not open until 1930. Up until that time, limited modern education was accessible only to aristocratic Malay girls.[40] Although the kind of education available to Malay girls before World War II was intended merely to improve their feminine skills, nonetheless a few of these

Malay women excelled in their studies and pursued teaching careers. A student of Lily Eberwein, Ajibah Abol, who studied at Sekolah Permaisuri, later pursued a teaching career in the same school. Malay women were not visible in career advancement until after the 1950s.[41]

The Japanese occupation gave women in Sarawak their first taste of being in associations and working together. Ethnic-based associations were encouraged during the Japanese occupation between 1941 and 1945.[42] These associations were responsible for organising demonstrations of loyalty and cultural events to celebrate the Japanese emperor's birthday and war heroes. The Japanese also sponsored the setting up of a women's association known as Kaum Ibu (Women's Group), which included representatives of the four major ethnic groups. Its leaders were Eberwein, the headmistress of Permaisuri Girls School, for the Malay section; Mary Ong, the daughter of Ong Tiang Swee, a trained nurse, for the Chinese; Barbara Bay (Bayang) of the Dayaks Cooperative Association (Syarikat Kerjasama Dayak) for the Ibans; and Mrs Gopal, the wife of an Indian doctor, to represent the Indians. Their tasks in Kaum Ibu were to collect unused and recyclable metal and to organise fairs to raise funds for Japanese soldiers. Kaum Ibu was also responsible for organising singing and dancing for such events. Apart from that, Kaum Ibu was responsible for encouraging women to grow tapioca as a substitute for rice, which was in short supply.[43]

These women from the four ethnic groups were given an opportunity to create networks in carrying out the tasks given to them by the Japanese. Furthermore, their involvement in the association indirectly gave them self-confidence and some encouragement to become interested in politics even if they did not know the meaning of politics and being political. With this experience behind them, some of the women — and for our case here, Eberwein — took a further step to become politically active in the anti-cession movement in 1946.

The Life of Lily Eberwein Abdullah

Lily Eberwein Abdullah was born in 1900 and passed away in 1980. Her father, John Eberwein, a Eurasian of Dutch and Scottish descent from Cocos Island, was a relative of the Clooney Ross family, rulers of that island. He worked with the Straits Steamship Company as the captain of the *Rajah Brooke*. Like many other European businessmen,

Eberwein's father looked for a local female partner when he was in Sarawak. The difference between John Eberwein and the others was that while the latter took local women as mistresses, John married a local Malay woman, Maznah bte. Ali bin Alang of Simanggang, and eventually brought her to live in Singapore, where they had two children, Lily and Edward. Although the family followed a Christian way of life in Singapore and the children had a Christian upbringing, Maznah continued to practise as a Muslim.

Eberwein attended St. Mary's Mission School in Kuching, Sarawak, until she was eight years old and then continued her studies at Raffles Girls School in Singapore. When her father died suddenly, however, she returned to Kuching with her mother and rejoined St. Mary's Mission School, where she completed standard seven (equivalent to form three, age 15).[44]

After John Eberwein died and the family returned to Kuching, their lifestyle changed completely. Eberwein had to adjust to a Muslim Malay upbringing, denoted by the addition of Abdullah to her name. In an interview, her daughter Hafsah Harun explained that her mother's upbringing was different from that of other Malay girls. Having had a European lifestyle in Singapore, when she returned to Kuching she missed her freedom and disliked being confined to the house. She had been accustomed to having male servants to serve her when her father was still alive in Singapore, but back in Kuching she had to serve her uncles. Furthermore, being an educated woman she was very outspoken and independent.

Eberwein converted to Islam in 1913 when she was just 13 years old. She took her time in making this decision, wishing first to learn about the religion. According to Hafsah, her friends in Singapore sent her papers and books to read on Islam, and she also learned from her immediate family members. Apparently her knowledge about her new religion impressed her neighbours, to the extent that many people in the village sent their sons to Eberwein to learn to read the Quran. This gesture showed how highly the people in the village trusted her and respected her, because at that time and in that setting, women were rarely consulted for religious teaching. Eberwein had become accepted, and identified herself, as a Muslim Malay, terms that were seen as inseparable. Hafsah explained that acceptance by people in the village was not really an issue because Eberwein was related to about half of them.

In 1927 Lily Eberwein became the first Malay woman to work in a government department when a Mr Tate, the director of the local telephone company, recruited her to work as a telephone operator (the telephone company was a government enterprise). She had an excellent command of both Malay and English, as was required of a telephone operator, and her father had been a family friend of Mr Tate's. In 1929 she resigned from this post when the Brooke government appointed her as the principal of the Permaisuri Malay Girls School, which was opened in Kuching in 1930. Through her educational activities, both religious and secular, she became known as Cikgu (teacher) Lily.

She was over the age for marriage by that time. She was a single woman until 1938, when she married and proceeded to have three daughters, with the first, Hasnah, being born in 1940. Her husband, Harun bin Haris, was ten years her junior, with only five years of primary education, and worked in the Sarawak Police Constabulary. Hafsah recalled that her father was very supportive of her mother's involvement in the anti-cession movement and her passion for education. He respected her as a woman and as a wife. In Sarawak at that time, being married at a later age and having a much younger husband would definitely have been controversial. However, Eberwein seemed to be able to take it all in her stride. She was highly respected, especially among Malay people, because of her dedication to educating Malay girls.

Lily Eberwein as a Nationalist Woman Leader in the Anti-cession Movement

Lily Eberwein's first step into the overtly political arena came when the women's wing of the Malay National Union, Kaum Ibu MNU, was established on 16 March 1947. Eberwein was elected the organisation's chairperson at its inaugural meeting of more than 1,000 Malay women members. Reece later commented, "In pre-war times, Malay women never appeared in public without covering their heads and it must have seemed an extraordinary development that they should now be speaking on a platform and taking part in politics."[45] Nonetheless, that platform was not new to Eberwein as she had led a public life for many years. An editor of *Sarawak Tribune*, describing the meeting as "History in the Making", was struck by the range of topics addressed by the speakers, which included Malay nationalist movements, Sarawak history, the backwardness of women in Sarawak and their demand for rights. The editor reflected:

> What a far cry the women of today are from their grandmothers…
> There is no trace of bashfulness that so characterized a woman in
> the old days when making a public appearance, and the woman
> of today stands out on just as firm and equal a ground as that of
> any man, in full realization of the part they have to play in the
> country.[46]

Reece stated that "like the younger group within the MNU, the leadership of the *Kaum Ibu* represented a movement towards social change".[47]

Eberwein appeared an obvious choice to be elected as the first chairperson of Kaum Ibu MNU. She was well educated and had leadership experience in a women's organisation established by the Japanese during the occupation. She also had full support from her husband and her family.[48]

As can be seen from the earlier description of political events in Sarawak, this was a highly charged period, when the British government faced opposition to cession within Sarawak. The colonial government in Sarawak attempted to curb the activities of local anti-cessionists by issuing an instruction (Circular No. 9) prohibiting all civil servants from getting involved in any way or being liable to instant dismissal from their post. Those who could not comply needed to inform their respective head of department by 31 December 1946. The anti-cessionists refused to acknowledge Circular No. 9 and organised campaigns in Kuching and Sibu to obtain as many signatures as possible to protest against the circular. About 400 government servants, of whom three were non-Malays, were served three months' notice till 1 April 1947 to quit when they made known their inability to comply with the circular to their superior.[49] Most of them were Malay schoolteachers, and this caused the closure of one-third of all government Malay schools.[50] On that day, all 56 teacher trainees of the Sarawak Malay Teachers Training College abandoned their studies in protest against the circular, and 500 other Malays working in schools and non-government occupations also took leave to manifest their displeasure.[51]

Eberwein as the headmistress of the Permaisuri Malay Girls School and her teaching colleague Ajibah Abol were among the Malay schoolteachers who resigned. Ajibah became Eberwein's secretary in the Kaum Ibu MNU, headed by the latter. Eberwein's husband, who was a corporal in the Sarawak Constabulary, resigned soon afterwards. In this case, Eberwein's resignation was her own decision and not governed by her husband's influence. According to Reece, for those who resigned it was a momentous personal decision as well as an act of political commitment, because there was very little prospect of obtaining employment outside government service. Among the 400 who resigned, there were only nine women.[52]

As the anti-cession struggle continued, the closure of these Malay government schools became a serious concern as affected students could not find places in other Malay schools. Four schools in Kuching and another in Sibu were established by those teachers who resigned. In order to assist children of resigned public servants who boycotted government schools, Eberwein helped to establish a religious school for girls and women (*sekolah rakyat*) in the premises of the Masjid Bintangor Haji Taha building.[53] Eberwein and teachers who had re-signed in protest against the circular taught in this and other schools without pay.[54] Hence Eberwein's actions appeared to be balancing two parallel concerns: fighting for Sarawak's political destiny as a nationalist, and providing an education for Malay women to effect social change as an educationalist.

In an interview with the *Straits Times* (Singapore) dated 21 July 1947[55] on the anti-cession movement, Eberwein expressed her con-cern for its impact on Malay education. In the article, titled "Education at a Standstill", she stated that the protest against cession had had the most serious effect on education, which was virtually at a stand-still. She emphasised that the position of education in Sarawak must remain a matter of gravest public concern "for as long as this unhappy controversy lasts", referring to cession. She also stated, "We Malays, in conjunction with the other indigenous races, will fight with unwavering purpose for the redress of the wrong that has been done to our people in the extinction of our nationhood and independence." In the article she clearly identified herself as a member of the Malay community and with the cause of Sarawak's national independence, but also expressed her concern about the effects of the nationalist struggle on education and thus on the people of Sarawak.

In his memoirs, Anthony Brooke clearly recognised the impor-tance of women's role in the anti-cession movement. He specifically highlighted Eberwein's effort, stating that "a new impetus was given to the movement due to the initiative of Chegu (head teacher) Lily

Eberwein, who formed a women's branch of the movement. This met with considerable support from women of all ages from throughout the country."[56]

The MNU sent a group of representatives to meet Brooke in Singapore in February 1947.[57] The Kaum Ibu organised events by petitioning the colonial government and taking part in demonstrations.[58] It also sent a three-member delegation, including Eberwein, to Singapore in July 1947 in anticipation of the arrival there of Kathleen Brooke (the wife of Anthony Brooke) before she proceeded to Sarawak in August 1947 for a tour of the state.[59] Representing her husband, who was banned by the British from entering Sarawak, Kathleen was a force for support of the anti-cession movement. She was accompanied by Eberwein as well as by male members of the MNU. The Kaum Ibu groups that had sprung up around the state since 1946 received Kathleen's tour group with enthusiasm.[60]

Together with Kathleen Brooke, Eberwein and other male and female leaders carried out an arduous rural anti-cession campaign on foot and by boat, travelling to remote longhouses to explain to the longhouse chiefs and get their thumbprints as affirming their opposition to cession. They also sold photos of Anthony Brooke and Sarawak flags to the villages to collect funds. The rural campaign managed to gain the support of 52 Iban penghulu, including Paramount Chief Temenggong Koh and Penghulu Jugah.[61] However, the British administration used its influence to get anti-cessionists, including the latter two, to withdraw their stand.[62]

Based on Hafsah Harun's recollections of her mother's activities during the anti-cession campaign, Eberwein to a certain extent had to sacrifice her time with her young children. Malay women in Sarawak at that time were groomed to be "famous for their skill in weaving sarongs, knitting"[63] and they were expected to stay home taking care of the children. Malay women's activities were all confined to the domestic domain. The anti-cession movement was an exceptional event for Eberwein and other Malay women at that time because they joined in the campaign along with their male counterparts, participating in demonstrations and petitioning the colonial government — and Malay women had their own section in Kaum Ibu even though it was under the male-dominated MNU. Significantly, Hafsah did mention that occasionally, after their meetings, Eberwein complained about her male colleagues, indicating that it was not always easy for her to deal with them.

It is difficult to determine the source of the commitment of Malay women in general and Eberwein in particular to the anti-cession movement, because of the speed of events. Kaum Ibu was created in March 1947, and within a few months women were rallied and campaigning against cession. Although the meeting with Kathleen Brooke in Singapore and her six-month visit to Sarawak until February 1948[64] may have spurred on the Malay women of Sarawak, by that time Kaum Ibu had already been established, with more than 1,000 Malay women members at the inaugural meeting.

Even for Eberwein, who had more exposure to the outside world than most other Malay women in Sarawak, political activity was not something she had dreamed of, according to her daughter Hafsah. However, she was accompanied to meetings by Ajibah Abol, and the two of them made a good team. Whether or not Eberwein saw herself as a political activist, she was committed to social change through education for Malay girls, as was shown by her lifelong leadership in teaching.

Eberwein's Legacy

After the failure of the anti-cession movement, Eberwein turned her attention mainly to education. In 1950 she established the Satok English School (SES). According to her daughter Hafsah, she started the school because she realised the importance of the English language as a medium of communication, especially in the government service. SES was a stepping stone for students to pursue their studies in government schools.

The school never received any funds from the government, and this showed Eberwein's true dedication to it. According to Hafsah, there were six classes up to form two, each having two sessions with five or six teachers, and the school survived solely on the sale of handicrafts and collection of funds from former students. The students were taught not just the normal curriculum but to be disciplined and determined. The school was multi-ethnic, taking Malay, Iban, Bidayuh, Chinese and Indian students. Although mainly for girls, the school also admitted a few boys from the boys' home who were sent to SES because they were too old to enter public school. The troublesome students from the boys' home were made to feel important, and gradually they became well behaved.

Although Eberwein was a very active anti-cessionist, she never joined any political party. Nevertheless, in 1950 she became the first woman to be appointed as a councillor of the Kuching Municipal Council — another occasion on which she was a pioneer for women in public life in Sarawak. She participated actively in various voluntary organisations, such as the Prisoners' Aid Society, Anti-Tuberculosis Association Sarawak and Red Cross. She remained the chairman of Kaum Ibu in the Malay National Union of Sarawak until 1960, when she also retired from her own school, Satok English School. After that she occasionally assisted Hafsah, who replaced her as the school principal.

In recognition of her services, Eberwein was given two Sarawak state awards after the Malaysian federation was formed, and she was named an exemplary teacher of Malaysia in 1977. After being a diabetic for 20 years, Cikgu Lily Eberwein died in 1980.

Although Eberwein was heavily involved in the anti-cession movement, her daughter claimed that from what she understood, her mother did not see herself as a politician and was probably unaware of being a nationalist leader: she just saw herself as a protester against the cession of Sarawak to British colonialism. According to Hafsah, Eberwein saw her role in the Malay National Union of Sarawak as participating in a non-governmental organisation, not a political movement. Evidence of her unwillingness to belong to a political party is seen also in her later life. As Hafsah said, "When Sarawak joined Malaysia, she [Eberwein] did not get involved in any political parties." Hafsah went on to point out that Eberwein's colleague Ajibah Abol "was one of her former students who were active in politics but it was easier for her because she was single", although she admitted that if a woman were single she could be subjected to gossip.

In Sarawak there is still only a limited place for women in the public sphere, especially in politics. Although Eberwein herself did not participate in public political life after the anti-cession movement ended, she inspired the few women politicians Sarawak had soon after it joined in the formation of Malaysia in 1963. Ajibah, Eberwein's former student and colleague whom she appointed as her secretary in Kaum Ibu MNU, became the first woman to win a seat in the state parliament — a feat she accomplished in 1970 and again in 1974. She was appointed the minister of welfare and culture for Sarawak but died in 1976 after a short illness. The second woman who entered the

Sarawak political scene was Hafsah Harun, Eberwein's daughter. In the 1976 election Hafsah took over the seat left empty by Ajibah's death. Subsequently, in 1981 she was appointed minister of culture, youth and sport. Her last position as a minister, before she retired as a politician in 1987, was in the Sarawak Ministry of Social Development.

Hafsah expressed fond memories of her upbringing and regarded her mother as an exceptional woman. She stated that her mother had instilled exceptional qualities in her and her sisters — to be independent and outspoken, and to have determination. She brought her daughters to meetings and left them in the next room. Hafsah claimed this experience caused her to perceive herself as a woman politician in the making. She had a very close relationship with her mother, especially after her mother established the Satok English School. Her mother was her role model. Hafsah was taught to speak her mind and was allowed to disagree on matters with a clear conscience. Her mother taught her daughters about religion. She was very strict, but at the same time she was more liberal than most Malay mothers in bringing up her daughters. They were allowed to go out at night but had to come back at a certain time and be escorted at all times.

Conclusion: Reflections on Eberwein's Evolving Identity

Eberwein was born Eurasian, and when her father was still alive she had the opportunity to travel and experience a European home and Christian upbringing, as well as an English-medium school in Singapore. Back in Sarawak, her life and identity changed when she converted to Islam. She obtained Islamic knowledge that made her a respected Quran teacher in her village, which was rare for a woman at that time. Eberwein dressed in Malay clothing — the long skirt and blouse called the baju kurung — covered her head when she went out in public, read and taught the Quran to village boys at the request of their parents, married a Muslim man and lived a Muslim life, and spoke Malay. This behaviour showed that she had adopted a Malay identity, and for that reason the Japanese appointed her as the leader of the Malay section of the women's association Kaum Ibu. Eberwein opened a religious school for Malay girls and women after her resignation from Permaisuri Malay Girls School in 1947, and she started the Satok English School in 1950 upon seeing the importance of English as a language of communication. She was concerned about

Malay women's education because she hoped Sarawak women could become educated and independent like herself.

Thus, Lily Eberwein Abdullah's life demonstrates her involvement in Malay society beyond her leadership of Kaum Ibu MNU in the unusual, brief and failed nationalist movement that was the anti-cession movement in Sarawak. More generally, she earned a place in Sarawak history by inspiring Malay women of her generation and afterwards to play a part in public life.

Notes

1. R.H.W. Reece, *The Name of Brooke: The End of White Rajah Rule in Sarawak* (Kuala Lumpur and New York: Oxford University Press, 1982), pp. 145–6.
2. Ibid., p. 274.
3. Sabihah Osman, "The Malay-Muslim Response to Cession of Sarawak to the British Crown 1946–1951", *Jebat: Malaysian Journal of History, Politics and Strategic Studies* 18 (1990): 145–74.
4. Haji Mohd. Hasbie Sulaiman, *Perjuangan Anti-cession Sarawak: Peranan utama Persatuan Kebangsaan Melayu Sarawak* [*Sarawak Anti-cession Struggle: The Important Role of the Sarawak Malay Nationalist Association*] (Kuching: PKMS/SAMASA Press, 1989).
5. Sanib Said, *Malay Politics in Sarawak 1946–1966: The Search for Unity and Political Ascendancy* (Singapore: Oxford University Press, 1985).
6. Reece, *Name of Brooke*.
7. In his academic exercise in 1997–98 Nordi Archie wrote a section on Lily Eberwein ("Wanita dan Politik Sarawak 1946–1996: Penglibatan, Peranandan Tokoh" [Women and Sarawak Politics 1946–1996: Involvement, Role and Leaders], Academic exercise, History Department, Universiti Malaya, 1997/98), among other women leaders in Sarawak, describing her background and involvement in the anti-cession movement in 1946.
8. Datuk Sri Hajjah Hafsah Harun started her career as a minister at the Chief Minister's Office in July 1976 and was appointed as Sarawak's minister of culture, youth and sport in 1981. Her last position as a minister before she retired as a politician in 1987 was at the Ministry of Social Development of Sarawak.
9. The source of statistics is Y.L. Lee, "The Population of British Borneo", *Population Studies* 15, 3 (Mar. 1962): 226–43.
10. Ibid., p. 348.
11. Ibid., p. 346; Sanib, *Malay Politics in Sarawak*, p. 8.
12. Lee, "Population of British Borneo", p. 347.

13. Sanib, *Malay Politics in Sarawak*, p. 11.

14. Sabihah, "Malay-Muslim Response", p. 145.

15. In the circumstances, "cession" is an odd word for what happened in 1946. Runciman states categorically that by the Order in Council on 26 June 1946, "Sarawak was 'annexed', not ceded to His Majesty's dominions" (Steven Runciman, *The White Rajahs: A History of Sarawak from 1841 to 1946* [Cambridge: Cambridge University Press, 1960]), p. 301.

16. According to Reece, the period of Anthony Brooke's administration of Sarawak from April until September 1939 is of some interest; but there are very few records, and those that have survived consist largely of complaints made about him by his critics (Reece, *Name of Brooke*, pp. 66–7).

17. Ibid., p. 192.

18. Sabihah, "Malay-Muslim Response", p. 148.

19. See Runciman, *White Rajahs*; Reece, *Name of Brooke*, chapter 8; and R.H.W. Reece, *The White Rajahs of Sarawak, a Borneo Dynasty* (Singapore: Archipelago Press, 2004).

20. Reece, *Name of Brooke*, p. 128.

21. Sanib, *Malay Politics in Sarawak*, p. 24.

22. The Merpati Jepang School opened in 1930. Enche Buyong School opened in 1931, and in the same year two existing schools were merged to form the government-sponsored Malay College, which was intended to train Malays as native officers and teachers. By 1933 enrolment had reached 400, bringing the number of students in Malay schools in Kuching up to 600 (three times the 1921 enrolment). Most important, Malay-language education was no longer restricted to the children of elite families. The first Malay girls' school, the Sekolah Permaisuri, opened in 1930; and by the late 1930s a handful of Malays had attended the Sultan Idris Training College in Malaya. The English-medium schools in Kuching, St. Thomas (Church of England) and St. Joseph (Roman Catholic), had become popular with the Chinese because of the growing importance of English. These two schools were also attracting some Malays. Clerkships in government departments required proficiency in English and were normally filled by mission school graduates. Christian missionaries were working among the Ibans in the Second Division, opening schools, and Reece stated: "Iban prosperity … had also brought about something of a social revolution since the early 1920s. St. Augustine's School …, St. Luke's …, St. Andrew's and other schools later opened … in response to Iban requests. Although reduced income from rubber in the early 1930s made it difficult for parents to send their children to school, the Iban demand for education was insatiable" (Reece, *Name of Brooke*, p. 129).

23. Ibid., p. 130.

24. Rakawi Yusoff, the driving force of *Fajar Sarawak*, was a former customs officer who died in 1936. He was a Malay representative on the Kuching Municipal Board in 1934–35 and was one of the few Sarawak Malays who had links with developments in Malaya. A member from 1934 of the Persaudaraan Sahabat Pena Malaya, the first vehicle of Malay cultural nationalism, he had probably been in contact with members of the Kesatuan Melayu Singapore (Singapore Malay Union), established in 1926 (Ibid., p. 132).

25. Ibid., p. 134.

26. Ibid., p. 160.

27. MNU objectives were similar to those of contemporary associations on the Malayan Peninsula (Ibid., p. 135).

28. Ibid.; Sabihah, "Malay-Muslim Response", p. 149.

29. Reece, *Name of Brooke*, p. 128.

30. Ibid.; Sabihah, "Malay-Muslim Response".

31. Reece, *Name of Brooke*, p. 135.

32. Ibid., p. 249.

33. Ibid.

34. Ibid., p. 250.

35. Ibid., pp. 236–7; Sabihah, "Malay-Muslim Response", p. 148.

36. Reece, *Name of Brooke*, p. 259.

37. Bertram's birthday on 8 August, which was designated as a public holiday, was marked by all government offices and most shops. Malay National Union members gathered at the Indian mosque, where the Sarawak anthem was sung and a number of speeches were made before the imam closed the meeting (Ibid.).

38. Ibid., p. 219.

39. Ibid., pp. 208–9. Christopher Dawson of the Malayan Civil Service, who was elected to act as chief secretary of the new colonial government if the cession went through, felt that as long as there was an undertaking that the rajah's replacement would visit them from time to time, "simple Dayaks" would accept cession (Ibid., p. 221).

40. See Margaret A.L. Brooke, *My Life in Sarawak* (London: Oxford University Press, 1913).

41. See Abg. Yusoff Puteh, *Portraits of Grace and Charm* (Kuching: SHOBRA, 1990); and Ministry of Culture, Sports and Youth, *Penyertaan Kita/Our Participation* (Kuching: State Government of Sarawak, 1983).

42. The Japanese attempted to garner support from the natives of Sarawak through the latter's participation in the Japanese-controlled government. Civil servants were asked (not forced) to remain in their administrative positions to help run the Japanese-controlled government. In fact, a Japanese military decree of 1943 emphasised "the political participation

of natives in the administration of North Borneo (including Sarawak)".
The Ken Sanjikai, or the Prefectural Advisory Council that had been
authorised by the military decree in 1943, chose its councillors from the
old elites. The councillors were supposed to advise the Japanese administration on social and political questions (Hasbie, *Perjuangan Anti-
cession Sarawak*; Sabihah, "Malay-Muslim Response").

43. Hasbie, *Perjuangan Anti-cession Sarawak*, p. 40.
44. There is conflicting information about her educational background. Abg.
    Yusof Puteh (1990) mentioned that she was the first Malay woman to
    be educated at Raffles Girls School in Singapore until standard seven,
    which was equivalent to form three, age 15. However, another source
    written in 1982 by her own daughter, who was then serving in the Chief
    Minister's Department of Sarawak, mentioned that after the untimely
    death of her father, young Lily returned to Kuching, Sarawak, and con-
    tinued her studies until standard seven at St. Mary's Mission School.
    The latter information seems to be more accurate, because the daughter
    still has Lily's school certificate given on completion of form three at St.
    Mary's Mission School.
45. Reece, *Name of Brooke*, p. 274.
46. Ibid., p. 275.
47. Ibid.
48. Interview with Lily's daughter Datuk Hafsah Harun at her residence,
    5 Nov. 2010.
49. Reece, *Name of Brooke*, p. 270.
50. Sabihah, "Malay-Muslim Response", p. 159.
51. Reece, *Name of Brooke*, p. 271.
52. This figure comes from the list of 338 with the names and their respec-
    tive departments published in *Sarawak Tribune* on 3 April 1947 (see
    Hasbie, *Perjuangan Anti-cession Sarawak*, pp. 107–21).
53. The school was closed after only a few months due to a lack of funds
    (Sabihah, "Malay-Muslim Response", p. 161).
54. Ministry of Culture, Sports and Youth, *Penyertaan Kita*.
55. Quoted from "Education at a Standstill", *Straits Times*, 21 July 1947.
56. Quoted from Anthony Brooke, "Operation Peace through Unity", http://
    www.peacethroughunity.info/background-anthonystory6.html. See also
    Hasbie, *Perjuangan Anti-cession Sarawak*; and Sabihah, "Malay-Muslim
    Response".
57. Hasbie, *Perjuangan Anti-cession Sarawak*, p. 103.
58. Ibid., p. 127.
59. Reece, *Name of Brooke*; Sabihah, "Malay-Muslim Response".
60. Reece, *Name of Brooke*; Hasbie, *Perjuangan Anti-cession Sarawak*.
61. Sanib, *Malay Politics in Sarawak*, pp. 49–50.

62. Ibid., p. 54. Evidently the Ibans and others upriver were not aware of the cession. Even many of the educated Ibans in Kuching did not respond positively to the anti-cession campaign. Robert Jitam (who resigned from government service) failed to persuade Iban government servants to do the same in relation to Circular No. 9, and as a response to that he reconstructed the SDA committee so that Alfred Jamuh, who resigned from the Forestry Department, was elected the new SDA president (Reece, *Name of Brooke*, p. 272).

63. Statement from *Jawi Peranakan* in *Sarawak Gazette*, 1 Oct. 1931 (quoted in Sanib, *Malay Politics in Sarawak*, p. 25).

64. "Mrs. Brooke back from Sarawak", *Straits Times*, 18 Feb. 1948, p. 5.

CHAPTER 8

"Minority" Women and the Revolution in the Highlands of Laos: Two Narratives

Vatthana Pholsena

This chapter focuses on two female war veterans of ethnic minority origin who conducted most of their revolutionary activities during the Second Indochina War (1961–75) in southeastern Laos along the "Ho Chi Minh Trail".[1] As women combatants from ethnic minorities, they are arguably the least-known participants of the Pathet Lao, the Communist movement that led the anti-colonial struggle in Laos in the second half of the 20th century.

In recent years, gender has emerged as a fruitful research area in war studies focusing on Asia. In particular, the participation of women in armed independence struggles and/or Communist insurgencies in Southeast Asia has been the focus of remarkable research. Works on "women warriors" have broadened our understanding of the experience of war by exploring the private sphere of combatants' lives, bringing to light the (often unattainable) balance female combatants sought between the traditional demands of their society, the sacrifices of a revolutionary life, and their own desire for freedom and independence. Books by Vina Lanzona[2] and Agnes Khoo[3] studying Huk female insurgents in the Philippines and women Communist fighters in the Malayan anti-colonial struggle, respectively, tackle such issues. Pioneering works by Karen Gottschang Turner and Phan Thanh Hao,[4] Sandra C. Taylor[5] and François Guillemot[6] on North Vietnamese female Communist fighters involved with Viet Minh forces also come to mind.[7] In fact, so important was Vietnamese women's role during

Manivanh. Courtesy of History Museum,
Savannakhet

the wars (especially in the struggle against the Americans) that Turner
and Phan Thanh Hao claim that "an accurate history of the war the
Vietnamese call the 'American War' must recognize Vietnamese
women's contributions to Hanoi's victory in 1975".[8] Yet, Taylor notes
in 1999 that "few books in English have mentioned the Women's Liberation Association, the Vietnam Women's Union, the role of women
in the National Liberation Front, or their participation in the war".[9]
Besides being essential for the writing of a more balanced and complete history of the Indochina Wars, the inclusion of women's voices
is also important as these voices often reflect different perceptions of
war to those of their male contemporaries.[10]

    This chapter aims to go beyond conventional diplomatic and
military histories of the Vietnam wars to examine war from below.
It is concerned with how people were shaped by their wartime experiences. To understand such processes, it is first necessary to explain
the strategic significance of the highlands and the role of ethnic
minorities on the anti-colonial side during the First (1946–54) and
Second Indochina Wars, in conjunction with the Communist ethnic
policy. In guerrilla warfare, the support of the local population is
essential. The local population discussed in this chapter consists of the
highland peoples of southeastern Laos.[11] During the Indochina Wars,
these highlanders were targeted as much by the Lao and Vietnamese

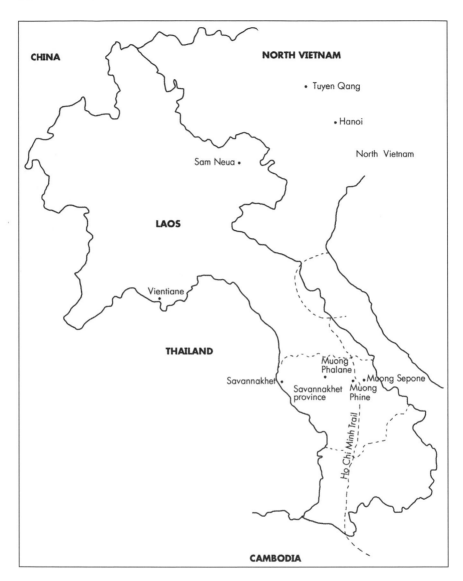

Map 9. Laos

revolutionaries as by the French and, later on, the Americans. All the belligerents saw the mountain areas of southeastern Laos as of crucial strategic importance: the areas became a Viet Minh (the Vietnamese Communist-dominated nationalist front[12]) stronghold during the First Indochina War and, beginning in the early 1960s, the conduit for the

Ho Chi Minh Trail, also known as Duong Mon Truong Son.[13] (For place names in this chapter, see map 9.)

Historical Context

Following the Japanese surrender at the end of World War II, the Lao Issara (Free Lao), the first Lao nationalist movement — founded in 1945 and led by Prince Phetsarath — unilaterally declared the independence of Laos from France and formed a government. However, unable to curb the French military effort to regain control over Laos, the Lao Issara leadership fled to Thailand within six months. Deep divisions in the ranks of the Lao Issara emerged rapidly in the late 1940s, between opponents and supporters of collaboration with France. Some Lao nationalist leaders adopted a policy of strict neutrality — among them was Prince Phetsarath, who until his death in 1959 opposed any foreign intervention in Laos' internal affairs and subsequently left the country and lived in exile for ten years in Thailand. Another member of the Lao royal family and a well-known nationalist leader, Souvanna Phouma (Phetsarath's brother), conversely, returned to Vientiane after the disbanding of the Lao Issara on 25 October 1949 to serve under Laos' constitutional monarchy within the French Union. His half-brother, Souphanouvong, rejected the new political leadership in Vientiane and, in February 1949, formed another political front from the guerrilla forces under his command, which in the early 1950s took the name of Pathet Lao (Lao Nation).[14] Following the dissolution of the Lao Issara in late 1949, he travelled to meet Ho Chi Minh at his headquarters in Tuyen Quang (North Vietnam) to ask for his support. The first congress of Lao Communist leaders was organised there on 13 August 1950, and it resulted in the election of a new resistance government. A subsequent meeting held in North Vietnam in November 1950 provided the Pathet Lao with a pro-Communist nationalist political movement, the Neo Lao Issara (Free Lao Front), which began building battalion-sized fighting forces. This was a broad-based movement designed to draw popular support to the radical faction of the Lao Issara that had abandoned exile in Thailand for the struggle against the French on home soil. It issued a new political programme directed towards every Lao: equality of all races in Laos, unified struggle against the French, and abolition of inequitable taxes.[15] Adoption of this policy for the first time also gave

Lao Communist-Nationalist Movement

1945   Formation of coalition of Lao nationalists, the Lao Issara, which creates a provisional government

1949   Prince Souphanouvong forms his own political movement in the north of Laos

1950   Creation of Neo Lao Issara and government of resistance of the Pathet Lao in North Vietnam

1953   Offensive in Laos of troops of Neo Lao Issara, together with Vietnamese "volunteers". Provinces of Huaphan and Phongsaly in the northeast pass under the control of the Pathet Lao. Total independence of Laos from France

1954   Signing of the Geneva Agreements and withdrawal of France from Indochina. Vietnam is divided at the 17th parallel. The independence and territorial integrity of Laos and Cambodia are reaffirmed. Pathet Lao forces are allowed to regroup in the provinces of Huaphan and Phongsaly while waiting for integration into the country's political system

1955   Creation of Lao Communist party, Phak Pasason Lao (Lao People's Party)

1959   North Vietnamese Communists begin armed struggle to take over South Vietnam by force via southeastern Laos

1968   Escalation of war: intensification of US Army bombings over northern and southeastern Laos

1973   Paris agreements between US and Democratic Republic of Vietnam; ceasefire in Laos; end of US bombardments

1975   Abolition of monarchy in Laos and proclamation of the Lao People's Democratic Republic. Kaysone Phomvihane, Lao Communist Party secretary general, becomes first prime minister of the new regime

the highland populations of non-ethnic Lao origin a role within a political movement where their interests were considered and promoted.

When the Viet Minh learned of Lao aspirations for independence, it sought to play an important role in guiding and supporting early Lao anti-colonialist and nationalist figures, such as Prince Souphanouvong, Kaysone Phomvihane and Nouhak Phoumsavanh. In fact, in the aftermath of World War II the Viet Minh had been active in recruiting Lao individuals along the western border of Vietnam.[16]

In the sparsely populated border regions of Laos and Vietnam, the political situation was extremely confused. Between the start of World War II and 1949, when the Lao Issara movement broke up, several small anti-French resistance groups operated in this area. Some of them were in close contact with the Lao Issara government-in-exile in Bangkok, while others, especially those led by highland chiefs, operated independently.[17] What they all soon had in common was their dependence on Viet Minh support. In some cases, this assistance took the form of rice, money, arms and ammunitions. In others, Vietnamese advisers attached themselves to lowland Lao or highland groups.[18]

By late 1947, it had become evident that the war between the French army and the Viet Minh was going to be a prolonged conflict. The Viet Minh had several reasons for intensifying their efforts to build up military forces and revolutionary bases in Laos (as well as in Cambodia). First, in developing close military and political collaboration with the local Communist movement, the Viet Minh were creating a buffer zone to protect their western flank from attacks by the French troops (especially in southeastern Laos) and to enable their troops to intervene freely in Laos.[19] Second, as in Cambodia, the Democratic Republic of Vietnam[20] considered it essential that the Communist movement expand its membership in Laos and train local cadres so they could lead the struggle side by side with the Vietnamese, thus carrying out a genuine Indochinese revolution. While strategic factors played a crucial part in this decision, the Vietnamese Communists were driven also by an ideological and cultural impetus. They felt a sense of belonging to a wider internationalist movement and believed they ought to play a role in spreading the revolution.[21]

Thus, anti-French resistance forces from late 1947 shifted gradually from western to eastern Laos, that is, away from Thailand and closer to Vietnam. Between the end of 1948 and early 1949, they set up military zones in the highlands of eastern Laos. Here they began to launch armed propaganda activities with the aim of establishing "peoples' power bases".[22] Once highlander support was secured, it was active, and often crucial, in the mountain areas.[23]

In some upland communities a legacy of resistance (some armed, others non-violent) to external control led them to be characterised and promoted as prime supporters of the patriotic revolution by the Communists.[24] There were a series of revolts in the highlands of eastern Laos beginning in 1896, reaching a peak between 1910 and

1916, and finally dying out in the 1930s, all of which expressed resistance to aspects of the French administration. Members of a Mon-Khmer group, the Loven, engaged in armed resistance against the French as early as 1901 led by their chief, Pha Ong Keo, in southeastern Laos. The latter was eventually killed in 1910, but the resistance sentiment was carried on by the Alak highland leader Ong Kommandan until 1937. The skilled chief was eventually shot by the French. However, his son, Sithone Kommandan, who would reach the rank of general in the Pathet Lao army, survived to rally armed opposition to French colonial rule after his release from the Japanese in 1945.[25] Although most of these early rebellions failed because they were scattered and isolated, they showed a desire for freedom and autonomy among some highlanders, as well as their responsiveness to their leaders.[26] The anti-colonial nature of these revolts was thereafter exploited skillfully by Communist agents to demonstrate the timeliness of their own anti-colonialist cause.

The Indochina Wars were as much a political as a military struggle. The Lao and Vietnamese revolutionaries understood that in order to carry through a war of independence, it was vitally necessary to mobilise the rural population by implementing immediate actions at the local level (for instance, providing medical care and schooling, and supplying staple foods) and making it clear through political training that the national revolution was the prelude to a wider social revolution from which the peasantry would largely benefit. Hence the Communists' strategy of involving the upland population in the war effort also included responding to local aspirations for concrete improvement in their general and material welfare. Moreover, the Communists' ethnic policy was not merely a by-product of their war strategy. The policy of national equality and unity was to a great extent influenced by Lenin's own prescriptions.[27] For example, in 1934 the External Direction Bureau of the Indochinese Communist Party warned the Laos section to remember Lenin's strategy of encouraging full liberation for ethnic minorities and of fighting against two dangers, one of which was "regional, patriotic, or chauvinist ideology, since communism recognizes only the class struggle, not the struggle of races".[28] Based on the socialist ideology, the highlanders were expected to follow the path to "progress" by going through all the evolutionary stages — from primitive Communism to feudalism, then to capitalism and finally to socialism.[29]

War and Revolution: Personal Narratives and Historical Experience

Although memoirs and biographies of former revolutionaries (mostly in Lao) began appearing in bookshops and markets in Vientiane in the early 1990s, they overwhelmingly portrayed the lives of male Lao leaders. Only one biographical memoir of a (lowland) Lao woman revolutionary, Khampeng Boupha, has been published (in Lao and English) in the last 15 years.[30] Khampeng Boupha, the first woman to be elected as a member of parliament and to the Central Committee of the Lao People's Revolutionary Party, was a Communist cadre who held mostly intellectual and political positions.[31] In her memoir, she mentions several other Lao women revolutionaries[32] who were awarded the highly prestigious Medal of National Heroes and Heroines for their military actions and courage. Unfortunately, their stories are unknown. To our knowledge, these women never published their memoirs, and none of them had their revolutionary lives narrated. Some of them no doubt died during the war: it is not uncommon for the title of National Hero to be granted posthumously as it is often associated with the sacrifice of one's life for the country.

Manivanh and Khamla[33] are the two "minority" women fighters in the Lao revolutionary movement whose oral testimonies will be examined in this chapter. These two militants belonged to the second generation of indigenous revolutionaries — the first one was formed by resistant fighters who participated in the struggle against the French (see above) — who were recruited between the mid-1950s and the late 1960s in Pathet Lao-controlled areas in southeastern Laos. Although their testimonies have historical value (they contain information on historical facts such as guerrilla-controlled areas, battle dates and guerrilla activities), this chapter is more interested in these revolutionary fighters for what their stories reveal about their own understanding of historical events. Their subjectivity plays an integral role in the constitution of their past: that is, what they believed they were doing, and what they now think they did. In other words, their narrated past matters also because of its relation to the present.[34] These two female war veterans' remembrances of their past are, of course, selective and subjective, evoking only certain memories. Yet, by analysing what such inconsistencies reveal in terms of deeper psychological and emotional significance, their narratives in the end unveil characteristics of the "good Montagnards ("highlanders" in

French)" that are not related in wartime propaganda literature and the carefully vetted memoirs of official leaders. The personal experiences of historical events and social changes that every personal narrative reveals in its own specific way are significant. As the anthropologist Roxana Waterson has stressed, "it is the combination of the deeply personal, and the social and political, embedded as it is in the manner of telling, which can make the life history such a special kind of document".[35] It is this unique positioning of the subject-narrator — linking the private and the public worlds of experience — that gives the narrative its authenticity, not some assessment of the individual's story as being "representative" or "typical".[36]

Motivations

Manivanh was a very well-known revolutionary figure in Savannakhet province. She was indeed the only female revolutionary cadre who was awarded the regime's highest military title of National Hero in the whole province (out of the total of three that were awarded to revolutionary fighters in Savannakhet; the two other National Heroes — both men — were Akum, a mobilising cadre of Bru Tri origin, and Sikhai, a Phuthai army officer).[37] Manivanh was born in a Katang village a few kilometres from the district centre of Muang Phine around the mid-1940s.[38] After some formal introductions, she began to unfold the story of her revolutionary life:

> I would like to tell you my story. Since I was 14, my parents ... as I told you, I was an orphan ... At the age of 14, I stayed with my uncles and aunts.... I was working for the revolution. Before that, to start with, soldiers, agents had been carrying out their underground propaganda activities in the forests ... At the very beginning they were our agents, *Issara* agents. Before getting involved, my motivations were as follows: first, I was an orphan — both my parents had died. I was living with my uncles and aunts. I wasn't angry; I didn't hold any sentiments of hatred. No, I didn't. But on that day ... at the age of 14, in 1957, on my way back from the *hay* [upland rice field] I met my uncle. He was already working for the revolution. He was in hiding. He asked me: "Do you want to get involved? Do you want to study?" I then replied: "Yes, I want to study!" He took me to another agent and told him: "Write her down and take her to study politics, solidarity and all that!" My uncle warned me: "If you meet strangers, people that you don't know, don't tell them that visitors came around." And that was how it really began![39]

The kind of motivation that pushed Manivanh onto the revolutionary path is not the stuff of stories of heroism. What seemed to persuade her to join the struggle was the disarmingly straightforward prospect (yet exceptional in those circumstances) of going to school, studying, and escaping an ordinary life. "Anti-imperialist" feelings of anger and hatred would come later:

> Later I understood, I reflected, I clearly saw that I wanted to join the Revolution, that I wanted above all to study. Secondly, I understood that ... in the villages ... the enemy was beating us, was threatening us.... I was full of hatred, of anger ... and this is why I joined the Revolution.... My uncle, my brother were arrested in 1958, 1959. I wanted to go with the soldiers. In my heart, I hated the enemy! At that time, I wasn't sure if they were French or Americans. But I was full of hatred. The date of my entry into the Revolution was around July 20, 1957.[40]

Khamla was born in Muang Phine, in Savannakhet province, in the middle to late 1950s. She also came from an "ordinary" peasant family (*khorp khoua pasason*), did not go to school in her childhood because "there wasn't any in the village", and could not (as a member of the Bru Katang ethnic group) speak Lao. Her first acquaintance with the Communist-nationalist movement, at the young age of eight, occurred when the area around her village was "liberated" around 1963–64. She was "restless as a child" and enjoyed helping with the collection of fruits and vegetables in the forest to feed guerrilla soldiers who entered the village to hold meetings and conduct their activities. As time went by, she gradually learned how to write and read in the company of revolutionary soldiers and cadres in makeshift evening classes. In fact, she explained her proper "entry into the Revolution" (*khaw hoam kan pativat*) in 1968[41] as partly the result of a desire to get a better education ("I was an ignorant girl, could even not speak Lao"), since she hoped that leaving her village and joining the revolutionary movement "out there" would help her in achieving this goal. Nonetheless, Khamla also linked her personal reason with a more collective motive: "resentment and hatred against foreign invaders", as she put it, employing commonly used anti-colonialist idioms.

Khamla and Manivanh's narratives reveal the complex nature of their motivations. The reasons for their involvement in the revolution were first personal (they came from underprivileged backgrounds, and they wanted to study) and subsequently collective (Manivanh fought to take revenge against an enemy who arrested and probably tortured her fellow fighters two years after she joined the guerrilla forces). Their motives were not initially ideological. They did not become revolutionaries because of a faith in Communism or socialist ideals, nor even for the liberation of women. These politically inspired reasons would mature progressively.

Revolutionary Activities

In its early days the Pathet Lao was a male-dominated organisation. Most of the women serving in the movement's administrative organs were spouses or daughters of cadres. However, this does not mean that the party did not have a policy stance on the role of women in society, as it formed a Research Committee on Lao Women's Activities in July 1955. In fact, many women were members of the party's underground cells and conducted numerous missions on its behalf.[42] Women in the "liberated zones" also served as couriers and spies. They were entrusted with the transmission of secret directives and took an equal share of the burden when carrying supplies on foot to military bases set up in the forest. Manivanh vividly remembers her first mission:

> I brought food and water to the agents. I was recruited into the women's secret organisation.... [She later recalled the name of the organisation] ... *seup khao, song khao* [literally, "information investigator"]. I was also recruited as an informant to check on the enemy's movements in Muang Phine, Muang Phalane — how many were they? I went three times to the enemy's military base of Muang Phine. Once I got the information, I gave it to Brother Khamla, who was a soldier. He's now retired. He was a soldier for the enemy, for the French. But he was also working for us, and he was also working for the French! I was getting the information from him. As well as from Uncle Khemly ... he's now deceased. Information on their weapons, big, small, and on the number of the enemy troops. The enemy never suspected anything; I was only 14 years old in 1957. I was collecting information on the enemy's position, after which I'd go back and submit my report. My third task was to inform the Issara soldiers when the enemy was about to go into the villages. I then would run to the forests to inform the Issara soldiers. Those were my revolutionary activities at the village level, in 1957, 1958 and 1959.[43]

With the inclusion in 1957 of the Pathet Lao's official political vehicle, the Neo Lao Hak Sat, into the government, supplementary elections were called to provide for representation of the new party in the Assembly and so complete the process of national integration that began at the first Geneva Conference in 1954. Twenty additional parliamentary seats were created to this end, and elections were scheduled for May 1958. But as the elections approached, hostilities between the conservative Royal Lao Government (RLG) and the Pathet Lao deepened, with the political struggle on the ground getting increasingly violent. The Neo Lao Hak Sat, with its electoral ally, the left-wing Santhiphab (Peace) Party, won 13 of the 21 seats that were contested in the 1958 election.

These results proved enough to alarm right-wing politicians and their American allies in Vientiane and to subsequently force Souvanna Phouma, who pushed for the political integration of Neo Lao Hak Sat, to resign as prime minister in July following the suspension of US aid. In actuality, the electoral gains obtained by the leftist camp merely reflected a reality already entrenched in some eastern parts of the country: the conviction among Lao Communist partisans (and the people sympathetic to their cause) of the existence of two opposed governments, the Vientiane-RLG side backed by the United States, and the Pathet Lao supported by the Viet Minh. Likewise, the eastern districts of Savannakhet province, where our two female protagonists originated, were then a disputed territory pitting Pathet Lao agents against RLG forces. By the late 1950s, the struggle between Communists and royalists had spread to the social and political sphere and had turned into a hide-and-seek pursuit where the Communist followers remained an elusive target by blending into the population, exacerbating the RLG forces' reprisals against civilians. In other words, Laos was turning into a politically and socially fractured country.

It was during the early years of her revolutionary life that Manivanh (not her birth name) adopted the name "Manivanh", which, significantly, is a lowland ethnic Lao name. As the war intensified and the Communists made territorial gains and won military battles, Manivanh moved up the ladder of responsibility and left the physically demanding work of a porter to assume the more enviable task of a propaganda agent at the provincial level, again driven by both personal desire and collective purpose. It was at that moment of her life that she became aware of the wider political issues and struggles. Her narrative clearly shows the intersection between her personal experience and historical events:

> In 1958, I sometimes stayed in the village, or when there was danger, lived in the forest. But 1959 was the most violent year.[44] My brother, my uncle were arrested. The enemy shot at my comrades, at our vehicles.... Then we lost our cover ... They arrested and tortured people ... I left and went into hiding in the forest. Then in 1961, it was the battles of Muong Phine and Muong Sepone. These were finally liberated. I was in the village at that time. I was carrying out the same task, I was still a porter [*lam lieng*]. I was carrying rice, cigarettes, oil and so on, up to Muang Phine. Then, in 1962, I left. My uncle and brother came to take me. At that point, I knew I wanted to leave! Because first, I was full of hatred, I hated the enemy! And secondly, I wanted to study, I especially wanted to study! At that time, I even didn't know to read [Lao]. I could only speak it. I sacrificed [*sala*] myself. I left the family, the village, around June 20, 1962. I joined the mobilising group [*korng kon kwai*] in the province of Muang Phine. I followed my uncle, my brother.[45]

Like other minority cadres' narratives I had the opportunity of hearing, Manivanh's is closely tied up with agency, reflected in her strong desire to acquire a formal education. This was clearly a determining factor in her decision to join the revolution, though the weight of fate never completely disappears in her story. During the period of renewed political turmoil in Laos, which began in 1959 and ended — temporarily — with the second Geneva Accords of 1962, the Pathet Lao and North Vietnamese forces made significant territorial gains, extending their control into new areas of the country. In January 1959, during the Fifteenth Plenum of the Vietnamese Workers Party's Central Committee, the North Vietnamese leadership authorised the use of armed struggle in the south, to be headed by the National Liberation Front for South Vietnam.[46] In early 1961, after negotiations with the Pathet Lao, Hanoi decided to extend the Ho Chi Minh Trail into Laos.[47] Muong Sepone, which became one of the most important centres for the North Vietnamese transportation network, fell in 1961.

Manivanh's life, meanwhile, was not getting any easier. In the years that followed, she indefatigably contributed to the war effort, travelling to wherever her help was needed and living with the villagers, mainly women and children, who had fled the bombings and lived scattered in the forests.

> I was sent with this group to the Tasseng Namchalo-Angkham [in the eastern region of present-day Savannakhet province]. I

followed the older sisters, they were more experienced. The people cultivated the upland rice fields, so did we! We were by their side. The people were pounding rice, so were we. The people went and fetched the water, so did we. They were looking for food, and we helped them. We never stopped, never had a break, we were by their side, with the children, with the grown-ups. We kept going! We also went with the soldiers. We were looking for food, bamboo shoots, and so on. People were living in the forest ... they were our informants, kids, women without their husbands, kept us informed on the enemy's movements.... The orphans, the widows, single women, they were trustworthy because we liberated them ... it was like that! In 1962, 1963, 1964, 1965, I was on the road with the comrades.... Then, in 1967–68, I sometimes went on my own to go and collect "rice for helping the nation", as we called it then, "rice to help the country".[48]

In a sense, the tasks Manivanh undertook during wartime provided her with an independent life and a sense of adventure she would not have experienced had she stayed in her village: moving about as a propagandist and proselytising for the party. Having been recruited into the struggle, she in turn mobilised children to join the revolution and, in the same manner as her own recruitment, promised them a bright, though elusive, future:

I was mobilising the population. I was recruiting children. I per-suaded them to go and study, to become teachers, soldiers, nurses, doctors. I wasn't alone in my work, there were several of us. We worked together. We worked in the rice field during the day and returned home in the evening. After dinner, there were dances.... The youth in villages in Namchalo, we all went, girls, boys, to become agents, soldiers, doctors, students ... that was my work in the emulation group.... Everyone was satisfied with my work. I was always the first to be chosen to carry out the work. Because I was young and hard working, because I never stopped working. I lived with the people, I fetched the water, I looked for food, for wood. I lived in places where life was tough, with widows, single women, orphans, it was with them I shared my life. Those were my tasks in the propaganda group from 1962 to 1968.[49]

In her exemplary narration, Manivanh never mentioned her personal suffering. The harshness of her life during the war is perceptible, though — particularly in the middle to late 1960s, when villagers and revolutionaries alike lacked food and more or less everything else and had to rely on the forest to subsist. Nevertheless, Manivanh never expressed anything other than collective ordeals. As an interesting comparison, when writing about war veterans and resistance fighters during World War II in Italy, Alessandro Portelli notes that "often, these individuals are wholly absorbed by the totality of the historical event of which they were [a] part, and their account assumes the cadences and wording of *epic*".[50] By these narratives of self, people are expressing the desire to impose an order, to form a "whole" out of "constituent parts" (that is, events), and thus to retain a sense of their life — past and present — that is reflective, coherent and meaningful.[51] At the end of her interview, Manivanh modestly expressed her contentment and gratitude towards the state for her house and her monthly war veteran's pension. She kept her revolutionary virtues pristine until the end.

Upon her "entry in the revolution" in the late 1960s, Khamla was immediately sent to carry out activities on the ground; she became, and remained for the duration of the war, a "foundation-laying cadre" (*phanakngan pheunthan*). As related in Manivanh's testimony, Communist cadres were assigned to accompany villagers — alone or in pairs depending on the size of the group — for periods of time from a few days to several weeks. One of the cadres' tasks was to provide practical advice and concrete support: in other words, to "educate" the population. Under their instructions, the villagers learned, for example, how to dig trenches covered with a steeply pitched roof of logs to deflect bombs. Revolutionary agents were also instructed to work in the upland rice fields and help in daily subsistence activities, such as the cultivation of potatoes, a crucial vegetable that could replace rice in times of shortage.

Their most important mission, however, was to keep mobilising the people in support of the revolution and war efforts. For instance, every household under the Communists' supervision had to pay a "rice tax" — although it was strictly forbidden to use this "counter-revolutionary" term during the war — which in official language, or "political phraseology", was known as "rice to help the nation" or, more concisely, "patriotic rice". The quantity to be donated depended on each household's production capacity. Every year, a cadre was tasked with assessing and monitoring the quantity of rice "paid" by each household. Khamla performed this work countless times, as she explained in detail:

For instance, one household produced 100 *meun* [one *meun* is equivalent to 12 kilos] per year. Then one counted how many members this household had and deducted accordingly the volume of rice needed for the family's own subsistence. The latter's share might be higher if the family included one or more revolutionary cadres. The remaining quantity of rice, if any and however small, was considered to be "patriotic rice". It was very fair.[52]

But the seemingly well-calibrated policy did not always go as smoothly as this and at times faced some (passive) resistance: "It happened that households, the richer ones, would lie to us and would declare a lower quantity. But neighbours would come and tell us the truth. We of course also carried out our own checks among households." Khamla spoke spontaneously of these "un-revolutionary" behaviours; unlike Manivanh, who was a National Hero, she may have felt less compelled to maintain a flawless narrative.

Khamla remained a ground-level cadre, her desire to be "better educated" remaining unfulfilled: "I never went anywhere. The 'central level' never sent me anywhere, neither in the North [of Laos] nor to Vietnam;[53] only some training of one month or two here and there. I learnt everything by myself and with the help of friends and comrades." Khamla's hint of bitterness must be understood in the wider context of the Communist revolution in eastern Laos during the war. At that time the Pathet Lao leadership began the building of a proto-socialist state. Thousands of children living in Pathet Lao-controlled areas were thus sent to study in Sam Neua or in North Vietnam between the late 1950s and the mid-1970s. These young boys and girls — many of whom were of ethnic minority origin — experienced various trajectories following the end of their studies and their return to Laos (for those who were sent to North Vietnam) in the 1970s: some went back to their home villages, while others became civil servants under the new regime after 1975. Others held, or still hold, influential positions within the state apparatus, while a few are members of the political ruling class and even sit on the Central Committee of the party (the Politburo, the highest political body in a Communist regime). In spite of divergent paths, one can argue that the Pathet Lao's recruitment campaigns in the highlands of Laos have produced a new generation of public servants: teachers, civil servants in ministries and local governments, medical personnel, senior officials, politicians (including members of parliament, provincial governors and district heads), all of whom benefited during their youth from the Communist education system during the First and (especially) Second Indochina Wars.[54] Meanwhile, on the ground, *phanakngan pheunthan*, such as Manivanh and Khamla, were the revolution's foot soldiers, fulfilling an often thankless and demanding, yet crucial, role in rallying and keeping villagers in line with the revolutionary cause and the party's doctrine.

After the Revolution

Manivanh never married and did not have any children. Towards the end of her life, unable to travel as much as she was used to because of declining health (she suffered from diabetes), she lived in downtown Savannakhet with her adopted daughter in a one-storey concrete house — a gift from the state for her accomplishments during the "30-year struggle" (1945–75). During the interview, the revolutionary cadre hardly mentioned anything about her private life. According to other war veterans (including Khamla), Manivanh was granted the "National Hero" title because she never refused or showed the slightest sign of dithering when tasked with carrying out a mission, including the riskiest ones, such as spying in the enemy's territories during the war or conducting political assignments in areas threatened by counter-revolutionary forces that continued to operate well after the 1975 Pathet Lao victory in some districts of the province. "She was so often away, carrying out an assignment, attending a meeting or following a political training. She didn't even have time to look after her adopted daughter. It was another female cadre who brought her up; the child ended up calling the two women 'mother,'" Khamla recalled. Through the lens of her personal narrative and life, Manivanh personifies the model patriot whose life demanded a high degree of self-sacrifice, if not total abandonment to the revolution. Manivanh did not hold any prominent political position at the national or provincial level: in the aftermath of the war she was elected as the head of a district-level office of the Lao Women's Union. The rationale underlying Manivanh's biography could concur with comments made by Sophie Quinn-Judge on the lives of early Vietnamese women revolutionaries: "For the generation of women who began the revolution in Vietnam, the traditional virtues of stoicism and self-sacrifice were the ones that dominated their lives."[55]

Manivanh passed away in 2007. A picture of her is displayed in the Savannakhet history museum, next to Akum's portrait (the third National Hero, Sikhai, who is still alive, may get this honour only after his death). The setting is bare: only their names are mentioned in the captions below the portraits. The lack of any mention of the ethnic group of each revolutionary (Bru Katang and Bru Tri, respectively) seems to be a missed opportunity for a regime that has constantly insisted on the inter-ethnic solidarity of "Lao people of all ethnic groups", a phrase often used in Lao official discourse to emphasise the multi-ethnic unity of the nation. Neither did ethnicity feature prominently in Manivanh's interview, though it does not mean that her ethnic origins did not matter. In fact, they greatly influenced the course of her revolutionary activities, because it was common for mobilising cadres of ethnic minority origins to operate in areas where they could use their cultural and language skills and knowledge; in other words, they were frequently assigned to mobilise their own "people". Khamla recollected recruiting "lots of soldiers", especially in "ethnic minority villages", because "parents [in those villages] were not keen on sending their children to school, whereas young men wanted to fight against the imperialists and to wear a nice military uniform!"

The former revolutionary cadre candidly explained that she was taught which ethnic group she "belonged" to only after joining the revolutionary movement: "I couldn't tell then the difference between a Makong or a Katang, I knew only that I was Bru. But my hierarchy told me that the name of my ethnic group was Katang, so the name stuck!" Despite accepting the official terminology, Khamla insisted that villagers, especially the elderly, in her native district would currently not be able to name any ethnic group and would still prefer to call themselves Bru (as she herself did at times, despite being told otherwise). More specifically, these villagers would identify themselves to a large extent by their village's name and territory. (According to the anthropologist Gábor Vargyas, "[the] word 'Bru' has two meanings: a narrow one, as autonym, and another broader one, meaning all the surrounding mountain people: 'Bru Van Kieu, Pakoh Bru, Bru Tau-Oi'. … [T]he same ethnonym [therefore] could have two meanings: all these people being 'forest people', they can use it to refer to themselves and to designate other neighbouring ethnic groups of the 'forest'.")[56] Khamla's sense of ethnic belonging (or, more broadly, sense of ethnic distinctiveness from the lowland Lao majority) may be also partly explained by the regime's ethnic policies.

The Communist leadership in Laos changed the discourse and policies on ethnicity. As against the policy of the Royal Lao Government, they substituted a majoritarian logic built around the lowland Lao culture with a policy of equality dominated by the class issue and the diktat of progress. During the war in the "liberated" zones and the first decade of Communist rule, the Communists attempted to create a loyalty greater than loyalties to particular ethnic identities. The ultimate goal for the Lao Communists, as it was for their Soviet, Chinese, and Vietnamese counterparts, guided by a historicist and evolutionist vision, was to eradicate "old" identities and replace them with a "Socialist" one.[57] In other words, these regimes' ultimate objective was not to build a society based on ethnic/national consciousness: the concept of class was thought to be the new society's main axis of identification. Antagonisms and mistrust between ethnic groups were to be dissipated by a period of national equality. This policy came to be known as "the flourishing of the nations". It was predicated upon the Marxist belief that "nationalities" (ethnic minorities) would naturally move closer together. The new Communist regime in Laos, accordingly, explicitly recognised the "the hill-tribe question" from the early years of its leadership. Kaysone Phomvihane, the late president of the Lao People's Democratic Republic, called for greater attention to be paid to promoting education among ethnic groups, improving their living conditions, and increasing production in remote minority areas. Furthermore, he insisted on respect being paid to the "psychology, aspirations, customs, and beliefs of each ethnic group".[58] The principle was to give every constituent group of the multi-ethnic state official recognition on an equal footing. In speeches, policies and textbooks, the Communists promoted a new image of the nation: from an apparent mono-ethnic portrait adopted under the "old regime" to a multi-ethnic representation of the national community in which equality, diversity and unity were now the new key parameters.

However, a disturbing trend, from the perspective of state-minority relations, is currently the government's embrace of Buddhism as a marker of national identity. For example, the religious Buddhist monument That Luang in Vientiane, which was the centrepiece of a tribute ceremony to royalty under the former regime, has replaced the hammer and sickle as the national symbol. The annual That Luang festival has become the locus of the state's representational project of the nation, a crossroads between socialist ideals, Buddhist rituals, exhibition of the multi-ethnic national culture, and the politics of opening to the world. The conflation of Buddhism and socialism is openly celebrated and benefits from extensive media coverage.[59] Symbols of nationhood are required to engender social cohesion by arousing a deeply felt sense of a shared community. They encompass what are claimed to be the unique and distinctive values of society. Functioning as collective representations, they aim at producing homogeneity from heterogeneity and integrating what is fragmented. With respect to majority-minority relationships, however, the revival of a Buddhist-orientated polity may widen the gap between the dominant Lao population (who are, in their vast majority, Buddhist followers) and the ethnic minorities (most of whom are non-Buddhist). The distinction is not solely religious: it also encompasses social organisation and world view. Thus, from the perspective of non-Lao citizens, the resurgence of state-sponsored Buddhist rituals as markers of national identity is troubling.[60] Neither Khamla nor her husband is Buddhist, as they told me; nonetheless, they (and their children) participate in Buddhist religious ceremonies and gatherings, although (as far as Khamla and her husband are concerned) they do so only, as she stressed in her interview, "to conform to the majority's urban social life". In other words, former revolutionaries such as Khamla and her spouse, who once were told — and believed — that they were at the forefront of the new secular and egalitarian socialist society, having defeated the "feudal" regime, now have to fit the culturally lowland Lao-dominated everyday urban life, as promoted by their Communist leaders.

Khamla retired in her early forties during the 1990s. At the time of writing, she was a member of the Lao Front for National Construction (Neo Lao Sang Saat), the regime's main mass organisation, which functions as an intermediary body between the party and the population. Not dissimilar to her activities during wartime, Khamla is sometimes called upon to explain the government's policies related to ethnic matters to villagers with whom she shares the same ethnic background. As during her revolutionary years, her relatively low level of education prevents her from undertaking higher-level assignments, which would require good (or better) literacy skills. Such was the explanation she gave me for her continuing grass-roots tasks, though a lack of good connections probably also accounted for the absence of opportunities. She never expressed any feelings of regret or sentiments of dissatisfaction during the interviews, however, although she was somewhat aware that perhaps she could have expected a better outcome from her years of devotion to the revolutionary cause. "My friends and colleagues keep saying that I'm stupid," she told me, sounding rather upset. "They think I could have asked for more with my revolutionary background. But I'm not stupid, I'm intelligent: I helped to liberate the country! I live in a state house,[61] and I'm not asking for anything else." Despite years of involvement in the revolution and in post-war reconstruction, Manivanh and Khamla barely saw any political career benefits from their self-abnegation.

In truth, politically active women in general have not fared well under the Communist regime. The statistics for 2010 show that women are still poorly represented at the executive level. There is no woman holding the post of provincial governor (one woman is deputy governor); two district chiefs (out of a total of 143) are women, as are 146 of the total of 8,726 village chiefs. The representation of women in the National Assembly is slightly better, at 25 per cent (29 out of 115). The proportion of women in the Lao People's Revolutionary Party's Central Committee (the regime's most powerful political organ, below the Politburo) is stagnating and has not increased from its peak of four members (out of 55 to 60) in 1982.[62]

Conclusion

Manivanh and Khamla were both recruited as young girls, went through the wartime educational apparatus and ideological circuit, and became cadres within the revolutionary movement. They both came from a materially poor and illiterate background. As guerrilla agents, these women broke from their own cultural and social norms to embrace socialist and nationalist ideals. They lived exceptionally independent lives under extraordinary circumstances for women of their background and origins. Manivanh literally gave her life to the revolutionary cause and was awarded for her sacrifice with the title of National Hero. Khamla might have followed a similar path had she been born a dozen years earlier. The war was over when she was still in her twenties, and the end of the conflict allowed her to regain a personal life — she got married and built a family ("During the war it was out of the question! You wouldn't have time to raise children moving around all the time like we did"). Neither woman went back to live in her village of origin. Both of them settled in Savannakhet town after the "liberation" in 1975 and carried on their duties as the regime's loyal militants. Both women kept being assigned to the same task again and again — liaising between the party and populations of their own ethnic background in their native province. In a sense, they never grew out of their ascribed "ethnic" role, perhaps because they were never given the opportunity to do so.

Notes

1. This chapter is a modified version of my article "Highlanders on the Ho Chi Minh Trail: Representations and Narratives", *Critical Asian Studies* 40, 3 (2008): 445–74. I thank the journal's editors for granting me permission to republish sections of this article, which is based on information gathered during research trips in the southern provinces of Sekong, Saravane and Savannakhet in 2003, 2004, 2008 and 2010.

2. Vina Lanzona, *Amazons of the Huk Rebellion: Gender, Sex and Revolution in the Philippines* (Madison: University of Wisconsin Press, 2009).

3. Agnes Khoo, *Life as the River Flows: Women in the Malayan Anti-Colonial Struggle* (Kuala Lumpur: SIRD, 2004).

4. Karen G. Turner and Phan Thanh Hao, "'Vietnam' as a Women's War", in *A Companion to the Vietnam War*, ed. Marilyn B. Young and Robert Buzzanco (Malden: Blackwell Publishing, 2002).

5. Sandra C. Taylor, *Vietnamese Women at War: Fighting for Ho Chi Minh and the Revolution* (Lawrence: University Press of Kansas, 1999).

6. François Guillemot, "Death and Suffering at First Hand: Youth Shock Brigades during the Vietnam War, 1950–1975", *Journal of Vietnamese Studies* 4, 3 (Fall 2009): 17–60.

7. Turner and Phan Thanh Hao (2002, pp. 94–5) estimate that among the (officially accounted for) 170,000 young people who joined the North Vietnamese volunteer youth (also called the "youth shock brigades") between 1965 and 1973, at least 70 per cent were women. Around a million more participated in local self-defence and militia units, and some 70,000 professional women — doctors, engineers, reporters — were recruited or volunteered to support the North Vietnamese Army.

8. Ibid., p. 93.

9. Taylor, *Vietnamese Women at War*, p. 18.

10. The Belorussian writer and journalist Svetlana Alexievitch, who has collected hundreds of testimonies of the former Soviet Union's female World War II veterans, eloquently explains: "Women's accounts contain nothing, or so little, about what we hear constantly, or perhaps rather,

what we have stopped hearing because we no longer pay any attention to it, that is, how some people heroically killed others and prevailed. Or lost. Women's stories are different in character and deal with another topic. The 'feminine' war possesses its own colors, odours, lighting and world of feelings. And, lastly, its own words" (Svetlana Alexievitch, *La guerre n'a pas un visage de femme* [*War Doesn't Have a Feminine Face*] [Paris: Éditions J'ai Lu, 2005], p. 9, my translation).

11.   In Laos, the ethnic Lao, who are the politically and economically dominant group (though they do not constitute an overwhelming majority), live mainly in the lowlands. Other lowland areas are inhabited by ethnic groups who speak a variety of Tai-Kadai languages. Tibeto-Burman speakers arrived recently from southwest China, while the Hmong-Mien (Miao-Yao) peoples, also recent arrivals, came from southern and southeastern China. These latter two families are confined primarily to highland areas in the northern provinces. Members of the Austro-Asiatic language family, generally acknowledged to be the first inhabitants of the country, are found throughout the country in both upland and lowland rural environments. Southeastern Laos — comprising the eastern districts of Khammouane, Savannakhet and Saravane provinces; the whole of Sekong and Attopeu provinces; as well as the Bolovens Plateau, located in the east of Champassak province — are by and large populated by Mon-Khmer (a sub-branch of the Austro-Asiatic family) language speakers. With the exception of the Katang and the Makong (called Bru-Van Kieu in Vietnam), none of these ethnic groups numbers more than 10,000 people, though ethnic minority peoples constitute the majority of the population in Sekong (Katu, Triang and Arak) and Attopeu (Oy and Brau/Brao) provinces.

12.   The League for the Independence of Vietnam (Viet Nam Doc lap Dong minh, or Viet Minh) was founded by Ho Chi Minh in May 1941 as a broad-based movement designed to draw popular support.

13.   The name indicates its geographic location in the Trường Sơn Mountains, which form the natural border between Vietnam and Laos.

14.   The term "Pathet Lao" gained international currency when it was used at the Geneva Conference of 1954, although representatives of the PL forces were not seated at the conference and it was a Viet Minh general who signed the ceasefire with the French on the PL's behalf. The name remained in common use as a generic term for the Lao Communists despite the fact that a "legal" political party, the Neo Lao Hak Sak (Lao Patriotic Front), was formed in early 1956. Therefore, although Pathet Lao is properly the name only of the armed forces of the Lao Communists, it is colloquially used to include all non-Vietnamese components of the Lao Communist movement to this day (Paul F. Langer and Joseph

J. Zasloff, *North Vietnam and the Pathet Lao: Partners in the Struggle for Laos* [Cambridge: Harvard University Press, 1970], p. 2).

15. Bernard B. Fall, "The Pathet Lao: A 'Liberation' Party", in *The Communist Revolution in Asia: Tactics, Goals and Achievements*, ed. Robert A. Scalapino (Berkeley: University of California, 1965), p. 178.

16. Motoo Furuta, "The Indochina Communist Party's Division into Three Parties: Vietnamese Communist Policy toward Cambodia and Laos, 1948–1951", in *Indochina in the 1940s and 1950s*, ed. Takashi Shiraishi and Motoo Furuta (Ithaca: Southeast Asia Program, Cornell University, 1992), p. 147; Jean Deuve, *Le Laos, 1945–1949: Contribution à l'histoire du mouvement Lao Issala* [*Laos, 1945–1949: A Contribution to the History of the Lao Issara Movement*] (Montpellier: Université Paul-Valéry, 1999), p. 248.

17. Martin H. Rathie, "The Historical Development of a Polyethnic Society and Culture in Laos from Independence and under Socialism", Honours thesis, Northern Territory University, 1996 (revised edition), p. 35.

18. Langer and Zasloff, *North Vietnam and the Pathet Lao* (Cambridge: Harvard University Press, 1970), p. 38.

19. By supporting anti-colonial movements in Laos, the Viet Minh gained access to and control of safe territorial bases, communication networks, and logistical corridors for external assistance to flow through. Indeed, Laos bordered 1,300 miles of highly permeable Vietnamese frontier, and later on it provided the best route for reaching southern Vietnam and avoiding the political and military problems involved in infiltrating directly through the demilitarised zone that divided the country in two in 1954. (The Vietnamese Demilitarised Zone was established as a dividing line between North and South Vietnam as a result of the First Indochina War [1946–54]. The Geneva Conference on 21 July 1954 recognised the 17th parallel as a "provisional military demarcation line" temporarily dividing the country into a Communist zone in the north and a non-Communist zone in the south.)

20. On 2 September 1945, Ho Chi Minh proclaimed the independence of Vietnam.

21. Christopher Goscha, "Vietnam and the World Outside: The Case of Vietnamese Communist Advisers in Laos, 1948–1952", *South East Asia Research* 12, 2 (2004): 151.

22. Martin H. Rathie, "Histoire et Evolution du Parti Révolutionnaire Populaire Lao" [History and Evolution of the Lao People's Revolutionary Party], in *Laos: Sociétés et Pouvoirs* [*Laos: Societies and Powers*], ed. V. Bouté and V. Pholsena (Paris: Les Indes Savantes-IRASEC, 2012).

23. My point is not to argue that the participation of highlanders in the war effort was the key factor in the Communists' final victory, either during

the Franco-Viet Minh war or the North Vietnamese-US conflict. Their role, nonetheless, should not be underestimated.

24.   State-sponsored nationalist historiographies in post-war Vietnam and Laos have portrayed their countries' ethnic minorities as early nationalists in conformity with the Communist principle of inter-ethnic solidarity. See Patricia M. Pelley, *Postcolonial Vietnam: New Histories of the National Past* (Durham: Duke University Press, 2002) for Vietnamese nationalist historiography.

25.   The most violent of all revolts occurred between 1914 and 1916 in the Tai-inhabited region around Sam Neua. When French troops from Vietnam recaptured the provincial capital from Tai rebels, the survivors retreated through Vietnam into Phongsaly province, where it required more than 5,000 colonial troops from Hanoi to drive them eventually into China. The Hmong people also launched a violent insurrection against French taxes and impositions in 1919. Starting in Vietnam and spreading to Xieng Khouang province, their revolt was led by Pha Patchay, who called for an independent Hmong kingdom. Both the Hmong and the Mien ethnic groups shared a long history of resistance activity, which had led them to develop highly organised units of resistance. The French colonial government granted the Hmong a special administration status as a result of this rebellion (MacAlister Brown and Joseph J. Zasloff, *Apprentice Revolutionaries: The Communist Movement in Laos, 1930–1985* [Stanford: Hoover Institution Press/Stanford University, 1986], p. 10).

26.   The release of Sithone Kommadan and his brother Kamphanh from prison in Phongsaly province in August 1945 was critical for the development of the Lao Issara and subsequently the Pathet Lao. Sithone was identified as the undisputed leader of the southern highland peoples, and thus his presence helped to unite them rapidly with the Lao Issara resistance forces. Sithone began to establish "resistance bases" in Phongsaly and Xieng Khouang. Then he entered southern Vietnam, where he met the militant Communist Tran Van Giau. He soon made contact with the Viet Minh leadership in northern Vietnam and the Lao Issara government in Vientiane. In 1948 Sithone began leading raids on the Bolovens Plateau, and in 1950 he regrouped with his son Sang Kham in their home province of Saravane. Sithone's experience in utilising and organising the support of highland and rural groups extended the nationalist activities of the Lao Issara on a countrywide scale (Rathie, *Historical Development*, pp. 34–5).

27.   Although for Lenin nationalism was a secondary problem, it was essential to keep it under control. His strategy for neutralising the national question was guided by his perception of nationalism as the result of past discrimination and oppression. Consequently, national antagonisms

and mistrust were to be dissipated by a period of national equality; this policy came to be known as "the flourishing of the nations". It was predicated upon the belief that nations would naturally move close together, a process described in the official Marxist vocabulary as the "rapprochement" or "coming together" of nations (W. Connor, *The National Question in Marxist-Leninist Theory and Strategy* [Princeton: Princeton University Press, 1984], p. 202).

28. Brown and Zasloff, *Apprentice Revolutionaries*, p. 15.

29. J. Michaud, "The Montagnards and the State in Northern Vietnam from 1802 to 1975: A Historical Overview", *Ethnohistory* 47, 2 (2000): 357.

30. Mayoury Ngaosyvathn, *Remembrances of a Lao Woman Devoted to Constructing a Nation: Khampheng Boupha* (Vientiane: Lao Women's Union, Vientiane, 1993).

31. Khampeng Boupha worked first as a teacher, then as a translator, before representing her country in various international conferences and congresses throughout the 1960s and 1970s as well as after the war.

32. They were Ms Nyaeng, Ms Buasy, Mother Mi, Mother Buakham, Mother Yongkay, Ms Su, Ms Buakham, Mother Phanh and Nang Trai Phet.

33. I am using a pseudonym for the second revolutionary cadre, who is still alive and lives in Savannakhet province, for the sake of her privacy.

34. E. Ochs and L. Capps, "Narrating the Self", *Annual Review of Anthropology* 25 (1996): 25.

35. R. Waterson, *Southeast Asian Lives: Personal Narratives and Historical Experience* (Singapore: NUS Press; Athens: Ohio University Press, 2007), p. 12.

36. C.W. Watson, *Of Self and Injustice: Autobiography and Repression in Modern Indonesia* (Singapore: NUS Press, 2006), p. 3.

37. The eastern districts of Savannakhet province are inhabited predominantly by Mon-Khmer peoples (accounting for approximately 70 per cent of the total population), who are classified into three subgroups (the Makong/Mangkong, Katang and Tri). However, there is also a significant minority of Tai-speaking Phuthai (about 30 per cent).

38. The Katang (also known as Bru Katang) are a Mon-Khmer speaking group. They mostly inhabit the highland areas straddling the border between the provinces of Savannakhet and Saravane, in southeastern Laos.

39. Interview on 26 February 2004 in Kaysone Phomvihane, the capital of Savannakhet province.

40. Ibid.

41. That is, approximately one generation of revolutionary cadres after Manivanh's generation.

42. Mayoury, *Remembrances of a Lao Woman*, p. 1993; Lao Women's Union, *Pavat mounsieu sahaphanmaenyinglao* [*History of the Origins of the Lao*

Women's Union] (Vientiane: Lao Women's Union's headquarters, July 2010).

43. Interview on 26 February 2004 in Kaysone Phomvihane, the capital of Savannakhet province.

44. The summer of 1959 marked a low point in the PL's military strength. Its two battalions had recently fled Luang Prabang and Huaphan provinces to reach North Vietnam and had hardly had any time to regroup by the time 16 of their leaders were arrested and detained in Vientiane.

45. Interview on 26 February 2004 in Kaysone Phomvihane, the capital of Savannakhet province.

46. Z. Qiang, *China and the Vietnam Wars, 1950–1975* (Chapel Hill: University of North Carolina Press, 2000), p. 81.

47. J. Prados, *The Blood Road: The Ho Chi Minh Trail and the Vietnam War* (New York: Wiley, 1999), p. 15.

48. Interview on 26 February 2004 in Kaysone Phomvihane, the capital of Savannakhet province.

49. Ibid.

50. Alessandro Portelli, "What Makes Oral History Different", in *The Oral History Reader*, ed. R. Perks and A. Thomson, 2nd ed. (London and New York: Routledge, 2006), p. 38, emphasis in original.

51. J. Bruner, "The Narrative Construction of Reality", *Critical Inquiry* 18, 1 (Autumn 1991): 8.

52. Interview on 1 March 2010 in Kaysone Phomvihane, Savannakhet province.

53. The Pathet Lao's headquarters were located in Huaphan province (formerly called Sam Neua), in northeastern Laos. Many Lao revolutionary cadres were sent during and after the war to North Vietnam for political and ideological training.

54. V. Pholsena, "L'éducation d'une génération de patriotes révolutionnaires, du Laos au Nord Viêt Nam" [The Education of a Generation of Revolutionary Patriots, from Laos to North Vietnam], *Communisme 2013*, "Vietnam, de l'insurrection à la dictature 1930–2012" [Vietnam: From Insurrection to Dictatorship, 1930–2012], Special issue coordinated by Christopher Goscha. Paris: Vendémiaire, 2013, pp. 230–58.

55. Sophie Quinn-Judge, "Women in the Early Vietnamese Communist Movement: Sex, Lies, and Liberation", *South East Asia Research* 9, 3 (2001): 269.

56. G. Vargyas, *À la recherche des Brou perdus, population montagnarde du centre indochinois* [*In Search of the Lost Brou: A Highland Population of Central Indochina*]. Les Cahiers de Péninsule, 5 (Geneva: Olizane [Études orientales], 2000), p. 133.

57. V. Pholsena, "Nation/Representation: Ethnic Classification and Mapping Nationhood in Contemporary Laos", *Asian Ethnicity* 3, 2 (2002): 191.

58. Kaysone Phomvihane, *La Révolution lao* [*The Lao Revolution*] (Moscou: Editions du Progrès, 1980), p. 233.

59. The examples usually cited are pictures taken of the party's senior members making merit during major Buddhist festivals.

60. V. Pholsena, "A Liberal Model of Minority Rights for an Illiberal Multi-ethnic State? The Case of the Lao PDR", in *Asian Minorities and Western Liberalism*, ed. Will Kymlicka and Baogang He (Oxford: Oxford University Press, 2005), pp. 96–7.

61. The government sold houses located in downtown Savannakhet (some of which had been abandoned by their owners, who fled to Thailand in the aftermath of the Pathet Lao's victory) to highly deserving war veterans at a (relatively) low price.

62. Lao Women's Union, *Pavat mounsieu sahaphanmaenyinglao* [History of the Origins of the Lao Women's Union], pp. 158–9. I thank Martin Rathie for sharing this book with me. Despite the dispiriting statistics, some women, who participated in the 30-year struggle (1945–75) and/or were educated in the Communist education system during the war, have nevertheless attained fairly prominent political positions under the Communist regime at both the central and local levels, the most well known example being Pany Yathorthou, president of the National Assembly and member of the Politburo at the time of writing. Lao women revolutionaries' trajectories during and after the war constitute an important area for further investigation.

CHAPTER 9

Bisoi: A Veteran of Timor-Leste's Independence Movement

Sara Niner

"What is very upsetting is that the discrimination is from our own partners in the struggle ..."[1]

Rosa de Camâra is better known by her *nom de guerre* or code name of Bisoi, a sad reference to being discarded, or perhaps disregarded (*bi* means "sister", and *soi* [or *soe*] means "to throw away or discard"). Born in 1963, Bisoi is a political activist who fought for both the self-determination of her people and equality for women. She is one of the surviving women who served the armed wing of the nationalist movement of Timor-Leste as a combatant with the guerrilla army Falintil from 1975, when Indonesia invaded and occupied her homeland, until the UN-sponsored ballot of 1999, which delivered the territory's independence. One journalist who interviewed Bisoi over a number of years described her as feisty, yet felt she hid her secrets and feelings behind a faint smile, dubbing her the "Mona Lisa in fatigues".[2] Today, Bisoi is a well-known member of the national parliament and continues to fight for women's rights in Timor's post-conflict society and for improved treatment of women combatants like herself. The treatment of women combatants is emblematic in the life of Bisoi because they have not been recognised or rewarded on a par with their male colleagues. This issue will be discussed here with some analysis about the implications for society in Timor-Leste today.[3]

This biographical chapter provides an exploration of Bisoi's political and military involvement from her own perspective, illuminating the experiences of women in the nationalist movement of East Timor,

Mana Bisoi and her uncle, Falintil Commander L7 Foho Rai Boot. Courtesy of Irene Cristalis

a small country of about a million people. This chapter will trace her personal story along with supplying the historical context for her comments and including a gender analysis of this evidence. Bisoi sees three clear phases to her biography, and this chapter is organised accordingly:

> I want to point out three phases of my life: first, the Portuguese time, when women didn't have the right to do anything; second, the resistance period, when women suffered a lot compared to men; and third, the independence period, when some women are still not free, such as those who have no education.[4]

Portuguese Timor (pre-1975)

In 1944 the anthropologist Mendes Correa described the Portuguese colony of Timor as a "Babel ... a melting pot", and a diverse mix of traditions is still strongly felt today. Although there are many differences between the distinct ethno-linguistic groups, most share similar cosmological beliefs and social structures. The largest Malayo or Austronesian groups are the Tetum (100,000), the Mambai (80,000),

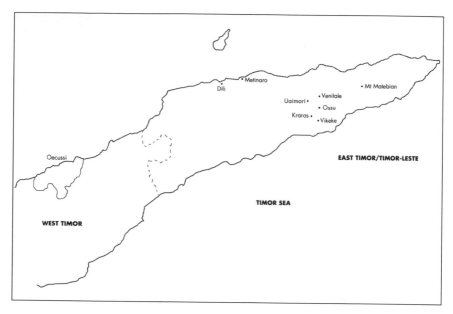

Map 10. East Timor

the Tokodete (63,000), the Galoli (50,000), and the Baikeno or Antoni people who live in the western enclave of Oecussi (20,000). The main groups of Papuan or Melanesian origin include the Bunak (50,000), the Fataluku (30,000), and the Makassae (70,000) living in the eastern end of the island.[5] Bisoi comes from a village near Ossu, in Vikeke District. (For place names in this chapter, see map 10.)

The diverse indigenous societies and their kingdoms cross the spectrum of matriarchal and patriarchal organisation. Women are accorded a sacred status within Timorese cosmology, and the divine female element is prominent in much indigenous belief. The sacred world is dominated by female spirits, while the secular world is dominated by men. Therefore, while women may hold power in a ritual context they generally do not have a strong public or political voice. According to this indigenous logic, women and girls are consigned to the internal or domestic sphere rather than the external or public sphere. Consequently, domestic duties and care of children are the sole domain of women and may explain the formidable positions some women hold within households. Yet this position carries the full burden of domestic chores and child-rearing, excluding women from a place in the wider society and in leadership roles. While the roles of women and men in indigenous society are understood by anthropologists as complementary and interdependent, it cannot be inferred that these roles are equal or equitable if we analyse them from a modern gender perspective. It is also an important observation that senior or elite women are powerful, and any gender analysis in Timor must be modified with this class awareness. Class, or caste, is very strictly observed, even today, so that elite and middle-class women are invested with much more power and privilege than the men who fall below them in the social hierarchy. Women's experience in the resistance may also be defined by class,[6] as illustrated by the experience of Bisoi.

Timor's Portuguese colonisers brought the Catholic Church to the island, and this had an enormous impact on Timorese culture. While other domains have been researched,[7] it remains unclear how much Catholicism degraded women's sacred power within indigenous religion and replaced it with its own more demure version of femininity and what impact it had on indigenous women's status. The argument advanced here is that the late colonial-era status of women, which Bisoi was brought up with, had been altered by colonialism and Catholicism and was a weaker one. The Portuguese influence had done little to improve the lives of women.

A famous Timorese rebel, Dom Boaventura, led an armed uprising against his Portuguese colonisers in 1911. One of his main grievances was over the sexual abuse and exploitation of Timorese women by Portuguese men. Due to such exploitation, the idea of protecting women and keeping them safe at home could only have become more firmly entrenched. For most of the 20th century East Timor was ruled directly from Portugal by the fascist dictatorship of Salazar, and the colony remained neglected and closeted from any modern liberalising trends such as the feminism of the 1960s and 1970s.

By the early 1970s, the Timorese independence movement Fretilin, inspired partly by Dom Boaventura, had begun opposing Portuguese colonialism and its racism and discrimination, while developing a revolutionary programme that included the emancipation of women. Rosa "Muki" Bonaparte was one of the founders of Fretilin — in fact, she was the only woman to hold a position on the Central Committee, which set political direction in the movement.[8] She was also the leader of its women's organisation, OPMT.[9] A statement of Rosa's from the early 1970s reads, "The creation of OPMT has a

East Timorese Nationalist Movement

1512	Portuguese explorers arrive in Timor
1912	Armed rebellion led by Dom Boaventura against Portuguese colonial control
Aug. 1975	Portuguese governor withdraws from territory amidst a civil war
Dec. 1975	Indonesia invades East Timor, and Timorese resistance movement is established
1978	Fall of last resistance base at Mt Matebian
1981	First National Council for Revolutionary Resistance; CRRN formed, and Xanana appointed leader
Mar. 1983	Regional ceasefire agreed upon by Xanana and Indonesian military
Aug. 1983	Uprising in Vikeke and Kraras massacre signal end of ceasefire
Sept. 1983	State of emergency declared. New Indonesian offensive launched
1991	Santa Cruz massacre of hundreds of East Timorese, bringing enormous international condemnation of the Indonesian occupation
1992	Resistance leader Xanana Gusmao captured in Dili amidst international protests
Aug. 1999	UN-sponsored referendum votes in favour of independence. After announcement, pro-Indonesian militias begin a massive campaign of murder and destruction
May 2002	Democratic Republic of Timor-Leste established

double objective: firstly, to participate directly in the struggle against colonialism, and second, to fight in every way the violent discrimination that Timorese women had suffered in colonial society."[10]

Bisoi recalled her early days and OPMT's part in her political awakening: "During Portuguese times and because of Timorese culture, East Timorese women were not allowed to express their ideas and say what they wanted. It was a challenge for me to contribute to and fight for women's rights...."[11] Bisoi recalled that her childhood during Portuguese colonial times was affected by the lack of opportunities for women. She said that Timorese indigenous culture combined with Portuguese influence precluded East Timorese women from expressing their ideas or from joining political parties:

> The main problem is there was no opportunity or equality for women. I saw the existence of inequality for East Timorese women compared to men. This is from our ancestors. Our traditional customs mean that women can't go out and achieve anything. Women and girls must marry even if they don't love the person: the parents agree to an amount, and the daughter must marry. Political leaders [in 1974–75] were starting to talk about these issues, and I thought, "This is a good moment for me to join in their campaign and political activities." From Indonesian times to the present, women's participation in meetings has been limited because of lack of support from the family, especially for married women. Their husbands do not allow them or give them opportunities to participate.[12]

The decolonisation period in 1974–75 was the first time Timorese women became involved in political issues. Bisoi remembers it was still very difficult for women to become involved in politics and that from her first moment as a political activist she felt she was criticised by her community and her own family.[13]

Invasion and Resistance: The First Phase of the Struggle (1976–79)

After the Indonesian invasion of 7 December 1975, much of the population of East Timor, including Bisoi, retreated to the mountains with Fretilin and became part of the resistance to Indonesian occupation. The ongoing conflict shifted women's economic, social and political roles, as war has done repeatedly around the world, and many women were challenged to act more independently than they had previously. In East Timor the war forced many women to take up roles outside the domestic sphere for the first time. Not only did women lose husbands, fathers, brothers and sons to the war, making it necessary for them to provide for their families and enter an economic sphere previously closed to them, but they also became a significant component of all the resistance fronts: military, political, civil and diplomatic.

Bisoi was 12 years old when Indonesian forces attacked her village in Vikeke and killed her mother.[14] Her education was halted, and she is still saddened that she had the opportunity to reach only second grade of primary school. By her own account, Bisoi was involved in the nationalist movement from the time of the Indonesian invasion.[15] She ran to the bush and ended up in the care of her uncle, the well-known Falintil Commander L7 Foho Rai Boot, and she eventually became a Falintil soldier also.[16]

From about 1977, when she was 14, after listening to campaigning by Fretilin activists she became more directly involved in the independence movement and became a member of OPMT. Fretilin's social and political programmes were predicated on an ideological revolution to overthrow colonial and traditional power structures, including gendered ones, in conjunction with mass mobilisation in a guerrilla-style military resistance. Bisoi travelled around as a "barefoot" teacher to illiterate farmers.[17] Women were encouraged to become part of OPMT rather than to take up roles within the Fretilin Central Committee, which was staffed almost entirely by men. Revolutionary rhetoric had had little time to impinge on traditional male-dominated power structures. Many of OPMT's roles were stereotypically gendered ones such as teaching, running crèches, and providing food and clothing, but the organisation was also committed to literacy classes for women and banning indigenous customary practices that it believed led to the oppression of women. In these first revolutionary years women were also trained in the handling and firing of weapons.

Bisoi says she "came down" to surrender in 1978,[18] meaning she was one of the hundreds of thousands of East Timorese who surrendered after a systematic Indonesian annihilation campaign had encircled the remaining resistance leadership and 140,000 civilians on Mount Matebian, in the east of the island. After three years of war, in November 1978 this was the last stronghold of Fretilin and Falintil, and these organisations were no longer able to protect civilians. Trapped and unable to retreat any farther, the weakened resistance advised civilians to surrender. The latter were placed in prisons and "resettlement camps" set up by Indonesian forces.[19]

Bisoi's resolve to work towards the independence of her country, and particularly for the liberation of East Timorese women, continued.[20] She was one of a dwindling number of women who had worked with Falintil since the beginning of the war. Bisoi said the number of women who lived and worked directly with the resistance guerrillas in the mountains varied:

> In 1974–1975, everyone was involved so it is difficult to know the number of women, but from 1980–1990 it was more or less 130

people. By 1996, only 40 or 50 remained and by the time of the UN Referendum in 1999 there were only around 10 remaining. Perhaps 30 or 40 were captured and killed by the enemy. Every region knows well about their women who were involved in the war.[21]

Reorganising the Resistance (1981–99)

Bisoi recounted that her involvement during the years following the destruction of the resistance in 1978 was in reviving resistance networks. She described being part of starting a new Milicia Popular de Libertacao Nacional (Miplin) group in 1980, in the Central East Region, where she had relocated. This group became part of the newly emerging resistance. One of Bisoi's main objectives in establishing this group was to build links between Falintil and the Indonesian military and work towards a peace plan.[22]

The Fretilin network of Miplin had been created prior to the 1975 invasion to assist Falintil and was slowly being revived.[23] Unlike most clandestine groups, Miplin had a military-type structure. Recruits were organised in unarmed teams and platoons. Taur Matan Ruak, a senior military leader in the Central region (currently the president of Timor-Leste), explained Miplin's role:

> The mission of those known as militia was usually to relay information about spies in their midst to prevent [the spies] from doing any harm, and about Indonesian army movements. Normally that is what we called a militia. But it wasn't necessary for them to carry weapons because there were no arms [to give them] ... Miplin is a concept we created and it is difficult to compare it to the classic understanding of the term [militia] ... We did not have arms ... we used [the militias] to motivate the population to remain alert.[24]

In the early 1980s a new leadership was emerging, including Ruak. Most of the original Fretilin Central Committee leadership had been eliminated; and their revolutionary politics, including the ideal of the emancipation of women, disappeared along with them. The revived resistance of the early 1980s had no such programme and little capacity to think beyond basic survival. They relied on traditional family and clan networks to survive and revive the resistance, and the position of women in these networks remained very traditional and was based on indigenous gender roles.

The much more nationalist, rather than revolutionary, struggle was led by Xanana Gusmao, who established a series of national resistance councils as platforms to unite various resistance factions to work together: CRRN from 1981, CNRM from 1986, then CNRT from 1998.[25] Like before, no women were to hold senior positions within these elite male hierarchies. Xanana's attempts to accommodate other groups caused ongoing tensions with the surviving Fretilin leadership.[26] It is still not yet documented what effect these political tensions had on OPMT, which remained the women's organisation associated with Fretilin, but it continued to operate locally and clandestinely to support the politically expanding resistance councils throughout the 1980s and 1990s.

With the change to CNRT in 1998, a new women's arm developed — Organização Mulher Timorense (Organisation of Timorese Women, or OMT). Most OPMT women co-joined this organisation as well to demonstrate political solidarity at this crucial time of negotiating for a UN-sponsored referendum. By 1998 OMT claimed 70,000 members in 3,000 secretariats in every little village in the country.

Women held political positions such as deputies, assistants and coordinators. Bisoi was one of them, rejoining the political front after 1981. In addition to their accepted roles as mothers, carers, community workers and educators, women performed a range of other roles during the occupation. They played a large role in clandestine networks: they collected and couriered intelligence and documents; supplied medicine, uniforms and ammunition; and hid guerrillas in their homes. One generally accepted estimate of women's participation in clandestine organisations is 60 per cent.[27]

Despite the generalised conservative gender culture, and the disruption of war, Bisoi was able to circumvent restrictive roles and carve out a different life for herself, though she avoided questioning outright traditional gender position. Bisoi spoke about what it was like for women balancing their political and domestic roles during resistance times:

> If I was organising OPMT activities, that was my responsibility at that time. But when I left this activity and returned to my normal [family] life then I had to act as a normal woman. These two lives were separate. When I did political activities I concentrated on those political issues, and when I was doing normal things I concentrated on that. I received support from my family: when I had an activity at night they always said, "That is her task, let her do this." They never intervened in my political activities.[28]

In March 1983 a regional ceasefire was agreed upon by Xanana Gusmao and Indonesian military representatives. However, the negotiations faltered by August and the ceasefire was broken by the Timorese with an uprising in Vikeke. Hundreds of Timorese members of Indonesian-sponsored militias rebelled and deserted, taking their weapons up to the mountains and jungles, rejoining the few remaining guerrilla forces. The Indonesian military retaliated with the brutal Kraras massacre, killing the entire male population of that village. By September 1983 the Indonesian military had declared a state of emergency and launched a new offensive.

Women, including Bisoi, also returned to the mountains with the rebel soldiers. Bisoi became a soldier again. "In the difficult times there was no food," she said, "but many refused to go back to the city — they stayed put. We can be as patriotic as men, you know. We knew we could do as men did: we stayed. We wanted to show that women, too had a strong sense of duty."[29] She recalled:

> We returned to the forest on 8 August 1983 to join Falintil again and immediately got involved in all operations of Falintil. The situation became difficult. The Commander [Xanana] released the statement [about the], "*Guerra dura e prolongada*" [the Long War] and announced that children and women should return to the town. The women all refused. Better to fight to the death in the forest. But the Commander's decision was for the children. It was decided also that elderly and pregnant women should be sent to the town.
>
> In 1983 we again made contact with Indonesian army battalion 713 and started to set our minds to delivering our small children to the battalion in Venilale. There were 27 children, the eldest about five years ... This time was very difficult. When the parents agreed, their children were handed over and [the parents] returned to the military battle. We only handed over the old and our children. Then we again set about trapping and shooting the Indonesian military.[30]

Bisoi became the "second wife" to a senior Falintil commander and had a child with him during her time in the mountains. She said that while she was pregnant she was shot in the stomach, and she believed the later safe birth of her daughter was a miracle. She said when the baby was born the bullet was found to be lodged in her wrist and remains there today. As was the custom for guerrilla women, Bisoi placed her baby daughter, Lekas Susar (meaning "quite a handful"), in the garden of a local convent, where the child was brought up by nuns.[31] The women who made such heartbreaking choices for the nationalist movement and the resistance army they were part of have received little acknowledgement for their roles and sacrifices.

After the collapse of the Suharto dictatorship in Indonesia, B.J. Habibie was appointed president and agreed to let the Timorese decide their future in a ballot. In the August 1999 referendum, nearly 80 per cent of East Timorese voted for independence by indicating the CNRT flag on the ballot paper. Extensive military and militia slayings followed the announcement of the vote — an estimated 2,000 East Timorese were killed and more than 200,000 forcibly displaced into Indonesia. Approximately 80 per cent of infrastructure was destroyed. Following the massive violence, Timorese struggled to find housing and food and look after their families while recovering from the mayhem.

As part of the agreement to hold the ballot, Falintil was assigned to temporary quarters in several camps around Timor. Bisoi was living at the Uaimori camp with most of the senior leaders of Falintil, including her uncle L7, who was to become marginalised in the Falintil hierarchy. In the camp she was the only woman active in political work and the only one to carry a weapon. All the other women in the camp worked in either the clinic or the kitchen.[32]

Women's Role and Discrimination in Falintil

During the Indonesian occupation OPMT provided women with a vehicle through which they could join the nationalist struggle, either militarily or as civilians. OPMT provided support and supplied the resistance with what it needed, as far as possible, and women in the main acted in these roles. It was clear to all that women made huge contributions under extraordinary circumstances. They understood the dangers of their actions but persisted, and many died or were captured and tortured as a result. As Bisoi says above, "We can be as patriotic as men."

Although women fighters such as Bisoi were respected and appreciated as OPMT members and gained a form of "second class" status within Falintil as military support and occasional combatants, they were not acknowledged as soldiers and there were no women in the Falintil command structure. There was little thought among male commanders about ideas of equality for women. Bisoi elaborated why she and other women did not lobby for change:

> During the guerrilla war we never knew for sure whether we were going to live or die, and every single man and woman concentrated only on how to survive. We had lost everything, and because we were on the move we had to leave the kids behind and just keep going. When the enemy wounded us, man or woman, the consequences were the same. We had to concentrate on surviving and continuing our activities to support and encourage Falintil, so they would not lose their spirit to fight for independence.
>
> The difference between the occupation and the independence period is that during the guerrilla war everything was limited, including information about equality and women's rights. We did not receive any information about women's rights during that time. At that time we didn't care about these issues and concentrated only on how we would survive if the Indonesians attacked. For this reason women were put in a secondary role with specific tasks. I knew how to organise things, and everyone treated me well within the movement.[33]

Throughout the occupation OPMT was treated by Falintil as a women's auxiliary for the war effort. Certainly no women were invited into senior positions in the resistance hierarchy. However, many motivated women such as Bisoi exceeded these expectations. This significant minority of women challenged the gender roles of women in Timorese culture. During resistance times, however, "at many levels these changes remained symbolic — the exception rather than the rule. In general women had no freedom to move and men continued to make the decisions."[34]

Bisoi believes that many male guerrillas have failed to acknowledge the role of the OPMT women in the military struggle and that this is still a story that needs to be told: "This inequality existed in the resistance movement and Falintil. The contribution of women to Falintil is obscured by the male Falintil. There were also women fighters, but the activities of the male fighters are more popular."[35]

A small number of women, such as Bisoi, served Falintil for most of the entire 24 years of the resistance. Many of the women engaged in armed conflict acted as assistants to their guerrilla fighter husbands or partners in the military camps and sometimes took up arms if their husbands were disabled or killed. Bisoi recalled that they were taking care of what was termed "nucleos" of injured soldiers, the children and the sick and were responsible for their security and food supply. These women, like men, who were discovered by the Indonesian authorities faced imprisonment, torture and death with the added terror of sexual abuse.[36]

During Falintil military assaults, women were often part of the "second wave" and had the duty of recovering weapons and other valuable items such as uniforms. Their instructions were to shoot only if they came under attack. The situation during the conflict was very fluid, especially during military engagements. Duties were performed according to capacity and conditions. Women whose main duties may have officially been logistics and support often switched to combat duties when conditions warranted.

Bisoi spoke about one incident of killing several Indonesian soldiers at Mount Matebian. She was resting in a camouflaged spot when she realised she had been surrounded by about 15 Indonesian soldiers. She believed the soldiers had been tracking her but had not realised they were so close. She shot at the soldiers with a machine gun, and said she must have killed up to five of them but because she fled she would never know.[37]

Bisoi was wounded several times:

> The worst phase was the second period [of the Indonesian occupation, 1979–80s]. It was a black moment that has not really been covered until now. Women were killed and suffered a lot. I was shot, eight bullets in my body and stomach and one in my foot. Only in 2002 did I have an operation to take out some of the bullets, but I am still suffering a lot.[38]

Yet the role played by women in these armed forces was undervalued. One clear indication that they were regarded as second-class soldiers was in the allocation of uniforms, as experienced by Bisoi:

> Life was very basic — we were lucky to possess two changes of clothes each, and had a bath about once a month. We got our clothing quite often from the bodies of Indonesian soldiers we had killed. Uniforms were first given to the male Falintils — they fitted better, and in any case the men, especially the commanders, did not want to give us uniforms.[39]

Hence, women were given political space and roles but only as dictated by the male leadership. The appreciation of their specific role and contribution in resistance was also skewed from the standpoint of the masculine experience. Despite documented evidence to the contrary, the official position of much of the resistance leadership and veterans' recognition bodies today is that women fulfilled only civilian roles, with its attendant practical and material implications. Bisoi recounted her experience of discrimination in the national parliament in gaining access to state-sponsored medical treatment for her war wounds in comparison to the treatment received by male veterans:

> In 2008 when I became a parliamentary member I used my own money to get medical treatment in Indonesia to take out bullets from my body. Then I found that discrimination exists also in parliament. For example, parliament provides allowances of $1,500–2,000 to parliamentary members to have medical treatment — but for me to have this operation to take out the bullets from the war I received only $500. I protested about this: I pointed this out at the plenary, but I was criticised by members of my own party [CNRT]. But I am trying to continue because these are my personal efforts to get recognition as a resistance member. I made a strong protest to other parliamentary members and pointed out that others had received [more than the full allowance]. When I presented my case to [Parliamentary] Vice-President Vicente Guterres for consideration, they only provided the $500 and advanced my salary for four months. When I returned five to six months later I wondered why that had happened, as there should not be a difference between the rights of parliamentary members.[40]

Bisoi was also indignant at the lack of due recognition of the contribution of female veterans in the demobilisation of Falintil fighters and spoke about her group's futile struggle to fight for just treatment. UNTAET, the UN transitional administration of East Timor, oversaw the establishment of the Defence Force of East Timor, ultimately to be called the Falintil-Forças Armadas de Defesa de Timor-Leste (F-FDTL) in February 2001. Male Falintil fighters were offered the option of joining the new Timor-Leste Defence Force or receiving the equivalent of US$100 along with language and computer training. Nothing comparable was offered to women.[41] Bisoi spoke of this new army in reference to the plight of a female comrade:

> Inequality exists in F-FDTL as an institution. Our resistance *colleaga* is Biralin. Today she is attempting to be recognised by the state. She was also a captain in FDTL [around 2004]. However, they offered positions to younger women and discontinued her duties

in the military because she was too old. She was replaced with younger women who had better capabilities [education and skills]. When they terminated her duties they didn't provide any support or demobilisation for her. This happened at the Metinaro military base, in a phase when FDTL were trying to recruit younger soldiers to replace the older ones.

Our women's group has sent a protest letter to F-FDTL Colonel Lere in Metinaro and also to Brigadier-General Taur Matan Ruak in Tasi Tolu, because Biralin was a Falintil member. We received an answer from Taur that the war had finished now and we should go and work on our farms. He said we didn't have rights any more because the army only needed women who were aged 25–35. We don't have any good adviser or capacity to organise any further protest, and so this continues until today....

... We understand that now that we are independent, we must give the opportunities to the most highly skilled, those with the skills to take on responsibilities for the whole society. I can accept that to enter to the military today you must be young and skilled. But we who fought for the resistance shouldn't be discriminated against. We recognise that we have very low formal education, and we feel hopeless because nobody listens to us.

What is very upsetting is that the discrimination is from our own partners in the struggle....[42]

Men are culturally, socially and politically dominant in Timor-Leste. The experiences of male Falintil fighters are prominently displayed. Women are startlingly absent from the displays in the Timorese Resistance Archive and Museum, which focus instead on the senior male leadership of the resistance, particularly those currently in power. Women important to the early struggle seem like ghosts: they appear occasionally in photos and documents, but mostly they are invisible in the telling of East Timorese history. There seems little capacity to imagine women in the roles of soldiers or leaders; stereotypically these heroic roles are assigned or imagined as only male.

Post-Independence Politics

Bisoi continued to be a member of Fretilin during the initial period of UN administration after 1999. She believed there was very little women's representation within the central Fretilin hierarchy and lobbied for more recognition and specific responsibilities at senior levels: "All of us who came from the hills [during resistance times] were illiterate and were not allowed to enter the main structure of the party...."[43]

On 30 August 2001, elections were held for a constitutional assembly. Fretilin won 57.4 per cent of the mandate and set about drafting a new constitution for the country. Bisoi noted that some of the Fretilin women lobbied to become part of the government as it was envisaged that the constitutional assembly would convert into the first parliament. As expected, Fretilin transformed into the first constitutional government of the new nation of Timor-Leste. Disappointed to be given no place in the new political structure, Bisoi resigned from the Fretilin party and withdrew from political life, starting a small business in Maubisse. She had been completely marginalised due to her protests:

> Because we participated in the resistance movement we are disadvantaged now, and support from the government is minimal. Yet everything today is a result of the resistance movement efforts: no one can deny it. My main problem now is my capacity, as I wasn't educated and I have very limited options. What I feel is that it is a little bit unfair for us women who were in the resistance in comparison to those who got themselves educated during that time. We concentrated only on the resistance, and now in the independence period we don't feel we have as much opportunity as those who got themselves a good education. They have more knowledge than us. We feel left behind.
>
> Discrimination still exists, because the state doesn't recognise or value women's role in the resistance. And because of their lack of background and education, women don't even have enough capacity to claim that they were resistance members. They are suffering, they don't have enough knowledge, they don't have enough capacity to represent themselves.[44]

However, in 2004, at the invitation of the new president, Xanana Gusmao, Bisoi became involved in the Commission for Veterans, collecting and assessing data on women veterans for their inclusion on commemorative lists and for veteran payments and access to resources. Then in 2006 she was invited by Gusmao to join his new CNRT political party, which would compete in the upcoming parliamentary elections. Bisoi believes Gusmao asked her to join CNRT because he supported the political participation of women but also because she was a well-known resistance and community activist who would attract supporters. Also, there was a quota for women representatives and every fourth name on party lists had to be a woman.

Gendered Recognition of Veterans

Involvement in the official veteran recognition process was an emotionally disconcerting experience for Bisoi. Bisoi, like other female combatants, was not initially recognised as such even though she had clearly engaged in combat. Additionally, since women did not serve the armed struggle in ways recognised by male guerrilla leaders, they were initially invisible in the demobilisation process. Bisoi and a small group of other women were recognised only post hoc — and in this way women were treated as something of an afterthought in the process of veteran recognition and again only as second-class soldiers.

The first round of the official veteran recognition process was restricted to those who had been formally part of the armed structure — and women, it was argued, had only been part of the civilian structure. Only 13 women registered for the combatant list, and their names were not included in the final list of names.[45] Other women said they had wanted to register but were advised by President Gusmao to wait for the second round, the clandestine civilian process.[46] Several senior resistance women were appointed as commissioners in these processes, and one observer noted that while the women were often critical of the criteria devised for combatants they finally agreed to them. The observer felt that these women had to "tread a fine line between protecting the interests of women and not marginalising themselves in the veteran community".[47] The small yet significant numbers of women such as Bisoi who served together with Falintil for all or most of the resistance period found this situation difficult to accept. After protests, Bisoi and some of these women who had registered as civilian clandestine veterans received the added designation: "located with the armed forces". Later, during the process of recognition and payment of pensions, these women successfully argued that they should be recognised in the same category as men who had served in the armed front.[48] Bisoi too received some of these benefits. However, there is a feeling that this recognition was forced and grudgingly given. In addition, the women have never been recognised for the unique roles they played in Falintil, their sacrifice in giving away their babies, their military logistical support roles, and their care and nurturing of male soldiers.

In what can be described as a campaign for recognition of women's actions during the struggle for independence, a series of documents has been published by Timorese women and their international supporters.[49] The work is being continued today by women concerned that their experiences and service to the nation are unrecognised, crimes against them remain unpunished, and their current needs and rights go unmet. The Timorese leadership has not pursued Indonesian military leaders for war crimes, due to pragmatic political considerations — and no international authority has the jurisdiction to pursue them.

The predominantly male leaders of East Timor's armed struggle were engaged in a brutal and bloody war for most of their adult life and suffered a variety of ill effects, including displacement, imprisonment, torture, and the loss of family and fellow soldiers, close friends and colleagues. They made dreadful sacrifices for their country's independence. It is these male elites who now head the government, military and police, and the society they have shaped is heavily influenced by their experiences and prejudices. These influential men have asserted their political dominance in Timor-Leste, which has precluded the full recognition of women's roles during the war and in turn excluded "women from full and assertive participation in post-war public life".[50]

Gender Disparity in Timor-Leste Today

While most Timorese women and men still live in the rural poverty of a life devoted to subsistence farming, indicators for the health and well-being of women and children are often worse. There is substantial gender inequity, as illustrated by the 2004 Human Development Index (0.426) and Gender Development Index (0.369), meaning women had a 13 per cent lower standard of living than men. Women overall have lower participation in the work force — around 36 per cent of the non-agricultural sector — and are usually in lower-level positions, meaning lower salaries, fewer benefits and less possibility of advancement.[51] In 2005, women represented around 25 per cent of the civil service but held only 2 per cent of the highest positions.[52] The gender wage gap is huge, with women earning one-eighth the income of men.[53] Disparity between men and women exists across the domains of landownership, political participation, access to education and economic activities, and domestic issues such as reproductive decision making.

Bisoi feels strongly that women, and particularly women veterans like herself, have a long way to go before they are equal partners with men in East Timorese society:

> Today my family or husband does not intervene in my political activities, but when I return home again I submit myself to the family structure. I have to listen to my husband. I recognise that in Timor-Leste it is like this. Some people do intervene in others' lives, especially in women's lives, and say she can't do this or that. But in my experience it didn't happen, from when I was young to when I was a married woman. Yet this conservatism still exists in East Timor. During the guerrilla war we never knew for sure if we were going to live or die, but during independence women are going to have their rights.[54]

The beliefs Bisoi expresses here about women still "submitting" to the family structure, where men are dominant, are common among women in Timor, especially older women. It is still socially unacceptable for women to privately or publicly contest men's power. Invisible social control is exerted using customary practices and by powerful people or institutions who define socially restricted roles for women. It also works to limit participation psychologically through an internalised feeling of subordination, social exclusion and inequality and devalues the concerns of the excluded group, in this case Timorese women. Women have to be more muted and skillful in getting around these cultural norms, and the situation of the war offered many women like Bisoi a way to do this. Post-independence politics too offers this hope. In the home, however, older women still maintain their traditional roles.

Conclusion

The unfinished life story of Bisoi is one of the lifelong struggle of a feminist nationalist. Her life journey was intertwined intimately with the fateful vicissitudes of her homeland and the nationalist movement fighting for its independence. Her relentless dedication to the cause, together with the sacrifice and commitment of thousands of her comrades, contributed to the liberation of her country from foreign occupation. Women veterans in Timor are well known and generally highly regarded in their communities. Yet the enjoyment of the fruit of nationalist struggle was not shared equitably. Victory over foreign domination was overshadowed by the continuation of feminine subordination and discrimination, not just in the domestic sphere but even in the veterans' recognition exercise. We have discussed how women combatants such as Bisoi who served the nationalist movement for independence (1974–99) have been treated with discrimination historically and received partial recognition as war veterans only after contestations by women activists. The prospects for female combatants such as Bisoi to be extended the same recognition and privileges as their male counterparts seems a long way off.

In the contested world of modern Timorese history the crucial and unique role of women in the resistance has not yet been fully acknowledged, and this affects women's full and active participation in the post-conflict society. This is significant because how a post-war society treats its female veterans is a powerful indicator of the current and future status of women in that society.[55]

It is understood that the struggle for women's rights was not possible during the difficult times of the war and was subsumed by the nationalist struggle, and women such as Bisoi accept this. However, this nationalist struggle created a pool of highly skilled and motivated women who no longer accept the status quo and who strive towards equity for women. Only now can women create and develop a separate identity alongside other international women's movements. Yet this process is fraught. Separating the recently concluded struggle for independence from the modern women's movement fighting for women's rights is still difficult. Such a separation would necessitate a cleaving and the voicing of opposition to the men — the fathers, uncles, brothers and husbands — alongside whom women fought the war, and with whom they formed families and communities during these hard times. Such a separation and shift in thinking, for both men and women, may well be impossible for the generation who suffered together during such a long and troubled war.

Notes

1. This quote is from an interview the author conducted with Rosa da Camâra (Bisoi) in the Gender Resource Unit of the parliament of

Timor-Leste in July 2010, and most of the quotations in this chapter are from that interview. Otherwise, as noted, quotes from Bisoi in this chapter are from other interviews by S. Ospina, "Participation of Women in Politics and Decision-Making in Timor-Leste: A Recent History" (Dili: UNIFEM, 2006); I. Cristalis and C. Scott, *Independent Women: The Story of Women's Activism in Timor-Leste* (London: Catholic Institute for International Relations, 2005); and I. Cristalis, *Bitter Dawn*, 2nd ed. (London: Zed Books, 2009).

2.   Cristalis, *Bitter Dawn*, p. 188.

3.   There is passionate debate about the name of the territory of East Timor. During the period of Portuguese colonisation it was usually referred to as Portuguese Timor in English-language contexts and Timor-Leste if referred to in Portuguese. After the Indonesian invasion it came more often to be referred to as East Timor in English-language contexts and RDTL — the República Democrática de Timor Leste (the Democratic Republic of East Timor), as it was declared by the independence movement — in resistance and Portuguese circles. It became widely referred to in the Tetun as Timor Loro'sae during the later resistance period of CNRM and CNRT, even in English circles. This reference fell by the wayside when the country was again declared the República Democrática de Timor Leste (RDTL) in 2002, or simply Timor-Leste (T-L). When referring to the country in English, it is now again common to call it East Timor. Some East Timorese object to this, arguing that everyone should use the country name they have chosen. English-language editors do not agree, complying with stylistic conventions that the English translation should be used when writing in English. I have tried to use the appropriate term in each context.

4.   Interview with Bisoi, 2010.

5.   These population figures are from the Timor-Leste government website, http://www.easttimorgovernment.com/demographics.htm, accessed Nov. 2010. However, considering the total population is now over one million, these figures cannot be accurate today — most figures must be at least double these numbers. The full range of languages spoken in Timor-Leste is shown on maps in Frederic Durand, *East Timor, A Country at the Crossroads of Asia and the Pacific: A Geo-historical Atlas* (Chiang Mai: Silkworm Books, 2006), pp. 46–8, 95.

6.   S. Niner, "*Hakat klot*, Narrow Steps: Negotiating Gender in Post-conflict Timor-Leste", *International Feminist Journal of Politics* 13, 3 (2011): 413–35.

7.   See S. Harris Rimmer, "The Roman Catholic Church and the Rights of East Timorese Women", in *Mixed Blessings: Laws, Religions and Women's*

Rights in the Asia Pacific Region, ed. Caroline Evan and Amanda Whiting (Leiden: Koninklijke Brill/Martinus Nijhoff Publishing, 2006).

8. Ospina, "Participation of Women in Politics", p. 18.

9. OPMT is the Organização Popular Mulher Timorense (Popular Organisation of Timorese Women), founded in 1974 as the women's wing of the nationalist political movement Fretilin.

10. H. Hill, "Fretilin: The Origins, Ideologies and Strategies of a Nationalist Movement in East Timor", MA thesis, Monash University, 1978, p. 192.

11. Interview with Bisoi, 2010.

12. Ibid.

13. Ibid.

14. Cristalis, Bitter Dawn, p. 188.

15. Interview with Bisoi, 2010.

16. Cristalis and Scott, Independent Women, p. 40.

17. Cristalis, Bitter Dawn, p. 189.

18. Interview with Bisoi, 2010.

19. S. Niner, Xanana: Leader of the Struggle for Independent Timor-Leste (Melbourne: Australian Scholarly Publishing, 2009), pp. 34–7.

20. Interview with Bisoi, 2010.

21. Ospina, "Participation of Women in Politics", p. 22.

22. Interview with Bisoi, 2010.

23. Comissao de Acolhimento, Verdade e Reconciliacao (Commission for Truth, Reception and Reconciliation), Final Report "Chega!" (Dili, 2006), http://www.etan.org/news/2006/cavr.htm, accessed March 2011, chapter 3, paragraphs 203:54 and 273:71, and chapter 5, paragraph 147:42.

24. Ibid., chapter 5, paragraph 148:42.

25. CRRN: Conselho da Resistência Revolucionário Nacional (National Council for Revolutionary Resistance) (1981–87); CNRM: Conselho Nacional da Resistência Maubere (National Council of Maubere Resistance) (1988–98); CNRT: Conselho Nacional da Resistência Timorense (National Council of Timorese Resistance) (1998–2001), not to be confused with the political party CNRT: Conselho Nacional da Reconstrucao Timorense (National Council of Timorese Reconstruction) (formed in 2007), also led by Xanana Gusmao.

26. Niner, Xanana, pp. 103–6, 111–9.

27. Cristalis and Scott, Independent Women, p. 39.

28. Interview with Bisoi, 2010.

29. Cristalis and Scott, Independent Women, p. 40.

30. Ospina, "Participation of Women in Politics", p. 23.

31. Cristalis and Scott, Independent Women, p. 41; Cristalis, Bitter Dawn, pp. 188, 279–80.

32. Ibid., pp. 189–90.
33. Interview with Bisoi, 2010.
34. Cristalis and Scott, *Independent Women*, p. 42.
35. Interview with Bisoi, 2010.
36. World Bank, "Defining Heroes: Key Lessons from the Creation of Veterans Policy in Timor-Leste", Timor-Leste, Papua New Guinea and Pacific Islands Country Management Unit East Asia and Pacific Region, 2008, p. 5.
37. Cristalis and Scott, *Independent Women*, p. 41.
38. Interview with Bisoi, 2010.
39. Cristalis and Scott, *Independent Women*, p. 40.
40. Interview with Bisoi, 2010.
41. E. Rehn and E.J. Sirleaf, *Women, War and Peace: The Independent Experts' Assessment on the Impact of Armed Conflict on Women and Women's Role in Peace-building* (New York: UNIFEM, 2002), p. 116.
42. Interview with Bisoi, 2010.
43. Ibid.
44. Ibid.
45. L. Kent, *Independent Evaluation Report: Commission on Cadres of the Resistance (CAQR)* (Dili: World Bank, 2006), p. 9.
46. Ospina, "Participation of Women in Politics".
47. Off-record interview 2010.
48. World Bank, "Defining Heroes", p. 15.
49. R. Winters, *Voice of East Timorese Women, Vol. 1* (Darwin: East Timor International Support Centre, 1999); M.D.F. Alves, L.S. Abrantes and F.B. Reis, *Hakarek no ran: Written in Blood* (Office for the Promotion of Equality, Prime Minister's Office, Democratic Republic of Timor-Leste, 2003); Cristalis and Scott, *Independent Women*; Rede Feto (with Fokupers and APSC-TL), *Hau Fo Midar; Hau Simu Moruk [I Gave Sweet; I Received Bitter]* (Dili: Rede Feto, 2007); APSC-TL (Asia Pacific Support Collective-Timor Leste with SEPI and MSS), *Segredu: Xáve ba Ukun Rasik-an [Secrecy: The Key to Independence]* (Dili, 2008); J. Conway, *Step by Step: Women of East Timor, Stories of Resistance and Survival* (Darwin: Charles Darwin University Press, 2010).
50. C.H. Enloe, *The Curious Feminist: Searching for Women in a New Age of Empire* (Berkeley: University of California Press, 2004), pp. 217–8.
51. M. Costa, R. Sharp and D. Elson, "Gender-Responsive Budgeting in the Asia-Pacific Region: Democratic Republic of Timor-Leste Country Profile", University of South Australia, 2009, www.unisanet.unisa.edu.au/genderbudgets, accessed Aug. 2010, p. 5.
52. Ospina, "Participation of Women in Politics".

53. Asian Development Bank (ADB)/UNIFEM, "Gender and Nation Building in Timor-Leste: County Gender Assessment", 2005, http://www.adb.org/documents/reports/country-gender-assessments/cga timor-leste.pdf, accessed June 2008, p. 23.
54. Interview with Bisoi, 2010.
55. See Enloe, *The Curious Feminist*.

CHAPTER 10

Karen Nationalism and Armed Struggle: From the Perspective of Zipporah Sein

Ardeth Maung Thawnghmung and Violet Cho

In late 2008 Burma watchers and members of Karen communities were taken by surprise when the Karen National Union (KNU), one of the oldest ethnicity-based organisations in Burma that has continued to engage in armed struggle against the current Burmese government, announced that Zipporah Sein would be its next general secretary. It was completely unprecedented for the historically male-dominated organisation to elect a woman. At the time, Zipporah Sein was serving as the general secretary of the Karen Women Organisation (KWO), the women's wing of the KNU. Who is Zipporah Sein? What are the circumstances that gave rise to her ascendance to one of the most important positions in the ethno-nationalist movement in Burma?

In this chapter, we will describe the life of Zipporah Sein within the context of the emergence and evolution of the Karen nationalist movement and armed struggle in Burma.[1] Particular emphasis will be placed on how Zipporah Sein perceives her role and articulates her political vision as a prominent civilian leader in an armed resistance organisation, how she believes her gender affects her relationships with her colleagues, and the role of women in the KNU struggle. The chapter is based mainly on interviews with Zipporah and her siblings and colleagues. A personal relationship between one of the authors of this article and Zipporah Sein has given us access to these primary sources of information, and allowed us to let Zipporah tell her story in her own way.

Zipporah Sein (second from left) with her mother, sister and nieces, 2009. Courtesy of Zipporah Sein

Zipporah Sein at KNU congress, 2009. Courtesy of Zipporah Sein

The armed resistance led by the KNU in 1949 emerged out of the desire to have genuine autonomy over Karen-populated areas and a distrust of the majority Burman population as a result of the communal violence during World War II. The KNU has articulated the concept of "nationalism" (known in Sgaw Karen as *hta eh kalu tha* or "love for one's nation") through the four principles articulated by Saw Ba U Gyi, the late president of the KNU. These four principles mainly emphasize the pursuit of an autonomous Karen State through armed revolt.[2] This interpretation of Karen nationalism has not been shared by some Karens, who stress non-violent approaches to maintain Karen identity and culture and to promote social, political and economic development.[3]

Zipporah Sein adheres to the official KNU interpretation of Karen nationalism, but perceives her role differently from those who took up arms at the inception of the Karen armed revolution. This chapter shows that while Zipporah's rise to power may have been a product of an internal power struggle within the KNU, her new leadership also reflects the KNU's broader strategy to adapt to current international trends and represents an attempt by second- and third-generation armed fighters to redefine the role of the KNU within the context of Burma's evolving external and domestic political landscape.

Emergence and Evolution of Karen Nationalism and Armed Struggle in Burma

Contemporary Myanmar/Burma, with a population of about 54 million, is made up of a diverse array of ethnic, cultural, religious and language groups, including Burman (the largest, constituting 68 per cent of the population), Shan (9 per cent), Karen (7 per cent), Arakanese (4 per cent), Mon (2 per cent), and more than 100 smaller language groups.[4] Burmans, along with Mons and pockets of Karens, live in lowland areas in the Irrawaddy Delta and central and southern Burma surrounded by minority populations inhabiting the highland areas bordering India, China, Laos and Thailand.

The term "Karen" is a polysemy for approximately 20 subgroups of the Karen language family that come from diverse religious, cultural and regional backgrounds. Their numbers in Burma are estimated at 3 million to 10 million.[5] The two major groups are the Sgaw (predominantly Christians and animists living in the hill regions) and the Pwo (mostly lowland Buddhists). About 15–20 per cent of Karens

Karen Nationalist Movement

1885 British occupy whole of Burma after waging three successive wars

1887 Founding of the Karen National Association, the first Pan-Karen organisation

1945 Establishment of the Karen Central Advisory Board, which makes the first demand to the British government to create a Karen State

1948 Independence of Burma

1949 KNU takes up arms for a separate state

1950 Assassination of Ba U Kyi, the KNU president

1976 National Democratic Front is formed in Manerplaw, the "capital" of KNU-controlled areas, bringing together key ethnic resistance groups

1990 First multiparty elections since the military took over power in 1962

1994 Democratic Karen Buddhist Army splits from the KNU

2004 KNU leaders engage in ceasefire negotiations with former Prime Minister Khin Nyunt. Talks break down when Khin Nyunt is placed under house arrest

2008 Assassination of KNU General Secretary Padoh Manh Shah

2010 Military-controlled multiparty elections in Burma

are Christians, 5–10 per cent are animists, and the remainder are Buddhists.[6] The Karens are spread all over lower Burma, from the Irrawaddy Delta region to the central Pegu Yoma mountain range and the eastern hills along the Thai border. In precolonial times, interactions between those who lived in the surrounding hills (including the Karens) and the majority Burman population were sporadic at best and hostile at worst. A popular Karen perception of precolonial history is that the Burmese monarchy looked down upon minority hill tribe populations as illiterate and uncivilised and occasionally employed them as protective shields against their enemies from neighbouring countries.[7]

The British, who colonised Burma in 1885, further separated Burmans from minority groups by resorting to a classic divide-and-rule policy. Minority groups, such as Karen, Chin and Kachin, were deliberately recruited in the army and police. Many Karen people welcomed the British as a protector against the majority population and a source of opportunities previously denied them. Some accepted Christianity and became the main beneficiaries of American and European missionaries who promoted literacy (in both Karen and English), education and healthcare for the newly proselytised populations. Under British rule, Karen Christians held a disproportionately large number of positions in the civil service, military and police.[8]

The resistance movement against British rule was initiated and dominated by Burman nationalists who secretly went to Japan and China in the early 1940s to get military training for their campaign against the colonisers. In 1942 the group formed the Burma Independence Army, and returned to Burma at the head of the invading Japanese. Some members of ethnic minority groups, including Karen, remained loyal and fiercely defended the British. Nearly 2,000 Karen (as well as Burman) civilians in Salween District in the east and in the Irrawaddy Delta were killed during communal violence, initially instigated by Burma Independence Army members who went after the local Karen population for their perceived privileged status and close association with the British.[9] While this collective memory of persecution had fuelled Karen nationalistic sentiment, Karen community leaders continued to uphold diverse views and approaches.[10]

Aung San and other nationalist leaders later turned against the Japanese and formed an anti-Fascist front in a secret meeting in 1944. They perceived support from Burma's ethnic minority groups as crucial to national independence.[11] After the end of World War II, nationalist leaders eventually negotiated the country's independence with the British government. Initially the Shan, Karen and Karenni preferred to keep their areas autonomous under British rule. However, after a series of meetings with the Burman nationalist leader Aung San at Panglong in Shan State, some ethnic leaders, such as from the Shan, Kachin and Chin groups, agreed to be a part of independent Burma on various conditions. Many Karen believed that their case for autonomy would be favourably considered due to the support they had provided to the British government and the sacrifices they had made in fighting against the Japanese army. It was a major blow for many Karen people when the British administration cancelled its original plan to retain the frontier areas under its direct rule. Instead, it allowed for the immediate election of a constituent assembly, leading to the country's independence.[12] The constitution of 1947 created three new states within the borders of Burma — the Shan, Karenni and Kachin — and established frameworks for the creation of new states in post-independent eras. The territories and status of the government's territorial authority over three other major ethnic groups — the Mon, Karen and Arakanese — were left open in the constitution, to be decided after independence in January 1948.[13] The current Karen State, which came into existence in 1952, encompasses only a minority of the Karen population.

From the very beginning of independence, the Burmese government led by the Anti-Fascist People's Freedom League party experienced internal dissension.[14] The government was also unable to accommodate demands by various ethnic groups for greater autonomy and independence. Towards the end of the 1940s, the Karen and Mon revolted. A decade later, the Shan and Kachin rebellions broke out. In 1962 the military took over power under the name of the Revolutionary Council, ostensibly to prevent the country from disintegrating into various units. It soon launched the "Four Cuts" policy, which forcibly relocated villages in areas controlled by resistance groups to deny them a source of food, funds, intelligence and recruits.[15] These strategies succeeded in wiping out Communist and KNU resistance groups in the Irrawaddy and Pegu Yoma. General Ne Win, the leader of the military coup, imposed restrictions on civil and political freedom and established a one-party system led by the Burma Socialist Programme Party. He introduced a socialist economy, nationalised private enterprises (including the previously vibrant media), and put restrictions on internal and external trade. However, ethnic armed organisations continued to control extensive territories along the border areas, partly as a result of the abundant natural resources and taxes imposed on goods that crossed the borders between Burma and its neighbours. The KNU formed an alliance with other armed resistance organisations to establish a nine-party National Democratic Front in 1976, which agreed in 1984 to adopt a common federal goal, dropping any demands for separate independent states.[16]

In the meantime, the isolationist and state-controlled economy in Burma soon resulted in a scarcity of basic food and consumer products, and poverty. It eventually culminated in the nationwide popular demonstrations that brought down Ne Win's regime in 1988. The military ruthlessly repressed the anti-regime demonstrations and staged a coup d'état in 1988 to govern under a new name: the State Law and Order Restoration Council (SLORC). Over 10,000 students and civilian activists fled underground into the resistance-controlled mountains, with many ending up in KNU-controlled areas.

The SLORC removed a few restrictions on foreign trade and investment and held a multiparty election in 1990 to promote its international image. The main opposition party, the National League for Democracy (NLD) led by Aung San Suu Kyi, the daughter of the leading nationalist Aung San who had been assassinated in 1947, won a landslide victory. The military junta refused to honour the results and instead cracked down on opposition parties. In the early 1990s a dozen NLD elected members of parliament fled into KNU-held territory, where they formed the exiled National Coalition Government Union of Burma.

By the early 1990s, the geopolitical situation was no longer favourable to armed resistance groups. The Thai government now adopted a "constructive engagement" policy towards Burma to secure lucrative logging, fishery and gas pipeline deals offered by the SLORC.[17] Funds from this emergency sell-off of natural resources to Thailand enabled the Burmese junta to buy much-needed arms, ammunitions and aircraft from neighbouring countries, particularly China. The SLORC was also able to conclude successful ceasefire negotiations with 17 armed groups by the mid-1990s, which enabled it to launch a stronger military campaign against the remaining armed resistance groups, including the KNU.[18] The biggest setback to the KNU was a major split that led to the formation of the Democratic Karen Buddhist Army. Some attribute the cause of the split to the reaction of disgruntled KNU soldiers, many of whom were Buddhist, against corruption, abuse and religious discrimination by the Christian-dominated leadership.[19] Many KNU members blame the Burmese military for enflaming these tensions to split the organisation. The formation of the Buddhist army organisation led to the collapse of the KNU's headquarters in 1995. This was soon followed by a number of smaller KNU breakaway factions signing ceasefire agreements with the Burmese military regime.[20]

By 2008, only four non-ceasefire groups — the KNU, Karenni National Progressive Party, Shan State Army-South and Chin National Front — maintained military forces of any strength, on dwindling economic and recruitment bases.[21] The State Peace and Development Council (SPDC), the new name for the SLORC, unilaterally proceeded with its "road map" by holding the National Convention, which drew up a new constitution that gave a dominant role to the military. The SPDC used a combination of coercive and incentive measures and outright manipulation of votes to procure a very high approval rate for the constitution and held nationwide legislative elections on 7 November 2010. Three Karen political parties contested the elections, emphasising a non-violent approach to promote Karen nationalism within the legal boundaries. The Union Solidarity and Development Party, a pro-junta party, whose high level positions were dominated by retired military and government personnel, won an overwhelming majority.

Former SPDC Prime Minister Thein Sein was appointed the new president. He soon embarked on a series of reforms, including negotiation with armed groups, releasing political prisoners (notably Aung San Suu Kyi), and relaxing control over the economy, politics and media. Suu Kyi's party then officially registered to participate in the by-elections in April 2012. She and 42 other members of her party won almost all the contested seats and have become the main opposition party in the parliament although they occupy only 6.8 per cent of the seats. The new government has adopted a more lenient approach towards ethnic armed resistance movements by signing provisional agreements with most of them, including the KNU but excluding those in northern Burma, where fighting recurred between government troops and the Kachin Independence Organisation. Detailed arrangements to end conflict with these resistance groups may take years, given their sheer numbers and the seemingly incompatible positions between them and the government.

It is during these critical years of Burma's history that Zipporah Sein has taken over leadership of the KNU. The decisions she and her movement make are likely to have a major impact not just on the future of the KNU and the Karen people but also on the nature of political reconciliation and institutional arrangements for Burma's diverse population.

Zipporah Sein's Childhood and Education

Zipporah was born in a hamlet called Saw Kha Der in Kler Lwe Htu (Nyaung Lay Bin) District on 27 March 1955, the fifth of eight children of General Tamalar Baw and Naw Laurel. By then, the Karen armed revolt was in full swing. Her family members had to flee from one area to the next to accompany the father, who was a leading figure in the Karen armed resistance movement. Zipporah's father joined the British Army at the age of 16 and took up arms against the Burmese government at the onset of the Karen armed revolt in 1949. Zipporah describes her precarious childhood growing up in a war zone as follows:

> I do not have any special place I call my home because I have been living in so many places in my life, particularly in the mountainous jungle areas of eastern Burma. Because my father is an active member of the Karen revolutionary movement, our family members constantly had to run for our lives to avoid Burmese government soldiers.
>
> Villagers did not usually let us stay with them for fear of government retaliation, so they built shacks in the field for us to stay outside the village. Quite a few of those in eastern Burma who knew nothing about the Karen revolution ultimately rejected us.[22]

Zipporah recalled growing up missing the presence of her father:

> I hardly saw my father, and I only knew a few things about him. When we asked for our father, my mother would tell us that he had to travel with a big mission to liberate his people. We were the happiest children when he came back, no matter how short the visit was. However, this happiness never lasted long because we knew that our father would have to go away again.

It was Zipporah's resourceful mother who was single-handedly responsible for the upbringing and early education of Zipporah and her siblings. As a soldier, Zipporah's father was not paid a salary. Her mother worked as a schoolteacher and was provided food to feed her children. Sometimes Zipporah and her brother helped people harvest paddy in exchange for food. A devout Baptist, she and her family continued to pray together every morning and evening. Zipporah also mentions that her traditional Karen Christian family background has influenced her principles, such as honesty, kindness and generosity. She sees God as her "true friend" and has found comfort in prayer and communication with God to gain emotional and spiritual strength whenever she has encountered challenges.

Zipporah's early awareness about Karen people and history came through her mother, who she says was a great night-time storyteller:

> My mother would tell us about the Karen revolution and our father's involvement in the struggle. She told us stories about Japanese colonisation, and how dominant Burmans oppressed Karen people, which led to the Karen armed insurrection. These stories played a very important part in my life as they inspired us and influenced our thoughts. My mother also said that if Karen gained autonomy we would not need to run away again and we could live happily with our father. I even had a dream of living with my parents and other siblings in a village where we settled permanently and did not need to move any more. As a child, I was deeply hoping for that special day to come. I am still waiting.

Zipporah acknowledges the powerful influence of her mother, who instilled a sense of duty and responsibility in the minds and hearts of her children. Most of Zipporah's siblings are currently serving in important leadership positions in the KNU as military personnel, teachers and administrators. In a 2010 interview with Violet Cho, Karenni National Progressive Party General Secretary Khu Oo Reh considered Zipporah's background as a strength: "In my view, their family's participation in the revolution has become a sort of ritual, that is passed down the generations. She has got a good background and foundation in the movement."

Zipporah and her siblings learned how to read and write the Karen language from their mother before going to formal primary, middle and high schools in the Karen-controlled area. In order to further her studies in a government university, Zipporah repeated her high school education in a government-controlled area. However, she gave up halfway when she heard that her friend who had sat for matriculation had to run for her life from local authorities who uncovered her familial connection with the Karen armed resistance. After giving up her dream to pursue a university education, Zipporah decided to go back to the Karen "liberated" area and dedicate her life to teaching.

Zipporah's passion for teaching came at an early age, and she recalls fondly the fun she and her elder sister had when they occasionally replaced their mother as teachers:

> I was only eleven years old when I first became a teacher. My older sister and I took over my mother's teaching responsibility in the small school she'd set up, when she went secretly to a city

for medical treatment for her abdominal pain. It was really fun because we registered all the students who attended our school and we started teaching. Some students were my friends and some were older than me. We were supposed to take a 10- or 15-minute break during school hours but sometimes we would let it drag on for an hour. When we thought we had had enough playing we went back to the classroom to teach again.

From Teacher to General Secretary of Karen Women Organisation

While she was teaching in one of the districts controlled by the KNU, Zipporah began to get involved in a local women's organisation that had been established to address the social and humanitarian needs of Karen residents. In 1985 she was elected general secretary of the Karen Women Organisation, a position she proudly accepted; but she soon realised that holding two jobs — as a teacher and the general secretary — was too much for her. She decided to leave the KWO and focus all her attention on teaching. Padoh Lah Say, Zipporah's former colleague and a KNU officer, remembered Zipporah as follows:

> I have known Zipporah since 1986 when I came to work as a schoolteacher in Hway Baw Lu. Zipporah had a passion for learning and teaching. She was a hard worker, and a dedicated public servant. I found her constantly learning new things and asking questions. She was also very patient and treated others with respect. Most people, including her colleagues, students and myself, loved her and enjoyed working with her.[23]

Zipporah's teaching career came to an end in 1995, when the KNU's main headquarters were overrun by government forces. Along with many Karen civilians who were now displaced, Zipporah and her family moved to Mae Ra Mu refugee camp, on the Thailand-Burma border. It was at the camp that she focused her attention on women's and children's issues.

The Refugee Camp: Working for Women and Children

By the time Zipporah got to the refugee camp the KWO was barely functional, due to the fall of the KNU's headquarters and the ongoing war and displacement of Karen residents. Some leaders went back to Burma, while others resettled overseas. Zipporah recalled that it was a challenging time for the KWO amidst many urgent needs that had to be fulfilled. In 1999, she quit teaching to dedicate herself to the KWO:

> When I came to live in Mae Ra Mu camp, I saw that it was neces-
> sary to reorganise the women's organisation to address the needs
> of refugee families. We used to live in the jungle, where we had
> unlimited space and freedom of movement. However, the refugee
> camp was cramped and crowded so we need to change our living
> style. I set up a women's group in each section of the camp to
> make a list of their needs in the household and coordinated collec-
> tion and distribution of essential items for pregnant women, new
> mothers and infants. I opened nursery schools and summer schools
> for children to learn basic reading and writing skills as well as to
> educate them with necessary health and hygiene knowledge.

She was also concerned with the prevalence of indiscriminate corporal punishment towards children:

> There is a need to change our traditional perception about the role
> of children in our society. I was disturbed to see, while living in
> the camp, how children were punished physically, regardless of the
> severity of their mistakes. There were no rules and guidance for
> child-rearing. So while in the camp, I also organised training and
> education for parents on child psychology and development and
> how to raise children.

Financial need was the most challenging part of the KWO activities. The then treasurer fled with all the KNU money to government-controlled areas in Burma, and collection of dues from local women's units was hampered due to the war situation. Zipporah began to send applications overseas to get financial aid to run activities for the camp and slowly reorganised the KWO office. She was later invited overseas to talk about the situation of Burmese women and refugees, an experience that exposed her to new perspectives and ideas:

> My first overseas trip was to Norway, where I made a presentation
> at the World Women's Conference. It was something I had never
> dreamt of. I started travelling regularly to Thailand. I worked very
> hard to speak, write and research in English in order to give pre-
> sentations at international conferences. I did not turn down the
> offer to go for an EU lobbying trip to advocate for my people, even
> though I didn't understand how lobbying and campaigning worked.
> After coming back from that lobbying trip, I set up lots of pro-
> grammes under the KWO.

Zipporah set up a women's rights school and other learning centres to train young women to work with local women's groups. Their programmes continue to encourage Karen women to participate in major decision making, empower them to be self-confident and outspoken, make them aware of their rights, and encourage them to get involved in the movement against the military government. Noting the low rate of political participation of women in nationalist struggle in the late 1990s, Zipporah tries to send her women staff for further training and education whenever opportunities arise. She believes that education is key to women's participation in politics.

Zipporah spent most of her time as KWO general secretary promoting education, health, family welfare and women's rights. She first attended the KNU congress in 2000 as a women's representative. When she attended the congress as a women's representative again in 2004, she was elected to serve on the KNU Executive Committee, which had 11 members consisting mostly of the highest-ranking authorities in the organisation. She nevertheless continued to devote much of her time to the KWO.

From the KWO to the KNU

On 14 February 2008, the charismatic KNU General Secretary Padoh Manh Shah was gunned down at his home in Mae Sot. He had fled to the KNU area in 1966 at age 22 after graduating from college with a major in history. He worked his way up to the highest level of the KNU political machinery by first serving as a soldier, like other KNU male leaders. As a Pwo Karen Buddhist, Padoh Manh Shah represented an anomaly within the KNU leadership dominated by Sgaw Karen Christians. Speaking fluent Burmese and advocating for a federal union in Burma, he was highly regarded for his diplomatic skill in building trust among disparate members of the resistance. However, his uncompromising "politics-first demand" policy towards the Burmese military regime was at odds with the "peace-through-development policy of mutual trust building" strategy adopted by other ceasefire groups.[24] This alienated some segments of the Karen population within and outside the resistance movement. The "politics-first demand" policy put political issues such as equal rights, the right to self-determination, and moves towards federalism as a precondition before negotiating a ceasefire arrangement.[25]

The KNU holds elections every four years for president, vice-president, general secretary as well as executive members. At the 14th congress in November 2008, Zipporah attended as a member of the executive committee. Tamalar Baw, Zipporah's father, became the president of the KNU, and Zipporah Sein was elected general secretary. This new development came as a surprise to many, including Zipporah herself. Though she felt unprepared for the responsibility, she gracefully accepted the mandate given by her supporters, with the hope to inspire more women to take up leadership positions.

Numerous accounts were offered as to how and why Zipporah was elected to the highest position in the KNU. A member of KWO who attended the KNU congress recalled that approximately 100 delegates voted for candidates in the election through a series of screening processes.[26] Zipporah Sein was one of the two most favoured candidates for the position of general secretary. The other candidate was reportedly Padoh David Taw (d. 2012), a former secretary of the KNU Foreign Department. The voting for David Taw and Zipporah was close, and therefore another round of elections had to be held, in which Zipporah emerged as a clear winner.

Zipporah and the KNU

It is difficult to uncover the motivations of delegates who voted for or against Zipporah Sein. Some suggested a possibility of vote rigging and manipulation by the KNU establishment, which was dominated by her relatives, while others speculated that she may have genuinely earned the votes due to her past accomplishments, experience and role as an internationally recognised humanitarian worker, which could potentially help the KNU's image and raise its international profile. In the view of some male delegates who voted for her, it may have been in the best interest of the KNU to have a KWO woman activist within its leadership.

Burma activists, members of the Karen community, and foreign scholars and experts have offered a number of reasons for Zipporah's ascendance to the KNU's dominant position, which had previously been held by men. Most pointed out the role of "dynastic" politics, since many of Zipporah's siblings occupied leadership positions in the KNU. Some common criticisms of Zipporah are that she lacks first-hand experience in politics; that she is the puppet of her father or brothers or other leaders; and that she is merely reactive, and not proactive enough to develop new and pragmatic visions and strategies for the KNU in accordance with the changing nature of Burmese domestic politics.[27]

Zipporah is well aware of these criticisms against her and her family. She said:

> Some people think that I got this position because of my father. I may not have a lot of experience with KNU work, but I have so much experience working with grass-roots populations in promoting education and health, and in working with international organisations. All of these should be counted as strengths, but nobody seems to acknowledge them. People elected me because of my work with KWO, not because I'm the daughter of a KNU leader.

Zipporah also claimed that her father did not vote for her to become general secretary of the KNU. In fact, she mentioned that her father strongly objected when she became a member of the KNU Executive Committee in 2004, reasoning that women in general and Zipporah in particular should continue to work for the women's organisations and help promote political awareness among women.

There are nonetheless others who view her victory in a positive light. Khu Oo Reh, general secretary of the Karenni National Progressive Party, for instance, thinks highly of her: "She became popular and gained recognition from ethnic armed groups, democracy forces and the international community since she was working with the Karen Women Organisation. As a single person with no familial responsibilities, she can devote her time to political work more than typical women."[28]

Others comment that Zipporah's gender and rich experiences at the grass-roots level helped improve the image of the KNU among the Burmese opposition movement as well as the international community. Ehna, the head of the KNU Dawei District Information Department and the editor of *Kwekalu*, said:

> ... the perception of women needing to be involved in the political movement is influenced by outsiders. The promotion of women's rights is very popular these days. People will applaud and show their admiration for an organisation that appoints a higher proportion of women in leadership positions. The KNU leadership added an additional constitutional amendment to establish a quota for

women's participation at every level of political leadership.... Since Zipporah was elected as KNU general secretary, the KNU's image has become good again, and the Western media really likes that. She is a role model for other women, and she can inspire women to be aware of and promote their rights.[29]

Khu Oo Reh also pointed out Zipporah's positive influence on women in the resistance movement and her impact on the image of the KNU: "She is a guiding star for women who want to be involved in political leadership. I'm really proud of her ... I also think that the KNU will get more support and recognition from the international community and from ethnic and democracy groups for being open-minded and giving women opportunities to become a leader." Zipporah speaks English and communicates well with the outside world, and she is the founder of the Women's League for Burma, which has brought together women of different ethnic groups. Her good relations with other ethnic groups in the resistance movement and her ability to communicate with foreign media and NGOs may have put her in a good position and made her a preferred candidate to serve the KNU now that its international links are so important for funding and diplomatic strategy.

Gender and Politics

It is difficult to generalise about gender relationships in Burma, as they vary across generational, cultural and religious groups and within individual households. Buddhism (the religion practised by the majority of Burmese) prescribes a superior status for men and states that a person can attain enlightenment or become a Buddha only after going through the life cycle as a man.[30] Although Christianity (mainly the Baptist Church) in Burma does not practise institutional discrimination against women leaders, there have so far been only a handful of ordained women ministers. Legal practices in Burma recognize equal inheritance between sons and daughters, but the Burmese government has exercised various forms of gender discrimination in higher education by setting a higher bar against women candidates for professional schools such as medicine and engineering. Women still occupy a minute proportion of high-level government and professional positions, and a greater degree of respect has continued to be accorded to men as heads of household in the majority of Burmese families.

Zipporah offered an explanation for the existing political apathy among Karen women:

> The majority of Karen women grew up in a society where politics is not openly discussed. Even in village-level meetings, women don't really get a chance to speak out. Those who attend community meetings are often husbands. There is also a popular Karen maxim that discourages women from participating and engaging in political organisations. Consequently, women in our community have less interest in politics.
>
> Those who live in rural areas and refugee camps always have to focus and think about their survival, so that stops them from getting involved in politics. When both wives and husbands work for the opposition movement it becomes difficult for the family to fulfil their basic needs. So it is difficult for a woman to be an active nationalist. Male politicians in the movement today don't need to think about that because they know that their wife will take full responsibility for the family. If we look back in Karen history, most politicians including my father are supported by their wives. I believe that women would do equally well in politics if they were encouraged and supported by their husbands. I have a colleague in KWO who got full support from her husband. She travelled regularly for her work, and left her child with her husband. This kind of practice is growing in the Karen community, but it is still rare. For example, men can listen to the radio every morning but most women can't do that because they have to prepare food early in the morning and do other stuff for their family, so they miss listening to news. It will be easier for young women to work in politics because they are free to make a decision and set goals.

Zipporah's active involvement in social and political fields is helped by the fact that she has never married. Following the death of her fiancé during a military operation, she vowed to remain single to honour his legacy. Zipporah also acknowledges the different ways Karen women have contributed to the nationalist struggle:

> Throughout the history of the Karen armed revolution, many women have been directly and indirectly involved in the struggle for freedom and self-determination. Women try to hold the family together while their husbands are supporting the movement as soldiers. There are so many women who are actively involved in the education sector by inspiring young people to love their people and become Karen nationalists. There are also women who work in the health, transportation and communication sectors, carrying

and delivering messages. In the past, a lot of women were involved in military operations and some even became officers and colonels. In addition, Karen women demonstrate strong interest in the community and social work.

Padoh Lah Say, a KNU official, also pointed out the crucial role of his wife, which enabled him to participate in armed revolution:

> When I was elected to work in the Karen education department, the KNU could not financially support me. However, my wife raised pigs and chickens and sold them for money, which she used to support my work. I can travel and work with the money she saved for me. So in this way, she is supporting the Karen movement as well. If a Karen woman says she loves her people and wants to work for them, even if she is not actively involved in the movement, she can stay home and support her husband, which can be counted as a way of working for her people.[31]

Zipporah, however, felt genuinely disadvantaged by her gender in her workplace, and expressed her frustration as a female general secretary:

> There are some male colleagues who hold the traditional views that women are not as competent as men, which really undermined my confidence. I felt like if I were a man I would be treated differently, with more respect. Most of the people who came and congratulated me on the day I was elected were women. A few male leaders came and congratulated me, but almost all of them just passed by without saying a word. I was very upset. Is that male culture that they don't know how to compliment women?

Zipporah said the use of a secret ballot during the election for the general secretary prevented her from identifying her supporters, but she seemed quite sure that most of the people currently working with her in a high position did not vote for her. The fact that another candidate came very close to winning the position also explains her lack of popularity among some segments within the KNU leadership.

> I often feel the superior attitudes held by some of my male colleagues even though they would not openly express their opinion. They demonstrated signs of unwillingness to work with me, or deliberately remained silent when I talked, raised and presented issues during our meetings. I don't feel good about this, but I can't do anything about it; all I can do is express my feelings. Sometimes male Karen leaders say that men and women have equal

opportunities and equal rights, but based on my experience, some still don't want to agree and accept female leadership.

I despair sometimes. But I don't want to give up because this is a duty and responsibility that I couldn't stop doing. I always think that I'm working for all Karen people. Of course I know that everything I do won't be perfect, but I have a motto that if people give me a duty, I will do my best. Sometimes when I'm feeling down, I pray to God to give me strength, intelligence to make good decisions. I also keep my own diary to write when I'm feeling upset. Fortunately, there are some people who understand me, respect me and try to work closely with me.... Because I have confidence and believe in myself, I can overcome whatever problem I encounter.

While gender may be an important factor in influencing the negative perception of Zipporah's male colleagues in the KNU, other factors, such as her lack of experience in politics and disagreement over her political orientation among the committee members, could also contribute to the prevailing animosity towards her leadership. She encounters great resistance against her position from some segments within the KNU leadership who do not share her vision.

Zipporah's Political Vision

As the general secretary of the KNU, Zipporah has the daily duties of addressing reports from the frontlines, responding to requests for information, finance and training, hosting members of allied resistance movements and journalists, attending meetings, and coordinating plans and urgent tasks. Unlike her predecessors and other KNU top leaders, she did not have any first-hand experience or involvement in KNU military operations. Zipporah has never fired a gun in her life, and would not give orders or suggestions related to KNU military operations. Professing her belief in non-violence, she nevertheless defends the Karens' armed struggle as a mechanism for self-defence against authoritarian rule, while admitting the importance of other political and peaceful means of struggle. She interprets Karen nationalism as follows:

I don't really think of myself as a nationalist who focuses on the interests of my community at the exclusion and expense of other communities. I believe in equal treatment of all ethnic groups, including Burman. As a Karen, I respect my culture and traditions. I also want people to respect my culture and traditions. At the same time, I also respect other people's cultures and traditions. I don't want Karen people to disappear one day. There are a few traditions and cultural practices that are not good to practise nowadays, and they should be discarded, but many good cultural practices should be maintained. Of course dominant groups have oppressed us for so many years, and their culture influenced some of our Karen people as well. When I talk about culture, I don't only mean clothing, music, literature, etc. … but values like honesty, sharing and hospitality, which should be maintained. This is a unique culture, but it has nearly disappeared. For example, in rural areas and refugee camps, people are losing the culture of hospitality because of continuing repression and hardship. Before, if you went to a Karen village, you'd be given food, but now it has become rare. I don't want this to become something that only exists on paper or in the national anthem. The main thing I want to see in my life is seeing my people develop and progress.

Zipporah measures progress for the Karen community through the protection of children and empowerment of women, equal rights, and the promotion of education, health and culture to improve overall living standards at the grass-roots level. She perceives and describes her role in the armed resistance movement not as an armed fighter who leads the battle, but as an educator who is responsible for promoting awareness about the adverse consequences of civil war:

> Good soldiers should not only be good at fighting, they should also have political views and they should make themselves understand contemporary politics. I always suggest and initiate the inclusion of political awareness training when there is a military training. We educate soldiers and officials to make them fully aware of international law, particularly related to landmines and child soldiers.

She disseminates information and conducts awareness training about landmines and child soldiers among Karen National Liberation Army soldiers.

Ceasefire Negotiations with the Burmese Government in the Post-2010 Period

A stalemate that characterised the relationship between the KNU and the government during the latter years of the SPDC regime came to an end when the new government made efforts to reopen negotiations after 2010. The KNU's army chief of staff led the first round of cease-fire negotiations with the government team in January 2011 in Karen State, Burma. This was followed in April by a high-profile second round of negotiations where the Karen team was led by Zipporah Sein to work out detailed arrangements for the ceasefire agreement. Zipporah recalled her encounter with Burmese government representatives as follows:

> I was greeted by a crowd of ministers, uniformed military officers, and civil servants. I shook their hands, but I stopped smiling when I saw uniformed military officers and skipped them. Their appearance brought back so many painful memories to me. Most of the ministers I met in fact were former division commanders and battalion commanders who fought in major battlefields against the KNU. And I feel the head of the Burmese negotiation team treated me differently than he treated my male counterparts in the KNU. He seemed to be more at ease, friendlier, and tended to share detailed information with my male counterparts. I think we have mutual distrust towards one another.

The second round of negotiations nonetheless resulted in a tentative agreement to establish a code of conduct for soldiers from both sides as well as international and local monitoring mechanisms to form peace-building groups, to set up liaison offices in various cities inside Burma, and to resettle and rehabilitate internally displaced people and refugees. The talks also covered demining, citizenship, implementation of rule of law and "sustainable development", land issues, and the release of all Karen political prisoners. The KNU team then travelled to the capital and Rangoon to meet with the president and Aung San Suu Kyi as well as Karen civil organisations.

Despite this progress, significant disagreements remain and mutual distrust persists. President Thein Sein, for instance, proposed a three-step plan that would begin with a ceasefire truce and ultimately bring various armed opposition groups (presumably without having to disarm) to participate in the "all inclusive political process" within the framework of parliamentary politics to begin building mutual trust and confidence for a long-term political solution. The KNU, on the other hand, perceives the ceasefire negotiation as an integral and initial step towards political dialogue that should take place outside the parliament to resolve outstanding issues such as economic opportunities and social equality. The KNU also advocates for a nationwide ceasefire, especially an end to hostilities and fighting in Kachin State.

Zipporah commented:

> While I personally welcome the government's initiative on the
> ceasefire agreement, I am deeply concerned that their action is
> economically driven. I believe that the government's motivation to
> end civil war in the country is based on their desire to entice
> foreign investment and to promote economic development in areas
> occupied by ethnic populations. I feel they do not understand
> the roots of ethnic armed struggles nor care about aspirations of
> minority ethnic groups. They seem to neglect the very fact that we
> are struggling for equal rights and opportunity.

Zipporah also commented that they still have to work out detailed
arrangements on the withdrawal of Burmese military troops from
areas previously occupied by civilians and villagers who are currently
internally displaced.

According to Zipporah, the role of the KNU (perceived by the
government as an illegal organisation) remains uncertain under the
current constitution, but it could be transformed into a parliamentary
political party. Zipporah concluded, "We will seriously consider if our
people think that the KNU should be a political party representing
Karen people in Karen State or the entire Karen population in the
country. If my people want, I am ready to represent Karen and be a
member of parliament."

Conclusion

The KNU has modified some of its official policies to respond to the
changing international and domestic environments and dwindling resources over the 60 years of its existence. For instance, it has softened
its demand for an independent separate Karen State and instead campaigned for an autonomous Karen State within a federal union in
Burma in a bid to win both international and Burman-majority support. The new government itself has taken a more accommodating
stance towards armed resistance groups by reopening dialogue with
the KNU and facilitating preliminary ceasefire agreements. Outstanding disagreements have yet to be resolved between the two sides
in terms of steps to be taken towards national reconciliation.

Zipporah's rise to power may have been a combination of her
gender, her past accomplishments, the broader strategy by the KNU to

show that it is pursuing a more peaceful negotiating strategy, and/or the result of factional struggle within the organisation which was won by those who were close to her. However, she has brought along her unique experiences to the KNU and redefined the means of pursuing Karen liberation. She may be perceived as part of the conservative and establishment force within the KNU, but she has continued to wage other equally important battles that are not necessarily defined in militaristic and militant terms. The KNU definitely is at an important crossroad where it will need to continuously redefine its role and strategies to position itself as a legitimate body representing the majority Karen populations in the new and evolving political landscape in Burma.

Postscript

At the KNU congress in December 2012, Zipporah Sein was elected vice-chairperson. It is debatable whether this means increased power for her in the organisation. Saw Kwe Htoo Win, a well-known "moderate" member of the KNU leadership, replaced her as general secretary, while General Saw Mutu Sae Poe, the KNU's commander-in-chief, replaced Zipporah's father, Tamalar Baw, who retired as chairman of the organisation. As of early 2013, the KNU continued its ceasefire negotiations with the Burmese government.

Notes

1. In 1989 the military junta replaced the existing English names for the country and its divisions, townships, cities, streets, citizens and ethnic groups with what it considered to be more authentic Burmese names. Thus, "Burma" became "Myanmar" and its citizens "Myanmars"; "Rangoon" became "Yangon"; and ethnic groups such as the Karen were renamed "Kayin". The choice to use the old or new names has become one method of indicating one's political stance towards the Burmese junta. We use the pre-1989 terms to avoid confusion, as these terms are commonly used in English-language publications, including the books, journals and other sources cited in this study.

2. The four principles of Ba U Gyi are as follows: (1) Surrender is out of the question; (2) The recognition of the Karen State must be completed; (3) We shall retain our arms; (4) We shall decide our own political destiny.

3. See, for example, Ardeth Thawnghmung, *The "Other" Karen in Myanmar: Ethnic Minorities and the Struggle without Arms* (Lanham: Lexington Books, 2012).

4. Central Intelligence Agency, *The World Factbook: Burma*, 2011, https://www.cia.gov/library/publications/the-world-factbook/geos/bm.html, accessed 6 May 2011.

5. Ardeth Maung Thawnghmung, *The Karen Revolution in Burma: Diverse Voices, Uncertain Ends*, Policy Studies 46 (Southeast Asia) (Washington, DC: East-West Center, 2008), 3. Zipporah Sein commented that attendees of the Karen Unity Seminar, an annual gathering of key Karen groups, estimated the Karen population in 2011 to be between 8 million and 10 million (Zipporah Sein 2011, personal correspondence).

6. Ibid.

7. Karen National Union, *History of the Karens and the KNU*, n.d., http://www.karen.org/knu/KNU_His.htm, accessed 15 Mar. 2009; Harry Marshall, "The Karens: An Element in the Melting Pot of Burma", *The Southern Workman* 56 (1927): 26–33.

8. John F. Cady, *A Modern History of Burma* (Ithaca: Cornell University Press, 1958).

9. Andrew Selth, "Race and Resistance in Burma, 1942–1945", *Modern Asian Studies* 20, 3 (1986): 491; Martin Smith, *Burma: Insurgency and the Politics of Ethnicity* (Bangkok: White Lotus; Dhaka: University Press; London and New York: Zed Books, 1999), p. 82; Dorothy Guyot, "Communal Conflict in the Burma Delta", in *Southeast Asian Transitions: Approaches through Social History*, ed. Ruth McVey (New Haven and London: Yale University Press, 1978).

10. Thawnghmung, *Karen Revolution*, pp. 6–7; Josef Silverstein, *Burmese Politics: The Dilemma of National Unity* (New Brunswick: Rutgers University Press, 1980), p. 115.

11. Thakin Tin Mya, *Fascist Taw Lan Yay Ta Na Chot Nhin Taing Seh Taing* [*The Headquarters and Ten Divisions of the Fascist Resistance*] (Yangon: Kyu Pyoh Sa Pay, 1968), pp. 17–8.

12. Thawnghmung, *Karen Revolution*, pp. 5–6.

13. Smith, *Burma*, p. 82.

14. Michael Charney, *A History of Modern Burma* (Cambridge: Cambridge University Press, 2009), pp. 84–6.

15. Smith, *Burma*, pp. 258–9.

16. Martin Smith, *State of Strife: The Dynamics of Ethnic Conflict in Burma*, Policy Studies 36 (Southeast Asia) (Washington, DC: East-West Center, 2007), p. 37.

17. Maung Aung Myoe, *Neither Friend Nor Foe: Myanmar's Relations with Thailand since 1988: A View from Yangon*, IDSS Monograph No. 1, Singapore, 2002.

18. For an assessment of the ceasefire process and conditions in ceasefire areas, see Zaw Oo and Win Min, *Assessing Burma's Ceasefire Accords* (Washington, DC: East-West Center, 2007); and Mary Callahan, *Political Authority in Burma's Ethnic Minority States: Devolution, Occupation and Coexistence*, Policy Studies 31 (Washington, DC: East-West Center, 2007).

19. Thawnghmung, *Karen Revolution*, p. 30.

20. Ashley South, "Governance and Legitimacy in Karen State", in *Ruling Myanmar: From Cyclone Nargis to General Elections*, ed. N. Cheeseman *et al.* (Singapore: ISEAS Publishing, 2010), pp. 63–89.

21. Smith, *State of Strife*, p. 48.

22. All interviews with Zipporah Sein were conducted between 15 and 30 May 2010 by Violet Cho via Skype. Cho was in Melbourne, Australia, and Zipporah Sein was in an undisclosed location in the Burma borderlands.

23. Interview with Padoh Lah Say conducted by Violet Cho by telephone on 12 August 2010. Cho was in Canberra, and Padoh Lah Say was in an undisclosed location in the Burma borderlands.

24. Martin Smith, "Burma: The Karen Conflict", in *Encyclopedia of Modern Ethnic Conflicts*, ed. J.R. Rudolph Jr (Westport: Greenwood Press, 2003), p. 20.

25. Interview with Padoh Mahn Shah by Ardeth Maung Thawnghmung, Mae Sot, Thailand, 2006.

26. The KNU organised itself into seven administrative districts (Thaton, Toungoo, Nyaunglaybin, Mergui-Tavoy, Papun, Dooplaya and Pa-an), which were further sub-divided into townships and tracts. Each of the districts administered by the civilian wings of armed resistance groups was also controlled by a corresponding brigade, a parallel military formation of the KNLA (Karen National Liberation Army). The KNU constitution stipulates that only official representatives from all seven districts and general headquarters (both administrative and military) can vote. Official delegates from the KNU district and KNLA brigades who attend the KNU congress nominate and vote for KNU's central committee members. The 35 candidates who receive the most votes form the central committee, with the next five becoming alternate members. The central committee members then vote for an executive committee (11 members), which in turn decides within itself by secret ballot the five main positions: chairman, vice-chairman, general secretary and two joint secretaries.

27. This criticism also comes from some low-ranking, district-level KNU officials who have had tensions with the central KNU leadership. Some KNU district leaders perceive Zipporah's father as authoritarian and a hardliner.

28. Interview with Khu Oo Reh conducted by Violet Cho by telephone on 8 August 2010. Cho was in Canberra, Australia, and Khu Oo Reh was in an undisclosed location in the Burma borderlands.
29. Interviews with Ehna were conducted by Violet Cho by telephone on 10 August 2010. Cho was in Canberra, Australia, and Ehna was in an undisclosed location in the Burma borderlands.
30. Melford Spiro, *Gender Ideology and Psychological Reality* (New Haven: Yale University Press, 1997).
31. Interview with Padoh Lah Say by Violet Cho, 2010.

Becoming Women Nationalists

Helen Ting

Introduction

This book examines individual women's experiences in nationalist struggles in Southeast Asia. A sceptical reader may wonder about the value of taking a biographical rather than a broader historical approach. Does it achieve anything more than just adding women into the equation? How can examining the life stories of individual women constitute a step towards a better knowledge of women's involvement in nationalist movements? If those women we study represent the exceptions rather than the rule, how can the biographical approach go beyond focusing on mere personalities to linking their life stories with the social and collective aspects of history?

Shifts in theoretical concerns and attention to new historical questions have led to renewed academic interest in biography and to changing approaches in writing biography.[1] The biographical approach offers a window into what Roxana Waterson described as "that space where history intersects with personal experience".[2] There is a growing effort "not only to understand the social and political contexts in which individuals lived but also to explore in much more detail the complex ways in which individuals relate to the worlds they inhabit".[3] This captures the intention of our biographical studies of individual women nationalists, within the limits of availability of information. Indeed, to look at life stories without the knowledge of their historical context impoverishes much of our understanding of their experiences.

Besides adding to our knowledge regarding women's role in nationalist movements in Southeast Asia, the underlying theoretical concern that inspired this book is to understand their political and personal trajectory from the point of view of identity and agency. To what extent and how did the ideas and perspectives of these women nationalists bear the imprint of the sociocultural context of their time, which was at the confluence of colonialism, patriarchal traditions and modern[4] ideals of national and personal emancipation? Despite being "products" of their eras and being women, how did they overcome the odds to push for new norms and practices and challenge existing structures through their sociopolitical involvements?

Theoretical discussions on the relations between identity and agency, structure and individual autonomy have always stimulated engaging debates and lie at the heart of our understanding of social change. It could be readily agreed that the identity of a person is shaped by the larger social and historical structures, notwithstanding the individuality of each person's life trajectory. How is this shaping manifested in the lives of our women nationalists? Conversely, to what extent is each of the women free to make her own decisions or to rise against structural forces such as colonialism and patriarchy? Nowadays it is fashionable to describe identity as fluid and situational. To what extent is the identity of our female protagonists changeable or rigidly determined by larger structural forces; and if their identity did evolve, how did that happen? These are the theoretical questions this short essay attempts to explore based on the preceding life narratives of our 12 heroines.

Historical Structures as Resources and Constraints

Many life events of the women nationalists described in this book were shaped by larger social forces, what Waterson described as the "intrusion of history"[5] into their lives. Various chapters illustrate how historical structures "intervened" *as a process*, in the form of providing resources or opportunity on the one hand and imposing social constraints on the other. Some of these historical events, such as growing up in a war zone, may have had dramatic consequences, while others, such as schooling, may seem to readers to be routine life experiences.

The life story of Bisoi from East Timor presents a case of how powerful larger structural forces brought her schooling to a premature end. The eruption of generalised armed conflict forced her to flee into the jungle and drew her into a Falintil squad in the footsteps of her uncle. In Laos, the impacts of the international and national socio-historical processes in the shadow of the Cold War were heavily consequential on the lives of highlanders such as Manivanh and Khamla. Laos during the 1950s and 1960s was embroiled in civil war, a victim of violent attempts by various international forces to influence the outcome of the political future of the country. Manivanh and Khamla decided that joining the Pathet Lao, which seemed to promise a better life through education, presented the best option to them.

Similarly, the life trajectory of Zipporah Sein simply cannot be understood without referring to the Karen people's historical struggle for autonomy from the Burmese state. More tragically, Zipporah recalls that she does not even have a place to call home, due to the nomadic life her family led fighting against the Burmese state. Her pursuit of higher education was blocked due to the problem of getting recognition from hostile state institutions of her schooling qualification obtained in the Karen-controlled area.

Anticipation of the eruption of an international conflict, in the shape of World War II, also led to the interruption of the education of Shamsiah Fakeh in Sumatra. Her return to Malaya led to her early marriage, which was a common practice then. As a consequence, she was not able to complete her high school education. Aishah Ghani would have suffered the same fate of being married off in her early teens, if not for the vehement opposition she staged, including a few days of hunger strike. She found an ally in the person of her Sumatran brother-in-law who was influenced by modernist Islamic thinking: he managed to persuade her parents of the importance of educating girls.

Historical structure also operated in the form of class relations. In the Philippines, historical conflicts between the landless and the landowners were carried over into the struggle for political independence, as illustrated by the struggle of Salud Algabre and her Sakdal peasant movement. Landlords maintained their grip on political power and were unsympathetic towards the efforts of peasants to fight for their welfare and improve their livelihood via anti-colonial struggle. The social position of the landlord class in Philippine society provided resources for this group's political dominance before and after independence. The impoverishment of Salud's initially landowning family bears witness to the exploitative impact of the larger socio-economic forces of the land tenure problem, leading to Salud's integration into the Sakdal peasant movement.

In many of the chapters, the education system represents an important institution of cultural reproduction, which may be part and parcel of the colonial project, or a creation of an indigenous socio-political movement, such as the case of the Thawalib school system in Sumatra based on a modernist understanding of Islam. Dissatisfaction with colonial education also led to the emergence of the "national education movement" in Burma, which emphasised Burmese language and literature as the rallying point for Burmese nationalism.

From the outset, the choice of the type of education experienced by our protagonists was often, though not always, a reflection of the socio-economic background and outlook of their parents and family, and constituted an important baseline in determining the subsequent life trajectory of these women. There is also the empowering dimension of having an educational qualification as a form of symbolic capital. Aishah Ghani from Malaya, who studied initially in Malay and Arabic, was unusual in her determination to further her studies in the English medium, which afforded her greater sociopolitical mobility. In the same light, the well-regarded Dutch education of Suyatin Kartowiyono differentiated her social position from that of Rasuna Said, who was a product of the Islamic reformist schooling system. Accordingly, it seems logical that Suyatin developed a secular political outlook while Rasuna inclined towards the Islamist groups.

Under Independent Daw San's pen, the Buddhist parents of the main character in her novel *Khin Aye Kyi* debated whether to send their child to the American Baptist mission school, and situated the debate at the level of the importance of female education to the nationalist struggle. Daw San no doubt appreciated the empowerment she gained through her Western education, herself belonging to the early generation of Burmese women who benefited from its expansion, eclipsing the role of Buddhist monastic schools. This illustrates the contradictory impact of colonisation, which may well favour one particular social group over another, be it based on gender, ethnicity, religion or class. More often than not, colonial education has historically been responsible for the emergence of the male political elites who became the leaders of the anti-colonial movement, while the first generation of educated women became the catalyst for the emancipation of women. In effect, without the expansion of female education during the colonial era, most of the women we studied would not have become teachers, writers, journalists and activists, taking the roles in nationalist movements that they did, except perhaps for Bisoi, Manivanh and Khamla, who lacked such educational advantages.

Nationalist Movements as Sites of (Re)Production of Cultural Forms

The previous section discussed how historical structures and processes intruded into our individual protagonists' lives, shaping their life trajectories, but also how the protagonists were the product of socialisation of their respective families and educational systems. This implies that they saw the world through the lenses of their parents, teachers, peers or significant others, appropriating and applying the existing norms, concepts, categories, idioms and practices that they were exposed to, what we may call "cultural forms".[6] Cultural forms are the medium through which we meaningfully carry out our daily activities and, through the process of doing so, become who we are and assume our identity.

We have read that Bisoi acquired her critical gender awareness as well as anti-colonial perspective from the nationalist movement she joined. In her autobiography, Shamsiah also credited the Malay Nationalist Party for her initiation to anti-colonialism, and traced the origins of her awareness of women's oppression to nationalist struggle. Just as family and school could be important vehicles of identity formation, the nationalist movement provided a social milieu where alternative ways of thinking that challenged the status quo were articulated, affirmed and propagated. In order for this social milieu to develop, appropriate cultural forms such as alternative political discourse and social practices needed to be developed and disseminated.

As a journalist and prolific writer of nationalist (and feminist) writings, Burmese Daw San played an active role in the creation of literary medium and public discourse (one type of cultural form) to interpret and influence popular thinking on what constituted the "protection of the interests of the nation" as well as the "woman question". Her first major publication, *Khin Aye Kyi*, was a pioneering effort to articulate a feminine model of the Burmese patriot. Reflecting the larger Burmese nationalist thinking of her time, she linked the survival of the Burmese nation to the revival and propagation of Buddha's teachings and Burmese language and literature. As was common in anti-colonial movements, Burmese traditional culture, language and religion served as a powerful mobilising force to demarcate the boundary with the "enemy" colonialists, who were Christian and English-speaking.

Nationalist movements did not invent their ideology and practices from scratch. The mode of organisation of the Viet Nam Quôc Dan Dang (VNQDD) is said to resemble Communist organisations, adopted through mimicking the Chinese nationalist party, Guomindang, which at one point received strategic advice from Soviet Union advisers. VNQDD began by establishing study groups and a bookshop, which effectively were means to spread their anti-colonial ideas. Modelled after the Guomindang, VNQDD leaders — unsurprisingly — derived their revolutionary inspiration from Sun Yat Sen and the 1911 Revolution in China. The VNQDD leader Nguyen Thai Hoc even drew a strategic comparison between the Vietnamese sociopolitical situation in 1929 and that of the 1911 Chinese Revolution in determining or justifying that the time was right to prepare for the general insurrection.

The case of the Philippine Independent Church, which united the Sakdalistas, is a good example of the transformative evolution of religious practices from the traditional Catholic Church. Its attraction to the masses was attributed to the similarity of its liturgy to the Catholic faith, minus the institutional control and link with Rome. Salud's home became a regular meeting place of the movement, where Mass was celebrated in the morning followed by prolonged political discussions. Salud described it as "exciting": "Religion in the morning and politics all day."

According to Salud, the Sakdalistas believed that independence, "as the United States had promised", was part of the answer to the plight of the peasants: that independence would render "the people" powerful and free, while the leaders would "cease to be powerful". Her perspective indicates that the Sakdalistas integrated the concept of democracy and nationalism as professed by the Americans themselves. In effect, Salud credited her American elementary education, which taught civics lessons for citizenship training, as contributing to her sense of patriotism and civic consciousness. In other words, nationalists have at their disposal not only those cultural forms derived from their local tradition and religion, but also those offered by other societies and cultures.

In the chapter on Rasuna Said, the Sumatran Thawalib school system and the Diniyah Putri School are fruits of the endeavour by a social movement to popularise new cultural forms, that is, to promote alternative ways of understanding and practising Islam. They emerged out of the attempts by young Islamic scholars to revitalise and modernise Islamic practice in the face of what was perceived as Christian colonialism at the beginning of the 20th century. They derived their inspiration from the Islamic modernist school of thought in the Middle East and were vehemently resisted by local traditionalists. The Thawalib and Diniyah schools also integrated selective organisational aspects of the Western schooling system, such as the introduction of secular subjects, graded classes, the use of textbooks, and more modern methods of teaching and curriculum. Reflective of Marxist influence, the methods of Thawalib schools encouraged students to analyse their social and political circumstances. There was also innovative thinking with regard to the importance of female literacy. The Islamic reformist movement argued that women were entitled to religious education in order to pass on their faith to other women and their children, and by virtue of the fact that they were answerable to God, just like men.

The Sumatran Islamic school reform represents a historical case of "localisation",[7] whereby outside ideas were progressively and eclectically integrated into educational institutions and successfully brought about significant social changes. The Thawalib school was instrumental in shaping a generation of religiously educated leaders who formed Permi, one of the nationalist organisations Rasuna joined. These reformist schools became the crucible of identity formation not just for Minangkabau Rasuna Said but also for Shamsiah Fakeh and Aishah Ghani from Malaya.

The ultimate case of localisation here, of course, is the idea of nation (and of reclaiming sovereignty in the name of the people) by nationalist movements. Liah Greenfeld described national identity as an empty conceptual framework, providing "an organising principle applicable to different materials to which it then grants meaning, transforming them thereby into elements of a specific identity".[8] The raw materials used by nationalist leaders were existing symbolic resources such as historical narratives and cultural practices in colonial society, as well as collective identities, be it ethnic (Burmese, Karen, Malay), territorial (Indonesia), provincial (Timor-Leste), or even social class (Sakdal Movement). They bore the imprint of prior layers of localisation of outside ideas and norms that were then regarded as an integral part of local social practices and "indigenous" tradition.

Nationalism thrives on historical nostalgia and the impulse to restore precolonial order, but the truth is that colonialism participated intricately in the very creation and formation of the nation.

As a territorial and political entity, the form of nation-states that nationalist movements in the various chapters envisaged owed much to the boundaries and social divisions carved out by colonialists. In the chapter on the Javanese Suyatin, it was suggested how revolutionary the idea of an Indonesian nation was, to unite the hundreds of disparate islands of the archipelago whose only point in common was Dutch colonialism. Suyatin stated that she was attracted to the idea as a means "to fight the Dutch". Ideas of nationalism among those Dutch-educated youth were picked up through their reading, from nationalist leaders who returned from their higher education in the Netherlands, as well as through the influence of nationalist movements.

We have also noted in the preceding paragraphs how nationalist movements, in their articulation of the idea of a nation, made innovative use of existing cultural forms, at times giving them new meanings, in their attempts to forge a collective sense of belonging and to mobilise the common people behind their nationalist struggle. Vatthana Pholsena in her chapter on Laos explained how the historical legacy of resistance to external control by highlanders was exploited by Communist propagandists to rally popular support among the former for the anti-colonial cause of the latter.

The outcome of the shape and content of a national identity is the fruit of negotiation with historical identities.[9] In effect, at the formation of new nation-states, historically existent social structures and divisions could also maintain some form of colonial continuity — as clearly illustrated in the case study of the Philippines and Malaysia — provided that the dominant social group was on the winner's side of history. Hence at independence, traditional norms and colonial practices were rarely evacuated of their influence once and for all, while the cultural and political transformation brought about by the process of localisation of the ideals of nation-states set off new powerful dynamics that might coexist, or at a later time come into contradiction, with "old" customs and practices.

Identity Formation as Social Practice and Process[10]

The life story of Lily Eberwein in Sarawak presents a striking case of how identity formation is not given once and for all, but developed as a social process whereby the changing cultural environment can bring about a radical personal transformation. Born Eurasian, and the recipient of an English-medium education, Eberwein became completely identified with the Malay ethnicity, despite her Eurasian complexion and name. The death of her Christian father in her early teens brought an end to her European lifestyle in Singapore. Following her Malay mother back from urbanised Singapore to a rural Malay social milieu in Sarawak plunged her into a completely alien cultural environment. We are told that young Eberwein had a hard time switching from being served by men servants to serving her uncles. But her mother was her window to the new social context, helping her to adjust and adopt new cultural practices and norms and to gain social acceptance. Eberwein embraced Islam soon after her return to Sarawak, adopting Malay etiquette and attire. Her appointment to head the Malay section of the women's group during the Japanese occupation is indicative of the general social acceptance of her Malay identity. Her intimate involvement with the predominantly Malay anti-cession movement could also be interpreted as her complete identification with the Malay ethnic group's perspective and interests in Sarawak. Eberwein's assimilation as a Malay woman, however, represents an unusual and extreme case of identity change. Inadequacy of information does not allow us to go very far in our understanding of Eberwein's identity transformation process, in particular the operation of agency on her part.

On the other hand, we can clearly see the exercise of agency in the case of Aishah Ghani in British Malaya. Her strong resistance to early marriage was crucial in opening up other life chances, such as enabling her to acquire higher educational qualifications and be exposed to political initiation and participation. Her choice to switch to a different strand of nationalist group effectively constituted a turning point in the development of her political identity.

Nonetheless, agency never worked in a straightforward way. In many cases, the initial motivation of the protagonists examined in various chapters to get involved was not even political in nature. We spoke about the more dramatic "intrusion" of historical process in the form of war and crisis into some of the protagonists' lives; for others it was a spontaneous response to a mundane opportunity, such as an employment offer at the Malay Nationalist Party office in the case of Aishah. Manivanh, the Laotian revolutionary cadre, explained clearly that she first decided to join the guerrilla forces because she wanted to study. The "hatred" and anger against the imperialist forces developed only later, after she joined the movement. Her revolutionary, anti-colonial identity developed over time, as the product of a social process of participation in the movement.

In the case of East Timorese Bisoi, we saw evidence of her distancing herself from the social norms in which she was brought up. When Bisoi stated in an interview that she perceived the source of gender inequality in East Timor as "from our ancestors", that "traditional customs" dictated how women should behave, she was referring to gender norms that were prevalent in her society. This was evidence of her looking back from a distance at her initial stage of "political awakening" after joining OPMT, the women's wing of Fretilin. Women's emancipation constituted one of the founding aims of OPMT, and Bisoi embraced the discourse and acquired a critical gender consciousness from it.

Bisoi described how she was criticised by her community and her own family for her participation in political activism. She subsequently came to a form of compromise with her family, by acting as a "normal woman" when she was at home. She won the support of her family for her political activities by avoiding the outright rejection of the traditional gender position, at the price of leading "separate lives" in the respective social realms. Currently, as a married woman and a parliamentarian, she continues with this compromise of convenience, acting independently in the public realm of politics but submitting herself "to the structure of family" and deferring to her husband's wishes in the domestic realm.

Attentive reading of the various chapters uncovers evidence, for Manivanh and Khamla, Aishah and Shamsiah, as well as Bisoi, that the identity of these women as anti-colonial fighters developed over the course of their increased participation in the nationalist movement they joined. Susan Blackburn, in her chapter on Suyatin, notes that "becoming a nationalist meant taking on a new identity, identifying with a huge archipelago rather than just one's own ethnic group, and learning what was for most people an entirely new language".

It was perhaps not a coincidence that the first responsibility assigned to many of the women when joining the nationalist movement was the role of "propagandist". To be successful propagandists, they had to be convinced of the aims and perspective of their nationalist struggle before they could persuade others to join or mobilise popular support. The more they did so, the more they themselves internalised the movement's perspective and identified with the movement. On the other hand, in order to stamp out the development of a "counter-revolutionary" perspective, armed nationalist movements facing high security risks also imposed heavy sanctions to punish those members construed to have committed acts of betrayal, as we have seen in the case of the Vietnamese Nationalist Party (VNQDD).

If we understand identity formation as a dynamic and inter-subjective *process* of practice, the role of nationalist movements as a site of reproduction and reinforcement of the political identity of our protagonists should be foregrounded. The women nationalists we studied in the preceding chapters devoted a significant part of their lives, if not the whole of their adult lives, to the nationalist cause. Not only did they persist in their commitment to the nationalist struggle, most of them displayed bold determination in carrying out their missions, ready to risk imprisonment or give up their lives for the cause. Behind such supreme adherence to the cause, which Craig Calhoun described as bordering on "apparent foolishness", these women perceived their personal integrity and honour in the eyes of their comrades to be at stake: the participation of these persons in the course of action "has over time committed one to an identity that would be irretrievably violated by pulling back from the risk".[11]

Discordance among the Nationalists: Open-endedness of the Localisation Process and Identity Formation

The chapters on Rasuna Said and Suyatin Kartowiyono help us understand how the anti-Dutch nationalism in the early 20th century, during what was referred to as "the age of *pergerakan* (movement)", was far from monolithic, even contradictory. Not only were there multiple strands of competing and overlapping ideologies, purported "nation"-wide organisations such as Muhammadiyah and PSII-manifested variations when transplanted from Java to Sumatra. This illustrates how the idea of "nation", when appropriated by a local society, may generate a whole spectrum of different articulations and interpretations, based on the specificity of local groups and the social processes they were involved in. The expulsion of Rachmany from the Indonesian Communist Party in Sumatra, the formation of Permi following the tension within Muhammadiyah, the controversies over the public role of

Muslim women, and responses to the controversial Marriage Ordinance tabled by the Dutch authorities are some examples of tension arising from such differences.

The political trajectory of Rasuna herself exemplifies an eclectic integration of political ideas from a variety of ideological sources, combining Islamic modernism, nationalism and socialism. Her public statements during her famous trial in 1932 reveal her creative combination of anti-colonialism and Islam, arguing that her nationalist party's struggle for a free nation was sanctioned by Islam and hence even if it was unsuccessful, "paradise still awaits". Her perspective against the 1937 Marriage Ordinance in defence of Islamic marriage laws, including provisions for polygamy and divorce which disadvantaged Muslim wives, put her in the camp of the Islamic women's movement and set her apart from the secular women's movement. (However, in subsequent years, Rasuna apparently became more closely associated with organisations with left-wing orientations as well as the secular women's organisation Perwari). Secular women's movements had been seeking marriage law reform and rejected the ordinance only because they saw it as a colonial device to drive a wedge between the Islamists and others, as noted by Susan Blackburn in her chapter. As a matter of fact, the success of the nationalist struggle depends on the effectiveness of bringing together different strands of nationalist groups under a common anti-colonial front or even suppressing brutally those whom others judge as "inadmissible", failing which the deep hostility of ideologically incompatible groups may become its gravest obstacle. Hence the battle line of conflicts (determination of who the enemy was) was more often than not multifaceted, and generally not as simplistic as just anti-colonial versus colonial.

In Burma, the historical emergence of the Karen National Union and its ongoing struggle against the Burmese state for an autonomous homeland is testimony to the ambivalent and contested nature of nationalist struggle. Despite helping Burma gain its independence from the British, the Burmese nationalist movement was not able to hold together competing, even incompatible, ideological and ethnic factions, and this led to prolonged armed conflicts that still continue today.

In the Philippines, at the heart of the struggle of the Sakdal peasant uprising was the sense of despair among landless peasants that their plight was overlooked by the dominant bourgeois nationalist movement led by Manuel Quezon, who negotiated with the American colonialists for independence. At times, it is even deemed desirable to collaborate with one colonising power against another. The strategic collaboration of Salud and her group with the Japanese during World War II, just as Rasuna's in Hahanokai and the political struggle of Lily Eberwein for the retention of White Rajah dynastic rule against the British takeover, manifested the ambivalent nature of ascertaining the "colonial enemy".

In Malaysia, due to the hegemonic and continued dominance of political power of UMNO in the federal government since independence, the historical recognition of the anti-colonial role played by the Malay Nationalist Party and, to a greater extent, the Malayan Communist Party (MCP), remains hotly contested. The Malaysian official historical narrative regarded UMNO leaders as nationalists, while the MCP leaders were labelled simply as "terrorists". History textbooks even make allusions to the MCP as a potential "coloniser".[12] This continues to fashion official and popular perceptions of Shamsiah Fakeh and Aishah Ghani. Official historians and MCP fighters clearly do not share the same view of the role of the latter, and MCP leaders in turn claimed that Malaya did not attain real independence as the British continued to maintain their military presence after independence. The dispute was over the very meaning of "what was going on".[13] This complexity of nationalist struggles on the ground is not unique to Malaysia, and cannot always be captured simply by drawing a clear line between a pre-categorised "oppressor" and "oppressed", as at times those who fight against a common oppressor may not see eye to eye with — or even acknowledge — one another.

The divergence of the political orientation of some of our protagonists appears to confirm Ranchod and Tétreault's statement that "there is no single 'woman's view' of the nation":[14] in the contrasting ways secular Suyatin and Islamic Rasuna articulated their nationalist discourses; the participation of Shamsiah and Aishah in antagonistically positioned factions of the Malayan nationalist movement; and finally, the commitment of Burmese Daw San and Karen Zipporah to the struggle for different forms of nation.

The "Woman Question" and Gendered Experience of Nationalist Struggles

The ideals of human autonomy, equality and emancipation inspire nationalist struggles as well as feminist movements. A number of the subjects of this book, such as Daw San, Zipporah, Shamsiah and Suyatin, expressed a strong conviction that the "woman question" went hand in hand with the "national question". In her autobiography, Suyatin explained that her parents had inculcated in her a strong sense of egalitarianism and passionate opposition to discrimination. She saw feminist struggle as "especially stimulated by the spirit of nationalism and the sense of justice". Her keen sense of justice was also consistently applied to her acceptance of people of all faiths and ethnic groups. To maintain her autonomy, she made clear that she chose a husband who truly respected her socio-political engagement. An interesting adaptation of her idea of gender equality was her reversal of the local concept of leadership roles in the household and in the public sphere: according to her, her husband was the head of the household while she was the leader in the public sphere.

Burmese Daw San also tried to hold together nationalism and feminism. In her writings, she stressed that the "protection of the interests of the nation" was inextricably linked to the liberation of women from inequitable gender relations in society and at home. She argued that female education was a crucial yardstick in the assessment of the readiness of a people for national self-determination. The most controversial position she took in gender terms was her declaration of personal rejection of married life after divorcing her drunkard husband, equating marriage with the subjugation and exploitative nature of colonisation and wage labour.

Shamsiah in Malaya, like Bisoi in East Timor, claimed that she became conscious of the oppression of women through her participation in the leftist nationalist movement that critiqued the feudalist, capitalist and imperialist systems as sources of women's oppression. She described her negative experience of marriage as an example of oppression in the name of traditional customs and religious rules. She reasoned that achieving political independence for her homeland constituted the first step towards the liberation of women. On a more ambivalent note, Shamsiah experimented briefly with a polygamous marriage arrangement, which she appeared to condone as permissible in Islam and justified as being for the furtherance of the nationalist cause. The struggle against female subordination did not seem to inspire all our protagonists in the same way as the nationalist endeavour, perhaps due to the selectivity and specificity of our focus here. A lack of sources, particularly in the case of Nguyen Thi Giang of Vietnam, did not allow us to ascertain the experiences and perspectives of all our protagonists on the women's situation, nor to discover how they imagined the nation for which they struggled, suffered and sacrificed their lives. Some chapters, however, do allow us glimpses into gender issues as confronted by these women in their participation in nationalist movements.

Bisoi's bitter post-independence experience is testimony to how her male comrades perceived women's role in the East Timorese armed struggle differently from women. The male-dominated leadership appeared to have decided on the criteria for recognition and compensation of war veterans based solely on masculine experience in the armed forces, overlooking the equally crucial though different roles played by women soldiers. The fact that Bisoi had learned from the nationalist movement that independence would bring women's liberation would have accentuated her disappointment and frustration. Sara Niner notes how the "revolutionary" and gender-emancipative agenda of the Fretilin was progressively lost in the succession of leaders and the challenging efforts to reorganise and unify various factions of the nationalist movement.

Given that the gender orientation of the nationalist movements involved was not examined in all the chapters, we are not in a position to discuss in depth or verify Kumari Jayawardena's contention that "revolutionary" nationalist movements were more receptive to the feminist agenda than "bourgeois" nationalist movements.[15] The East Timorese case nonetheless illustrates the practical difficulty of categorising nationalist movements as "revolutionary" or "bourgeois". It shows how a movement's ideology may evolve over time and according to historical circumstances, especially if a longer time frame is involved.

Contrary to the metamorphosis experienced by the Fretilin, the 60-year-old Karen National Union is confronted with a different dilemma. Its founding nationalist principles, which have remained unchanged, are now subject to contestation and blamed as an obstacle to the search for a viable peace settlement with the Burmese state. The KNU is affected adversely by the current modified international and domestic geopolitical context and evolving evaluation of past military practices such as the recruitment of child soldiers and the use of landmines. The unprecedented election of a civilian woman as its general secretary was probably made possible by the increasing importance of international lobbying and foreign funding as a means to achieve the KNU's nationalist cause. But the macho militaristic culture among Zipporah's male colleagues remains. Zipporah barely concealed her frustration as she shared her first-hand experience of the condescending attitude of her male colleagues who purportedly professed their belief in equal opportunity and equal rights.

The 1937 Dutch Marriage Ordinance controversy is an example of how nationalist and feminist agendas may sometimes appear incompatible. Between her nationalist and feminist commitments, Suyatin had to decide where she put her priority. Interpreting the proposal as a means to split the nationalist movement, Suyatin supported Sukarno's suggestion to defer marriage law reform until after independence. This was to delay it for almost four decades to come. The episode is a good illustration of how, in a particular context, women nationalists may have to prioritise the nationalist cause over feminist struggle.

In the same light as our discussions on political identity, the development of feminist consciousness and critical gender identity by these women may also be understood as a social process, at times in tandem with other aspects of social identity. Divorcing her alcoholic husband must have been a defining moment in Daw San's life, as indicated by her declaration, through the naming of her paper as *Independent Weekly*, that she would never return to the shackled life of a married woman. Aishah and Shamsiah both experienced family pressure to be married off as young teenage girls; while Shamsiah docilely obeyed her father, Aishah rebelled. Shamsiah learned the hard way to recognise the vulnerability of women's position in traditional gender relations. Bisoi, in her interview by Sara Niner, summarised her life as a journey in three progressions: "first, the Portuguese time, when women didn't have the right to do anything. Second, the resistance period, when women suffered a lot compared to men; and third, the independence period, when some women are still not yet free, such as those who have no education". It is interesting that she spoke of her personal life as reflective of the overall East Timorese women's experience.

The localisations of nationalism and feminism, despite their common source of inspiration, do not in reality always share the same trajectory in their interaction with local norms. As a whole, we saw how female rights to education and universal suffrage were less contested, while domestic relations remained murky and subject to negotiation, as illustrated by the variable strategies deployed by Suyatin, Shamsiah, Daw San, Zipporah and Bisoi. Over the long term, the generalisation of female literacy should in principle have an empowering effect. On the other hand, the evolution of gender relations need not be linear and unidirectional. The struggle of feminists in pushing the frontier of women's emancipation against the tide of gender conservatism continues, and the obstacles they face in building a united front is different but no less challenging than those of nationalists.

Conclusion

Biographical studies of women leaders are not meant to replace conventional historical studies of women's participation in nationalist movements on a larger scale. They are complementary in helping us to understand better the issues at hand.

The relevance of biographical studies in understanding historical change has always been recognised with regard to important historical personalities. What is new is an increased awareness of how posing thoughtful questions about life stories of ordinary people could also help scholars understand historical process and human agency.[16] This book certainly does not exhaust the potential offered by biographical studies of different women's lives in understanding women's involvement in nationalist movements in the region. Comparison of different women's lives focusing on a specific subject of enquiry, such as identity issues, differences in gender perspectives, leadership styles or the strategy in pursuit of women's rights can be fruitfully carried out. One can make comparative biographical studies within the same movement, among different movements, among those living through the same era, across a geographical region, and so forth. Through careful examination of individual lives in their larger social and political contexts, we can gain insights into the subject of enquiry as well as both the individuals' lives and the eras they lived through.

Notes

1. Barbara Caine, *Biography and History* (Basingstoke and New York: Palgrave Macmillan, 2010).
2. Roxana Waterson, "Introduction: Analysing Personal Narratives", in *Southeast Asian Lives: Personal Narratives and Historical Experience*, ed. Roxana Waterson (Singapore: NUS Press; Athens: Ohio University Press, 2007), p. 2.
3. Caine, *Biography and History*, p. 3.
4. The term "modern" here is intended to be descriptive, as opposed to "traditional", without value judgement.

5. Waterson, *Southeast Asian Lives*, p. 9.

6. Dorothy Holland and Jean Lave, "History in Person: An Introduction", in *History in Person: Enduring Struggles, Contentious Practice, Intimate Identities*, ed. Dorothy Holland and Jean Lave (Santa Fe: School of American Research Press; Oxford: James Currey, 2001), pp. 3–33.

7. Anthony Milner, "Localisation, Regionalism and the History of Ideas in Southeast Asia", *Journal of Southeast Asian Studies* 41, 3 (2010): 541–9.

8. Liah Greenfeld, *Nationalism: Five Roads to Modernity* (Cambridge and London: Harvard University Press, 1993), pp. 12–4.

9. Prasenjit Duara, "Historicizing National Identity, or Who Imagines What and When", in *Becoming National: A Reader*, ed. Geoff Eley and Ronald Grigor Suny (Oxford and New York: Oxford University Press, 1996), p. 158.

10. Dorothy Holland, William Lachicotte Jr, Debra Skinner and Carole Cain, *Identity and Agency in Cultural Worlds* (Cambridge, MA, and London: Harvard University Press, 2001).

11. Craig Calhoun, "The Problem of Identity in Collective Action", in *Macro-Micro Linkages in Sociology*, ed. Joan Huber (Newbury Park, London and New Delhi: Sage Publications, 1991), p. 51.

12. Helen Ting, "Malaysian History Textbooks and the Discourse of *Ketuanan Melayu*", in *Race and Multiculturalism in Malaysia and Singapore*, ed. Daniel Goh, Philip Holden, Matilda Gabrielpillai and Khoo Gaik Cheng (London and New York: Routledge, 2009), pp. 36–52.

13. Holland and Lave, *History in Person*, p. 22.

14. Sita Ranchod-Nilsson and Mary Ann Tétreault, "Gender and Nationalism: Moving beyond Fragmented Conversations", in *Women, States, and Nationalism: At Home in the Nation?* ed. Sita Ranchod-Nilsson and Mary Ann Tétreault (London and New York: Routledge, 2000), p. 7.

15. Kumari Jayawardena, *Feminism and Nationalism in the Third World* (London and New Jersey: Zed Books, 1994), pp. 10, 258.

16. See Waterson, *Southeast Asian Lives*; and Caine, *Biography and History*.

Abbreviations

AWAS	Angkatan Wanita Sedar, women's wing of MNP
BWA	Burmese Women's Association
CNRM	Conselho Nacional da Resistência Maubere (National Council of Maubere Resistance)
CNRT	Conselho Nacional da Resistência Timorense (National Council of Timorese Resistance) 1998–2001; also Conselho Nacional da Reconstrucao Timorense (National Council of Timorese Reconstruction) from 2007
CRRN	Conselho da Resistência Revolutionário Nacional (National Council for Revolutionary Resistance)
GCBA	General Council of Burmese Associations
ICP	Indochinese Communist Party
KNU	Karen National Union
KWO	Karen Women Organisation
MCP	Malayan Communist Party
MNP	Malay Nationalist Party
MNU	Malay National Union (Sarawak)
MPAJA	Malayan People's Anti-Japanese Army
OMT	Organização Mulher Timorense (Organisation of Timorese Women, CNRM/CNRT)
OPMT	Organizacao Popular Mulher Timorense (Popular Organisation of Timorese Women); women's wing of Fretilin
PSII	Partai Sarekat Islam Indonesia (Indonesian Islamic Union Party)

PUTERA-AMCJA	The first multi-ethnic alliance formed in Malaya. Pusat Tenaga Rakyat (PUTERA) was a coalition of several Malay grass-roots organisations as well as the MNP; the non-Malay AMCJA stood for All Malaya Council for Joint Action.
SDA	Sarawak Dayak Association
UMNO	United Malays National Organisation
VNQDD	Viet Nam Quôc Dan Dang (Vietnamese Nationalist Party)
YMBA	Young Men's Buddhist Association

GLOSSARY

a myo	nation, race, kin, lineage (Burmese)
bada	Burmese language and literature
cedula	poll tax (Philippines)
cikgu	teacher (Malay)
Dobama Asiayone	Burmese Association
Falintil	Forças Armadas de Libertação Nacional de Timor-Leste (Armed Forces for the National Liberation of East Timor)
Fretilin	Frente Revolucionária de Timor Leste Independente (Revolutionary Front for an Independent East Timor)
Kaum Ibu MNU	Women's wing of MNU
Issara	see Lao Issara
kaum muda	young group (Indonesian)
kaum tua	old group (Indonesian)
Lao Issara	"Free Lao" nationalist movement
Muhammadiyah	Indonesian modernist Islamic organisation
Pathet Lao	"Lao Nation" pro-Communist guerrilla movement in Laos
perabangan	Malay aristocratic elite (Sarawak)
Permi	Persatuan Moeslimin Indonesia (Union of Indonesian Muslims)
Perwari	Persatuan Wanita Republik Indonesia (Union of Women of the Indonesian Republic)
Sakdal	Philippine radical peasant organisation
Sakdalista	member of Sakdal

sasana	teachings of the Buddha
thakin	master (Burmese); term employed by members of Dobama Asiayone to refer to themselves, not the British, as the rightful masters of Burma
Thawalib	West Sumatran radical Islamic education organisation
Viet Minh	Vietnamese Communist-dominated nationalist front
wunthanu	protector of national interests (Burmese)
wunthanu athin	patriotic associations (Burmese)

BIBLIOGRAPHY

Books

Abdullah, T. *Schools and Politics: The Kaum Muda Movement in West Sumatra (1927–1933)*. Ithaca: Cornell Modern Indonesia Project, Cornell University, 1971.

Agoncillo, Teodoro. *History of the Filipino People*. Quezon City: Garotech Publishing, 1990.

Aishah Ghani. *Memoir Seorang Pejuang* [*Memoirs of a Fighter*]. Kuala Lumpur: Dewan Bahasa dan Pustaka and Malaysian Education Ministry, 1992.

Alexievitch, Svetlana. *La guerre n'a pas un visage de femme* [*War Doesn't Have a Feminine Face*]. Paris: Éditions J'ai Lu, 2005.

Alfian. *Muhammadiyah: The Political Behavior of a Muslim Modernist Organization under Dutch Colonialism*. Yogyakarta: Gadjah Mada University, 1989.

Alves, M.D.F., L.S. Abrantes and F.B. Reis. *Hakarek no ran: Written in Blood*. Democratic Republic of Timor-Leste: Office for the Promotion of Equality, Prime Minister's Office, 2003.

Andaya, Barbara Watson. *The Flaming Womb: Repositioning Women in Early Modern Southeast Asia*. Honolulu: University of Hawaii Press, 2006.

Anderson, Benedict. *Imagined Communities: Reflections on the Origin and Spread of Nationalism*, 2nd ed. London: Verso, 1991.

APSC-TL (Asia Pacific Support Collective-Timor Leste with SEPI and MSS). *Segredu: Xáve ba Ukun Rasik-an* [*Secrecy: The Key to Independence*]. Dili, 2008.

Atkinson, Jane Monnig and Shelly Errington. *Power and Difference: Gender in Island Southeast Asia*. Stanford: Stanford University Press, 1990.

Aye Kyaw. *The Voice of Young Burma*. Ithaca: Southeast Asia Program, Cornell University, 1933.

Ba Maw. *Breakthrough in Burma: Memoirs of a Revolution, 1939–1946*. New Haven: Yale University Press, 1968.

Badan Pemurnian Sejarah Indonesia Minangkabau (BPSIM). *Sejarah Perjuangan Kemerdekaan Republik Indonesia Di Minangkabau, 1945–1950* [*A History of the Independence Struggle for the Indonesian Republic in Minangkabau, 1945–1950*], Vol. 1. Jakarta: Badan Pemurnian Sejarah Indonesia — Minangkabau, 1978.

Blackburn, Susan. *Women and the State in Modern Indonesia.* Cambridge: Cambridge University Press, 2004.

_____. *The First Indonesian Women's Congress of 1928.* Clayton: Monash University Press, 2008.

Blom, Ida, Karen Hagemann and Catherine Hall, eds. *Gendered Nations: Nationalisms and Gender Order in the Long Nineteenth Century.* Oxford: Berg, 2000.

Boekoe Peringatan 15 Tahoen "Dinijjah School Poeteri" Padang Pandjang [*Commemorative Book for the 15th Anniversary of "Dinijjah Girls' School" Padang Pandjang*], 2nd ed. Padang Pandjang: Dinijjah School Poeteri, 1936.

Brooke, Margaret A.L. *My Life in Sarawak.* London: Oxford University Press, 1913.

Brown, MacAlister and Joseph J. Zasloff. *Apprentice Revolutionaries: The Communist Movement in Laos, 1930–1985.* Stanford: Hoover Institution Press/Stanford University, 1986.

Burma, Government of. *Report of an Enquiry into the Standard and Cost of Living of the Working Classes in Rangoon.* Rangoon: Labour Statistics Bureau, 1982.

Burma Socialist Programme Party. *Myanmar nainngan amyothami mya e nainnganyay hlouk sha mhu* [*The Political Movements of Women in Myanmar*]. Yangon: Sape Beikman, 1975.

Burton, Antoinette. *Burdens of History: British Feminists, Indian Women, and Imperial Culture, 1865–1915.* Chapel Hill and London: University of North Carolina Press, 1994.

Cady, John F. *A Modern History of Burma.* Ithaca: Cornell University Press, 1958.

_____. *A History of Modern Burma.* Ithaca: Cornell University Press, 1969.

Caine, Barbara. *Biography and History.* Basingstoke and New York: Palgrave Macmillan, 2010.

Callahan, Mary. *Political Authority in Burma's Ethnic Minority States: Devolution, Occupation and Coexistence.* Policy Studies 31. Washington, DC: East-West Center, 2007.

Chapuis, Oscar. *The Last Emperors of Vietnam: From Tu Duc to Bao Dai.* Westport: Greenwood Press, 2000.

Charney, Michael. *A History of Modern Burma.* Cambridge: Cambridge University Press, 2009.

Chatterjee, Partha. *Nation and Its Fragments: Colonial and Postcolonial Histories.* Princeton: Princeton University Press, 1993.

Chong, Natividad Guttierez. *Women, Ethnicity and Nationalisms in Latin America.* Aldershot: Ashgate, 2007.

Cockburn, Cynthia. *The Space between Us: Negotiating Gender and National Identities in Conflict.* London: Zed Books, 1998.

Connor, Walker. *The National Question in Marxist-Leninist Theory and Strategy.* Princeton: Princeton University Press, 1984.

Conway, J. *Step by Step: Women of East Timor, Stories of Resistance and Survival.* Darwin: Charles Darwin University Press, 2010.

Cooper, Nicola. *France in Indochina: Colonial Encounters.* Oxford: Berg Publishers, 2001.

Cristalis, I. *Bitter Dawn,* 2nd ed. London: Zed Books, 2009.

Cristalis, I. and C. Scott. *Independent Women: The Story of Women's Activism in Timor-Leste.* London: Catholic Institute for International Relations, 2005.

Dancz, Virginia Helen. *Women and Party Politics in Peninsular Malaysia.* Oxford: Oxford University Press, 1987.

Deuve, Jean. *Le Laos, 1945–1949: Contribution à l'Histoire du Mouvement Lao Issala* [*Laos, 1945–1949: A Contribution to the History of the Lao Issara Movement*]. Montpellier: Université Paul-Valéry, 1999.

Dommen, Arthur J. *Conflict in Laos: The Politics of Neutralization.* London: Pall Mass Press, 1964.

Dube, Leela. *Women and Kinship: Comparative Perspectives on Gender in South and Southeast Asia.* Tokyo: United Nations University Press, 1997.

Durand, F. *East Timor, A Country at the Crossroads of Asia and the Pacific: A Geo-historical Atlas.* Chiang Mai: Silkworm Books, 2006.

Edwards, Louise and Mina Roces, eds. *Women's Suffrage in Asia: Gender, Nationalism and Democracy.* London and New York: RoutledgeCurzon, 2004.

Enloe, C.H. *The Curious Feminist: Searching for Women in a New Age of Empire.* Berkeley: University of California Press, 2004.

Enloe, Cynthia. *Bananas, Beaches and Bases: Making Feminist Sense of International Politics.* London: University of California Press, 1989.

Ensiklopedi Minangkabau. Padang: Pusat Pengkajian Islam dan Minangkabau, 2005.

Forbes, Geraldine. *Women in Modern India.* Cambridge: Cambridge University Press, 1996.

Freeman, Mark. *Rewriting the Self: History, Memory, Narrative.* London and New York: Routledge, 1993.

Greenfeld, Liah. *Nationalism: Five Roads to Modernity.* Cambridge, MA, and London: Harvard University Press, 1993.

Hadler, J. *Muslims and Matriarchs: Cultural Resilience in Indonesia through Jihad and Colonialism.* Ithaca: Cornell University Press, 2008.

Hanifah, Abu. *Tales of a Revolution.* Sydney: Allen & Unwin, 1972.

Hasbie Sulaiman, Hj. Mohd. *Perjuangan Anti-cession Sarawak: Peranan Utama Persatuan Kebangsaan Melayu Sarawak* [*Sarawak Anti-cession Struggle: The Important Role of the Sarawak Malay Nationalist Association*]. Kuching: PKMS/SAMASA Press, 1989.

Hayden, Joseph Ralston. *The Philippines: A Study in National Development.* New York: Arno Press, 1972.

Herbert, Patricia M. *The Hsaya San Rebellion (1930–1932) Reappraised.* London: Department of Oriental Manuscripts and Printed Books, British Library, 1982.

Hla Pe. *U Hla Pe's Narrative of the Japanese Occupation of Burma.* Recorded by U Khin. Vol. 14. Ithaca: Southeast Asia Program, Cornell University, 1961.

Hoang Van Dao. *Viet Nam Quoc Dan Dang: A Contemporary History of a National Struggle, 1927–1954,* transl. Huynh Khue. Pittsburgh: Rose Dog Books, 2009.

Holland, Dorothy, William Lachicotte Jr, Debra Skinner and Carole Cain. *Identity and Agency in Cultural Worlds.* Cambridge, MA, and London: Harvard University Press, 2001.

Htin Aung. *The Stricken Peacock: Anglo-Burmese Relations, 1752–1948.* The Hague: Martinus Nijhoff, 1965.

Ikeya, Chie. *Refiguring Women, Colonialism, and Modernity in Burma.* Honolulu: University of Hawaii Press, 2011.

India, Government of. *Census of India, 1921, Vol. 10: Burma.* Rangoon: Office of the Superintendent, Government Printing and Stationery, 1923.

———. *Census of India, 1931: Part One, Report, Vol. 11: Burma.* Rangoon: Office of the Superintendent, Government Printing and Stationery, 1933.

Inheemsche Vrouwenbeweging. *De Inheemsche Vrouwenbeweging in Nederlandsch-Indie en het aandeel daarin van het Inheemsche Meisje* [*The Native Women's Movement in the Netherlands Indies and the Role in It of the Native Girl*]. Batavia: Landsdrukkerij, 1932.

Jayawardena, Kumari. *Feminism and Nationalism in the Third World.* London and New Jersey: Zed Books, 1986.

Jones, Gavin W. *Marriage and Divorce in Islamic South-East Asia.* Kuala Lumpur: Oxford University Press, 1994.

Kahin, A. *Rebellion to Integration: West Sumatra and the Indonesian Polity, 1926–1998.* Amsterdam: Amsterdam University Press, 1999.

Kartowijono, Sujatin. *Mencari Makna Hidupku* [*Searching for the Meaning of My Life*]. Jakarta: Penerbit Sinar Harapan, 1983.

Kartowijono, Suyatin. *Perkembangan Pergerakan Wanita Indonesia* [*The Growth of the Indonesian Women's Movement*]. Jakarta: Yayasan Idayu, 1977.

Kasturi, Leela and Vina Mazumdar, eds. *Women and Indian Nationalism.* New Delhi: Vikas Publishing House, 1994.

Kaysone Phomvihane. *La Révolution lao* [*The Lao Revolution*]. Moscou: Editions du Progrès, 1980.

Kent, L. *Independent Evaluation Report: Commission on Cadres of the Resistance (CAQR).* Dili: World Bank, 2006.

Khin Myo Chit. *Colorful Burma: Her Infinite Variety; A Collection of Stories and Essays*. Rangoon: KMCT Sazin, 1976.

Khin Yi. *The Dobama Movement in Burma, 1930–1938*. Ithaca: Southeast Asia Program, Cornell University, 1988.

Khoo, Agnes. *Life as the River Flows: Women in the Malaysian Anti-Colonial Struggle*. Monmouth: Merlin Press, 2007.

Kongres Wanita Indonesia. *Sejarah Setengah Abad Pergerakan Wanita Indonesia* [*History of Half a Century of the Indonesian Women's Movement*]. Jakarta: Balai Pustaka, 1978.

Kwantes, R.C. *De Ontwikkeling van de Nationalistische Beweging in Nederlandsch-Indie: Bronnenpublikatie: Derde stuk 1928–1933* [*The Development of the Nationalist Movement in the Netherlands Indies: Sourcebook, Vol. 3, 1928–1933*]. Groningen: Wolters-Noordhoff, 1981.

Kwon, Insook. "'The New Women's Movement' in 1920s Korea: Rethinking the Relationship between Imperialism and Women", *Gender and History* 10, 3 (1998): 399.

Lang Nhan. *Nhung tran danh Phap: Tu Ham Nghi den Nguyen Thai Hoc, 1885–1931* (*Fighters against France: From Ham Nghi to Nguyen Thai Hoc, 1885–1931*). Houston: Zieleks, 1987.

Langer, Paul F. and Joseph J. Zasloff. *North Vietnam and the Pathet Lao: Partners in the Struggle for Laos*. Cambridge: Harvard University Press, 1970.

Lanzona, Vina A. *Amazons of the Huk Rebellion: Gender, Sex, and Revolution in the Philippines*. Madison: University of Wisconsin Press, 2009.

Lao Women's Union. *Pavat mounsieu sahaphanmaenyinglao* [*History of the Origins of the Lao Women's Union*]. Vientiane: Lao Women's Union headquarters, July 2010.

Mai Thi Thu and Le Thi Nham Tuyet. *Women of Vietnam*. Hanoi: Foreign Languages Publishing House, 1978.

Manderson, Lenore. *Women, Politics, and Change: The Kaum Ibu UMNO, Malaysia, 1945–1972*. Kuala Lumpur: Oxford University Press, 1980.

Marching, Soe Tjen. *The Discrepancy between the Public and Private Selves of Indonesian Women*. Lewiston: The Edwin Mellon Press, 2007.

Marty, Louis. *Contribution à l'histoire des mouvements politiques de l'Indochine française* [*Contribution to the History of French Indochinese Political Movements*]. Hanoi: Imprimerie d'Extrême Orient, 1933.

Maung Maung. *From Sangha to Laity: Nationalist Movements of Burma, 1920–1940*. New Delhi: Manohar, 1980.

Mayer, Tamar, ed. *Gender Ironies of Nationalism: Sexing the Nation*. London: Routledge, 2000.

Mayoury Ngaosyvathn. *Remembrances of a Lao Woman Devoted to Constructing a Nation: Khampheng Boupha*. Vientiane: Lao Women's Union, 1993.

McConnell, Scott. *Leftward Journey: The Education of Vietnamese Students in France, 1919–1939*. New Brunswick: Transaction Books, 1989.

McHale, Shawn Frederick. *Print and Power: Confucianism, Communism, and Buddhism in the Making of Modern Vietnam*. Honolulu: University of Hawaii Press, 2004.

Mendelson, E. Michael. *Sangha and State in Burma: A Study of Monastic Sectarianism and Leadership*. Ithaca: Cornell University Press, 1975.

Menon, Visalakshi. *Indian Women and Nationalism: The UP Story*. New Delhi: Shakti Books, 2003.

Mi Mi Khaing. *The World of Burmese Women*. London: Zed Books, 1984.

Ministry of Culture, Sports and Youth. *Penyertaan Kita/Our Participation*. Kuching: State Government of Sarawak, 1983.

Moghadam, Valentine M., ed. *Gender and National Identity: Women and Politics in Muslim Societies*. London: Zed Books, 1994.

Myoe, Maung Aung. *Neither Friend Nor Foe: Myanmar's Relations with Thailand since 1988: A View from Yangon*. Singapore: IDSS Monograph no. 1, 2002.

Nana Nurliana Soeyono and Sudarini Suhartono. *Sejarah untuk SMP dan MTS* [*History for Secondary Schools*]. Jakarta: Grasindo, 2006.

Niner, S. *Xanana: Leader of the Struggle for Independent Timor-Leste*. Melbourne: Australian Scholarly Publishing, 2009.

Noer, D. *The Modernist Muslim Movement in Indonesia, 1900–1942*. Kuala Lumpur: Oxford University Press, 1973.

Nu, U. *Burma under the Japanese: Pictures and Portraits*. New York: St. Martin's Press, 1954.

Ospina, S. *Participation of Women in Politics and Decision-Making in Timor-Leste: A Recent History*. Dili: UNIFEM, 2006.

Overzicht van den Inlandsche en Maleisch-Chineesche Pers [*Survey of the Native and Chinese Malay Press*]. Batavia: Landsdrukkerij.

Panitia Peringatan 30 Tahun Kesatuan Pergerakan Wanita Indonesia. *Buku Peringatan 30 Tahun Kesatuan Pergerakan Wanita Indonesia, 32 Des. 1928–22 Des. 1958* [*Commemorative Book for the 30th Anniversary of the Indonesian Women's Movement Association, 22 Dec. 1928–22 Dec. 1958*]. Djakarta: Pertjetakan Negara, 1958.

Pelley, Patricia M. *Postcolonial Vietnam: New Histories of the National Past*. Durham: Duke University Press, 2002.

Phut Tan Nguyen. *A Modern History of Vietnam, 1802–1954*. Hanoi: Nha San Khai Tri, 1964.

Prados, John. *The Blood Road: The Ho Chi Minh Trail and the Vietnam War*. New York: Wiley, 1999.

Premalatha, P.N. *Nationalism and the Women's Movement in South India: 1917–1947*. New Delhi: Gyan Publishing House, 2003.

Pringgodigdo, A.K. *Sedjarah Pergerakan Rakjat Indonesia* [*A History of the Indonesian People's Movement*], 3rd ed. Djakarta: Pustaka Rakjat, 1950.

Qiang, Zhai. *China and the Vietnam Wars, 1950–1975*. Chapel Hill: University of North Carolina Press, 2000.

Ranchod-Nilsson, Sita and Mary Ann Tétreault, eds. *Women, States, and Nationalism: At Home in the Nation?* London and New York: Routledge, 2000.

Rasid, Gadis. *Maria Ullfah Subadio: Pembela Kaumnya* [*Maria Ullfah Subadio: The Defender of Her Race*]. Jakarta: Bulan Bintang, 1982.

Rede Feto (with Fokupers and APSC-TL). *Hau Fo Midar; Hau Simu Moruk* [*I Gave Sweet; I Received Bitter*]. Dili: Rede Feto, 2007.

Reece, R.H.W. *The Name of Brooke: The End of White Rajah Rule in Sarawak*. Kuala Lumpur and New York: Oxford University Press, 1982.

————. *The White Rajahs of Sarawak, a Borneo Dynasty*. Singapore: Archipelago Press, 2004.

Rehn, S. and E.J. Sirleaf. *Women, War and Peace: The Independent Experts' Assessment on the Impact of Armed Conflict on Women and Women's Role in Peace-building*. New York: UNIFEM, 2002.

Reid, A. *The Indonesian National Revolution, 1945–1950*. Studies in Contemporary Southeast Asia. Hawthorn: Longman, 1974.

————. *Southeast Asia in the Age of Commerce 1450–1680, Vol. 1: The Lands below the Winds*. New Haven: Yale University Press, 1988.

————. *Imperial Alchemy: Nationalism and Political Identity in Southeast Asia*. Cambridge: Cambridge University Press, 2010.

Ricklefs, M. *A History of Modern Indonesia since c. 1300*, 2nd ed. Basingstoke: Macmillan, 1994.

Runciman, Steven. *The White Rajahs: A History of Sarawak from 1841 to 1946*. Cambridge: Cambridge University Press, 1960.

Rupp, Leila J. *Worlds of Women: The Making of an International Women's Movement*. Princeton: Princeton University Press, 1997.

Salim, Agus. *S.K. Trimurti*. Bandung: Jembar, 2007.

Sanib Said. *Malay Politics in Sarawak 1946–1966: The Search for Unity and Political Ascendancy*. Singapore: Oxford University Press, 1985.

Sastroamijoyo, Ali. *Milestones on My Journey: The Memoirs of Ali Sastroamijoyo, Indonesian Patriot and Political Leader*. St. Lucia: University of Queensland Press, 1979.

Saw Moun Nyin. *Bamar amyothami* [*Burmese Women*]. Yangon: Thiha poun hneik htaik, 1976.

Scott, James C. *The Moral Economy of the Peasant: Rebellion and Subsistence in Southeast Asia*. New Haven: Yale University Press, 1976.

Shamsiah Fakeh. *Memoir Shamsiah Fakeh: Dari AWAS ke Rejimen Ke-10* [*Memoirs of Shamsiah Fakeh: From AWAS to the 10th Regiment*]. Bangi: Penerbit UKM, 2004.

Shiraishi, T. *An Age in Motion: Popular Radicalism in Java, 1912–1960*. Ithaca: Cornell University Press, 1990.

Silverstein, Josef. *Burmese Politics: The Dilemma of National Unity*. New Brunswick: Rutgers University Press, 1980.

Smith, Martin. *Burma: Insurgency and the Politics of Ethnicity*. Bangkok: White Lotus; Dhaka: University Press; London and New York: Zed Books, 1999.

_____. *State of Strife: The Dynamics of Ethnic Conflict in Burma*. Policy Studies 36 (Southeast Asia). Washington, DC: East-West Center, 2007.

Snow, D.A., S.A. Soule and H. Kriesi, eds. *The Blackwell Companion to Social Movements*. Oxford: Blackwell Publishing, 2004.

Soebagio. *S.K. Trimurti: Wanita Pengabdi Bangsa [S.K. Trimurti: A Woman Devoted to Her Nation]*. Jakarta: Gunung Agung, 1982.

Soekarno. *Sukarno, an Autobiography as Told to Cindy Adams*. Indianapolis: Bobbs-Merrill, 1965.

Spiro, Melford. *Gender Ideology and Psychological Reality*. New Haven: Yale University Press, 1997.

Sturtevant, David. *Popular Uprisings in the Philippines (1840–1940)*. Ithaca and London: Cornell University Press, 1976.

Subardjo, Ahmad Djojoadisuryo. *Kesadaran Nasional: Otobiografi [National Consciousness: An Autobiography]*. Jakarta: Gunung Agung, 1978.

Subido, Tarrosa. *The Feminist Movement in the Philippines 1905–1955*. Philippines: National Federation of Women's Clubs in the Philippines, 1989.

Sutjiatiningsih, Sri, ed. *Biografi Tokoh Kongres Perempuan Indonesia Pertama [Biographies of Leaders of the First Indonesian Women's Congress]*. Jakarta: Departemen Pendidikan dan Kebudayaan, Direktorat Sejarah dan Nilai Tradisional, Proyek Inventarisasi dan Dokumentasi Sejarah Nasional, 1991.

Taylor, R.H. *The State in Myanmar*. London: Hurst, 2008 (rev. and expanded; originally published in 1987).

Taylor, Sandra C. *Vietnamese Women at War: Fighting for Ho Chi Minh and the Revolution*. Lawrence: University Press of Kansas, 1999.

Team Fact Finding Badan Pembina Pahlawan Pusat. *Haji Rangkayo Rasuna Said: Kesimpulan Team Fact Finding, Badan Pembina Pahlawan Pusat [Haji Rangkayo Rasuna Said: Conclusions of the Fact Finding Team, Working Group for Selection of National Heroes]*. Jakarta: No publisher, 1974.

Tin Mya, Thakin. *Fascist Taw Lan Yay Ta Na Chot Nhin Taing Seh Taing [The Headquarters and Ten Divisions of the Fascist Resistance]*. Yangon: Kyu Pyoh Sa Pay, 1968.

Thawnghmung, Ardeth. *The "Other" Karen in Myanmar: Ethnic Minorities and the Struggle without Arms*. Lanham: Lexington Books, 2012.

Thawnghmung, Ardeth Maung. *The Karen Revolution in Burma: Diverse Voices, Uncertain Ends*. Policy Studies 46 (Southeast Asia). Washington, DC: East-West Center, 2008.

Thein Pe Myint, Thakin. *Ko twe mhattan* [*Memoirs*]. Yangon: Taing Chit, 1950.

Thu Ha, ed. *Danh Nu Trong Truyen Thuyet va Lich Su Viet Nam* [*Women in Legend and History of Vietnam*]. Hanoi: Nha Xuat Ban Lao Dong, 2009.

Trinh Van Thao. *Vietnam: Du Confucianisme au Communisme* [*Vietnam: From Confucianism to Communism*]. Paris: L'Harmattan, 1990.

Turner, Kathleen Gottschang and Phan Thanh Hao. *Even the Women Must Fight*. New York: John Wiley and Sons, 1998.

Ueno, Chizuko. *Nationalism and Gender*, transl. Beverley Yamamoto. Melbourne: Trans Pacific Press, 2004.

Vargyas, Gábor. *À la recherche des Brou perdus, population montagnarde du centre indochinois* [*In Search of the Lost Brou: A Highland Population of Central Indochina*]. Les Cahiers de Péninsule 5. Geneva: Olizane (Études orientales), 2000.

Vreede-de Stuers, Cora. *The Indonesian Woman: Struggles and Achievements*. 's-Gravenhage: Mouton, 1960.

Waterson, Roxana, ed. *Southeast Asian Lives: Personal Narratives and Historical Experience*. Singapore: NUS Press, 2007.

Watson, C.W. *Of Self and Nation: Autobiography and the Representation of Modern Indonesia*. Honolulu: University of Hawaii Press, 2000.

————. *Of Self and Injustice: Autobiography and Repression in Modern Indonesia*. Singapore: NUS Press, 2006.

West, Lois A., ed. *Feminist Nationalism*. New York: Routledge, 1997.

Williams, Brackette F., ed. *Women out of Place: The Gender of Agency and the Race of Nationality*. New York: Routledge, 1996.

Winters, R. *Voice of East Timorese Women, Vol. 1*. Darwin: East Timor International Support Centre, 1999.

Woodside, Alexander B. *Community and Revolution in Modern Vietnam*. Boston: Houghton Mifflin, 1976.

Woolf, Virginia. *A Room of One's Own and Three Guineas*, 2nd ed. Oxford: Oxford University Press, 1992 [originally published in 1938 by Hogarth Press, London].

World Bank. *Defining Heroes: Key Lessons from the Creation of Veterans Policy in Timor-Leste*. East Asia and Pacific Region: Timor-Leste, Papua New Guinea and Pacific Islands Country Management Unit, World Bank, 2008.

Yin Yin Htun. *Independent Daw San*. Yangon: Pinnya than saung poun hneik taik, 2009.

Yusuf Puteh, Abg. *Portraits of Grace and Charm*. Kuching: SHOBRA, 1990.

Yuval-Davis, Nira. *Gender and Nation*. London: Sage, 1997.

Yuval-Davis, Nira and Floya Anthias, eds. *Woman-Nation-State*. London: Macmillan, 1989.

Zaw Oo and Win Min. *Assessing Burma's Ceasefire Accords*. Washington, DC: East-West Center, 2007.

Zöellner, H-B., ed. "Material on Ba Khaing, *Political History of Myanma*" (annotations and translation of book extracts). Myanmar Literature Project, Working Paper no. 10:5. Passau: Southeast Asian Studies, Universität Passau, 2006.

Book Chapters

Allott, Anna J. "Thakin Ko-daw Hmaing", in *Far Eastern Literatures in the 20th Century: A Guide*, ed. Leonard S. Klein. New York: Ungar Publishing Company, 1986.

Anderson, Benedict. "A Time of Darkness and a Time of Light: Transposition in Early Indonesian Thought", in *Perceptions of the Past in Southeast Asia*, ed. Anthony Reid. Singapore: Heinemann, 1979.

Bystydzienski, Jill M. "Conclusion", in *Women Transforming Politics: Worldwide Strategies for Empowerment*, ed. Jill M. Bystydzienski. Bloomington and Indianapolis: Indiana University Press, 1992.

Calhoun, Craig. "The Problem of Identity in Collective Action", in *Macro-Micro Linkages in Sociology*, ed. Joan Huber. Newbury Park, London and New Delhi: Sage Publications, 1991.

Carey, P. and V. Houben. "Spirited Srikandhis and Sly Sumbadras: The Social, Political and Economic Role of Women at the Central Javanese Courts in the 18th and Early 19th Centuries", in *Indonesian Women in Focus: Past and Present Notions*, ed. E. Locher-Scholten and A. Niehof. Dordrecht and Providence: Foris Publications, 1987.

Curaming, Rommel A. "The State and the Historians in the Construction of Nationalist Historical Discourses in Indonesia and the Philippines: A Preliminary Consideration", in *Asian Futures, Asian Traditions*, ed. Edwina Palmer. Folkestone: Global Oriental, 2005.

Dobbin, Christine. "The Search for Women in Indonesian History", in *Kartini Centenary: Indonesian Women Then and Now*, ed. Ailsa Thomson Zainu'ddin. Clayton: Monash University, 1980.

Duara, Prasenjit. "Historicizing National Identity, or Who Imagines What and When", in *Becoming National: A Reader*, ed. Geoff Eley and Ronald Grigor Suny. Oxford and New York: Oxford University Press, 1996.

Dufour, Pascale, Dominique Masson and Dominique Caouette. "Introduction", in *Solidarities Beyond Borders: Transnationalizing Women's Movements*, ed. Pascale Dufour, Dominique Masson and Dominique Caouette. Vancouver and Toronto: University of British Columbia Press, 2010.

Fall, Bernard B. "The Pathet Lao: A 'Liberation' Party", in *The Communist Revolution in Asia: Tactics, Goals and Achievements*, ed. Robert A. Scalapino. Berkeley: University of California, 1965.

Fatimah, Siti. "Perspektif Jender Dalam Historiografi Indonesia" [Gender Perspective in Indonesian Historiography], in *Titik Balik: Historiografi di Indonesia* [*Turning Point: Historiography in Indonesia*], ed. Doko Marihandono. Jakarta: Wedatama Widya Sastra, 2008.

Furuta, Motoo. "The Indochina Communist Party's Division into Three Parties: Vietnamese Communist Policy toward Cambodia and Laos, 1948–1951", in *Indochina in the 1940s and 1950s*, ed. Takashi Shiraishi and Motoo Furuta. Ithaca: Southeast Asia Program, Cornell University, 1992.

Guyot, Dorothy. "Communal Conflict in the Burma Delta," in *Southeast Asian Transitions: Approaches through Social History*, ed. Ruth McVey. New Haven and London: Yale University Press, 1978.

Harris Rimmer, S. "The Roman Catholic Church and the Rights of East Timorese Women", in *Mixed Blessings: Laws, Religions and Women's Rights in the Asia Pacific Region*, ed. Caroline Evan and Amanda Whiting. Leiden: Koninklijke Brill/Martinus Nijhoff Publishing, 2006.

Holland, Dorothy and Jean Lave. "History in Person: An Introduction", in *History in Person: Enduring Struggles, Contentious Practice, Intimate Identities*, ed. Dorothy Holland and Jean Lave. Santa Fe: School of American Research Press; Oxford: James Currey, 2001.

Jahroni, J. "Haji Rangkayo Rasuna Said: Pejuang Politik dan Penulis Pergerakan" [Haji Rangkayo Rasuna Said: Political Fighter and Movement Writer], in *Ulama Perempuan Indonesia* [*Indonesian Women Islamic Scholars*], ed. J. Burhanuddin. Jakarta: Penerbit PT Gramedia Pustaka Utama bekerja sama dengan PPIM IAIN Jakarta, 2002.

Kartowijono, Sujatin. "The Awakening of the Women's Movement of Indonesia", in *Indonesian Women: Some Past and Current Perspectives*, ed. B.B. Hering. Bruxelles: Centre d'étude du Sud-Est asiatique et de l'Extreme Orient, 1976.

———. "Ny. Sujatin Kartowijono: Tokoh Pergerakan Wanita Indonesia" [Ny Sujatin Kartowijono: A Leader of the Indonesian Women's Movement], in *Sumbangsihku Bagi Pertiwi: Kumpulan Pengalaman dan Pemikiran* [*My Contribution on Behalf of Women: A Collection of Experiences and Reflections*], ed. Lasmidjah Hardi. Jakarta: Yayasan Wanita Pejoang, 1981.

Kartowiyono, Suyatin. "Pengalaman Seorang Pemimpin Organisasi" [Experience of an Organisation's Leader], in *Perjuangan Wanita Indonesia 10 Windu Setelah Kartini 1904–1984* [*The Indonesian Women's Struggle 80 Years after Kartini 1904–1984*]. Jakarta: Departemen Penerangan RI, 1984.

Kasetsiri, Charnvit. "The Construction of National Heroes and/or Heroines", in *Southeast Asia over Three Generations*, ed. James T. Siegel, Audrey Kahin and Benedict Anderson. Ithaca: Cornell University Press, 2003.

Kyan. "Amyothami mya ne sanezin lawka" [Women and the World of Journalism], in *Sanezin htamain sa tan mya* [*Essays on the History of Journalism*]. Yangon: Sape Beikman, 1978.

Lessard, Micheline. "More than Half the Sky: Vietnamese Women and Anti-French Political Activism, 1858–1945", in *Vietnam and the West: New*

Approaches, ed. Wynn Wilcox. Ithaca: Southeast Asia Program, Cornell University, 2010.

McCoy, Alfred W. "Introduction: Biography of Lives Obscure, Ordinary, and Heroic", in *Lives at the Margin: Biography of Filipinos Obscure, Ordinary, and Heroic*, ed. Alfred W. McCoy. Quezon City: Ateneo de Manila University Press, 2000.

Miller, David. "Nationalism", in *The Oxford Handbook of Political Theory*, ed. John S. Dryzck, Bonnie Honig and Anne Phillips. Oxford: Oxford University Press, 2006.

Mya Sein. "Myanmar amyothami" [Burmese Women], in *Myanmar amyothami kye moun* [*A Looking Glass of Burmese Women*]. Yangon: Myanmar nainggan sape hnik sanezin ahpwe, 1998 (originally published in 1958).

Olzak, Susan. "Ethnic and Nationalist Social Movements", in *The Blackwell Companion to Social Movements*, ed. D.A. Snow, S.A. Soule and H. Kriesi. Oxford: Blackwell Publishing, 2004.

Pandoe, M. "Dua Singa Betina Dibuang" [Two Female Lions Jailed], in *Jernih Melihat Cermat Mencatat: Antologi Karya Jurnalistik Wartawan Senior Kompas* [*Watching Clearly and Noting Carefully: An Anthology of Senior Kompas Journalists' Writings*], ed. Julius Pour. Jakarta: Penerbit Buku Kompas, 2010.

PERTIWI (Pertubuhan Tindakan Wanita Islam, Organisation of Muslim Women's Action). "Aishah Ghani, Tan Sri Datin Paduka Seri (Dr)", in *Biografi Tokoh Wanita Malaysia* [*Biographies of Female Personalities in Malaysia*]. Petaling Jaya: Pelanduk Publications, 2004.

Pholsena, Vatthana. "A Liberal Model of Minority Rights for an Illiberal Multi-ethnic State? The Case of the Lao PDR" in *Asian Minorities and Western Liberalism*, ed. Will Kymlicka and Baogang He. Oxford: Oxford University Press, 2005.

Phuong Bui Tranh. "Femmes Vietnamiennes pendant et après la Colonisation Française et la Guerre Américaine: Réflexions sur les Orientations Bibliographiques" [Vietnamese Women during and after French Colonisation and the American War: Reflections on the Bibliographical Orientations], in *Histoire des Femmes en Situation Coloniale* [*History of Women under Colonialism*], ed. Anne Hugon. Paris: Karthala, 2004.

Poeze, H. "Inleiding" [Introduction], in *Politiek-politioneele overzichten van Nederlandsch-Indië: bronnenpublikatie* [*Political Police Reports on the Netherlands Indies: A Sourcebook*], ed. H. Poeze and Koninklijk instituut voor taal-, land- en volkenkunde (Pays-Bas). Dordrecht and Providence: Foris Publications, 1988.

Portelli, Alessandro. "What Makes Oral History Different", in *The Oral History Reader*, ed. Robert Perks and Alistair Thomson, 2nd ed. London and New York: Routledge, 2006.

Rathie, Martin H. "Histoire et Evolution du Parti Révolutionnaire Populaire Lao" [History and Evolution of the Lao People's Revolutionary Party], in *Laos: Sociétés et Pouvoirs* [*Laos: Societies and Powers*], ed. Vanina Bouté and Vatthana Pholsena. Paris: Les Indes Savantes-IRASEC, 2012.

Ray, Bharati. "The Freedom Movement and Feminist Consciousness in Bengal, 1905–1929", in *From the Seams of History: Essays on Indian Women*, ed. Bharati Ray. Delhi: Oxford University Press, 1995.

Roces, Mina. "Is the Suffragist an American Colonial Construct? Defining 'the Filipino Woman' in Colonial Philippines", in *Women's Suffrage in Asia: Gender, Nationalism and Democracy*, ed. Louise Edwards and Mina Roces. London and New York: RoutledgeCurzon, 2004.

Said, R. "Pidato Rasuna Said" [Rasuna Said's Speeches], in *Tidak ada kontra revolusi bisa bertahan: Amanat Presiden Soekarno dan Pidato Rasuna Said pada Rapat Pantja Sila di Bandung tanggal 16 Maret 1958* [*Counter-revolution Cannot Last: The Address of President Soekarno and the Speech of Rasuna Said to the Pantja Sila Meeting in Bandung on 16 March 1958*]. Djakarta: Kementrian Penerangan RI: Penerbitan Chusus, 1958.

Sape Beikman. "Myanmar konmaryi athin mya" [Burmese Women's Associations], in *Myanma swe soun kyan* [*Myanmar Encyclopaedia*]. Yangon: Sape Beikman, 1966.

─────. "Daw San, Independent", in *Myanma swe soun kyan* [*Myanmar Encyclopaedia*] 4. Yangon: Sape Beikman, 1967.

Saydam, G. "Rasuna Said: Tokoh Politik, Singa Betina yang Orator Ulung" [Rasuna Said: Political Leader, a Lioness Who Was an Excellent Orator], in *55 tokoh Indonesia asal Minangkabau di pentas nasional* [*Fifty-five Indonesian Leaders from Minangkabau in the National Arena*] (Cet. 1.). Bandung: Alfabeta, 2009.

Smith, Martin. "Burma: The Karen Conflict", in *Encyclopedia of Modern Ethnic Conflicts*, ed. Joseph R. Rudolph Jr. Westport: Greenwood Press, 2003.

South, Ashley. "Governance and Legitimacy in Karen State", in *Ruling Myanmar: From Cyclone Nargis to General Elections*, ed. N. Cheeseman, M. Skidmore and T. Wilson. Singapore: ISEAS, 2010.

Sulasiah Munajir. "Aishah Ghani, Tan Sri: Menjaga Kebajikan Masyarakat" [Aishah Ghani, Tan Sri: Taking Care of Social Welfare], in *20 Tokoh Wanita* [*Twenty Female Personalities*]. Bangi: Medium Publication, 2009.

Tetreault, Mary Ann. "Women and Revolution in Vietnam", in *Vietnam's Women in Transition*, ed. Kathleen Barry. London: Macmillan, 1996.

Thakur, Bharti. *Women and Gandhi's Mass Movements*. New Delhi: Deep and Deep, 2006.

Ting, Helen. "Gender Discourse in Malay Politics: Old Wine in New Bottle?" in *Politics in Malaysia: The Malay Dimension*, ed. Edmund Terence Gomez. London and New York: Routledge, 2007.

_____. "Malaysian History Textbooks and the Discourse of *Ketuanan Melayu*", in *Race and Multiculturalism in Malaysia and Singapore*, ed. Daniel Goh, Philip Holden, Matilda Gabrielpillai and Khoo Gaik Cheng. London and New York: Routledge, 2009.

Tiongco-Enriquez, Carmen. "Revolt within the Grassroots", in *Filipino Heritage*, ed. Alfredo Roces. Metro Manila: Lahing Pilipino Publishing, 1978.

Turner, Karen G. and Phan Thanh Hao. "'Vietnam' as a Women's War", in *A Companion to the Vietnam War*, ed. Marilyn B. Young and Robert Buzzanco. Malden: Blackwell Publishing, 2002.

Walby, Sylvia. "Woman and Nation", in *Mapping the Nation*, ed. Gopal Balakrishnan. London and New York: Verso, 1996.

Wilford, Rick. "Women, Ethnicity and Nationalism: Surveying the Ground", in *Women, Ethnicity and Nationalism: The Politics of Transition*, ed. Rick Wilford and Robert Lee Miller. London: Routledge, 1998.

Zainah Anwar. "What Islam, Whose Islam? Sisters in Islam and the Struggle for Women's Rights", in *The Politics of Multiculturalism*, ed. Robert W. Hefner. Honolulu: University of Hawaii Press, 2001.

Journal Articles

Aung-Thwin, Maitrii. "Genealogy of a Rebellion Narrative: Law, Ethnology and Culture in Colonial Burma", *Journal of Southeast Asian Studies* 34, 3 (2003).

Barnard, Timothy P. "Local Heroes and National Consciousness: The Politics of Historiography in Riau", *Bijdragen tot de Taal-, Land- en Volkenkunde* 153, 4 (1997).

Basu, Aparna. "A Nationalist Feminist: Mridula Sarabhai (1911–1974)", *Indian Journal of Gender Studies* 2 (1995).

Brown, Colin. "Sukarno on the Role of Women in the Nationalist Movement", *Review of Indonesian and Malayan Affairs* 15, 1 (1981).

Bruner, Jerome. "The Narrative Construction of Reality", *Critical Inquiry* 18, 1 (Autumn 1991).

Chapman, Jean. "A Khmer Veteran Remembers: Herstory and History", *Indian Journal of Gender Studies* 17, 1 (2010).

Cheah Boon Kheng. "Sino-Malay Conflicts in Malaya, 1945–1946: Communist Vendetta and Islamic Resistance", *Journal of Southeast Asian Studies* 2, 1 (March 1981).

Djaja, T. "Rasuna Said (1910–1965): Srikandi Indonesia yang Pertama Masuk Penjara Karena Politik" [Rasuna Said (1910–1965): The First Indonesian Heroine to Be Jailed for Political Reasons], *Nasehat Perkawinan* [*Marriage Advice*] 75 (1978).

Doran, Christine. "Women, Nationalism and the Philippine Revolution", *Nations and Nationalism* 5, 2 (1999).

Geiger, Susan. "Tanganyikan Nationalism as 'Women's Work': Life Histories, Collective Biography and Changing Historiography", *Journal of African History* 37 (1996).

Goodman, Grant. "An Interview with Benigno Ramos", *Philippine Studies* 37 (1989).

Goscha, Christopher. "La Guerre pour l'Indochine? Le Laos et le Cambodge dans le Conflit Franco-vietnamien (1948–1954)" [War over Indochina? Laos and Cambodia in the Franco-Vietnamese Conflict (1948–1954)], *Guerres Mondiales et Conflits Contemporains* [*World Wars and Contemporary Conflicts*] 211 (2003).

————. "Vietnam and the World Outside: The Case of Vietnamese Communist Advisers in Laos, 1948–1952", *South East Asia Research* 12, 2 (2004).

Guillemot, François. "Death and Suffering at First Hand: Youth Shock Brigades during the Vietnam War, 1950–1975", *Journal of Vietnamese Studies* 4, 3 (Fall 2009).

Hill, David T. "In the Shadow of Other Lives: Reflections on Dan Lev and Writing Biography", *Review of Indonesian and Malaysian Affairs* 42, 2 (2008).

Ikeya, Chie. "The 'Traditional' High Status of Women in Burma: A Historical Reconsideration", *The Journal of Burma Studies* 10 (2005/2006).

Judge, Joan. "Talent, Virtue, and the Nation: Chinese Nationalisms and Female Subjectivities in the Early Twentieth Century", *American Historical Review* 106, 3 (June 2001).

Kaung. "A Survey of the History of Education in Burma before the British Conquest and After", *Journal of Burma Research Society* 46, 2 (Dec. 1963).

Kelly, Gail P. "Education and Participation in Nationalist Groups: An Exploratory Study of the Indochinese Communist Party and the VNQDD, 1929–1931", *Comparative Education Review* 15, 2 (1971).

Kintanar, Thelma B. and Carina C. David. "Salud Algabre, Revolutionary", *Review of Women's Studies* 6, 1 (1996).

Laungaramsri, Pinkaew. "Women, Nation, and the Ambivalence of Subversive Identification along the Thai-Burmese Border", *Sojourn: Journal of Social Issues in Southeast Asia* 21, 1 (2006).

Lee, Y.L. "The Population of British Borneo", *Population Studies* 15, 3 (March 1962).

Lessard, Micheline. "The Colony Writ Small: Vietnamese Women and Political Activism in Colonial Schools during the 1920s", *Journal of the Canadian Historical Association* 18, 2 (2007).

————. "We Know the Duties We Must Fulfill: Modern 'Mothers and Fathers' of the Vietnamese Nation", *French Colonial History* 3 (2003).

Linh Vu. "Drowned in Romances, Tears and Rivers: Young Women's Suicide in Early Twentieth Century Vietnam", *Explorations* 9 (2009).

Marr, David. "The 1920s Women's Rights Debates in Vietnam", *Journal of Asian Studies* 35, 3 (1976).

Marshall, Harry. "The Karens: An Element in the Melting Pot of Burma", *The Southern Workman* 56 (1927).

Michaud, Jean. "The Montagnards and the State in Northern Vietnam from 1802 to 1975: A Historical Overview", *Ethnohistory* 47, 2 (2000).

Milner, Anthony. "Localisation, Regionalism and the History of Ideas in Southeast Asia", *Journal of Southeast Asian Studies* 41, 3 (2010).

Mya Sein. "Towards Independence in Burma: The Role of Women", *Asian Affairs* 59, 3 (Oct. 1972).

Niner, S. "*Hakat klot*, Narrow Steps: Negotiating Gender in Post-conflict Timor-Leste", *International Feminist Journal of Politics* 13, 3 (2011).

Ochs, Elinor and Lisa Capps. "Narrating the Self", *Annual Review of Anthropology* 25 (1996).

Pholsena, Vatthana. "Nation/Representation: Ethnic Classification and Mapping Nationhood in Contemporary Laos", *Asian Ethnicity* 3, 2 (2002).

————. "Highlanders on the Ho Chi Minh Trail: Representations and Narratives", *Critical Asian Studies* 40, 3 (2008).

————. "L'éducation d'une génération de patriotes révolutionnaires, du Laos au Nord Viêt Nam" [The Education of a Generation of Revolutionary Patriots, from Laos to North Vietnam], *Communisme 2013* ("Vietnam, de l'insurrection à la dictature 1930–2012" [Vietnam: From Insurrection to Dictatorship, 1930–2012], Special issue coordinated by Christopher Goscha), 2013.

Quinn-Judge, Sophie. "Women in the Early Vietnamese Communist Movement: Sex, Lies, and Liberation", *South East Asia Research* 9, 3 (2001).

Rottger-Rossler, B. "Autobiography in Question: On Self-Presentation and Life Description in an Indonesian Society", *Anthropos* 88 (1993).

Sabihah Osman. "The Malay-Muslim Response to Cession of Sarawak to the British Crown 1946–1951", *Jebat: Malaysian Journal of History, Politics and Strategic Studies* 18 (1990).

Selth, Andrew. "Race and Resistance in Burma, 1942–1945", *Modern Asian Studies* 20, 3 (1986).

Ting, Helen. "The Politics of National Identity in West Malaysia: Continued Mutation or Critical Transition?" *Southeast Asian Studies* (Kyoto University) 47, 1 (June 2009).

Tusan, Michelle E. "Writing *Stri Dharma*: International Feminism, Nationalist Politics, and Women's Press Advocacy in Late Colonial India", *Women's History Review* 12, 4 (2003).

Van Klinken, Gerry. "The Battle for History after Suharto: Beyond Sacred Dates, Great Men, and Legal Milestones", *Critical Asian Studies* 33, 3 (2001).

Vu Van Thai. "Vietnam: Nationalism under Challenge", *Vietnam Perspectives* 2, 2 (1966).

Wazir Jahan Karim. "Malay Women's Movements: Leadership and Processes of Change", *International Social Science Journal* 35, 98 (1983).

Theses and Dissertations

Braun, Eric Christopher. "Ledi Sayadaw, Abhidhamma, and the Development of the Modern Insight Meditation Movement in Burma". PhD diss., Harvard University, 2008.

Carlson, Richard James. "Women, Gender, and Politics in Burma's Nationalist Movement, 1900–1931". MA thesis, Cornell University, 1991.

Dhammasami, Khammai. "Between Idealism and Pragmatism: A Study of Monastic Education in Burma and Thailand from the Seventeenth Century to the Present". PhD diss., Oxford University, 2004.

Hill, H. *"Fretilin: The Origins, Ideologies and Strategies of a Nationalist Movement in East Timor"*. MA thesis, Monash University, 1978.

Nordi Archie. "Wanita dan Politik Sarawak 1946–1996: Penglibatan, Peranan dan Tokoh" [Women and Sarawak Politics 1946–1996: Involvement, Role and Leaders]. Academic exercise, History Department, Universiti Malaya, 1997/98.

Rasyad, A. "Perguruan Diniyyah Puteri Padangpanjang: 1923–1978. Suatu Studi Mengenai Perkembangan Sistem Pendidikan Islam" [Diniyyah Puteri Padangpanjang Teachers' Training: 1923–1978. A Study of the Development of the Islamic Education System]. PhD diss., Institut Agama Islam Negeri, Syarif Hidayatullah, Jakarta, 1982.

Rathie, Martin H. "The Historical Development of a Polyethnic Society and Culture in Laos from Independence and under Socialism". Honours thesis, Northern Territory University, 1996 (revised edition).

White, S. "Reformist Islam, Gender and Marriage in Late Colonial Dutch East Indies, 1900–1942". PhD diss., Australian National University, 2004.

Online Resources

Asian Development Bank (ADB)/UNIFEM. "Gender and Nation Building in Timor-Leste: Country Gender Assessment", http://www.adb.org/documents/reports/country-gender-assessments/cga-timor-leste.pdf, 2005, accessed June 2008.

Brooke, Anthony. "Operation Peace through Unity", http://www.peacethrough unity.info/background-anthonystory.html, accessed 4 June 2010.

Central Intelligence Agency. *The World Factbook: Burma*, https://www.cia.gov/library/publications/the-world-factbook/geos/bm.html, accessed 6 May 2011.

Comissao de Acolhimento, Verdade e Reconciliacao (Commission for Truth, Reception and Reconciliation). *Final Report "Chega!"* http://www.etan.org/news/2006/cavr.htm, 2006, accessed Mar. 2011.

Costa, Monica, Rhonda Sharp and Diane Elson. "Gender-Responsive Budget-
    ing in the Asia-Pacific Region: Democratic Republic of Timor-Leste
    Country Profile", University of South Australia, www.unisanet.unisa.edu.
    au/genderbudgets, 2009, accessed Aug. 2010.
Karen National Union. "History of the Karens and the KNU", http://www.
    karen.org/knu/KNU_His.htm, n.d., accessed 15 Mar. 2009.
Timor-Leste Government Website, http://www.easttimorgovernment.com/
    demographics.htm, accessed Nov. 2010.

Archival Papers and Documents

French *Archives nationales d'outre mer*: Intelligence reports and police investi-
    gation papers.
India Office Records: archival papers.
National Council of Women in Burma. 1927. In file "Papers of Sybil Mary
    Dorothy Bulkeley", MSS EUR D1230/5, India Office Records.
_____. 1929. *Report by the National Council of Women in Burma on Condi-
    tions Affecting Labour in and near Rangoon*. MSS EUR D1230/6, India
    Office Records.
Riot Inquiry Committee. *Interim Report of the Riot Inquiry Committee*. Ran-
    goon: Office of the Superintendent, Government Printing and Stationery,
    1939.
University of the Philippines Main Library: People's Court Files.
Vietnam Virtual Archive, Texas Tech University: archival papers.

Newspapers and Magazines

Adil
Atlantic Monthly
Dewan Masyarakat
Independent Weekly
Kompas
La tribune indochinoise
Le petit parisien
MASSA
Phu Nu Tan van
Straits Times
Sunday Tribune Magazine
Thuriya Magazine
Tjaja Sumatra
WHO Magazine
Yuwadi Gyanay

Contributors

Susan Blackburn

After teaching at two other Australian universities, Susan Blackburn returned to Monash University, where she had gained her PhD in Indonesian political history. Currently Associate Professor in the School of Political and Social Inquiry there, she teaches Southeast Asian Politics, supervises postgraduate students, and conducts research, mainly concerning Asian women. Her publications include *Women and the State in Modern Indonesia* (Cambridge University Press, 2004), *The First Indonesian Women's Congress of 1928* (Monash University Press, 2008) and "Feminism and the Women's Movement in the World's Largest Islamic Nation" (in *Women's Movements in Asia: Feminisms and Transnational Activism*, ed. Mina Roces and Louise Edwards, Routledge, 2010).

Maria Luisa Camagay

Maria Luisa Camagay is a faculty member of the Department of History, College of Social Sciences and Philosophy, University of the Philippines. She obtained her Doctorat de Troisieme Cycle at the Ecole des Hautes Etudes en Sciences Sociales in Paris. Her research interests are the history of women in the Philippines and the social history of the Philippines. She recently edited a work titled *More Pinay than We Admit: A Social Construction of the Filipina* (Quezon City: Vibal Foundation, 2010).

Violet Cho

Violet Cho is a Visiting Fellow in the Department of Political and Social Change at the Australian National University, College of Asia and the Pacific. In 2009, she completed a Bachelor of Communication Studies (Hons) degree at Auckland University of Technology, where she was the inaugural Asian Journalism Fellow.

Chie Ikeya

Chie Ikeya is Assistant Professor in the Department of History at Rutgers University (she was previously at the National University of Singapore). She received her PhD in modern Southeast Asian history from Cornell University and maintains an active interest in the related fields of women's and gender history, race, gender and sexuality studies, colonial and postcolonial studies, and Asian history/studies. Her recent publications include *Refiguring Women, Colonialism, and Modernity in Burma* (University of Hawaii Press, 2011) and "The Modern Burmese Woman and the Politics of Fashion in Colonial Burma" (*Journal of Asian Studies* 67, 4 [2008]).

Welyne Jeffrey Jehom

Welyne J. Jehom is a senior lecturer in the Gender Studies Program at the University of Malaya. Her research focuses on issues of gender in the context of development in Malaysia, particularly concerning the displacement of indigenous communities in Sarawak because of development programmes. Her latest publication is "Compensation Crisis on *Adat* Land and Properties: State vs. Natives" (in *Negotiating Local Governance: Natural Resources Management at the Interface of Communities and the State*, ed. Irit Eguavoen and Wolfram Laube, LIT Verlag, 2010).

Micheline Lessard

Micheline Lessard is Assistant Professor of History at the University of Ottawa. Her area of specialisation is Southeast Asia, and her research focuses on Vietnamese history, particularly Vietnamese women's history. She received a PhD in Southeast Asian history in 1995 at Cornell University and has a BA and an MA from Concordia University. She has published chapters in *Essays into Vietnamese Pasts* (Cornell University Press, 1995) and *Women's Suffrage in Asia* (RoutledgeCurzon, 2004) as well as articles in *Vietnamologica* and *French Colonial History*. She is a co-editor (with Tamara Hunt) of *Women and the Colonial Gaze* (New York University Press, 2002). She is currently working on a manuscript on human trafficking in Vietnam during the French colonial period.

Sara Niner

Sara Niner is a researcher and teaching associate at the School of Social and Political Inquiry at Monash University. She is the editor of *To Resist Is to Win: The Autobiography of Xanana Gusmão with Selected Letters and Speeches* (Aurora Books, 2000) and author of *Xanana: Leader of the Struggle for Independent Timor-Leste* (Australian Scholarly Publishing, 2009); the latter has recently been translated into Portuguese. Her current research focus is on development and gender.

Vatthana Pholsena

Vatthana Pholsena is a research fellow at the French National Centre for Scientific Research (CNRS). Currently based in Singapore, she is also the representative for the Institute of Research on Contemporary Southeast Asia (IRASEC) (Bangkok). She is the author of *Post-War Laos: The Politics of Culture, History and Identity* (ISEAS and Cornell University Press, 2006). Her current research projects include the study of the process of war and state making in the borderlands between Laos and Vietnam.

Ardeth Maung Thawnghmung

Ardeth Maung Thawnghmung is Associate Professor of Political Science at the University of Massachusetts, Lowell. She has an MA in International Relations from Yale University and a PhD in Political Science from the University of Wisconsin, Madison. Ardeth's areas of teaching and research interests include international relations, comparative politics (Third World politics, Southeast Asian politics and Myanmar politics), political economy, ethnic politics, and democracy and democratisation. She has written numerous books and articles on Myanmar economy and politics, including *Behind the Teak Curtain: Authoritarianism, Agricultural Policies and Political Legitimacy in Burma/Myanmar* (Columbia University Press, 2004). Her latest works on Myanmar include "The Politics of Everyday Life in Twenty-First Century Burma/Myanmar" (*Journal of Asian Studies* 70, 3 [Aug. 2011]); *Beyond Armed Resistance: The Non-insurgent Members of Ethnonational Groups in Burma/Myanmar* (East-West Center, 2011); and *Struggle without Arms: The "Other" Karen in Burma and the Dilemmas of Ethnic Minorities* (Lexington Books, 2012).

Helen Ting

Helen Ting is a research fellow at the Institute of Malaysian and International Studies at the National University of Malaysia. Her publications include "Khadijah Sidek and Fatimah Hashim: Two Contrasting Models of (Malay) Feminist Struggle?" (in *Malaysia: Public Policy and Marginalised Groups*, ed. Phua Kai Lit, Persatuan Sains Sosial Malaysia, 2007); "Gender Discourse in Malay Politics: Old Wine in New Bottle?" (in *Politics in Malaysia: The Malay Dimension*, ed. Edmund Terence Gomez, Routledge, 2007) and "Social Construction of Nation: A Theoretical Exploration" (*Nationalism and Ethnic Politics* 14, 3 [July 2008]). She heads a research project to study women leaders in Malaysia during Independence.

Sally White

Sally White is a senior research associate in the College of Asia and the Pacific at the Australian National University, where she gained a PhD in Indonesian history. Her main research interests are the historical development of ideas concerning Islam and gender in Indonesia and their contemporary manifestations. Her current research is focused on women and gender among jihadist groups in Indonesia. She is a co-editor (with Greg Fealy) of *Expressing Islam: Religious Life and Politics in Indonesia* (ISEAS, 2008).

INDEX

historiography, 4, 6, 9, 20
    Burmese, 23–5, 35, 40, 253, 266
    Indonesian, 13, 14, 75, 90, 91,
        96–7, 118
    Lao, 199, 215, 222
    Malaysian, 15, 152, 168, 288
    Philippine, 14, 124–6
    Sarawak, 177, 193
    Vietnamese, 12, 48, 50–2, 61, 64,
        69, 199, 222
history
    historians, 9, 12, 13, 40, 51, 58,
        70, 91, 126, 130
    historical structures and
        processes, 277–92
    life history, 7, 206
    of nationalist movements, 2, 3,
        4, 35, 40, 48, 52, 69, 90, 91,
        126, 152, 177, 240, 266, 292
    oral history, 144, 205
Ho Chi Minh Trail, 198, 201, 210
husband, 44, 51, 167, 171, 189, 211,
    231, 237, 245, 266–7
    of Bisoi, 244, 285
    of Daw San, 28, 32, 94, 289, 291
    of Khamla, 217
    of Lily Eberwein, 186–8
    of Nguyen Thi Giang, *see*
        Nguyen Thai Hoc
    of Rasuna Said, 106, 111, 114–5
    of Salud Algabre, *see* Generalla,
        Severo
    of Shamsiah Fakeh, *see* Ahmad
        Boestamam *and* Wahi
        Anuwar, 158–9, 168–9
    of Suyatin Kartowiyono, 83–4,
        89, 92, 289

identity, 170, 277, 280, 282–6, 291–2
    ethnic, 192, 252, 284
    feminist, 40, 245, 291

    national, 51, 81, 132, 216–7,
        282–3
    nationalist, 79, 285
    political, 284, 286, 291
    religious, 11, 2, 6, 113, 192, 282
ideology
    communist, *see* communism
    in Indonesia, 90, 100, 118
    of nationalist, movements, 281,
        290
    of VNQDD, 54, 67
imprisonment
    of East Timorese nationalists,
        232, 238, 243
    of Filipino nationalists, 135, 137
    of Indonesian nationalists, 111
    of Malayan nationalists, 169
    of Rasuna Said, 14, 83, 109–10
    of Salud Algabre, 124, 140–1
    of Shamsiah Fakeh, 151
    of Vietnamese nationalists, 62,
        64–5, 67–9, 74
independence, national, 2, 3, 4, 7,
    86, 283
    Burmese, 12, 14, 24, 29, 32,
        37–9, 253–5, 287
    East Timorese, 17, 226, 229,
        230, 232, 236–7, 243–5, 290
    Indonesian, 13, 14, 79–80,
        84–90, 98, 103–6, 108–10,
        114–6
    Karen, 17, 29, 271
    Lao, 198, 201–2, 204
    Malayan, 15, 147, 154–5, 159,
        161–4, 167–70, 288
    Philippine, 124–7, 129–31,
        134–5, 137–8, 140–1, 143,
        278, 281, 287
    Sarawak, 175, 177, 180, 188
    Vietnamese, 198, 201–2, 204
Independent Weekly, 25, 32, 36–7,
    291